TEN DAYS
IN AUGUST

TEN DAYS IN AUGUST

THE SIEGE OF LIÈGE 1914

TERENCE ZUBER

First published 2014
by Spellmount, an imprint of The History Press
The Mill, Brimscombe Port
Stroud, Gloucestershire, GL5 2QG
www.thehistorypress.co.uk

British Library Cataloguing in Publication Data.
A catalogue record for this book is available from the British Library.

ISBN 978 0 7524 9144 8

Typesetting and origination by Thomas Bohm, User design
Printed in Great Britain

Contents

Acknowledgements

This book would probably not have been possible without the support of Daniel Neicken, who lives near Liège. On hearing of my project, he was kind enough to approach me and offer to assist in obtaining source materials. He was of inestimable help and I cannot thank him enough. Dan bears no responsibility for the conclusions I have drawn.

I conducted much of the research while at the University of Würzburg, thanks to the hardworking and efficient interlibrary loan section.

I received invaluable support from West Virginia Northern Community College, especially the librarian, Janet Corbett and the dean, Larry Tackett.

Once again, Heather Wetzell drew the maps.

Sources

All the records of the German units that fought at Liège were located in the military archive at Potsdam, which was destroyed by a British firebomb raid on the night of 14 April 1945, two weeks before the end of the war. The principal German sources will therefore be the German infantry and artillery regimental histories as well as *Das Ehrenbuch der Deutschen Schweren Artillerie* (The Book of Honour of the German Heavy Artillery).[1]

There are two German monographs concerning the attack on Liège. *Lüttich-Namur* (Liège-Namur), book one of the series *Der Grosse Krieg in Einzeldarstellungen* (The Great War in Individual Campaigns).[2] The purpose of this series was not to present a scientific military history, but to explain the course of the war in general terms to the German soldiers and populace. Work was begun in the fall of 1917, and *Lüttich-Namur* was published in 1918. It is ninety-six pages long and hardly goes below regimental level. Sketch 2, showing the attack routes of the German brigades at Liège, is frequently reproduced. It is practically worthless concerning the siege itself. It also contains numerous errors. The heroic deeds of a member of the Guard Foot Artillery Regiment were mentioned prominently, and the regiment was supposed to have taken heavy casualties.[3] In fact, the story is pure invention, the Guard Foot Artillery Regiment was never engaged at Liège.

Ernst Kabisch began the war commanding an infantry regiment in Lorraine, but was wounded at the beginning of September. He was then chief of staff at increasing levels, and commanded a brigade and a division. His *Lüttich* (Liège) is more an apologia for the attack, along with his recommendations which would have made the attack more effective, than it is military history.[4] It is about 180 pages long but surprisingly quite general: his discussion of the attack and the siege contain no tactical details; it also contains numerous errors. However, Kabisch does make some interesting judgements.

The German official history, *Der Weltkrieg*, contains a short (nine-page) and accurate summary of the infantry attack on the night of 5–6 August.[5] But it too, makes errors, for example putting a German 38cm mortar at Liège, which never happened.[6]

The Belgian Army historical records concerning 1914–18 were in two railcars which were destroyed in a fire at the rail station in Dunkirk on 25 May 1940. All that survived concerning Liège is 'a short and completely inadequate summary'.[7] The after-action reports of all the fort commanders were also destroyed. The Belgian 3rd Division (3 DA) post-war chief of staff, Colonel De Schrÿver, 'probably' used the historical records in his 1922 book, *La Bataille de Liège*, but we can't be sure, because De Schrÿver unfortunately did not cite his sources.[8] De Schrÿver's book is the most complete Belgian source, with 258 very dense pages, but he did not include any tactical maps.

Laurent Lombard wrote a series of five monographs on the battle at Liège in the 1930s. Lombard was a high school teacher who lived near Liège and was involved in the Belgian resistance in both world wars, escaping execution in the Great War only because he was under-age. Lombard's strength is in his description of Belgian tactical operations and tactical maps, which are far better than those of the German regimental histories. Lombard looked at all the published work in both French and German, but did not use the Belgian archives. His use of the German sources is selective and tendentious. His prose is far too wordy, emotional and florid. His description of the battle from the Belgian point of view is invaluable, but has to be treated very carefully. His judgement is unreliable, influenced by intense Belgian patriotism and his ignorance of tactics.

An important and brutally honest source concerning the fortifications at Liège is the highly-detailed 800-page Belgian official history, *Défense de la Position Fortifiée de Namur en Août 1914*.[9] Robert Normand published *Défence de Liége, Namur, Anvers en 1914* in 1923.[10] A French engineer officer, his book contains a technical description of the fortresses, which, however, missed some very important factors concerning armament and tactical defensive capabilities. Its account of the battle is largely a translation of the German *Lüttich-Namur* and Ludendorff's memoirs, but does include some valuable snippets concerning Belgian operations.

One of the most valuable sources is the report of the Belgian commander, General Leman.[11] Leman pulled no punches, and his critique of the state of the pre-war Belgian Army and the fortress of Liège is scathing.

Emile Joseph Galet's *Albert, King of the Belgians in the Great War* (translated by Major General Sir Ernst Swinton)[12] is very informative concerning the pre-war Belgian Army and Belgian strategy and is also the only detailed source on the Belgian Army in English. *Du Haut de la Tour du Babel* (From the Summit of the Tower of Babel) by the 1914 Belgian Chief of Staff, Lieutenant General Selliers de Moranville, is an excellent source concerning Belgian strategy in the two months before the war and the significance of the attack on Liège.[13] Another useful source is B. Duvivier/B. Herbiet, *Du Rôle de l'Armée de Campagne et des Fortresses Belges en 1914*.[14] The modern guidebooks to the individual forts are frequently valuable gems.[15]

One of the few accounts of the battle in English is C. Donnell, *The Forts of the Meuse in World War I*.[16] Insofar as the German Army is concerned, Donnell is completely unreliable. Rather than use German sources (he did not, and apparently doesn't speak German), he invented 'facts' about the German equipment and operations out of whole cloth. His most egregious absurdity is that on the night of 5–6 August the Germans took 42,712 casualties, unlikely since only about 25,000 German infantry were attacking. Donnell attributes to the Germans 28cm guns that they never had. In total, 457 shells were fired by I/ Foot Artillery 9 against Chaudefontaine. Donnell also says that the Germans were firing 2–300 shells an hour, and so on, including a pencil drawing of German infantry being overrun by Belgian cavalry.[17]

German time was an hour ahead of Belgian time: 0900 German time was 0800 Belgian time. Where confusion might arise, German time is listed as (G), Belgian as (B). Times stated are, however, generally approximate.

Notes

1. F.N. Kaiser (ed.), Das Ehrenbuch der Deutschen Schweren Artillerie (Berlin: Kolk, 1931).
2. Marschall von Bieberstein, Lüttich-Namur (Oldenburg: Stalling, 1918). Bieberstein was a Rittmeister (cavalry captain) and at Liège an assistant adjutant in 14 ID. Stalling was the publisher of the influential Deutsches Offiziersblatt (German Officers' Journal).
3. Bieberstein, Lüttich-NAMUR, 52.
4. E. Kabisch, Lüttich. Deutschlands Schicksalschritt in den Weltkrieg (Berlin: Schlegel, 1934).
5. Reichsarchiv, Der Weltkrieg I (Berlin: Mittler, 1925) 108–117.
6. Weltkrieg I, 119.
7. G. Leman, Le Rapport du général Leman sur la defense de Liège en août 1914. (Brussels: Palais des Acadêmes, 1960). Notes 16 and 25 by the editor of General Leman's report, Major Hautecler.
8. Colonel De Schrÿver, La Bataille de Liège (Liège: H. Vaillant-Carmanne, 1922).
9. Ministère de la Défense Nationale – Etat-Major Général de l'Armée. Section de l'Historique. Défense de la Position Fortifiée de Namur en Août 1914 (Brussels: Institut Cartographique Militaire, 1930).
10. R. Normand, Défense de Liége, Namur, Anvers en 1914 (Paris: Fournier, 1923).
11. Leman, Le Rapport du général Leman sur la defense de Liège en août 1914 (Brussels: Palais des Acadêmes, 1960).
12. E.J. Galet. Albert, King of the Belgians in the Great War (Boston: Houghton Mifflin, 1931).
13. Selliers de Moranville, Du Haut de la Tour du Babel (Paris: Berger-Levrault, 1925).
14. B. Duvivier/B. Herbiet, Du Rôle de l'Armée de Campagne et des Fortresses belges en 1914 (Bruxelles: l'Institut Cartographique Militaire, 1928).
15. Christian Faque, Henri-Alexis Brialmont. Les Forts de la Meuse 1887–1891 (Les Amis de la Citadelle de Namur, 1987). L. Ruther, Fort de Loncin (Ans: Front de Sauvegarde du Fort de Loncin, 2009). Ruther is the administrator of the 'Front to Safeguard the Fort de Loncin'. Comite de Sauvegarde du Patrimonie Historique du Fort de Hollogne, Le Fort de Hollogne dans la Position Fortifiée de Liège en 1914 (No publisher, no date).
16. C. Donnell, The Forts of the Meuse in World War I (Oxford: Osprey, 2007).
17. On page 41, Donnell captions a picture with 'Civilians flee as German troops cross the border into Belgium.' The troops and civilians are, however, moving in the opposite direction, so if the civilians are 'fleeing' they're fleeing into Germany. The occupants of the nearest automobile appear to be in a pleasant discussion with some German Jäger.

Mission

Siege Warfare

Shortly after the Napoleonic wars the increasing range and effectiveness of siege artillery had forced engineers to abandon the bastioned trace, exemplified by Vaubaun, and construct detached forts some distance from the point to be defended, frequently but not always a city. The detached forts would be linked by field fortifications – trenches – dug at the commencement of hostilities, if not somewhat before. This was called 'arming' a fortress. The detached forts would serve as strongpoints for the defence. The attacker would concentrate his main point of effort against what he considered a weak point. The attacker would have to engage three forts: one in the centre (the main point of attack) and the forts on each side that would provide supporting, and ideally flanking, fire for the centre fort. The defender would move additional forces, particularly artillery, to reinforce the threatened area. Fortresses like Metz had massive parks of mobile and semi-mobile 15cm heavy howitzers and long-range 10cm and 13cm cannon, backed up by full munitions bunkers, with which to conduct a protracted artillery duel at the decisive point.

Each major fortress was provided with a dedicated infantry reserve to occupy the trenches in the intervals between the fortresses and to conduct counterattacks to eliminate enemy breakthroughs – in German terminology the *Hauptreserve*. In 1914 each of the six major fortresses on the Western Front – Metz, Strasbourg, Verdun, Toul, Épinal and Belfort – had an entire reserve infantry division. In Metz this division (33 Reserve Division – RD) was particularly strong, including a Bavarian active army brigade (BDE) and an entire 15cm heavy howitzer regiment. These divisions were permanent parts of the fortress garrisons and would leave only if there was no threat to the fortress. Having left, if a threat materialised, they would return to the fortress.

The attacking artillery would attempt to suppress the defending artillery, destroy both the forts and the infantry in the intervals between the forts, and move his approach trenches and artillery forward observers (FOs) closer to the defensive works. Again, primarily using artillery fire, the defender would attempt to destroy the attacking artillery and infantry.

Fortress warfare doctrine anticipated the trench warfare that set in almost immediately on the Western Front.

To prevent a stalemate, it was essential to surround the fortress and cut it off from being reinforced and resupplied. Nevertheless, it had to be assumed that the siege of a first-rate fortress, even if cut off, would go on for months and consume vast numbers of heavy artillery shells.

In 1881 the French held a siege exercise against Verdun.[1] This was surely a mix of map exercise and staff ride – it is unlikely that troops were involved. The siege army was six divisions strong, and employed 460 heavy guns, three pioneer battalions and a large equipment park. The attack was directed at two of Verdun's detached forts, which held out for three months. It took another month to breach the city wall. Some 450,000 shells were expended.

Siege warfare doctrine against a fortress with detached works was uniform in all west-European armies, and was unchanged through 1914, in spite of improvements in both fortress armour and siege artillery.

By the Franco-Prussian War, the permanent fortress faced a crisis: the introduction of highly accurate rifled artillery, whose conical shells replaced cannon balls, and swung the scales in favour of the besieger. Rifled artillery could pick out the firing ports of the defenders' guns and silence them. The besieger could also walk shells across the walls of the fortifications and cause entire masonry walls to collapse. The guns had sufficient range to reach beyond the detached forts and engage the wall of the fortress (*enceinte*) directly.

An additional complication arose for the Belgians. In 1874 the French chambers approved the initial credits for Séré de Rivière's famous system of fortifications on France's border with Germany, which, based on the four great forts of Verdun, Toul, Épinal and Belfort, would make a direct German attack on France unlikely, if not impossible. Together with the increasing size of the French and German conscript armies, it appeared less and less likely that the next Franco-German war, widely anticipated by all of Europe, would be fought on their common border, which was also restricted by the Vosges mountains. The likely Franco-German battlefield was Belgium.

A further complication was presented by the discovery of high explosives around 1883, which could disassemble masonry fortifications in short order. Fortresses now had to be moved below ground, protected by a deep layer of concrete and earth, with the guns protected by iron and steel.

History of Belgian Fortifications[2]

Belgium became independent in 1830 and her borders were finalised in 1839. The first defence plan was drawn up between 1847 and 1851. The most important military decision was that Antwerp was to be transformed into an entrenched camp and the base of operations for the field army. Small fortresses were maintained all over the country. Based on these fortifications, the Belgian Army would conduct a delaying action against the invader, retreating to Antwerp if necessary. In 1859 Antwerp was designated the national redoubt. In 1876, given the increase in artillery capabilities, the first line of defence of Antwerp was pushed south.

The entire Belgian fortress system – Antwerp, Liège and Namur – was the work of the Belgian fortress engineer, Henri Brialmont. He was born in 1821, the son of Laurent Brialmont, a Belgian general officer and, for a short time in 1850–51, the Belgian Minister of War. Brialmont was commissioned in the engineers in 1843. In 1855 he made an inspection trip to the 'New Prussian system' of fortresses, which, breaking with Vaubaun's bastioned trace, inaugurated the system of detached forts and entrenched camps, and was deeply impressed. His rise from major (1861) to major general (1874) was rapid. In 1875 he was named inspector general of fortifications and the corps of engineers.

Brialmont's contribution to fortress engineering was to move the entire installation below ground and encase the guns in armoured turrets.

Liège and Namur: Mission

The dominating terrain feature in eastern and central Belgium is the Meuse River, an unfordable water obstacle which extends 70km from the Dutch border at Lixhé to the fortress of Namur.

Liège is located at the confluence of the Meuse, a significant obstacle 140m wide, the Ourthe and the Vesdre.[3] In 1914 it was an industrial city, the centre of Belgian arms manufacture, with 164,000 inhabitants, in a very strongly Walloon (French) portion of Belgium. On 27 June 1887 the Belgian government charged Brialmont with fortifying Belgium against both a French and a German attack. Namur would block the famous 'Trouée de l'Oise' between the Sambre and the Meuse. Liège would block the choke point between the Dutch border and the Ardennes.

Liège and Namur would replace fortresses constructed at these sites by the Dutch between 1816 and 1825, which the development of rifled artillery in 1860 had rendered obsolete. The new fortifications would therefore consist of a ring of detached forts encircling the city. At Liège this eventually meant twelve detached forts from 6,000–8,750m from the city centre and from 1,900–6,350m apart. The fortress perimeter would extend about 60km.

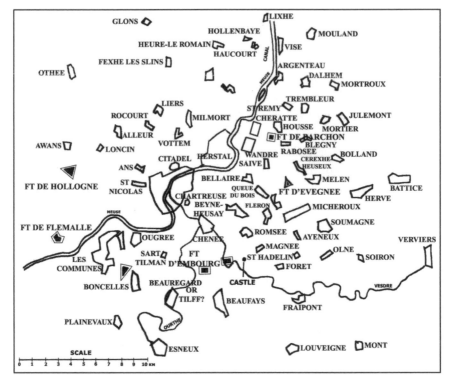

Liège, forts and towns.

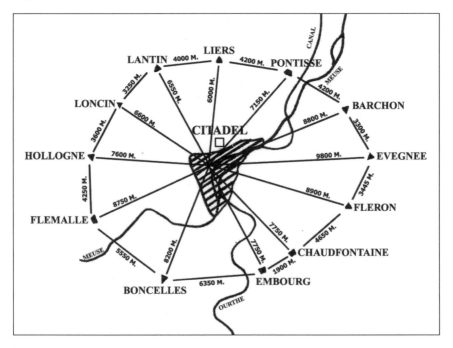

Liège, distances.

On 2 March 1887, General Pontus, the minister of war, explained the concept of the forts to the chamber of deputies:

Belgium has less to fear from an attack against its independence than a violation of its territory necessitated by the strategic interests of one of the belligerents [...] [crossing] either the lower Rhine or the north of France, utilising the Meuse as the route across Belgium [...] since we are obligated to defend the access to this route, it is necessary to give our army bridgeheads. In a word, the Meuse must be fortified.

Which Pontus identified as Namur and Liège, and to a lesser degree Huy, which were at once population centres, communication chokepoints, and important river crossings. On 7 July Pontus said:

Suppose that a war breaks out between our two powerful neighbours and consider how the Germans and the French might violate Belgian neutrality.

In the first case, the German northern army or right wing would assemble at Aachen and, given our hypothesis, direct the greater part of his forces towards the Sambre–Meuse and the valley of the Oise, attempting to take in the rear the French forces concentrated between Verdun and Stenay to block the German centre armies massed between Metz and Thionville.

It must be recognized that the chances of success for the strategic movement of the German right wing increase with the speed of its movement. If Namur and Liège are not fortified, the excellent communications along the Meuse allow the invader to move under optimal conditions along the most direct routes, while detaching forces to protect his right flank against the Belgian army in Antwerp. If this movement succeeds, not only is the way to Paris open to the Germans, they will have at their disposal a railhead 160 kilometres from the capital.

If, however, the line of the Meuse is fortified, the German forces could not march on a single route – a marching German corps is 24 to 28 kilometres long and under these conditions it would be impossible for a second German corps to follow the first. They would be forced to march all their forces north of the Meuse, or march on both banks.

In the first case they would cross the river by violating Dutch territory. To provide a route of march for each corps they would have to extend into the interior of our country. This flank march past the Meuse fortifications on the one hand and the Belgian army [in Antwerp] on the other would become exceptionally dangerous if a French army, coming to our support, was able to reach Namur. This converging movement [towards Verdun] would take too long and one can expect that it would fail.

If the German army decided to march on both banks of the Meuse the dangers are greater yet. The two halves would be separated by the Meuse fortifications, unable to unite, and risk defeat in detail.

The same considerations apply to a French invasion. Under this hypothesis, the objective of the French army would be to cross the Rhine between Cologne and Wesel and advance across the north German plain to Berlin. Once again, the line of the Meuse is the shortest and most advantageous route.

If Liège and Namur are not fortified, the French forces concentrate at Maubeuge and Givet and the march of the French columns on both banks of the river would be executed under the best strategic conditions from the point of view of speed and mutual support.

If, however, the line of the Meuse is fortified, the French army would be based at Lille, Valenciennes and Maubeuge, crossing the Meuse north of Liège and violating Dutch neutrality. This would be most dangerous, for a German army would stand on their left flank while Namur and Liège would menace the right, and these bridgeheads would facilitate the intervention of a German army assisting Belgium.

The situation would be no better for the French army if it advanced on both banks of the Meuse, separated by the fortifications.

These are the most probable hypothesis; it would take too long to consider all of them. I will limit myself to the situation in 1870, the only time that the Belgian army has mobilized. Our army deployed beyond Namur in the Ardennes. If one of the belligerents had moved into Belgium and pushed us back, our line of retreat would have been through Namur to Antwerp. Namur would have been called on to play the role of bridgehead […] A Belgian army might hold the line of the Meuse while waiting for support from the other belligerent.

In the face of a new war between France and Germany, Liège and Namur, properly fortified, will have a capital importance for Belgium.

Défense de Namur said that Liège and Namur would have three strategic/operational functions:

First, as blocking positions, depriving the invader of roads, rail lines and bridges. *Défense de Namur* said that the individual forts at Liège and Namur were therefore located to perform their principal function, which was to block the all the roads. De Schrÿver agreed.[4] General Pontus said:

After the enemy has broken through [the field fortifications in the intervals between the permanent fortifications] he can take possession of the city, but what advantage does that give him? Will he be the master of the routes of communication? Will his strategic advance be facilitated? Obviously not. He must first take the forts, and the immediate arrival of the Belgian army, or the army of the friendly power, or both, will place him in a critical situation.

As *Défense de Namur* and De Schrÿver both point out, there was no intention to even seriously defend the intervals. The permanent garrison was weak (garrison of the forts plus a regiment of overage fortress infantry at Namur and one or two at Liège, with no artillery worth the name) was not sufficient even to stop a *coup de main*.

The only way the individual forts could be defended is if they were supported by the field army, so here we encounter the fundamental contradiction between fortress doctrine, which called for a field force to support Liège, and the impossibility of providing such a force. If the Belgian Army tried to defend Liège against the Germans, or Namur against the French, the only likely outcome would have been the destruction of the Belgian Army. Belgium's neutrality prevented it from conducting defence co-ordination with either power, to bring a relief army to either fortress. In the event, in 1914 the French had no interest in sending an army to relieve Liège.

Second, Liège and Namur were to serve as bridgeheads, permitting the garrison or the field army to cross from one side of the Meuse to the other, even if in the presence of the enemy. Brialmont described the fortifications as 'a double bridgehead'.

Third, as bases for manoeuvre, permitting the Belgian Army to take positions and conduct offensive and defensive operations on both sides of the Meuse. The French fortress engineer, Normand, said the Belgians did not have a manoeuvre army capable of using it properly against a formidable German opponent, which reduced the forts to inert defence, which could hardly be successful. The forts could, however, also facilitate such operations by the army of the friendly power, with which the Belgian Army could co-operate. *Du Rôle de l'Armée de Campagne et des Fortresses Belges* said that Liège and Namur provided both the Belgian Army, and other friendly armies, a means of manoeuvring on both banks of the Meuse.

This is an important point, and one that is never recognised. Liège, Namur, and other 'entrenched camps' like the four great French fortresses of Verdun, Toul, Épinal and Belfort, and the German forts at Metz and on the Vistula, had an *offensive* mission. They provided a secure offensive springboard to screen and support attacks by army-sized units, especially against enemy flanks and rear. Liège could be used to support an attack into northern Germany as well as against the flank of a German advance into the Ardennes, and the Germans were well aware of this fact, as shown by the fact that they continually modernised Fortress Cologne.

In all three cases there is an explicit statement that the isolated forts had to be supported by a field army; indeed, two of the three reasons for building the forts were to assist the manoeuvre and operations of a field army.

The Belgians had another, more logical, reason for building Liège and Namur. In the late 1880s, when the fortresses were planned and constructed, a Franco-German battle in Belgium was considered by European military opinion to be likely, but it would take place in the Ardennes, south of the Meuse. It must also be remembered that 1888–89, when the fortresses were being built, were the years of the Boulanger crisis, with the French war minister openly talking of *revanche*.

In the 1890s neither Germany nor France were strong enough to send major forces north of the Meuse. Schlieffen did not even consider an advance in the Ardennes until 1897, and then only to reject it because the Germans did not have enough troops.[5] *Du Rôle de l'Armée de Campagne et des Fortresses Belges* said that Liège and Namur would also deny the invader use of the Meuse valley, forcing him to remain south of the river, and preventing central Belgium from becoming a battlefield. By making an advance north of the Meuse risky, and an advance on both sides of it impossible, the *actual* mission of Liège and Namur was to keep the opposing armies in the lightly-populated Ardennes Forest south of the Meuse, out of the Belgian plain north of the river and away from the centres of Belgian population and industry. This was for the Belgians a best-case scenario.

We therefore encounter a fundamental inconsistency between siege warfare doctrine, which demanded a large force of infantry and mobile artillery to hold the intervals, and Belgian resources. At Fortress Liège, as we shall see, doctrinal defence of the intervals required 60,000 men and hundreds of heavy guns. The Belgian command knew full well that such a force would never be available. It would require the entire Belgian field army just to hold the national redoubt at Antwerp, leaving nothing for Liège and Namur. In thirty years, the Belgians never made any attempt to resolve this inconsistency.

In the event, this would result in the Belgians adopting the worst possible solution to the problem. They made no preparations to defend the intervals or to support the forts with the field army. Then, at literally the last minute, they committed a completely inadequate and woefully unprepared force to try to hold the intervals. After one night of combat, they withdrew that force, leaving the practically defenceless individual forts on their own.

The Forts

Work commenced in 1888 and was mostly concluded by 1892, with the armoured searchlights being installed in 1893 and 1894. The construction of Liège and Namur were seriously over budget. The cost was originally estimated at 24 million francs, but rose to 73.5, and as a consequence Brialmont was forced to resign in 1892. It seems that the willingness of the Belgian parliament to pay for serious defensive preparations was exhausted, for there were no serious improvements in Belgian defensive arrangements until immediately before the Great War.

The concept of the individual forts was fourfold:[6]

- The forts needed to keep the attackers at a distance sufficient to prevent them from observing or bombarding Liège and Namur. Both cities were in defilade in the valley of the Meuse.
- The forts must be within medium artillery range from each other, to provide mutual support.
- The forts had to command their zone of action with artillery fire, particularly the intervals between the forts.
- The cost of the forts had to stay within budgetary constraints. Brialmont therefore did not construct small permanent works in the intervals between the forts.

Brialmont established two criteria for his forts:

- The artillery had to be armoured, protected by cupolas of iron and steel, and proof against the heaviest existing siege artillery.
- The routes of communication and troop quarters had to be protected by concrete and a deep layer of earth.

Brialmont did not leave this to guesswork[7]. He conducted firing tests with shells containing 30kg and 60kg of dynamite fired from a howitzer at 2,500m range against a concrete arch 2.5m thick. Nine direct hits at the same place were necessary to achieve penetration. Given that siege artillery had to be horse-drawn, the largest practical siege gun was a 21–22cm howitzer weighing 3,000 to 3,500kg. Brialmont therefore decided to protect his forts with 2.5m of Portland cement (but *not* reinforced with rebar) covered by 3m of earth. The forts would be below ground level, only the gun turrets/cupolas rising slightly above it.

Brialmont constructed four types of forts (see fort sketches). At Liège there were five large triangular (Barchon, Fléron, Boncelles, Loncin, Pontisse) four small triangular (Evegnée, Hollogne, Lantin, Liers), one large quadrangular (Flémalle) and two small quadrangular (Chaudefontaine, Embourg). The triangular fort was favoured in principle, for reasons of economy: it had the minimum number of flanks to be protected. The salients were numbered from the gorge, left to right. The most endangered salient, number II in the triangular forts, was called the principal salient. In rectangular forts the principal salient faced the enemy.[8]

The fort proper consisted of a central citadel protected by concrete, which contained most of the armament and fire control, including magazines, ventilators, a petrol generator and cisterns fed by rainwater. In a large fort there were two armoured turrets, each with two 12cm cannon, one turret with two 15cm cannon and two cupolas each with a single 21cm howitzer. Behind the 15cm turret was a searchlight in a disappearing turret, with a range on a clear night of 2 or 3km (sources differ). During the day it served as an observation post. There were also four more

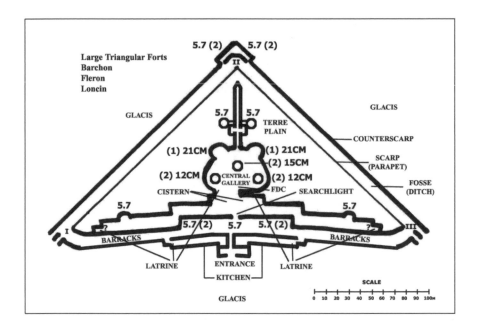

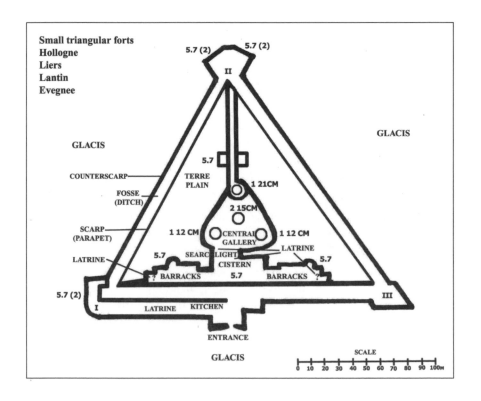

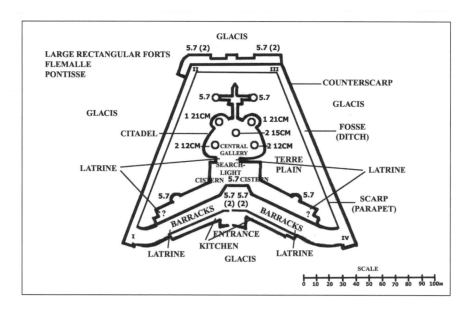

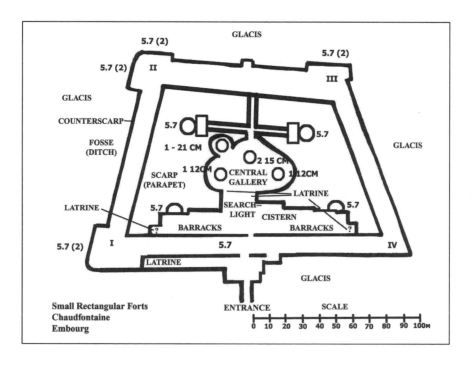

disappearing turrets with a fast-firing 5.7cm cannon, two in front of the citadel and one at each of the angles at the base. In a small fort there was only one 21cm howitzer cupola and three 5.7cm fast-firing cannon turrets.

The heavy artillery (12cm, 15cm, 21cm) was slow firing, using *black powder* shells and *black powder* charges.[9] On the night of 5–6 August, Fort Pontisse fired a salvo every three minutes against German infantry directly to its front.[10] The 5.7cm also employed black powder. This technology had been obsolete since 1883. When these guns fired, the enormous clouds of black powder smoke would blind observation from the fort of the fall of shell. In addition, some of this smoke was sure to work its way back into the fort. *Défense de Namur* said that the effectiveness of the black powder shells was 'insignificant'. Maximum effective range for the 15cm was 8,500m, for the 12cm, 8,000m. The commander of Fléron, Mozin, said that the maximum effective range of the main gun armament was 7,500m;[11] *Défense de Namur* also said that the theoretical maximum effective range of the heavy artillery shell was irrelevant: due to the clouds of smoke generated by the black powder charge and the great variations in the point of impact, it was difficult to observe the fall of shot beyond 1,500m.

Which brings up the question of fortress gunnery, which is never addressed. Until the advent of smart munitions at the end of the twentieth century, the first artillery rounds never hit their targets. Problems of actually identifying the target accurately on the map (and the gun's firing chart), barrel wear, temperature, wind, humidity and varying ammunition, meant that the first round always missed. An observer would have to see the fall of the shot and then adjust fire onto the target. The most common method of fire adjustment was 'bracketing'. The first round landed beyond or short of the target. A large correction would be made, so that the second round landed on the opposite side of the target, which was now 'bracketed'. The third round split the difference. Frequently corrections would have to be made for deflection left to right in addition to range. For this reason a four- or six-gun battery would usually adjust fire with one gun: when this gun landed on target, the entire battery would fire several rounds 'for effect'.

At Liège the forts all had preplanned targets, which were numbered, a common practice for artillery or mortars. But since the forts were surrounded by a heavily-inhabited area, there was no way that they could have 'shot in' their preplanned targets, that is to say, fired live rounds to determine if the calculations were correct. By 1914 the guns were 25 years old, during which time they had *never* fired live ammunition, and since they were firing inherently inaccurate black powder, the forts' first rounds in any fire mission would have been wildly inaccurate. It would have often been difficult to see where the shells had landed. Belgian accounts, which frequently speak of first-round direct hits by entire salvoes, are a fantasy.

The 12cm and 15cm turrets were based on the same model, similar to turrets in warships, a cylinder 4.8m in diameter with an armoured roof of 20cm of iron between two sheets of steel each 2cm thick. Around the turret proper was another ring of six curved sheets of hardened iron, 35cm thick at the top, 24cm at the bottom, called the *avant-cuirasse*. The turret occupied a hole lined with concrete, 8m deep, on three levels. These were not disappearing guns, but the turret was mounted on rollers. The turret was capable of turning 360 degrees. Gross movements were made in the lower level, delicate movements on the gun; the turret restricted the ability to elevate the weapon and so prevented it from firing at its maximum range. All of the turret mechanisms, gun direction and elevation, ammunition supply, loading and ventilation, were hand-powered.[12] It had a twenty-five-man crew. There were eight men in the turret: a turret commander, who was an officer or non-commissioned officer (NCO,) a gun captain and three gunners for each gun. On the intermediate level was the assistant turret commander. On the bottom level and the central gallery were sixteen men: an NCO, a corporal, six men to operate the turret training mechanism, two on the ventilator, two on the ammunition hoist, four for the ammunition supply. There were four different types of ammunition: explosive shells of normal iron or hardened iron; steel; shrapnel and canister.

The 21cm howitzer was protected by an armoured cupola (not a turret) sitting on two steel columns. (This is a technical distinction and for the sake of simplicity we will call all the gun positions on the citadel 'turrets'.) The armour rested directly on the *avant-cuirasse* and had to be lifted slightly in order to be turned in the direction of fire. The howitzer and cupola weighed 39 metric tons (39,000kg). At the time of the construction of the fort (1888) it was one of the most powerful pieces of artillery in existence, firing a 91kg shell 6.9km, as well as shrapnel. The howitzer crew was made up of an NCO howitzer commander and four men on the upper level; on the lower level a corporal, two men on the ventilator, two on the ammunition hoist and two on the ammunition supply.

To direct fire, the fort had observation posts connected with telephones: for Fort Loncin the bell towers of the churches at Alleur, Ans-Sainte-Marie, Loncin and the towers of the châteaux of Awans and Waroux. The fort also received information from patrols, including a group led by Corporal Polain in a requisitioned automobile.

For each 21cm howitzer there were 200 explosive shells and 300 shrapnel, for the 15cm and 12cm guns, 230 explosive, 20 canister and 300 shrapnel. For a large fort this comes to 4,300 shells, not a great deal considering that the forts contained the only heavy artillery Liège possessed, and would have to carry the entire load if the Germans launched a deliberate attack or began a formal siege.

The forts were protected by a dry ditch from 7–10m across and 5–8m deep. The gorge (entrance) and counterscarp were vertical and revetted with concrete. The scarp had a 4 in 5 slope of earth covered with spiked plants. Between the ditch and the armoured citadel was the grassy terreplein.

To provide flanking fire of the two lateral (Λ) sides of the ditch there were two 5.7cm fast-firing cannon in casemates in the counterscarp. Each of the casemates was two stories high. The cannon were mounted on the ground floor, but, if their field of fire was blocked by debris, could be moved to the second storey. If the gorge was bastioned (indented at the entrance), then flanking fire was provided by two cannon in one-storey casemates in the flanks of the bastion. If the gorge was straight, there was a casemate in the gorge counterscarp. At the other end of the ditch was a 'back-stop' to smother the shells and prevent damage to the walls. There was also a casemate and cannon above the access gate, firing down the access ramp. There were also four disappearing 5.7cm turrets topside on the large forts, three in the small ones. The gun crew consisted of an NCO gun commander, three-man crew and two ammunition handlers. The guns could fire at a rate of thirty-six rounds per minute. In a large fort there were four two-gun casemates, a single-gun casemate and four single-gun turrets, thirteen fixed 5.7cm guns; in a small fort ten. The 5.7cm turrets had 10cm of armour. There were also mobile 5.7cm stored in the counterscarp. The turrets for the search-light were protected by 10cm of cast steel sandwiched between two 4cm sheets of steel.

In case of infantry attack the fort's infantry company and some of the artillerymen would man a parapet behind the ditch, a feature so old that even Vaubaun would have had no trouble recognising it.

By 1914 the forts' defences against infantry attack were completely obsolete. When the forts were planned there were no machine guns (MGs). The German Army did not make widespread use of MG until 1909. In an attack on a fort the MG was par-ticularly effective against defending infantry behind the parapet, the 5.7cm turrets and the fort's observation posts (OPs). Prior to the introduction of the French Lebel 1886, infantry rifles were single shot and fired low-velocity black powder. The Lebel was magazine-fed and fired a smokeless round with far higher muzzle velocity and therefore greater range and accuracy. The standard German rifle was introduced in 1898 (hence the designation Karabiner 98, K98). Infantry defending the parapet was now likely to take significant casualties. To make matters worse, many of the forts were poorly sited, with dead ground just beyond the glacis, and over time civilian dwellings had been built in close proximity to the forts, offering attacking infantry cover, concealment, and offensive strongpoints.

As *Défense de Namur* said, 'The ventilation [of the individual forts] was not assured [...] they were not very hygienic'. The forts were extremely humid, from condensa-tion on the cold concrete walls and rainwater seeping through cracks in the concrete. In peacetime, the garrison lived in barracks on the glacis behind the gorge, which were burned down at the beginning of hostilities.

The forts were equipped with a 20hp gas generator, which supplied power to the searchlight, to spotlights in the fosse and limited illumination in the interior. Ventilation was supposed to have occurred by opening the windows into the rooms of the scarp and counterscarp. In wartime these were closed with armour plate. This did not prevent gas from exploding shells and the Belgian black powder charges from entering the fort, and there was no means to blow the gases back out. The turrets had hand-pumped ventilators, which were both ineffective and extremely tiring.

Several forts had a few electric ventilators. At Fléron the fire direction centre and machine room had power ventilation. The complete ventilation system planned by Brialmont was not installed, for reasons of economy.

The fort's own barracks were in the scarp at the rear of the fort, the food storage, kitchen, bakeries and latrines and such in the counterscarp. They were located here to keep unpleasant odours from the living quarters. This would have been perfectly suitable, had these been connected to the main fort by underground passages, but for reasons of economy they were not. When the fort came under bombardment, the citadel was cut off from the counterscarp facilities, including the food and kitchens, but especially the latrines, and the smell of excrement from some 300 or more men filled the armoured citadel. There were apparently two small latrines in the citadel, but these were inadequate, and may have overflowed or been broken. When access to the main latrines was lost, extemporaneous latrines needed to be made out of buckets and such.

The sole means of direct communication between the forts, or with the HQ, was an overhead telephone line to the main city telephone exchange.

In peacetime, the fort artillery crews and infantry and a few engineers were active-army. The artillerymen of each fort were organised into a battery, recruited from the surrounding area. The infantry company was also equipped with mobile 5.7cm cannon that could fire from positions topside. The glacis was covered with barbed wire.

On mobilisation, the fort artillery batteries were brought to full-strength –five Officers (OFF) and 317 enlisted men (EM) for the large forts, five OFF and 269 EM for the smaller forts) from reservists of the classes of 1912 to 1906. The older artillery reservists went to the mobile artillery batteries. The infantry platoon numbered one OFF and 82 EM. Each fort also had two doctors and several stretcher bearers.

In 1914 the only unit of the Liège mobile reserve was an active-army engineer battalion. On mobilisation Liège and Namur were each assigned four regiments of fortress infantry, to construct and hold field fortifications to defend the intervals between the permanent forts. The fortress infantry regiments were made up of the oldest age groups of the militia (reservists) comparable to Territorial troops in other armies. Generally, the fortress infantry regiments were composed of three battalions of four companies, each company with an authorised strength of three OFF and 260 EM, plus a fortress MG company, total authorised strength of fifty OFF and 3,150 EM. This remained a fond wish: the fortress regiments never came to anywhere near this strength and the MG companies were not formed.

Liège Obsolete

Once built, the Liège forts were frozen in amber. There were no MG positions. In 1914 there was not a single MG in either the fortifications or fortress regiments at Liège.[13] The concrete was not reinforced. The compound iron and steel armour was hopelessly outdated by 1914. In 1891 the American engineer, H.A. Harvey, introduced 'cemented' armour heated in contact with carbon – which was then cooled with water – giving it a hard face. The plate was then annealed, giving it a tough back.[14] 7½in of Harvey armour provided the same protection as 12in of compound (iron and steel, as in the Belgian fortresses), or 15in of wrought iron. In 1896 Krupp improved on the Harvey method with a steel alloy, requiring only 5½in of armour. Harvey and Krupp steel, and reinforced concrete, provided some protection against modern high-explosive armour-piercing shells; Liège's compound armour and unreinforced concrete did not. Moreover, as we shall see, the German introduced a mobile, more effective and highly accurate 21cm mortar.

Modern fortifications adapted to the increased effectiveness imparted by high-velocity smokeless powder, and the most modern fortress in 1914 was Metz; indeed Metz was arguably more effective than the Maginot fortifications.[15] The distinguishing characteristic of Metz was the use of widely dispersed *I-Werke*, company-sized infantry strongpoints constructed out of reinforced concrete. Rather than a parapet, the infantry defences consisted of blockhouses (bunkers) and *Schnecken,* concrete fox-holes. In the fall of 1944 Georgie Patton found to his dismay that the *I-Werke* were tough nuts to crack

Normand doubted that Liège was capable of withstanding a serious siege, nor did he think that the Belgians were prepared to conduct one. There was no munitions arsenal, nor narrow-gauge rail line to resupply the forts. Normand's evaluation was:

> Liège was a great fortified camp[16] composed of a number of blocking forts which were in fact isolated and unable to support each other. They could not place flanking fire on the intervals between the forts, which constituted a single, discontinuous line of uncertain effectiveness. The forts themselves were vulnerable from the rear. The forested and hilly Meuse valley contained considerable dead ground, which could not be covered by the very small number of howitzers available. The entire area, plateaux and ravines both, was covered by very large trees which limited visibility. Ravines even provided avenues of approach to the front and sides of several forts (Chaudefontaine, Embourg, Flémalle, Barchon). Some of the artillery forward observation posts were placed up to two kilometres in front and could not be protected. On the contrary, the plateau from Pontisse to Hollogne was completely open.

For all the vast expenditure in providing protection for the forts, their offensive firepower was insufficient: a 'large' detached fort had only four 12cm guns, two 15cm guns and two 21cm howitzers, all of mid-1880s vintage. The guns were flat-trajectory weapons and quite worthless against the predominant siege weapon, the 21cm mortar, which would fire from a defilade position. If the Germans launched a doctrinal attack against three fortresses, Liège would have to conduct the artillery duel with at the very most six 21cm howitzers. In 1914 the Germans brought up two 21cm regiments – thirty-two 21cm mortars, all a generation newer and far more accurate than the mortars Liège had been designed to face.

If the Germans had foregone an *attaque brusquée* and begun a doctrinal siege attack on the 11th day of mobilisation, Liège would not have held out much longer than it did in 1914 (as Namur did not). The fortress would have been cut off by an entire German cavalry corps. The defending heavy artillery would have been outnumbered five to one. The German infantry would have launched well-prepared attacks that would have blown through any resistance the fortress infantry tried to put up with little trouble.

Liège was incapable of performing its mission.

General Leman

As of 1911, the Governor of Liège was given operational control over 3 DA (*Division d'Armée* – Infantry Division) and Namur 4 DA. In the beginning of February 1914 the commander of the 3 DA, the 3 DA conscription area, and commandant of the Liège fortress was General Gérard-Mathieu-Joseph-Georges Leman. Major Hautecler, who served under General Leman as the fortress artillery officer before and during the battle and then was with Leman in captivity, and published Leman's after-action report in 1960, wrote that General Leman was 'one of the most attractive figures in our [Belgium's] military history.'

Leman was born at Liège on 8 January 1851, had entered the Belgian Army as a lieutenant of engineers, first in his class at the military academy, in 1872.[17] In Leman's entire career he had *never* commanded troops, but served in various capacities at the military academy. Leman began as a tutor in military construction and fortification, then taught geology, construction and architecture. He wrote widely, including one article on resistance of materials that was brought out as a second edition in 1910 and a third in 1926. From 1894 to 1899 he fought and won a scholarly battle with General Tilly on the best method of teaching infinitesimal calculus. In 1899 he became the director of education and reinforced the scientific emphasis of study, requiring chemistry and physics in the entrance examination. In 1905 he became the commandant of the military academy. In his notes on Leman's report, Hautecler says that Leman emphasised science 'to the detriment, it appears, of the purely military. In addition, Leman saw everything in terms of mathematics'. Leman wrote:

> When one decides to erect a fortress, the principal consideration is the length
> of time that it must resist; the second is the strength of the garrison [...] the

fundamental principle then: to the last shell and the last loaf of bread. Siege warfare is a problem for industrial engineering.

'These phrases', said Hautecler, 'were entirely characteristic: Leman took no account of the individual, his wavering morale and weaknesses. Confronted with the realities of commanding a fortress in the face of the enemy, he would have to modify them, though continued to apply them to his own person'.

On 31 December 1913 the commander of 3 DA died suddenly. The war minister recommended to the king that Leman replace him. Leman objected to the war minister that he had never commanded troops and that appointing him commander of 3 DA was a mistake, 'At the end of my career a brusque and complete change'. He also did not understand why the commander of 3 DA was at the same time commandant of Liège: these two positions, in his mind, should have been separate.

Leman's designation to command in Liège was strongly criticised. The journal *Belgique Militaire* wrote on 1 February 1914 that:

[Leman was] two years from mandatory retirement and it would seem more advantageous to leave him at the head of the military academy, where he had already passed 34 years of his career, rather than confer on him an active command, where he must familiarize himself with everything. We regard with considerable apprehension the appointment of technical officers, who have never had the least tactical experience, to command our divisions and brigades.

Brialmont had been impressed by Leman and gave him his first position in the military academy as a tutor. Together with Leman's experience as an instructor of fortification, construction and architecture, then as commander of the fortress, Leman must be considered to be one of the most knowledgeable officers in the Belgian Army concerning Fortress Liège.

Leman began his report with a startling assertion: Liège's forts had been designed to resist 21cm black powder artillery. This directly contradicts other sources which either state outright or strongly imply that Brialmont had protected Liège against the far more destructive high-explosive shells. Leman immediately followed this with a second startling revelation: that the fort's artillery also fired black powder charges and shells.

Leman calculated that for each 4km of front the permanent fort's artillery provided an average of 3 12cm and 2 15cm guns and 1.5 21cm mortar. Each of these had 500 shells. Leman did not carry his analysis further, but this was not enough artillery and shells to conduct a successful duel with the attacking artillery: on this 4km front the Germans would deploy at least one modern 21cm mortar regiment with sixteen mortars, and perhaps two. Moreover, the siege guns, now firing smokeless powder, would be defilade and hidden, and the fortress artillery would never find a target, while the location of the fortresses was a matter of public record.

According to European siege doctrine the fortress mobile artillery was to reinforce the fort's artillery at the main point of the enemy attack. The Belgians had at least made an attempt to provide the national redoubt at Antwerp with mobile siege artillery: 132 12cm guns (Krupp, Model 1889) and 96 15cm howitzers (Krupp, 1887 and 1890), providing 2.5 guns per kilometre of front. This material was completely obsolete by 1914, heavy and firing black powder charges, but at the least it shows that the Belgians recognised the necessity for mobile field artillery.[18] The mobile artillery at both Liège and Namur was so obsolete and ineffective as to call into question the military value of the two fortresses.

Leman gave a detailed description of the mobile artillery reserve, all but the 7.5cm once again firing black powder, '114 worthless old pieces which I mention only for the record':

12 15cm cast iron (!) guns with 500 shells per gun

8 12cm steel guns, model 1862 (!) with 300 shells per gun

16 8.7cm guns with 195 shells per gun

12 8.7cm howitzers with 500 shells each

48 8cm guns, Model 1862 (!) with 200 rounds each

18 7.5cm guns with 439 rounds each.

The 7.5cm horse guns and 8.7cm guns were Krupp Model 1877, had been issued to the field army between 1887 and 1890, replacing the 8cm and 9cm guns. They were slow firing (a shell a minute) with black powder charges and shells. The maximum effective range against infantry was 3,000m; total maximum effective range, 5,000m. Both were withdrawn from the field army in 1905, when the rapid-firing Krupp 7.5cm was adopted. The 7.5cm guns had been retrofitted with brakes on the wheels, and not recoil brakes, which nevertheless kept the gun relatively stable and increased the rate of fire to four shells a minute, and also with smokeless powder and high-explosive shells. There was no change in the 8.7cm guns.

The 8.7cm howitzers were adopted in 1900 specifically to engage dead space at Liège and Namur and entered service in 1904. They still fired black powder, 3 rounds per minute, maximum effective range 3,800m. The 8.7cm and 7.5cm guns and 8cm howitzers were not only obsolete, but were field-gun calibre and worthless in a siege artillery duel. Given the age of the guns, the condition of the ammunition had to be suspect, if not outright dangerous.

The 15cm guns were cast iron, the 8cm guns and 12cm guns were model 1862, all from the era of the US Civil War, which says all one needs to know. The 8cm had been withdrawn from the field army in 1890, twenty-four years previously.

All of these guns had to fire direct lay, which meant they would be visible to their targets, and the black powder would give their positions away. Only the 7.5cm had a gun shield, which meant that the crews had a very short life expectancy in combat.

These antiquated guns were to form twenty-four batteries, but only four of these had any officers and twenty had none. Leman noted that he therefore had no artillery with which to defend the intervals or conduct the artillery duel: the completely inadequate fortress artillery was on its own.

Leman said that Liège never had much value as a fortress because it was constructed on the basis of incorrect principles. He said that he had no need of pointing this out: it was perfectly well understood. The individual forts were never designed to be defended independently; the protection for the rear was only 1.5m thick, the other fronts 2.5m. Liège had always been intended to serve as a double bridgehead. The forts were to support each other and serve as strongpoints for the field fortifications that were to be constructed in the intervals.

The first major weakness at Liège was that these intervals were 'inconceivably weak', often with more than 3,500m between forts, 'enormous gaps in which the artillery of the forts was impotent' and which made up two-thirds of the defensive perimeter.

The second major weakness was that the forts were so poorly located on the ground that (except for Lantin, Loncin and Hollogne, all located on the west side of Liège) their immediate field of fire extended only 600m. Especially on the side facing Germany there were deep valleys which led directly up to the glacis 'as though the enemy had dug them to provide a covered avenue of approach'. This situation was aggravated by the fact that, when the forts had been constructed, a military zone 600m around the forts had been created, which forbade the construction of permanent buildings or modification of the terrain. Over the course of time these restrictions were not observed.

Third weakness: in order to conduct the long-range artillery duel, the forts needed artillery observers 3,000m from the defensive line. These had to be located in fortified positions just as strong as the forts themselves. None such were ever constructed.

Fourth weakness: once the forts were besieged, they immediately became uninhabitable. The kitchens and latrines were not located in the armoured citadel, but on the opposite side of the rear fosse. It was too dangerous to cross the fosse when the fort was under fire (the sole exception being Loncin). The principal cause for the fall of the forts, according to Leman, was the fact that the air inside the citadel was made foul, indeed unbreathable, by the excrement of 300 to 400 men.

The fifth weakness, 'perhaps the most serious of all', was the lack of an *enceinte* around the city. In this, the Germans agreed with Leman. Such an *enceinte* would have served as a rally point for the troops in the intervals, as well as have prevented an attacker from penetrating the line of forts and then bombarding them from the rear. Leman said that the very nature of the ring of forts around Liège implied an *enceinte* around the city. Once inside the city, the attacker was secure: it was unthinkable that the governor would have fired on the citizens of Liège. To make matters worse, the citadel in Liège should therefore have been reinforced and modernised, to provide the governor with a secure headquarters. Instead, the citadel was demilitarised.

Leman then returned to the fact that Liège was designed to resist 21cm mortars firing black powder shells. Not only were the Germans now using much more powerful high explosives, but Leman, like many other Belgian sources, was convinced that the Germans had 28cm mortars on a wheeled chassis capable of defeating 4–5m of concrete, double that at Liège, and said as much in a report concerning the reorganisation of the military academy to the war minister on 28 May 1913. He did so based on a report by General Deguise concerning Russian firing tests at Otchakoff on the Black Sea in October 1912, in which 15cm fire prevented a Cockerill turret, similar to the ones at Antwerp, from rotating, while 28cm fire collapsed the concrete and made the guns unserviceable without, however, penetrating the steel cupola. Leman said that everyone who read the report could no longer have the least confidence that the Belgian forts would stand up to such fire. The only hope was that the guns would not be mobile enough to follow the German troops closely, or that they would be employed against French fortresses rather than Liège. Leman said that he went to great lengths to keep the garrison ignorant of the fort's vulnerability, lest their morale collapse.

The Problem of Defending Liège

Given that Liège was made up of twelve detached works on about a 50km front, and that the prevailing fortress warfare doctrine called for the employment of both infantry and artillery to defend field fortifications, it would seem axiomatic that the Belgians would be prepared to conduct just such a defence. The Germans certainly assumed that the Belgians would. It comes as a considerable surprise that the Belgians prepared for no such thing.

The Belgian Chief of Staff in 1914, Selliers de Moranville, said that a garrison of 60,000 men, or 1¼ men per metre of front, would have been required to defend the perimeter of Liège, which he said was 49km long, 21km of that on the west bank of the Meuse.[19] In 1913 he said the garrison consisted of 8,000 men from the oldest age groups. While headquartered in Liège, 3 DA was not part of the garrison, and 8,000 overage men were clearly incapable of offering a serious defence of the intervals between the forts. Sixty thousand men would have amounted to half of the Belgian field army. A defence of Namur would have required a somewhat smaller number, but according to Moranville the national redoubt at Antwerp by itself required the entire field army. The three great Belgian fortresses looked formidable, but the Belgians had failed completely to raise the forces necessary to hold them.

Between 1905 and 1910 the Belgian Army had come to the conclusion that the intervals would not be seriously defended and that Liège, instead of being a single fortress, was to be considered as twelve isolated works. The Germans would be able to occupy the centre of Liège, but that would avail them nothing, because the individual forts would still block the lines of communication. The individual forts and the fortress infantry at

Liège were therefore provided with enough rations and ammunition for a month of combat. No provisions were made for rations or ammunition for a larger garrison.

Antwerp[20]

After the completion of Liège and Namur 1892, these two fortresses were the most powerful and modern in Belgium. The 1876 decision to construct an advanced line at Antwerp had been carried out only in part, and the fortifications were not as strong as at Liège and Namur. However, in 1906 it was decided to transform Antwerp into one of the largest and most powerful fortresses in the world. A principal defensive line 100km long would be constructed with seventeen forts, eleven of them new, and eleven new redoubts, with a fortress infantry garrison of 77,000 men and a siege park of 132 12cm guns and 96 15cm howitzers.

The expansion of Fortress Antwerp had by no means been completed by 1914. Nevertheless, there was now a real element of tension and uncertainty in Belgian war planning, which rested wholly on fortifications.

Liège and Namur had been designed to work closely with the field army: together they would block the line of the Meuse and the two fortresses would offer the option of a counterstroke south of the river.

The very size of Antwerp, and the resources it required, meant that the field army would orient itself on Antwerp. This, together with the increased probability that the Germans would attack north of the Meuse, meant that Liège's bridgehead function was far less viable, and Liège would probably serve solely as a blocking position.

Nevertheless, the contradiction between the concept behind Fortress Liège and the competing concept behind Fortress Antwerp was not resolved before the war, and became clear in the uncertainty in the beginning of August as to exactly what mission Liège was to perform.

The War Plan, Command and Control at Fortress Liège

The commander of 3 DA was also the governor of Fortress Liège. A major general was attached to 3 DA to serve as deputy governor and command of the fortress would have devolved to him. When Leman arrived there was friction between the division and fortress staffs, which he had to smooth over. Aside from sharing the same commander, the two organisations were completely separate.

The Belgian Army had only a mobilisation plan. The scheme of manoeuvre that it would conduct after the mobilisation was concluded was completely up in the air. There was no guarantee that 3 DA would remain at Liège: it might operate with the rest of the field army, wherever that might be. Leman said that in the fortress archives he found instructions from the General Staff dated 12 March 1913 concerning Liège's wartime function, which were so vague they could hardly be called a 'war plan':

> If, either at the beginning or during the course of the campaign, the commander in chief determines that he will use one of the Meuse fortifications [Liège and Namur] in their role as bridgeheads, strongpoint, pivot of maneuver or even entrenched camp, he will move the necessary troops and materials there.

As for Fortress Liège itself, Leman found a message from the War Ministry to the effect that the defence might be restricted to the individual forts, or the forts plus the fortress infantry regiments, or the forts, fortress infantry and an active-army brigade, or part or all of 3 DA, or perhaps even a portion of the field army. Galet also unofficially briefed Leman on the war plan that he and the king were trying to impose on the army, that is, hold the left bank of the Meuse with Liège being the strongpoint on the right bank. This state of affairs made serious war planning by Leman impossible.

When Leman arrived in February 1914 the 3 DA staff consisted of a lieutenant colonel as chief of staff and five staff officers, and was short a deputy chief of staff. Fortress Liège did not have a chief of staff and the staff consisted of only two officers. A major was sent as the deputy chief of staff in March, but on 15 July was sent to the Congo. Another major was designated chief of staff of Fortress Liège and then sent on 20 July to be chief of staff of 1 DA.

This was a lean enough staff in peacetime: it was completely inadequate in wartime, when all the staff sections had to be operational twenty-four hours a day. Leman said that he also did not have the ten liaison officers necessary to carry orders and receive reports to the twelve forts, the troops on the intervals and in the interior of the city.

On Leman's arrival, the deputy commander was a general who knew the fortress intimately. He was replaced on 6 July by a very capable general officer who did not understand fortress warfare because he had spent his entire career with manoeuvre units, and was of course unfamiliar with Liège.

The civil governor in Liège was housed in a 'celebrated palace'; the military governor did not even have government housing. Nor did he have an automobile. When Leman asked for one, he was told to rent it, so long that it did not cost more than 1,000 francs, which Leman said was 'humiliating'. The staff offices were 'a miserable hovel, in a middle-class house that would rent for 2,000–2,500 francs'. Leman's office was located on a corridor, which led directly to the street; there was no antechamber.

The only telephones available from the fortress headquarters passed through the civilian telephone exchange, which was not under military authority, so putting through a call 'took an enormous amount of time'. There was no direct means of communication between the forts, only signalling by means of the single searchlight, which must have been a laborious process.

There is no evidence that the Belgians ever conducted training to defend Liège above the individual fortress level. There is no mention of a fortress field training exercise, command post exercise, or even a map exercise to practise fortress defence. Armies fight the way they have been trained to fight; poor training, or even worse, no training at all, will lead to ineffective performance in combat. This was borne out in full measure at Liège. Command and control at Liège on the night of 5–6 August was abysmal. Aside from messengers, there was no communication with the manoeuvre units in the intervals between the forts. Reporting was so inaccurate it approximated to rumour control. Bizarre orders appeared out of nowhere. Leman was presented with tactical problems which he had not studied beforehand and he overreacted to every single tactical situation.

It would appear that Leman had six months, from 3 February to 27 July 1914, to correct the deficiencies he had found. Leman said that this was hardly the case: he was continually diverted by routine bureaucratic duties, particularly officer promotion, 'the nightmare of the army', so that he barely had three months in which to perform operational planning.

His principal priority was drawing up a war plan for the defence of Liège, as nothing at all had been done. All he could find in the archives was an out-of-date directive entitled 'Summary of a defence plan', and an 'ancient' work concerning curtain walls to be established between the forts which did not correspond to current conditions, as well as works he called 'treatises' which dealt with principles but offered no concrete solutions because the means they required were not available.

On the other hand, the commander of Fort Fléron said that in 1912–13 the staff had walked the terrain and, together with the commanders of the forts, prepared a detailed plan which provided for field fortifications in the intervals, well-covered by flanking fire from the forts. He was surprised on 3 August to find positions being prepared in locations different than those of the 1912–13 plan, and not nearly so well sited.

There was clearly serious confusion in preparing the Liège war plan.

Leman said that by the end of June he had completed a map of the permanent fortifications, with protection against field artillery, to be constructed to cover the intervals; the planned field fortifications being completely inadequate. He also wanted to construct fortifications around the town proper, construct an adequate fortress HQ and acquire mobile heavy artillery. He began to finalise this plan on 7 July; it was not completed on 27 July, when the point became moot.

There was no appreciation of possible German courses of action, and the General Staff never supplied any information. Leman put his own staff to work on the problem, but they were continually interrupted by the need to work on other projects.

The deputy fortress commander analysed four possible defence scenarios:

Case A: 3 DA (actual situation to 7 August)
Case B: More than a division from the field army

Case C: Fortress regiments only

Case D: No field forces; just the garrisons of the forts (actual situation 8–16 August)

Case A: There was enough infantry, but insufficient engineers and utterly inadequate artillery, in particular no mobile artillery or engineer equipment parks and almost no reserve of shells.

Leman did not say so, but without heavy mobile guns to conduct the artillery duel or engineers to prepare and repair field fortifications, the superbly trained and equipped German siege forces were going to blow through Liège within days, perhaps hours, of their arrival.

As for the forts themselves: if they were modernised, they could not be taken by assault; in their current condition, they would be completely ground down in a few days.

Case D: Under this hypothesis, there was no longer a question of Fortress Liège, merely individual forts defending themselves without mutual support. The forts could not conduct a long-range artillery duel and the attacking artillery could easily destroy them. The enemy would also penetrate into the town and seize the principal installations, such as the food supplies.

Leman envisaged two possible forms of attack against Liège, though he did not use standard military terminology to describe them, which is odd for a man who was an engineer at the head of the military academy. The first was an attack 'foot by foot' (*pied à pied*), that is, formal siege, which in European pre-war doctrine still involved the attacker moving infantry entrenchments slowly forward, covered by large volumes of fire from heavy artillery. The second was an assault (*vive force*) which probably meant a standard deliberate attack, with infantry relatively quickly crossing some considerable stretch of open ground.

Leman said that he based his actions at the beginning of August 1914 on case studies A and D, in particular his August 6 decision to withdraw 3 DA from Liège. Leman recognised before the war that Liège was not only indefensible, but that it would fall quickly, and if 3 DA remained in the fortress then one-fifth of the Belgian Army was going into captivity at the very beginning of the war. *Delaying the German advance for a few days by keeping 3 DA in Liège was too high a price to pay.* The minute it looked like the Germans were going to surround Liège, 3 DA had to leave. Withdrawing 3 DA from Liège meant that the isolated forts would fall almost immediately.

Leman said he demonstrated in April that Liège was not secure against an assault, contrary to previous opinion, which had elevated Liège's invulnerability to assault to a dogma. Between 7 and 21 July he convened eight conferences with the fortress artillery and engineer officers, which brought into question the covered and concealed avenues of approach available to the Germans, especially on the east side, and the lack of artillery OPs 2,500–3,500m in front of the fortress line.

On 15 April the General Staff instructed the fortress to come up with a plan to clear the fields of fire 600m from the forts. The deputy commander of Liège said that this was senseless unless steps were also taken to cover the concealed avenues of approach available to the Germans. His plan therefore involved the construction of additional fortifications, at a total cost of 8,617,000 francs. On 17 June Leman was informed by the General Staff that 'Liège did not have the importance that he attributed to it, that this plan was too ambitious and aimed at making Liège into "the ideal fortress"'. He was granted 300,000 francs to clear the fields of fire at Fort Fléron and Chaudefontaine

No planning had been conducted to co-ordinate with the civilian government, installations and population of Liège: judiciary, police, transportation, fire, electricity and gas, hospitals, food supplies, finance, construction and transportation, evacuation of unnecessary personnel, counter-espionage. Work was begun on 16 April, but apparently not completed in time.

The military engineers at Liège 'had sunk to the lowest level. They had lost the ability to perform their mission [...] projects were executed with unimaginable torpor' and contractors 'flouted the contracts with impunity'.

Leman and the Belgian Army

Leman said that the officer corps knew that their troops were not as well trained as those of 'their powerful neighbours, and in consequence were painfully aware that it was not possible for them to be victorious against an equal-sized enemy force'.

Leman said that in his youth, in 1870, the Belgian Army was the equal, man for man, of any in Europe. The artillery was as good as the German and proportionally as numerous, the number of effectives was, compared to the population, equal to that of France, and as well trained. Antwerp was 'the strongest fortress in the world'. But since war did not come to Belgium in 1870 'the nation went to sleep in belief of the dogma of neutrality [...] perpetual immunity against invasion and war'. From 1870, when the Belgian Army was one-fifth the strength of the French, it declined to one-twentieth in 1914. There were neither heavy artillery nor howitzers, few MGs, and the aircraft were useless.

Leman evaluated the Belgian 3 DA thus:

> The division's garrisons were scattered all over Belgium, but two (of four) brigades, Artillery R 3 and the engineer battalion, were stationed at Liège.

Leman arrived on 3 February 1914. He was horrified. Individual soldiers, dirty and unkempt, wandered around the city. When they saw an officer approaching they would move away so as to avoid saluting. If surprised, with no way out, the salute was badly performed, demonstrating the ill-will with which it was executed. Soldiers should move with a purpose and proper military bearing; these dragged their feet along the ground, heads down, slouching, hands on their stomachs, behind their belt or clasped behind their backs. The infantrymen did not wear their equipment belt or carry their weapons and looked so miserable they inspired pity. The officers did not correct these deficiencies. When the troops marched in formation the same negligence was evident. The distances between soldiers and units was not maintained, the soldiers gawked left, right and behind. The officers' turn-out was just as varied and lacked uniformity. In March Leman had several units pass in review and they looked no better. Leman sent a circular to his subordinate commanders, saying that while the troops did not look like regulars, they were a little better than the French National Guard under Napoleon III, which was hardly a compliment. He added that fundamental recruit training ('school of the soldier': military courtesy, wear of the uniform, individual movements, as well as movements under arms and in formation) which had been carefully conducted twenty-five years ago, was now merely quick and superficial. The soldier had to learn discipline in order to be effective in the field.

With the serving year group and three year groups of reservists, 3 DA went to the training area at Beverloo in May to conduct exercises up to brigade level, and range firing. He concluded that the officers were ignorant of both gunnery and tactics, or rather, they knew the letter of the regulations, but were unable to apply them properly in practice. They were therefore little capable of training the individual soldier. Instead, 'everybody from corporal on up argued about strategy and tactics as though they were scholars at [the medieval university of] Salamanca arguing the dialectic of cause and effect.' Leman said that this problem was endemic in the Belgian Army and actually facilitated by the promotion system.

Leman argued to his superiors that 3 DA should not have been conducting manoeuvres at Beverloo in the first place, but rather in the line of forts at Liège, especially those on the east bank of the Meuse, and in front of them. However, the Belgian leadership had not made a determination that 3 DA should defend Liège, so how could it order 3 DA to conduct exercises there?

Leman said he hadn't mentioned the artillery because it lacked the techniques necessary to maintain contact with its own infantry. It could therefore only fire at random or adjust fire only from the battery position.

Like the rest of the Belgian Army, 3 DA was reorganising, Leman said, and the strength of the unit in enlisted men, cadres and officers was insufficient, and the quantity of artillery, munitions and supply vehicles inadequate.

A small squadron of four aircraft had been attached to 3 DA at Beverloo. Leman said they had undoubtedly tried their best, but accomplished almost nothing. The aircraft were often non-operational, needed 'an incredibly long time to get airborne', and required landing pistes that could be put into communication with 3 DA HQ only with difficulty. He decided that the aircraft could not be relied on in combat, an opinion which was in the event confirmed.

Leman was motivated by the conviction that war was imminent. He said it was clear that a complete transformation in the training of troops and officers was a long-term proposition and not one that could be completed in several months. While some claimed to have seen results, Leman said that in this time he had not seen any profound improvement.

The law of 1902 provided that the army be recruited voluntarily: only when the number of volunteers was insufficient was recourse made to conscription. The period of infantry service was twenty months, which counted as twenty-four. In fact, the second year of service was spent on leave or in routine duties. The annual contingent was set at 13,300 men, which reduced the peacetime strength by 25 per cent, providing a wartime army of 187,000.

The law of 1909 substituted conscription by lot for one son per family. The annual contingent was ostensibly raised to 20,000 men, though in three years the actual contingent was 14,000, 16,000 and 19,000. There was a further reduction in the length of service, from twenty months to fifteen for the infantry, twenty-eight to twenty-one for the artillery, and from thirty-six to twenty-four for cavalry, while the European standard was two years for infantry and artillery, three for cavalry. Training was in practice conducted only for twelve months; after that the troops were put in a badly misnamed 'training company'. As in most European countries, the rising Belgian Socialist Party complained loudly about abuse of soldiers, undermining authority.

Men from ages 21 to 45 who were not inducted into the army were to be organised into the *Garde Civique* (National Guard) which was not subordinate to the war minister but to the minister of the interior. This meant that the *Garde Civique* mission and command arrangements were not at all clear. In towns of over 10,000 the *Garde Civique* was 'active', which is to say it had a limited degree of leadership in training, the 'inactive' *Garde Civique* in the smaller towns was armed but had no training or command and control.

Défense de Namur said that the troops' training was defective because the units were severely understrength 'skeletons'. The reduction in the period of service and the failure to increase the size of the annual contingent exacerbated the situation, discouraging the officers and seriously lowering morale.

By 1911 the European arms race, fuelled by recurrent crises in Morocco and the Balkans, was going into overdrive. At the end of that year the precarious state of Belgian defences was brought to the attention of the population and politicians in a series of newspaper articles titled '*Sommes-nous prêts?*' (Are we ready?) On 30 August 1913 universal conscription was introduced and the annual contingent increased to 33,000 men. The field army would be made up of the six youngest year groups of militia (reservists), reaching a strength of 180,000 men in 1919, but not reaching its full authorised strength of 350,000 men until 1926.[21]

Galet said:

> The Army had no tradition. It had never seen active service, and the exception of veteran African officers, who were unfortunately all collected in an autonomous corps, few officers even possessed a combatant spirit. Apart from the younger ones, they performed their duties as conscientious officials, not as comrades destined to lead their men in action. And how could it have been otherwise? For a great part of the year they commanded phantom battalions and skeleton companies.[22]

In 1913 and 1914, Albert instructed Galet to evaluate the French and German armies. Galet said that, 'given equal numbers, our infantry could not compete with German regular infantry, whose discipline and high standard of training impressed me deeply'. The king attended the Belgian manoeuvres in 1913. He wrote that the army was not even getting the fundamentals right: marches and billeting were poorly organised and undisciplined. In 1914 he saw almost all of the divisions at the Beverloo training area. After the 4 DA manoeuvres he wrote, 'I am convinced that where our Army fails is in discipline and cohesion.' Lombard said that the Belgian soldier was an indifferent marksman, due to insufficient live-fire training.[23]

Du Rôle de l'Armée de Campagne et des Fortresses Belges, written in 1928 by two professional Belgian soldiers, was just as gloomy. The army in 1914 was 'seriously imperfect', weaknesses which led to a drop in the morale of the officers and a decline in discipline.[24] The army didn't even have mobile field kitchens, and ration problems frequently affected troop morale.

> The [Belgian] army, composed ¾ of reservists, lacking cohesion, badly equipped (only 6 MG per brigade, ⅓ that of the German brigade) [actually ½] with half the number of artillery pieces, no heavy artillery, empty depots, unsuitable for offensive operations, had to face the best trained, best disciplined, best equipped, most formidable army ever seen, abundantly provided with artillery of all calibres and sure of its invincibility.

Fortunately, they said, the individual Belgian soldier was excellent, brave and patriotic.

Selliers de Moranville, Belgian Chief of Staff[25]

Antonin Selliers de Moranville was commissioned a lieutenant in Artillery Regiment 3 in 1874, the only time he served with troops. He entered the War College in 1877, served two years with the General Staff, returned to the War College as an instructor in 1881 and then joined the staff of the war minister in 1884. In 1886 he returned to the General Staff and in 1893 was back in the War Ministry, 1896 the War College, 1889 War Ministry. In 1900 he was the Chief of Staff of the 4th Conscription District, where he showed 'tact and firmness' during the industrial actions in 1902. 'For this reason, and because he was one of the rare Catholic senior officers' he was appointed commander of the gendarmerie in December 1904. He became the temporary Chief of the General Staff on 25 May 1914, and the permanent chief on 15 July, the third chief of staff since 1910. He had held no unit command or staff positions, his knowledge of military operations was purely theoretical, and in any other army would be unqualified to be chief of staff; his appointment was due to competition between cliques in the Belgian Army. The king much preferred the advice of his adjutant, Major Galet.

After the war Moranville wrote extensively concerning the lack of Belgian preparedness and the internal dissension in the Belgian government, command and General Staff. He was blistering concerning 'panegyrics' and 'fabricators of legends':[26]

[who] were not content to present a tendentious narrative of the Great War, deforming the truth, but also conceal the less glorious, indeed reprehensible, facts. They slide quickly over our insufficient preparation for the war, the profound weakness in our military organization, number of effectives, officers, fortresses, armament and artillery. Above all they failed to criticize the governments, legislative chambers and political parties responsible for these shameful deficiencies.

The authors of these Belgian panegyrics included well-intentioned men influenced by a misplaced patriotism. Others wanted to repay debts incurred by favours they had received, or to ingratiate themselves to the government. They:

Magnified the exploits of the Belgians and Allies both, competed with each other in addressing extravagant eulogies to the King, extolled the endurance and patriotism of the civilian population under the brutal yoke of our Teutonic oppressors.

And while many men had served honourably, had even given their lives, many others had been excused from active service, and passed the war tranquilly in front of their hearths. The panegyrists omit to reproach this population for having failed to establish and maintain an army of 600,000 to 700,000 men during the entire war, providing only, under diverse categories, 387,000 during four years of war.

The Belgian people therefore remained blind to their lack of preparedness before the war, and their heavy responsibility for their own misfortunes. It was therefore the duty of public opinion, enlightened by 'severe critics', to take the measures necessary to preserve Belgian independence during a second such test.

Moranville went on to describe Belgian deficiencies in detail.[27] The Belgian Army had been surprised in the middle of a fundamental reorganisation. Its strength was insufficient. There was a massive shortage of officers, in particular reserve officers, a 'derisory' number of MG, no howitzers or heavy artillery, and rudimentary aviation. The fortresses were incomplete or obsolete, and incapable of resisting the 'terrible' new German heavy artillery. Discipline was slack and there was a lack of road-march training for the infantry, which resulted, together with the shortage of officers, in an inability to conduct mobile offensive operations. Under these circumstances, it was hardly surprising that troop morale suffered from a sense of inferiority to the Germans. At the highest level, the General Staff had been created only in 1910, and since then had three chiefs: there was no unity of doctrine and training.

The Belgian Army, said Moranville, had always been inclined to adopt French ideas, good, bad and indifferent. Given the lack of stability at the General Staff, the French *offensive à outrance* filled the doctrinal vacuum, promoted, as in France, by a group of ardent young General Staff officers, who had scant respect for the old-fashioned ideas of their nominal superiors. They would use their access to the king, war minister and politicians to relieve general officers who did not attack as aggressively as they thought necessary.

Major Galet, ADC to King Albert

The king's aide-de-camp (ADC), Major (later Major General and Chief of the General Staff) Galet was born in 1870, the son of a worker. He studied at the village school until age 13, and at age 17 he enlisted in the artillery. As a student at the military academy in 1891 and 1892 he met Crown Prince Albert. In 1894 he was commissioned in Artillery Regiment 1 (AR 1) and served there for three years, apparently his only troop duty, before attending the Ecole de Guerre for two years. In 1903 he was promoted to captain in the General Staff, was made chief of the map section as well as given the Chair of Military History at the Ecole de Guerre and delivered two lectures to Albert on current military topics. He lectured on the campaigns of 1796 and 1805 and read the works of Frederick the Great, Guibert, Napoleon and Clausewitz, which led him to conclusions that did not agree with those being taught at the Ecole de Guerre. He accompanied Albert during the 1906 annual manoeuvres and was given the opportunity to critique them. In the 1908 manoeuvres he again accompanied the prince and apparently discussed Clausewitz's theory that war is a continuation of political policy.

Chapter X of Galet's *Principles of War* concerned the fundamentals of Belgian defence policy, as set down by the former war minister, General Renard, in 1851.[28] There were two schools of thought: (1) that the Belgian Army should immediately fall back to the national redoubt at Fortress Antwerp, or (2) that the army would move to the threatened frontier and conduct a delaying action back to Antwerp.

The problem with immediately moving to Antwerp was that it surrendered the entire country to the invader. This was dangerous for the continued existence of Belgium as an independent state:

> The Powers which are to-day guarantors of our independence, having discovered our inability to defend our own soil, would seek another political combination in place of that which had been found wanting. The loss of our autonomy would be the inevitable result of our lack of national spirit [...] *to condemn the country to a permanently passive defence would be almost as disastrous as not to resist at all* [italics in the original].[29]
>
> If the contrary policy which we advocate be adopted none of the belligerents would wish to be the first to violate our frontier. This possibility of averting the evils of war by a firm attitude is an advantage of inestimable value.

To this, Galet added that Liège and Namur had mobile garrisons of only a line infantry regiment each – of what use, he asked, would one regiment be on a 40km perimeter? Concentrating at once at Brussels–Antwerp and leaving the borders undefended would actually encourage any enemy to make an immediate surprise attack, to seize the rail lines and disrupt Belgian mobilisation, 'If it is Germany who has designs on us, *she will never have a more favourable opportunity for attempting a* coup de main *on Liège* [italics in the original].'

Before the war there were two competing schools of strategy in the Belgian General Staff, Galet said:

> The older members considered that to maintain our neutrality we must take up a position and fight on it or, in other words, let ourselves be beaten on it. The younger generation, ardent and enterprising, thought it derogatory to occupy positions which the enemy might ignore or avoid, and considered that for an outraged nation the offensive was the only course possible [...] French doctrine, completely permeated by the spirit of the offensive, mobility and audacity, should be our guide. '*Attack and attack quickly*' should be our motto [...] In short, in the name of honour, both young and old dedicated the army to immediate battle at all hazards.

In peacetime the king had little influence on military affairs, which were the purview of the government. Galet said that on Albert's accession the 'responsible authorities' had decided to concentrate the army in the centre of the country, in the area from Louvain to Brussels. The army would march there at peacetime strength and be joined by its reservists. If the threat was from Germany, the army would move halfway between Brussels and Liège, to Tirlemont (Tienen)–Hannut, by the sixth day of mobilisation. It might also move far into the Ardennes to the south, at

Marche–Rochefort, Libramont–Recogne or even Neufchâteau. On the one hand, this recognised that the German attack could well stay south of the Meuse. On the other hand, it is not clear what the Belgians thought they would accomplish by placing themselves in heavily wooded and mountainous terrain directly in front of the German Army, beyond their own annihilation. Nevertheless, Galet said that 'army staff tours, generally based on a supposed invasion of Upper Belgium, were carried out in the Province of Luxembourg' (the central Ardennes). If the threat were from France, the army would assemble at Enghien, halfway between Brussels and Mons. If the threat came from Britain, it would move to the south of Brugge. Apart from mobilisation these were 'vague proposals. We had no plan of operations [...] the whole conduct of the war was left to be improvised at the last moment.'

Galet said that the first of King Albert's reforms was to create a true General Staff, on 26 June 1910, with his former ADC, General Jungbluth, as the first chief of staff. The chief of the operations section was Lieutenant Colonel Baron de Ryckel, who produced a draft of a Belgian defence plan in 1911. Ryckel noted that the first task was to identify friends and enemies: during a period of international tension each of the neighbouring powers would be asked to reaffirm its adherence to Belgian neutrality. Refusal to do so would show Belgium where the danger lay. In addition, Ryckel recommended that the divisions mobilise at home station and then concentrate.

High-level dissension halted any progress in war planning. The war minister, who had lost functions to the new General Staff, was uncooperative. General Jungbluth reached mandatory retirement age and was replaced by an officer 'opposed to the new ideas, whose first act was to transfer Colonel de Ryckel away from Army Headquarters [...] Thus, after two years of effort [...] the plan of operations had not progressed a step'.

In France, Grandmaison's theory of the *offensive à outrance* was beginning to gain adherents, which Galet said 'claimed to reduce the whole Art of War to a few cut and dried sentences: "Victory is a matter of the will." "To manoeuvre is to succeed." "Inaction is disgraceful." "To wage war is to attack."' Galet said that these ideas were popular in the Belgian Army due to the passivity of Belgian doctrine, which consisted of taking up a defensive position north of the Meuse while watching the invading army march through the Ardennes. The enemy would merely mask the Belgian position; once he had transited the Ardennes:

the masking force would be withdrawn, and we should be left gazing into the blue, under the stigma of having allowed our soil to be profaned with impunity and having failed in our obligations to Europe. Therefore, to avoid making ourselves the laughing stock of the world we should have to fight at once; and to insure that we were not ignored it was essential that we should attack.

In 1910 General Count de t'Serclaes de Wommerson became the head of the Ecole de Guerre, and his motto on the title page of the new Belgian doctrine was '*Attack and swift attack*'.

Galet said that:

> What I sought to teach was that the offensive is not an immutable principle of universal applicability; that immediate battle should be sought only if there be the prospect of an important success; that the attack calls for a superiority of means; and that the degree of vigour with which operations should be conducted depends to a great extent on the quality of the troops available.

When told to bring his instruction into line with Ecole de Guerre doctrine, Galet resigned his professorship and returned for the next two years to the map section, while continuing his studies. In November 1912 Galet was made military advisor to Albert, an interesting development considering Galet's opposition to the current Belgian doctrine.[30]

Galet said that, 'the King, faced by the bankruptcy of ideas of the Military Authorities, decided with my assistance to take up the question of working out our plans of operations.' This was based on two principles: first, provide Liège and Namur each with a division as a garrison; second, assemble the army near the threatened frontier.

In the winter of 1912–13 Galet drew up an operations plan, oriented solely against Germany.[31] Galet said, 'we had long been distrustful of Germany, and had a complete plan of operations prepared against her, and at this time [he is speaking on 2 August 1914] our plan against France was no more than outlined.'[32] If the threat were from Germany, then the army should assemble around Liège. Galet then provided four options. In Case 1, the German Army was inferior to the Belgian: the Belgians should attack. Case 2, if the Germans were equal or slightly superior, the Belgians should conduct an 'active defence on the east bank of the Meuse'. In Cases 3 and 4 the defence would begin on the Meuse. In Case 3, the Germans had three corps: the Belgian 3 DA would defend Liège, forcing the Germans to invest it, while 'the main body [of the Belgian Army] withdrawn three marches to the rear' [about 45–60km], would be held in readiness to give battle at any favourable opportunity. In Case 4 the Germans had five or more corps north of the Meuse, and the best the Belgians could do was to delay back to Antwerp. If it appeared the Germans were going to transit Dutch Limbourg, the Belgians would defend with 3 DA at Liège, a division at Visé, three to the north opposite Maastricht and one division immediately north of Maastricht. If it did not appear that the Germans would transit Dutch territory, 3 DA would be at Liège, 4 DA at Namur, a division east of Namur at Andenne, three at or near Huy. In the event, Galet advocated a Belgian defence on the Meuse:[33]

It is perhaps not out of place to ask what might have happened if, as the King had desired, the concentration of the Army on the Meuse had been carried out completely?

Early on the morning of the 3rd August the movement of the troops would have begun, and the trains would have continued to run without pause till the night of the 4th. On that same day, towards 7 p.m., the Governor of the Liège position would have reported that there was no enemy in front of Dutch Limbourg, and that the German VIIth Corps was concentrating at Aix-la-Chapelle [Aachen] Moresnet and Herbesthal, and that there were many troops of the IVth and Xth Corps at the Camp of Elsenborn and also near Recht [Sankt Vith]. On the morning of the 4th the Frontier Guards would have reported that hostile bodies of the enemy of all arms would have crossed our frontier at 8 a.m. by Gemmenich, Henri-Chapelle, Limbourg, Spa, Stavelot. The Governor of Liège would have reported that there were in front of him the VIIth, IXth and Xth Corps, and another Corps unidentified. We should then have realized that we should very soon be confronted by the active elements of at least four corps. The plan of operations had laid down that in such a case the 3rd Division would have to defend the forts on the right bank, the other divisions holding the Meuse on the left bank.

On the 5th, at dawn, our six divisions, all complete, would have been in line of battle from Lixhé to Huy. There is little doubt that by such a disposition von Emmich's army would have been checked absolutely. We should have maintained our positions and not a German soldier would have reached the left bank; we should have avoided the isolated action of the 3rd Division, and we should have started the War with a resounding success, the effect of which on the German plan of campaign would have been incalculable.

Kabisch said that the real reason that the Belgian Army did not advance to the Meuse was that the rail minister said at 0900 on 1 August that no planning had been done to move the army by rail and that it was impossible to create such a plan extemporaneously.[34] In particular, no loading ramps had been built at Tirlemont. The most that could be accomplished was to move the two divisions in Flanders by rail to Tirlemont and Perwez, 25km to the south-west, and that would take two days. The order for this move was given 3 August. The divisions at Antwerp and Brussels would footmarch to Louvain and Wavre, the cavalry division to Waremme, 25km west of Liège.

Actually, the job of drawing up the war plan was the responsibility of Moranville, who was scathing concerning the war planning of the Young Turk '*offensive à outrance*' staff officers. It is now clear that, though he did not explicitly say so, the object of Moranville's displeasure was Galet's war plan.[35] Moranville said that:

during the war and even after the armistice, some contended that it would have been better to have concentrated the army on the Meuse, in the quadrilateral Visé–Liège–Waremme–Tirlemont, in spite of the danger that this position could be enveloped through the Maastricht Appendix. From this position, they maintain, the army would have been able to participate in the defence of Fortress Liège, and in particular defeat the attack on the night of 5–6 August.

Moranville does not doubt that the German 14 Brigade, which had penetrated into Liège, would have been destroyed and the Belgian Army could have taken up a position on the west bank of the Meuse. If it accepted combat on this advanced position, it would have been practically impossible to break contact and withdraw, and even if it had succeeded in doing so the effect on morale would have been 'most unfortunate'.

Moranville contends that it had been argued that the Belgian Army could have even conducted a spoiling attack on the east bank of the Meuse to disrupt the German mobilisation (Galet's Case one), a course of action which he easily shows would have encountered overwhelming German forces.

In either case, by 10 August the Germans would have been reinforced by 154,800 fresh troops. Given superior German combat power and mobility, the Belgians would have suffered a 'bloody defeat, followed by a pursuit that would have at least put the Belgian army out of action for a considerable period, perhaps for the duration of the war'.

Moranville then examines a Belgian advance from the Gette assembly area to the Meuse. The Germans would have been pushed out of Liège and back to the east side of the Meuse. But then the Belgian Army would have been exposed to a German counterattack, in particular to an advance by the German 2nd Army to Huy–Andenne by 13 August, followed by a march of 20–30km to St Trond–Waremme, which would have taken the retreating Belgians in the flank or rear.

Moranville contends that the presence of the Belgian field army at Liège would have done nothing to prevent the German siege artillery from pounding the permanent forts flat. Moranville presented his own war plan. He said that there were three possible German courses of action.[36]

German course of action one: the Germans would advance both the north and south of the Meuse, respecting Dutch neutrality. This implied immediately laying siege to and taking Liège. This seemed therefore to be the least likely German course of action, because *the Belgians assumed that Liège would hold out for a month*. The garrison of Liège included only the troops in the permanent fortresses and the regiments of fortress infantry, and these were provided with a month's supply of provisions and ammunition.

Moranville is the only source to emphasise that Liège was to hold out for a month, and the reason is not far to seek: Moranville was on a self-appointed quest to smoke out the panegyrists, and the biggest Belgian national myth was the heroic resistance of Liège, which, rather than holding out for a month, was taken by the German siege artillery in a week.

German course of action two: the Germans would invade Belgium, staying south of the Meuse, screening Liège, Namur and the Belgian field army. This was considered the most likely German course of action.

German course of action three: the Germans would invade Belgium both to the north and south of the Meuse, violating Dutch neutrality by passing through the Maastricht Appendix. The Germans would either lay siege to Liège or blockade it. The Dutch would not oppose the German movement and the Dutch Army would remain behind the Water Line, where they might remain permanently. This was considered the second most likely German course of action.

Moranville drew up plan one for a concentration if Germany were the likely enemy. The Belgian Army would occupy an assembly area in front of the Gette and south of St Trond–Tirlemont with all six divisions, from which position it would be able to 'respond to either German course of action 2 or 3'. Fortress Antwerp could only be held if supported by the entire Belgian field army. 'In case the army were threatened' it would withdraw there: in other words, the Belgian Army would avoid contact and pull back to Antwerp as soon as possible.

Moranville also drew up a plan two for war against France and a plan three if the enemy were uncertain. This was a pro forma exercise: Moranville did not discuss their contents and never mentions them again. War against Germany was the only possibility seriously considered. All three plans were complete six weeks after Moranville assumed his duties as chief of staff.

Belgian war planning was in chaos. There were at least three principal actors – the king and Galet, Moranville the chief of staff, and Leman the commander of 3 DA and Liège, who did not co-ordinate with each other and often worked at cross-purposes. Moreover, none of these had a firm concept of the operation. In part, this was because none of them had any experience as troop leaders or planners, in part, because they were all acutely aware of the poor state of the Belgian Army.

German Attack Plan

In the 1913–14 war plan, the younger Moltke determined that Germany would concentrate the mass of her army – sixty-eight divisions – against France and only nine against Russia (with two reserve divisions watching the North Sea coast against a British landing). Unless the French attacked first, and in strength, in Lorraine, the main German attack would be made through Belgium north of the Meuse. Moltke could not risk having an intact Liège cutting the supply lines of the German 1st and 2nd Armies.

Heereskavalleriekorps 2 (HKK 2 – 2nd Cavalry Corps) would advance with 2 and 4 *Kavalleriedivision* (KD – *Kavalleriedivision* – cavalry division) to cross the Meuse north of Liège to take up a position north-east of the fortress and send patrols into Belgium. 9 KD would operate south of Liège.

To take Liège quickly, six brigades, that had not had time to mobilise and were still at peacetime strength (about 25,000 infantry, 124 field artillery pieces and four 21cm mortars)[37] would conduct a quick attack on the night of the fourth to fifth mobilisation days in order to pass between the individual forts, before the Belgians had time to prepare field fortifications between them. The routes had been reconnoitred and established by German General Staff officers in peacetime, who were to act as guides in wartime. In almost all cases the routes followed a major road; little or no attempt was made to infiltrate cross-country. They would seize the city – which was not protected by a wall – and the individual forts would *presumably* see the futility of further resistance and surrender. 'Presumably' because the only notes that still exist concerning the *coup de main* against Liège are in 1913–14 German deployment orders (1913–14 *Aufmarschweisungen*),[38] which do not state why or how, if the forts did not surrender outright, that five brigades of infantry (six in 1914), supported by four 21cm mortars, were going to take twelve forts.

The only logical explanation is that Moltke was assuming that Liège would be completely unprepared to defend itself. Moltke apparently expected that in addition to the garrison of the forts, the Belgians would have the peacetime garrison of 6,000 men and 3,000 *Garde Civique*.[39] Not only would there be no Belgian forces in the intervals between the forts, allowing the German brigades unopposed passage into the city proper, but that the forts too would be unready: best case, still in peacetime caretaker status, worst case without their complete garrison and store of munitions and supplies. Under such circumstances, one or two forts might be overrun or surrender and the rest of the forts would recognise the futility of further resistance. Moreover, it was no state secret that the Belgian 3 DA HQ was at Liège. The German attack had to be made before 3 DA was combat-ready.

The General Staff brochure, *Liège-Namur*, written in 1918, says that Ludendorff was responsible for 'the concept and preparation of the attack'.[40] Ludendorff says that the *coup de main* against Liège was his idea, with the caveat that, once inside the central city and in possession of the citadel it would be possible to easily reduce the individual forts.[41] Ludendorff said that in 1914 he was assigned to the 2nd Army, which had the responsibility of conducting the operation, because of his knowledge of the Liège attack,[42] which was otherwise a closely guarded General Staff secret.

In fact it seems likely that Ludendorff, who had no particular expertise in fortress warfare and was the chief of the *Aufmarschabteilung* (deployment section) of the General Staff, had no more responsibility for planning the attack than preparing the rail-march tables. Kabisch says that the detailed plan for conducting the attack was written by Brigadier General Schwarte and Section 4 (Western Fortresses) of the great General Staff.[43] The plan was first developed in the 1908–09 *Aufmarsch* (deployment plan).[44]

If the first attack failed, it would be repeated on the tenth day of mobilisation. If Liège had not fallen by the twelfth day of mobilisation, it would be necessary to transit Dutch territory at Maastricht.[45]

The Younger Moltke

Practically no part of this plan worked as intended. Considering Moltke's career, this was hardly surprising. He became an officer candidate in 1869, and took part in the Franco-Prussian War as the second adjutant (not a troop leader) in an infantry regiment. He was given frequent special absences from his unit to ride out with his uncle, the Chief of the General Staff. The elder Moltke was childless and practically adopted his nephew, and in Wilhelmine Germany nepotism was quite common (Bismarck clearly intended that his son should succeed him). The younger Moltke began his General Staff training in 1875, and was appointed to the General Staff in 1880. He did not stay there long, for in 1882 he became his uncle's adjutant and on his uncle's death in 1891 adjutant to Kaiser Wilhelm II. In 1893 he was also commander of the Palace Guard Company. In 1896 he nominally returned to troop duty as commander of Guard Regiment I. In 1899 he was promoted to general and made the commandant of the Potsdam garrison and a guard brigade commander, in 1902 commander of I Guard Division, in 1904 *Generalquartiermeister* (executive officer) of the General Staff.

The distinguishing characteristic of Moltke's career was the almost complete absence of troop duty. From 1882 to 1893, eleven years when he should have been a division Ia (operations officer) and corps Ia and chief of staff, he was the adjutant to the elder Moltke or the kaiser. From 1893 to 1904 he commanded units in the Prussian Guard, which was heavily committed to ceremonial functions. In any case, the operations officer and chief of staff did the real work in any German troop unit.

'Common knowledge' holds that when Moltke became Chief of the General Staff in 1906 he adopted the 'Schlieffen Plan', later 'modifying' it. One of these 'modifications' was the *attaque brusquée* on Liège.

This presents two problems for the 'Schlieffen Plan' myth. The first is that Schlieffen obviously had no influence on Moltke or his career. Schlieffen became Chief of the General Staff in 1891: Moltke did not serve under Schlieffen until 1904, and only when it was obvious he was to be Schlieffen's successor. Then there is the famous Moltke quote that he and Schlieffen 'did not agree on anything'.

The second problem is that it is obvious that the most important influence on Moltke's career was not Schlieffen but the elder Moltke. The younger Moltke was following the elder Moltke's planning, not Schlieffen's. This is made clear by the *attaque brusquée* on Liège: Schlieffen never planned any such thing, ever. It is, however, is a carbon copy of the *attaque brusquée* that the elder Moltke wanted to conduct against Saxony and Fortress Mainz in 1865–66.[46]

That the younger Moltke was following the elder Moltke's planning, not Schlieffen's, is made even clearer in Moltke's first general order in the Marne campaign order on 27 August 1914, for a general pursuit 'towards Paris'.[47] In none of Schlieffen's two-front war games did he ever do any such thing. Having won the initial battle against the French, Schlieffen always stopped and sent massive reinforcements to counterattack against the Russians. However, this is completely consistent with the elder Moltke's war planning against France. It is, moreover, a carbon copy of Moltke's actual decision-making process after Gravelotte–St Privat. In August 1870 the elder Moltke decided to march on Paris with the vague idea that the French would be forced to fight somewhere: he had no idea what he would actually do when he got to Paris.[48] In August 1914 the younger Moltke did exactly the same thing.

German Doctrinal Night Attack

A night attack posed any number of difficulties. The first was land navigation: during night movement it was difficult for leaders to maintain the direction of march, to be sure of their location, or to estimate how far they had moved. It was difficult to send orders or receive reports. There was an increased possibility of friendly-fire incidents, while on the other hand, it was not possible to gain fire superiority or receive artillery support.

The German Army therefore concluded that large-scale night attacks were nearly impossible, but that night attacks could be conducted against limited objectives. The requirement was to gain surprise, which favoured dark nights. Such attacks had to be well prepared. Routes of march had to be easily recognisable in the dark, reconnoitred in daylight by officer patrols, marked and provided at frequent intervals with guides. Deployment lines also had to be easily recognisable and secured by a line of outposts. Troops had to wear a recognition badge, such as a white armband, and know the password and countersign. A dry-run practice attack in daylight never hurt.

The attack troops would usually move out after dark in close march column, with unloaded weapons and fixed bayonets, to reduce the possibility of friendly fire. In addition to the guides on the approach march route, the leaders would maintain orientation by compass. On the secured deployment line, the troops would fan out left and right. The plan of attack was to be kept as simple as possible. Battalions would advance with two companies in the first line, preceded by a weak skirmisher screen, followed by the other two companies, with the companies themselves in company or platoon column.[49] The intent was to avoid a firefight and close in to immediately attack with the bayonet. Once the objective was secured the units would hold in place and consolidate.

It was often advantageous to conduct night approach marches, particularly in order to cross open ground, to close in on a strong position, or to cross an obstacle, so that the firefight could begin at close range at dawn. In fact, given strong enemy field fortifications, the night approach march/dawn attack might be the only possible offensive option. Again, the key was to reconnoitre, mark, and secure as much of the approach march as possible in daylight. If an attack position was to be occupied, the same applied.

These German doctrinal procedures for night operations would be adopted by practically all armies and would change little for the next seventy years.

The General's Staff's plan for a night attack on Liège violated every particular of the German doctrine for the conduct of a night attack. There was no useful reconnaissance, in spite of the fact that four columns had a Jäger battalion attached, the masters of patrolling. The brigade did not deploy before reaching the objective but each brigade, some 2,500 men, advanced in march column four abreast.

This plan was predestined to disaster. It bears all the hallmarks of General Staff officers, like the younger Moltke himself, who had spent far too much time in Berlin and far too little with troops.

German Doctrinal Deliberate Attack[50]

A 'deliberate attack' is generally used to take a dug-in position, which requires that the attacking unit conduct careful reconnaissance and planning. These procedures were developed from siege warfare techniques, themselves the product of some 300 years of progress in siege warfare tactics. German pre-war doctrine held no illusions: attacks on dug-in positions would be long and hard and there would be no breakthroughs. An attack against a well dug-in enemy would be conducted with a night approach march followed by a daylight attack. An attack against a less well dug-in enemy might take place in daylight. An attack against a moving enemy, or one that had not had time to dig in, would be conducted as an immediate hasty attack out of march column.

Prior to deploying the force for a deliberate attack, infantry, cavalry, artillery and engineer units would all send out daylight reconnaissance patrols. For his part, the defender would seek to slow the attacker's progress towards the entrenchments as much as possible, using advanced positions, artillery fire, and counter-reconnaissance patrols. When the sector to be assaulted had been identified, the infantry would move forward to establish a defensive position for the artillery, which would then occupy previously reconnoitred battery positions.

The infantry attack on a fortified position could not begin until the defending artillery had been suppressed to the degree that the infantry could begin the forward movement without excessive casualties. Determining whether this had been achieved or not would be difficult, for if the defender saw he was losing the artillery duel, he could order his batteries to ceasefire, saving them so that they could engage the attacking infantry. Artillery preparation bombardment of infantry defensive positions was considered to be a waste of ammunition: the defender would just hunker down in his trenches, especially if they had overhead cover.

The infantry attack would force the defending infantry to come out of cover and man the trenches, providing the attacking artillery with targets. The defending artillery would unmask and open fire, and the German heavy howitzers would engage them. The attacker would choose a main point of effort and those entrenchments would be given priority of fire, including heavy howitzer fire. Positions with overhead cover presented a particular problem. They could only be engaged with high-angle fire, howitzers or trench mortars (a pre-war German innovation) using delayed-action fuses.

Supporting infantry, MG and artillery fire on the entrenchments would seek to prevent the defender from exposing his head above the parapet. The infantry would gain fire superiority and advance by fire and movement. This could be a slow, time-consuming process. Doctrinally, the assault on the enemy would be conducted when the attacking troops had closed to 100m or less from the defensive line. Artillery would be brought forward to be used in the direct-fire role. Skirmisher lines would provide close fire support, followed by combat engineers with assault tools.

In 1895 Field Artillery Regiment (FAR) 69 participated in a week-long field-fortification exercise which included a live-fire shoot against trench systems.[51] Such exercises became a regular part of the regiment's summer training programme. The regimental historian for Infantry Regiment (IR) 109 says that, as a result of the Russo-Japanese War, attacks on field fortifications at night and including the use of entrenching tools to dig skirmisher holes and offensive strongpoints, were practised extensively.[52] The Foot Guard R 1 regimental history reported practising attacks on field fortifications in September 1912 and 1913 (with a four-hour exercise critique!) and that such attacks became commonplace in the last peacetime manoeuvres.[53]

Moltke's decision to conduct night attacks with brigade-sized march columns was a poorly thought-out violation of German doctrine for both the night attack and the attack on a dug-in position.

Notes

1. H. von Müller, Geschichte des Festungskrieges von 1885–1905 (Berlin: E. S. Mittler und Sohn, 1907) 13.
2. Duvivier/Herbiet, Du Rôle de l'Armée de Campagne et des Fortresses Belges en 1914, 13–22.
3. Normand, Liège, Namur, 9–21.
4. De Schrÿver, Liège, 204.
5. T. Zuber, Inventing the Schlieffen Plan: German War Planning 1871–1914 (Oxford: OUP, 2002) 151.

6. Faque, Brialmont, 27–38.
7. Faque, Brialmont, 33.
8. Ministère de la Défence, Namur, 12.
9. Confirmed by Mozin, the commander of Fléron, 'La défence du fort de Fléron' in: Bulletin d'Information des Officiers de Réserve, 1er Trimestre 1937, 12.
10. L. Lombard, Face à l'invasion (Stavelot: Vox Patriae, 1939) 112.
11. Mozin, 'La défence du fort de Fléron', 12.
12. Mozin, 'La défence du fort de Fléron', 12.
13. Duvivier/Herbiet, Du Rôle de l'Armée de Campagne et des Fortresses Belges, 26.
14. D.K. Brown, Warrior to Dreadnought. Warship Development 1860–1905 (London: Chatham, 1997) 150.
15. Rudi Rolf, Die Deutsche Panzerfortifikation: die Panzerfesten von Metz und ihre Vorgeschichte (Osnabrück: Biblio 1991).
16. 'grande place d'arrêt'. In light of Brialmont's comment above, 'fortified camp' is preferable to the literal translation, 'blocking position'.
17. G. Leman, Le Rapport du général Leman sur la defense de Liège en août 1914. (Brussels: Palais des Acadêmes, 1960).
18. Duvivier/Herbiet, Du Rôle de l'Armée de Campagne et des Fortresses Belges en 1914, 29.
19. Moranville, Babel, 228–31.
20. Duvivier/Herbiet, Du Rôle de l'Armée de Campagne et des Fortresses Belges, 20–22.
21. Other sources say 1922 or 1926.
22. Galet, Albert, 72–3.40
23. L. Lombard, Face à l'invasion (Stavelot: Vox Patriae, 1939), 63.
24. Duvivier/Herbiet, Du Rôle de l'Armée de Campagne et des Fortresses Belges, 23–4.
25. De Selliers de Moranville.mht 25 June 2013
26. Moranville, Babel, 8–10.
27. Moranville, Babel, 189–93.
28. Galet, Albert, 305–10.
29. This would be especially damaging to the Belgian elites, who would be demoted from their positions as representatives of a sovereign country to the status of provincial officials – if they kept their jobs at all.
30. He retained that position during the war, then served as military advisor to the Belgian delegation at the Paris Peace Conference. From that point until 1926 he was the commandant of the Ecole de Guerre, when he was appointed by Albert to be Chief of the General Staff. A career spent at the military academy, followed with a terminal assignment as a high-level commander, seems very strange but was common in the Belgian Army.
31. Galet, Albert, 15–16.
32. Galet, Albert, 30.
33. Galet, Albert, 48.
34. Kabisch, Lüttich, 49.
35. Moranville, Babel, 204–10.
36. Moranville, Babel, 194–6.
37. Reichsarchiv, Der Weltkrieg I, 109.
38. Bundesarchiv-Militärarchiv (BA-MA) Freiburg im Breisgau RH61/v96 Aufmarsch 1913/14.
39. Reichsarchiv, Der Weltkrieg I, 108.
40. Bieberstein, Lüttich-Namur, 12.
41. E. Ludendorff, Mein militärischer Werdegang (Munich: Ludendorffs Verlag, 1933) 128.
42. Ibid. 158. E. Ludendorff, Meine Kriegserinnerungen (Berlin: Mittler, 1919) 27, 30.
43. Kabisch, Lüttich, 143, 162.

44. T. Zuber, The Real German War Plan 1904–1914 (Stroud: The History Press, 2011) 74.

45. Zuber, The Real German War Plan 1904–1914, 132–4.

46. T. Zuber, The Moltke Myth. Prussian War Planning 1857–1871 (Lanham: University Press, 2008) 108–110.

47. Zuber, The Real German War Plan 1904–1914, 168–9.

48. Zuber, The Real German War Plan 1904–1914, 290.

49. A tactical column is not a march column. In a tactical company column the company has platoons on line, one behind the other. In a platoon column the platoon is on line, operating independently.

50. Exerzier-Reglement für die Infanterie vom 29. Mai 1906. Neuabdruck mit Einfügung der bis August 1909 ergangenen Änderungen (Deckblatt 1–78). (Berlin, 1909) § 375–391. General-Inspektion des Militär-Erziehungswesens (bearbeitet), Leitfaden für den Unterricht in der Taktik auf den Königlichen Kriegsschulen (Berlin, 1910) 154–9. F. Immanuel, Handbuch der Taktik (Berlin, 1910) I , 207; II, 22–35, 284–7, 294.

51. Wilhelm Marx, Die Glückhafte Batterie, mit der 2. Batterie Feldartillerie-Regiments Nr. 69 im Bewegungskrieg 1914 (Potsdam: Voggenreiter, 1937) 10.

52. Rudolf von Freydorf (ed.), Das 1. Badische Leib-Regiment Nr. 109 im Weltkrieg 1914–1918 (Karlsruhe i. B., 1927) 11.

53. Friedrich von Friedenberg, Geschichte des Königlich Preussischen Ersten Garde-Regiments zu Fuss: 1871 bis 1914 (Berlin, 1933) 225–6.

2

Approach March

Belgian Mobilisation and Deployment

The Belgian constitution provided that the king was the commander in chief. Nevertheless, in the only preceding crisis, in 1870, the direct command of the field army had been entrusted to General Chazal. On 2 August 1914 Albert decided to exercise his command in fact.[1] Galet said that Albert did so because he was well informed of the state of the Belgian Army and did not trust either the General Staff nor its chief, Moranville.

The Dutch foreign minister approached the Belgian ambassador on 27 July, proposing a joint defence in case the Germans transited Dutch Limbourg and asking that the Dutch Minister of War be kept informed concerning Belgian decisions. The Dutch had considered such a scenario in the winter of 1913.[2]

On 29 July the Belgians decided that war between Austria and Serbia was inevitable. There were rumours that German active-duty personnel on leave were being recalled and that the five regiments at the German Major Training Areas (MTA) at Elsenborn, near the Belgian border (east of Malmedy, now part of Belgium) had returned to garrison. At 1300 the Belgians ordered a partial mobilisation, recalling the three youngest reservist year groups (1912, 1911, 1910), buying horses and uploading ammunition and equipment. Galet said that 'it was important that we should take action before our neighbours'.[3] All the Powers, including the Dutch, were advised of these actions.

On 30 July Moranville had submitted a plan to the king to concentrate the entire Belgian Army in the centre of the country, in two lines, the easterly with 1 DA in the north at St Trond, 3 DA in the centre, 5 DA at Hannut and 4 DA in the south, at Éghezée, just north of Namur. The second line had 2 DA in the north at Tirlemont and 6 DA to the south of Tirlemont. The cavalry division was south-east of 5 DA.[4]

Moranville's Plan, mid July.

On 31 July the Belgians learned that Austria had declared war on Serbia. Russia and Austria were mobilising and had broken off diplomatic relations. The German VIII AK (*Armeekorps* – army corps) supply units were 'about to mobilize'. The French were moving elements of II CA (*Corps d'Armée* – army corps) eastwards, and horse owners had been warned that their animals would be requisitioned. At 1400 it was learned that the Germans had ordered 'Period Preparatory to War' and closed the frontier. Holland was mobilising. The French Foreign Ministry declared to Belgium and Great Britain that France would respect Belgian neutrality.

Full Belgian mobilisation was ordered at 1900 on 31 July, first day of mobilisation 1 August, a day ahead of the Germans and French. On 31 July the king assumed de facto, if not *de jure*, command of the army, and 'out of concern for German sensibilities' and, 'so as to not stir German sensibilities' moved the deployment a day's

The king's plan, 31 July.

march to the rear, from the east side of the Gette to the west side. At 1150 31 July, Moranville telephoned Leman with instructions not to fortify the intervals between the forts 'out of concern for German susceptibilities'.[5] 'In any case, the work was soon ordered begun'.

Lombard's argument, that Liège covered the mobilisation and deployment of the Belgian Army, is absurd. Belgium is a little country, the Belgian Army was small, and Belgian mobilisation and deployment were completed by 5 August. The Germans could never have attacked before then. To cite just one example, the Guard Corps deployed to its assembly area at Malmedy (then German territory) between 10 and 12 August.

On 29 July only 12 and 14 Brigades and Lancer R 2 of 3 DA were at Liège; 11 Brigade was at Hasselt, 9 Brigade at Brussels, the artillery at Tirlemont.[6] On 30 July

Leman went to the war minister to ask that his division be concentrated at Liège; at the same time Moranville wanted to move 3 DA to St Trond. The king intervened on 1 August to keep 3 DA at Liège. At 1900 on 1 August the war minister informed Moranville that 3 DA would remain at Liège, 4 DA at Namur.[7] A considerable time afterwards (not further specified) Leman told Moranville that 'on 31 July or 1 August' he, Leman, had an interview with the king and received permission to keep 3 DA as the garrison of Liège. Leman said: 'But this did not end the trouble, for there was an [unsuccessful] attempt to retain the 9 Brigade in Brussels.' At 0300 1 August Moranville instructed Leman to move a brigade to St Trond to act as a covering force for the assembly of the army. Leman appealed to the king to get the order countermanded. On 4 August the Belgian General Staff found that 3 DA had not sent a brigade to St Trond and again ordered it to do so; Leman again appealed to the king, who sent an officer with an order written in the king's own hand to 'hold to the end with your division the position which you have been entrusted to defend'.

What did Albert expect to achieve with such an order? Apparently, he believed that Liège would be able to hold out for a considerable period, and that this would enable French forces to arrive, relieve Liège and stop the German invasion. Galet would be shocked when, in spite of this order, Leman would pull all of his troops out of the fortress on the morning of 6 August. The Belgian high command was far too optimistic concerning its own forces, and French intentions, and failed to comprehend the combat power of the German Army.

Moranville had just lost eight of his twenty manoeuvre brigades, 40 per cent of his total force, and was losing control of the army to the king, which is to say, to the king's principal advisor, Major Galet. Moranville's complaints about the excessive influence of young staff officers were perfectly justified.

This is a strange deployment. The Gette position was two days' march from Liège. On the one hand, in spite of Galet's bravado, it was clear that by deploying the main army on the Gette, the Belgians were not going to oppose a German crossing of the Meuse; it was likely that the Belgian intent was to fall back to Antwerp as soon as necessary. None of the principal Belgian officers state why the 3 DA was left at Liège, or its mission. What was it supposed to accomplish? No preparations had been made to support the division logistically in Liège, so it was dependent on an open line of supply to the west. That being the case, at the very best it was going to delay the German penetration between the intervals for a few days, at the risk of losing the division outright. This seems to have been a last-minute, poorly thought-out brainstorm that Leman (and perhaps Galet) sold to the king.

The Belgians received the German ultimatum, demanding free passage across Belgium, at 1900 2 August and held a full-scale council of war at 2130.[8] At 1100 3 August the Belgian HQ issued 'Instructions for the concentration of the army'. The 3 DA was to 'provisionally' concentrate at Liège and defend there; 4 DA had the same mission at Namur. Neither division was committed permanently to their fortress, nor given a mission or an operations order. The rest of the army would deploy between the Gette and Dyle rivers: 1 DA at Tirlemont, 5 DA at Perwez, with 2 DA at Louvain and 6 DA at Wavre, well to the rear. The cavalry division would move to the right rear of 5 DA, at Gembloux, not in front of the army, where it belonged. On 3 August, Belgian cavalry saw German troop concentrations at Aachen and to the north. Galet's analysis of the weaknesses of Moltke's plan was quite perceptive:[9]

If the [German] Imperial General Staff had really intended to send its armies across Belgium why did it disclose its plans so soon as the first day of mobilization, before concentration had begun? It was tantamount to a kindly warning to give the French time to take measures to meet the move.

When thinking over matters before the War, we had always considered that in order to dispose of France quickly the Germans ought to act by their left, as von Moltke did in 1870. It was only in this way that they could hope to cut off the French army from the interior of France, sweep it up against the sea or the neutral territories to the North and force it to a decisive battle. Any offensive on the right, especially across Belgium, besides in all probability causing the extra complication of British intervention, would leave to the French Army the whole of France with which to manoeuvre, and so lead sooner or later to an indecisive campaign, which would degenerate into a protracted war of exhaustion inevitably fatal to Germany [...] Was it [the German ultimatum] a colossal feint? Was it not possible that the Great General Staff was only trying to provoke the French Army to a deployment in the wrong direction by attracting its centre of gravity to the North? And if this were correct, and the Germans did not invade our territory, where should we be, with the French and British Armies on our soil? Could we avoid being dragged by them into the war?

Only after German forces had crossed the Belgian border, on 4 August, did Belgium ask the guarantor powers, France, Britain and Russia, to assist in the maintenance of her 'independence and integrity'. Belgium would never become an Allied power, but remain associated with the Allies.

Galet said that on 4 August, 'As a business man works out a balance sheet, I made out the following estimate of the opposing forces'.[10] Russia had thirty-nine active corps, France twenty-one, Serbia five, Belgium three, Germany had twenty-five, Austria sixteen. So, sixty-eight Entente active corps against forty-one for the Central Powers [the reserve corps would be in the same proportion], a three to two superiority for the Entente.

From this we argued that any attempt on the part of Germany to undertake an offensive would be an act of folly. This conclusion was strengthened next day when we learned that the British Empire would join in the struggle on our side, with all her military and naval might.

Having thus weighed our chances, it was in good heart that we left Brussels at 2 p.m. on 5 August to join the General Headquarters at Louvain. We did not conceal from ourselves that many difficulties lay before us. But of the issue of the World War we had high hopes.

The Belgian mobilisation made the serious deficiencies in Belgian military preparations glaringly evident.

There was only one year group under arms, 33,000 men from the class of 1913. During mobilisation the war minister instructed each Belgian infantry regiment to form a second active-army regiment.[11] In 3 DA, 9 L (*de ligne* regular infantry) formed 22 L, 11 formed 31, 12 formed 32, 14 formed 34. In the line regiments of most armies, the ratio of active duty to reservists was one-to-one. By creating an entirely new regiment, the ratio became one-to-four. By European standards, all the Belgian units became, in effect, reserve units, with weak cadres, unit cohesion, and training. The number of battalions increased from 78 to 120, but the effective strength of the battalions did not rise above 700 to 800, while the European standard was 1,000. Since there was no increase in artillery, fire support was diluted. Belgium also increased the field army from six to the eight youngest year groups of militia, which, Galet said, 'increased the average age of the unit, decreased its activity and broke up the already weak cohesion'. These would form six infantry divisions and a weak cavalry division, 117,000 men, of whom 85,000 were infantry.

> The infantry was insufficiently supplied with tools, and was unpractised in entrenching. It had only just received its machine guns, the number of which – 102 for the whole army – was calculated at half the scale on which the Germans were supplied. And there was *no reserve*. There was no heavy artillery. The telephone equipment was negligible. Aviation was in an embryonic stage.

The garrisons of the fortresses of Liège, Namur and Antwerp were composed of the eight oldest year groups, had barely one officer per company and, Galet said, 'were of absolutely no military value.' The result was an army strong in numbers of infantry, nothing more. Galet said this was the cause of 'the extremely poor tactical performance of our troops in 1914, which can only be characterised as disastrous'.[12]

Mobilisation brought 18,500 volunteers, which is not insignificant, but, given twenty infantry brigades, only about 900 men per brigade (a 20 per cent increase). In the last eight year groups, given the 1913 class of 33,000 men as the standard, 100,000 eligible men had not performed national service.[13] This was about the same as the field army possessed. The class of 1914 was not called up. German regimental histories frequently remarked on the number of military-age young men they saw still at home.

The cadres were utterly insufficient to lead the mobilised army. The most serious deficiency was the lack of reserve officers. Prior to 1909 the only reserve officers were former career NCOs who had returned to civilian life. Only under the reform of 1909 was it possible to train educated young men to be reserve officers. For lack of cadres, the infantry companies were organised into two oversized and unwieldy platoons (a German company had three). Most companies had only two or perhaps just one officer (a typical German company generally had four: an active-duty captain and three lieutenants, one active duty and two reservists).[14] For lack of guns and personnel, only three-quarters of the planned field artillery could actually be fielded, and the artillery lacked the fire control and communications equipment necessary to effectively conduct indirect fire.

Leman said:

> The men of the older classes of militia were a lamentable sight: they had lost all soldierly spirit.[15] But was it not to be expected? Out of the ten classes six were of older men who had long left the army, had ceased to be amenable to discipline, and had forgotten how to march or to hold a rifle. Was it not almost criminal to allot troops of this calibre to the defence of a frontier fortress, liable to attack 24 hours after the expiration of an ultimatum?

On 5 and 6 August the king made an inspection tour of the four divisions assembling near Louvain.[16]

> The men meandered about anyhow. They knew neither their officers nor their comrades. The non-commissioned officers, unused to exercising authority, did not attempt to do so; so the officers, as in peace, strove to take everything on themselves and were overwhelmed by having to handle units brought up to war strength [...] Battalions, companies and even platoons, were lodged at hazard in farms, large buildings and private houses, and the men thus escaped the observation of their seniors. All control, the communication of orders, and parades with arms were difficult. Guard-mounting, roll-calls, fatigues and any assembly of troops necessitated infinite preparation and much moving to and fro. The troops could not bivouac, for they had neither tents nor waterproof sheets. Moreover, there were no field-kitchens, and cooking utensils had to be collected from farm to farm [...] The soldiers strolled about with their friends and relations who had come to see what war meant. Parents joined their sons as a matter of course, even when on outpost duty. There was amazing cheerfulness. Soldiers and civilians were mixed together enjoying themselves, and were full of confidence [...]
>
> There were many stragglers in the 2nd Division, which had come back from Antwerp to Louvain in two short marches. The men walked in herds, the reservists, devoid of enthusiasm and overcome by heat, crumpling up under the weight of their packs and rifles.

By the 5th August the men of the classes of 1904 to 1909 had rejoined their units. Nevertheless, on the following morning certain formations were still not up to war strength [...]

The condition of the 6th Division was not more reassuring. The dearth of infantry officers – two per company – was already making itself felt on all sides. The men who joined in 1913 had not been instructed in musketry, and they were hurriedly put through a course of a few rounds to show them what it felt like to fire ball ammunition. Some of the machine gun companies had never fired ball ammunition! [...]

The tour made a deep impression on the King. It convinced him that our troops had no solidarity, and that some order and coherence must be instilled into them before they could be entrusted to undertake any operations. On every count the handling of them called for the greatest care. And if disaster were to be avoided it would be better for some time to rely upon the moral effect of their existence, rather than their utility in action.

It may be an unhappy confession, but at that time nobody troubled over these weaknesses. Officers and men aflame with patriotism declaimed indignantly against the enemy, boasted most fatuously, and tasted in anticipation all the joys of vengeance. The higher the rank, the louder the note of bellicose exuberance [...] at the different headquarters it savoured of the ridiculous, and was beyond all reason at General Headquarters and in the Ministry of War. In these last places the words 'offensive' and 'manoeuvre' punctuated all conversation, and uncontrolled imaginations pictured lightning-stroke operations on this or the other side of the Meuse. If the German Army had been no stronger than our Civil Guard, and if our Army had been as powerful as that of the Germans, confidence could not have been greater. What ignorance of the facts!

Galet said that this attitude was reinforced by Grandmaison's theory of the *offensive à outrance*, which had gained a following in the Belgian officer corps, government and press, 'What did the condition of our troops matter to them? Would not moral force, confidence in the justice of our cause, and the magic virtue in the offensive be all sufficing?'

Plan to Take Liège by *Coup de Main*

On 29 August the German Army ordered all units to remain in or return to garrison and recalled officers on leave. On 30 August all personnel on leave were recalled. At about 1400 on 31 August the regiments received notification the 'Period Preparatory to War' had been ordered. This involved preparation for mobilisation and securing important rail installations, ammunition and equipment dumps with standing guard posts. Horse purchases began. Active-army units released cadres for units to be formed on mobilisation: IR 20, for example, detached four staff officers, ten captains and a large number of lieutenants to form RIR (Reserve Infantry Regiment) 20 and 35, Landwehr IR 20 and Ersatz (Replacement) Battalion 11.[17] In the 11 Brigade area, about 400 reservists for IR 20 and IR 35[18] reported to the district recruiting headquarters on 31 August along with horses. Ammunition, food and equipment were uploaded on the regimental vehicles. Inspections of weapons, uniforms and equipment were conducted.

The infantry companies that were to conduct the attack on Liège would do so at peacetime strength. The exact determination of what this constituted was made by the corps headquarters.[19] IR 74 moved out with 135 men per company, IR 165 with 175. Beginning at 2100, 2 August, IR 20 rolled out of the rail station, each company at what was effectively peacetime strength of two or three officers and 130 men, or roughly half the wartime strength. The regiment consisted of fifty officers and 1,666 men. To bring it up to wartime strength it would be joined by seventeen officers, 1,546 NCOs and men and eighteen vehicles, which would not reach the regiment until 11 August.

When the German assault units left the home station rail yards they had no idea what their destination was or what their mission would be. Each brigade was joined en route or at the Aachen rail station by a General Staff officer, who carried secret orders. For 27 Brigade this was First Lieutenant Nida, originally from IR 25.[20] These specified the brigade's actions in great detail: bivouac on the night of 3–4 August, approach march route on 4 August, bivouac on 4–5 August.

The General Staff officer would also serve as a guide for the attack on the night of 5–6 August. Lieutenant Nida had reconnoitred the route exactly, 'Here over the rail line, then a sharp left, at the crossroads take the middle trail, etc.'

Nevertheless, it is doubtful that many of these officers had actually walked the ground under the conditions that would actually obtain, that is, in the rain at night. It is axiomatic for military operations that you fight as you have trained to fight. Failure to follow this rule will always have serious consequences, and the German night attack on 5–6 August was no exception: many of the guides got lost. Worse, at least one guide was a casualty before the attack even started.

The orders themselves were absurd, the product of Moltke's tactical incompetence. They did not prescribe infantry reconnaissance of the objective. They did call for an attack by an entire brigade in march column, instead of a tactical movement with an advance guard followed by well-spaced companies and battalions.

This left the brigade commanders with no decisions to make, and rather than fight their brigades tactically they acted like platoon leaders, putting themselves at the heads of their columns, where they often became casualties.

Comparison of Forces at Liège

Belgian Order of Battle:[21] Fortress Liège

22,000 men:

Fortress Infantry: Regiments 9, 11, 12, 14. Approximately 6,570 infantry in total.

Each fortress infantry 'regiment' therefore had 1,650 infantry. Each of its three battalions had 550 men and each of the four companies 135 men, about half the European norm for an infantry company.

Each of the six large forts had a garrison of around 550 men (300 artillery, 200 infantry).[22]

Each of the six small forts 350 men (230 artillery, 120 infantry).[23]

The fortress infantry platoons came from specially designated excess units in 14 L

The total garrison of the twelve forts therefore came to 5,400 men.

As mobile artillery to defend the intervals (all batteries four-gun): six 8cm batteries; three 8.7cm howitzer batteries; two 12cm batteries (Model 1862). Three 15cm batteries were never formed. Three 8cm batteries were to defend the citadel. It was intended that two 12cm batteries and three 15cm batteries first defend the intervals, then fall back to cover the Liège bridges. Three 8cm batteries were to defend the Chartreuse. Two six-gun batteries of 7.5cm horse artillery and one four-gun battery of 8.7cm horse artillery. As De Schrÿver notes, none of these guns engaged in combat.

A battalion of fortress engineers, 5 and 6 Squadron/ Lancer R 2, perhaps 1,000 men.

Garde Civique: infantry, artillery and a squadron of mounted police: 27 OFF and 463 EM.

Numerous support personnel.

3 DA

23,000 men:

9 Brigade (Bde): 9 L, 29 L (2,350 men per regiment).

11 Bde: 11 L, 31 L.

12 Bde: 12 L, 32 L.

14 Bde: 14 L, 34 L.

Each brigade had an MG company and three batteries of artillery.

In total approximately 19,000 infantry.

15 Reserve Brigade

Chasseur 1, Chasseur 4, three batteries of artillery. (Arrived 5 August), 4,700 men.

The five infantry brigades included approximately 23,500 infantry.

Lancer Regiment 2 (-).

FAR 3 (three batteries).

An engineer battalion with an engineer company and a bridge company .

Total strength for Fortress Liège – 50,000 men, including 30,000 mobile infantry (not including fortress infantry garrisons and *Garde Civique*).

German Order of Battle

Commander: General von Emmich, Commander X AK

Heereskavalleriekorps 2 (HKK, 2nd Cavalry Corps): 4 *Kavalleriedivision* (KD), 2 KD, 9 KD.

34 Bde: IR 89, IR 90, IR 25 (on 5 August to 27 Bde.), Jäger 9, II/ FAR 60 (how).

27 Bde: IR 16, IR 53, Jäger 7, II/ FAR 43 (howitzer – how), platoon (two 21cm mortars, guns), 2/ Foot Artillery 9.

14 Bde: IR 27, IR 165, Jäger 4, II/ FAR 4 (how), platoon 7/ Foot Artillery 4 (21cm).

11 Bde: IR 20, IR 35, Jäger 3, II/ FAR 39 (how).

38 Bde: IR 73, IR 74, Jäger 10, I/ FAR 26 (gun).

43 Bde: IR 82, IR 83, I/ FAR 11 (gun).

Comparison of Forces

This was to be a straight infantry close-range night battle. Field artillery was significantly involved only in the German 14 Brigade sector.

The six German brigades (thirteen regiments) at peacetime strength, plus five Jäger battalions, amounted to 25,000 infantry, according to the German official history.[24]

They would be opposed by five Belgian brigades and four fortress infantry regiments, (fourteen regiments), all fully mobilised, about 30,000 infantry.

But a comparison of forces is not just about numbers. Most of the Belgian troops were reservists who had a year of training. The German troops had no reservists at all: they were all active-duty conscripts who had served under the same officers and NCOs, half having a year's service, half two years. Almost all of the officers and NCOs were active-army professionals. In 1914 this was the gold standard. These troops would have been considered to be of higher quality than even the British Expeditionary Force or the French Colonial Corps, both of which contained large numbers of reservists.

The German Plan Collapses

The German 29 July intelligence estimate reported that the Belgians had mobilised, begun 'arming' the fortresses (digging field fortifications in the intervals between the permanent fortifications) and preparing bridges and rail lines for demolition. On 30 July intelligence estimates reported that the Meuse bridges were prepared for demolition, and on 31 July that Liège had been armed and the eastern viaducts and tunnels were ready for demolition.[25] It should have been evident to Moltke by 31 July, even before Germany took any military measures whatsoever, that the *attaque brusquée* on Liège – and a night attack at that – had little or no chance of success, while it had serious negative political consequences. Worse, the attack would telegraph the right wing's punch, and if Joffre had not been thinking about the threat to his left flank, the *attaque brusquée* on Liège would change all that. The Germans were also not going to be able to 'bounce' the Meuse bridges and the rail net near Liège was going to be rendered unusable for a considerable period.

The German official history maintained that 'The German General Staff [Moltke] estimated the garrison of Liège at 6,000 *peacetime troops* [emphasis mine] and 3,000 *Garde Civique*. This meant, as it soon became apparent, considerable underestimate of the number of troops and their combat power'.[26] First, Moltke's plan assumed that the Belgian Army as a whole had not mobilised. Moltke also assumed that the Belgian 3 DA, which was headquartered at Liège, had either not mobilised or had moved out. German intelligence reported that the Belgians had begun mobilising on 29 July, so both assumptions were no longer valid. In particular, there was no reason whatsoever to assume that 3 DA had left Liège. Indeed, on 3 August the intelligence estimate reported that the garrison of Liège had been reinforced. The only logical assumption was that 3 DA was at Liège and digging in. Moltke ordered the attack to proceed anyway.

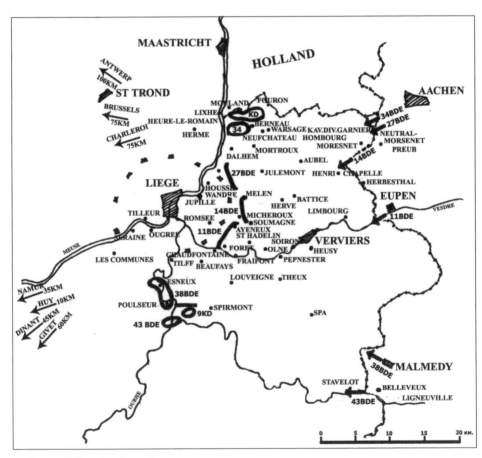

Siege of Liège situation, 5 August.

The German orders to the brigades on the evening of 5 August said that Liège was 'armed' and estimated the garrison at four regiments. This presents two problems. First, the very premise of the attack was that Liège would *not* be armed and the German brigades would be able to pass through the undefended intervals between the fortresses. If the intervals were undefended, there might be some justification in sending entire brigades in march column between them. If there was going to be any kind of fight, then a brigade column was tactical insanity; the attack should have been conducted by the Jäger battalions, alone. The entire operation was also in direct violation of German tactical doctrine for a night attack, which called for careful reconnaissance and preparation. The second problem is that, even though the German intelligence said that Liège had been reinforced, the four regiments the order referred to were still probably the four fortress infantry regiments; the attack order was based on an old pre-war estimate and not actual intelligence. In fact, the Belgians had twelve regiments in Liège

At several points between 31 July and 5 August it was clear that the assumptions that the Liège attack plan were based on no longer applied. It is a fundamental principle of troop-leading at any level that when this occurs the entire decision-making process has to be conducted based on the new situation. Had this been done, it would have been clear that the pre-war plan had to be discarded and a new order given based on the changed circumstances. Instead, Moltke continued with the pre-war plan, unchanged. This was the first of a series of decisions that would show that Moltke was unequal to his position as chief of staff.

Failed *Coup de Main* at Visé Bridge

On the German right, the Provisional Cavalry Division Garnier (elements of 2 KD and 4 KD) was to seize the Meuse bridge at Visé intact. It would be followed by 34 Bde. In the centre, from north to south, 27 Bde, 14 Bde and 11 Bde advanced directly on Liège. 38 Bde and 43 Bde, led by 9 KD, approached from the south.

Jäger 9 crossed the Belgian border at 1130 4 August and turned sharply right towards Visé. It had formed a task force made up of the bicycle company with 1/ Jäger 9 and attached engineers loaded onto requisitioned lorries, which had the mission of pushing rapidly forward and securing the Meuse bridges at Visé.[27] They never had a chance. The 'motorised' advance was delayed considerably by the road obstacles that would become familiar to all the troops of the German 2nd Army: overturned vehicles tied with cable, trees fallen over the roads, blown bridges, road signs removed. They did not reach the Meuse bridges – which had also been blown – much before the main body. Crossing was impossible. The bicycle company and 1/ Jäger 9 encountered resistance on the east side of Visé, which it said came from 'Gendarmes and elements of the Belgian 12 Line.' The Jäger battalion history does

not mention either a particularly heavy firefight or casualties. The commander of
1/ Jäger 9 reported to battalion that the far side of the Meuse was being held by an
estimated two enemy companies. Corporal Stuckert of the Jäger 7 Bicycle Company
wrote home that evening:

> [The Belgians] destroyed the most beautiful tree-lined *allée*; magnificent pop-
> lars were sawn down over the roads. We caught several civilians at work and
> shot two. We then reached Visé. There were barricades and wire obstacles at
> the edge of town, but we were quickly through these. The captain, my brother
> (a senior sergeant in 1/ Jäger 9) and 12 Jäger and I cycled up to the bridge,
> but we hadn't gone 200 metres when we reached the destroyed Meuse bridge.
> Not a soul was to be seen in the town. But when we got off our bicycles
> to decide what to do, we took fire from several houses; we barely had time
> to take cover. (The commander of 1/ Jäger 9 said that the houses his troops
> took fire from had hung out white flags). Baptism of fire! We replied in kind
> to this friendly greeting of bullets from ambush. Any window that appeared
> suspicious was fired on. Part of my brother's left index finger was shot off. We
> were ordered to pull back from the village so that the artillery could soften
> it up. Soon it was quiet in the village, which was burning in several places.
> Several volunteer patrols moved back in; I went with my brother and two
> other Jäger. We saw three Belgian soldiers standing on a street corner and
> killed two, wounding the third; a strange feeling, intentionally shooting at
> another human being.[28] We bandaged the wounded man, a Belgian border
> guard; he moaned a great deal, his calf wound being quite painful. The firing
> in the town by civilians armed with revolvers, hunting weapons and other
> unlikely shooting irons would not stop: we killed eight, wounded 13. We had
> five wounded.

De Schrÿver devotes four pages to an hour-long firefight between the Belgian
II/ 12 L on the west side of the Meuse and all of Jäger 9, companies of IR 25, and
'copious quantities' of German artillery.[29] Fire from Fort Pontisse 'spread devastation
in the German ranks'. The Belgian battalion was forced to retreat at 1645, satisfied
that it had prevented the German from crossing. II/ 12 L suffered two killed in action
(KIA) and 'a dozen' wounded in action (WIA).

   This is curious because the relevant German histories emphasise the fight in Visé
and hardly mention a firefight across the river. Only two companies of Jäger 9 were
engaged at Visé and no elements whatsoever of IR 25. It was obvious to the Germans
once they reached the river that they were not going to be able to cross. No German
artillery units were engaged, and according to the 1/ Jäger 9 history the fire from
Pontisse 'did not do any damage worth mentioning'. The two accounts had one thing
only in common: both sides reported the enemy had MG, and neither had any.

The withdrawal of II/12 and with it the Pontisse OPs worried Leman, who feared an attack on the west bank of the Meuse. He therefore moved 11 Brigade from the east bank to the west, and it bivouacked at Vottem, only to move it back to the east bank the next morning.[30]

The Jäger main body reached the area east of Warsage at 1800 and took fire from gardens, hedges and farms, deployed and swept without much difficulty to the other side of the village. The Jäger had no kind words for *francs-tireurs*:

It soon became clear that the aforementioned firing did not come from the rifles of Belgian soldiers, but the more-or-less questionable shooting irons of cowardly, treacherous, *francs-tireurs*. As is common with the despicable scum (*lichtscheue Gesindel*) on God's green earth, when faced with their just punishment, they disappeared without a trace. Whether the man with grim face, hunkered down on the side of the road as we passed, was innocent as a pigeon, or shortly before had been a sniper, we had neither any way of knowing nor time to find out.

The battalion history said, 'Yesterday we were in Ratzenberg (the Jäger's garrison), today we are in enemy territory in front of Liège. Practically incomprehensible, but nevertheless quite true'.

Hussar R 15 was the advance guard for 4 KD, and sent three long-range patrols to the Meuse.[31] One of the patrol leaders reported that the first half of his mission passed without incident; 'the only unusual thing was that the inhabitants of the towns looked at us with curiosity, shaking their heads and making fun of us, as though no one thought that the war was serious'. They then encountered civilians blocking the roads with wagons, equipment and fallen trees, who ran and hid in their houses when the hussars approached. The patrol leader sternly ordered them out to explain themselves. The inhabitants, who spoke perfect German, said that a gendarme had told them to do it. The patrol leader said that if the barricade was not gone in two hours, the town would be tried by court martial. As he left, he saw the civilians begin to clear the road. In a larger town numerous civilians shouted their dissatisfaction, which the patrol ignored. They then saw a Belgian cavalry patrol race out of the town towards the Meuse at full gallop, while a Belgian lancer stepped out of a house carrying a case of beer. He dropped the beer and jumped on his horse but the patrol captured him, which caused 'extraordinary agitation' in the crowd. As they reached the heights above the Meuse they heard a massive detonation – the Belgians had blown the bridge.

North: 34 Brigade

At 0700 on 4 August 2/ Uhlan R 16 crossed the Belgian border.[32] A cavalry patrol that had gone ahead a short time before was stopped by a Belgian policeman who took down the patrols leader's name so that he could press charges. A patrol encountered Belgian lancers, and two of the Germans hit Belgians with their lances and unhorsed them, but the Uhlan 16 troopers took infantry fire and had to withdraw, with one being wounded in the stomach. The squadron met the usual obstacles: fallen trees, ditches and cables across roads, bridges blown. The inhabitants repeatedly fired on the uhlan bivouac: a number were arrested and three, who were caught while armed, were shot.

IR 25 was stationed in Aachen, so when the order 'imminent hostilities' was received at 1500 31 July, the regiment immediately sent troops to act as security on the border with Belgium – they moved by electric streetcar.[33]

On 4 August, 34 Brigade crossed the Belgian border in order of march IR 89, II/ FAR 60, IR 90.[34] IR 89 moved out at peacetime strength – 37 OFF and 1,631 EM.[35] IR 90 noted that each battalion received 10,000 marks in gold – 2,000 gold marks per company commander, so that he could pay for whatever the unit needed, rather than requisition it. The regimental historian said that the countryside, meadows surrounded by hedges, looked like Holstein and the population of the villages was 'conspicuously friendly'. At 1730 the brigade reached Warsage, and after dark bivouacked north of Berneau. The IR 90 historian said that the bivouac site was 'not well chosen', in enclosed meadows immediately north of the village, as close as the vegetable gardens, divided by wire, fences and thick hedges from each other, all six battalions close together, yet completely isolated from each other by the hedges. 'Only this situation', he said, 'could explain the night's events.'

Towards midnight a guard called out 'Halt – who's there?' followed by firing. Bullets flew through the bivouac, hitting trees and ricocheting between the tents. Excited IR 90 men fired into the night, as did the IR 89 MG. The officers commanded ceasefire, fell the companies into formation at order arms. Finally it was quiet. Hardly had the troops returned to their tents than the firing began once again, stronger than before. A company of I/ 90 began to assault II/ 90, and was stopped by the personal intervention of the II/ 90 commander. Order was re-established again and so far as possible the rifles unloaded and ammunition counted to prevent further firing. As after the first incident, patrols were sent out and at dawn the entire area was thoroughly searched. A half-dozen residents of Berneau were caught wandering through the bushes without good reason, but there were no grounds to connect them with the night's events and they were released. Weapons and ammunition from IR twenty-five were found, and someone had shot horses through the windows of the stalls. Two NCOs, seven men and eleven horses were dead, the regimental adjutant, thirty-one men and two horses wounded.

At 0900 4 August, IR 25 crossed the border north of Aachen and marched straight to Visé, where it found Jäger 9 and the blown bridge.[36] Since it was not possible to cross the Meuse, the regiment bivouacked in Visé. The guns of Fort Pontisse began to shell the town, and at 0230 the regiment, which was in alarm quarters (ready to move), shifted its bivouac to the east of the town. Fléron shelled the area near Hervé.

It should be noted that the Belgian heavy fortress artillery, 12cm, 15cm and 21cm guns, was firing blind near and even directly into Belgian towns. However, none of the Belgian histories mention such casualties. This was probably an intentional omission, for one first-person account, the testimony of Abbé Madenspacher (Appendix), notes that Belgian civilians were killed by fortress artillery fire, and this was surely not an isolated incident.

North: 27 Brigade

The 'supplementary' troops began to arrive at the IR 53 barracks during the early morning on 1 August. Each company received twenty-five to thirty supplementary personnel, bringing the companies to a strength of 140–150 men. They moved the short distance to Aachen, arriving between 0100–0200, 3 August.[37] The regiment crossed the Belgian border at 1130 and made another short march to bivouac at Mortroux at 1530. II/ FAR 43 reported sending a platoon forward twice to shell houses that patrols had taken fire from. The artillery bought rations from a large farm.[38]

Centre: 14 Brigade

The IR 165 history said that the companies were not allowed to be stronger than 175 EM, but that a blind eye was often turned towards the fact that they moved out 'with a few more men than permitted'.[39] IR 27 moved out unusually strong: 56 OFF and 2,235 EM: 6/ 27 had 246 EM, 7/ 27 242 (near full-strength).[40]

In the early morning of 4 August the lead elements of 14 Brigade, 1/ Hussar R 10 and the Jäger 4 Bicycle Company, crossed the border and immediately encountered the Belgian obstacles.[41] The brigade had sent engineers forwards in automobiles to clear them out. The cavalry tried to move off-road, but were frequently prevented from doing so by pastures lined with hedges. Locals caught preparing obstacles were sent to the rear by Jäger 4. The cavalry point patrol leader, Sergeant Müller, said:

After about an hour and a half we were ordered to halt. I found a good spot, a fork in the road about 800 metres from Battice, and after a bit an observation post (OP) reported a cavalry patrol approaching, Belgian lancers, a lieutenant and nine men in 4-2-4 march order; I had used 2-4-3, then connecting riders.[42]

I could have let them come on and opened fire with carbines at short range, but we were Hussars, German cavalrymen. I pulled back the OP, mounted up and deployed my patrol, and when the first four lancers reached the fork, charged, yelling 'Hurra!' The four lancers immediately turned around and ran, taking the rest with them. I followed at full gallop. The old comrades know my horse then, 'Vesta': she would not allow another horse to be in front of her! I drew my pistol and with the third shot brought down a Belgian horse; the lancer jumped behind a hedge and fired his pistol at me. I had difficulty stopping Vesta, who reared up several times. I yelled to the Belgian in French 'Surrender!' but he continued firing – and missing. I fired and the Belgian soldier fell to the ground. My patrol had stopped with me, about 300 metres from Battice, from which we began taking fire. 'Off the road!' I ordered, and my men took cover in the hedges. By this time the bicyclists of Jäger 4 and the infantry point had come up. A half-hour later the bicyclists shot up the Belgian lancers.

After a 30km march the brigade bivouacked between 1600 and 1700 in Hervé, a small town 15km east of Liège, or in Battice further east. The brigade was accompanied by the X AK commander, General Emmich, and his staff.

Some Belgians had locked their houses and left. On the one hand, the IR 27 historian says that the remaining inhabitants were 'restrained and cold and made a suspicious impression'. In the next sentence he says that the inhabitants brought beer, water and cigarettes, which were accepted by the troops with pleasure, until the priest told them to stop, because Belgium was neutral.

During the night there was continual firing from the woods and houses against the bivouacking troops, though the 14 Brigade troops could never determine exactly where the fire was coming from. The exits to the town were put under guard, and IR 27 established an interior guard of an officer and eighteen men, and the corps HQ with a platoon. In Battice, a soldier from 9/ 27 was killed by such fire, and the priest and mayor were taken as hostages. Hussar R 10 was ordered to clean out the *francs-tireurs*, captured several armed men and turned them over for court-martialling.

II/ 165 was sent forward as security against the forts on a line Bolland–Mélen–Soumagne; 7/ 165 had to take Soumagne from elements of the Belgian 11 L. These troops also continually took sniper fire. An attack on one of the outposts resulted in the regiment's first fatal casualty.

Centre: 11 Brigade

IR 20 unloaded north-east of Eupen, near midnight on 3 August. At 0545 on 4 August the regiment began to footmarch towards Eupen. At 0850 the brigade order was given at the rail station at Eupen. It stated that Belgium was Germany's enemy. At 0900 the brigade would march to the west of Verviers. Only weak Belgian forces were expected on the border; the garrison of Verviers had probably withdrawn to Liège. Liège was 'armed' and had a four-regiment garrison. As the IR 35 historian noted, this order was highly unusual, in that the intent of the advance, the mission, was not stated. The troop commanders were not briefed on the General Staff order for the attack. Only in private conversations did they learn that the intent was to take Liège by *coup de main*.

As much as possible, the brigade was to avoid antagonising the civilian population: the battalions were given 7,500 marks in gold to pay the Belgians for provisions. On the other hand, Germans that had been expelled from Belgium told IR 20, 'much to their surprise', that the civil population intended to take part in the fighting. The road was blocked by the usual obstacles. Nevertheless, by 1300 the brigade had reached Verviers, where lunch was served from the field kitchens. The population thickly lined the streets, but was quiet and frequently offered the troops food and drink, refusing payment. The march objective, Soiron, about 5km west of Verviers, was reached between 1800 and 1900, where the brigade bivouacked. The heat and hilly terrain caused many troops to drop out, particularly the reservists.

Towards midnight an exterior guard post fired on what it thought was an enemy patrol. At midnight exactly firing began from everywhere in the town, which led to wild return firing. IR 35 reported that the situation in the castle, where the brigade staff, the command groups of I/ IR 35 and II/ FAR 39, and 2/ and 4/ 35 were bivouacked, was particularly hot. The castle took fire from all sides. Moving to help, 1/ 35 became involved in a blue-on-blue firefight. Finally officers stopped the firing with shouted commands and signals and assembled the troops at their alarm posts. Lieutenant Rittershaus, the commander of 7/ 35, reported:

My company had been assigned quarters in houses around the market. I spoke in French with the inhabitants and their furtive, nervous behaviour convinced me not to occupy the houses. In addition, in the dark, this close to the enemy fortress, I wanted to keep my company under tight control. I ordered my men to set up their tents on the market place and reported my decision to battalion, which was approved. When the firing began, shortly after midnight, in a few minutes 7/ 35 was assembled in the market with bayonets fixed. I ordered several squads to occupy the entrances to the village and I assembled the troops who were moving around and firing in the market. Once under my control, none of those troops fired a shot. 7/ 35 did not take any casualties. By the time the commander of II/ 35 arrived, three companies were there in closed formation.[43]

IR 20 did not take any casualties, but IR 35 lost a captain and 12 EM KIA, 30 EM WIA. The IR 35 historian admitted that some of the casualties were blue-on-blue, which he said always occurred in combat in towns or woods. Others were due to buckshot, which could only have come from a civilian weapon. There was no sign of Belgian troops. The IR 35 historian said, 'The *franc-tireur* war had begun, and often enough the regiment, while marching or resting, would take fire from cowardly ambush[es] in hedges, attics and cellars. Even medical aid stations'. The IR 20 historian claimed that it was later established that the attack had been the work of *francs-tireurs* from Liège and residents of the town. The brigade spent the night at their alarm positions. Three armed civilians were tried by the II/ 35 commander in courts martial and shot.

South: 38 and 43 Brigades

The 38 Brigade battle group was made up of IR 73, IR 74, Jäger Bn 10, 4/ Hussar R 17 and I/ FAR 26, and, along with 9 KD, unloaded from rail cars at Malmedy. The 43 Brigade battle group, of IR 82 and IR 83, 1/ Cuirassier R 6 and I/ FAR 11, unloaded at Ligneuville to the south. Both artillery sections were equipped with 7.7cm guns. The IR 83 history noted that each battalion received 10,000 gold marks in order to pay for all purchases in Belgium immediately in cash.[44]

At 0700 4 August, 4/ Hussar R 17, with the Bicycle Company of Jäger 10 attached, was near the border with the mission of preventing the destruction of the Belgian tunnels on the Stavelot rail line, but these had been destroyed the previous day. The squadron resumed its advanced guard mission and marched through Spa and Theux to bivouac Louveigné, which appeared deserted; the roads leading into the town had been blocked with tar barrels.[45]

At 0900, 38 Bde crossed the border. The last combat unit in the column, IR 74, took a two-hour lunch break just on the other side of the Belgian border. The troops took the opportunity to put the first letters home 'from the front' in the post box at the rail station; the IR 74 history said that it probably had never been so full. They only arrived weeks later.[46] Such almost childlike innocence would not last long.

The lead unit of the 38 Bde main body was IR 73. It noted that the beautiful *allée* leading down into Spa had been cut down to block the road and had to be cleared by 1/ Engineer Bn 10. IR 74 reported especially large trees felled on the road to Theux.

There were still guests at the baths in Spa. The brigade marched 35–40km under a burning sun, but IR 74 reported that few dropped out, and bivouacked between Theux and Louveigné. The houses were locked, many were unoccupied, and since the troops had been instructed to be careful dealing with the local population, finding billets was difficult.[47]

At 0215 a security element from 8/ 73 fired on a Belgian cavalry patrol, capturing the officer and five lancers with their horses, but five others escaped. West of Theux I/ FAR 26 bivouacked in the open; during the night a Belgian cavalry patrol was detected and a lieutenant and six men captured.[48]

On 5 August, IR 74 was awakened by silent alarm at 0200, because of a report (soon shown to be false) that Belgian forces were advancing from the north against Theux; the troops therefore had only a few hours' rest. This was followed by a difficult night march from the alert assembly areas to Mont (5km east of Louveigné), up steep hills and over fallen trees which was concluded at 0315, and then a further march to join 38 Brigade at Louveigné.

At 0640 the brigade continued the march south-west to Sprimont, and Poulseur, with IR 73 continuing on to bivouac at Esneux. There was contact with Belgian cavalry patrols and Fort de Boncelles and d'Embourg fired some shrapnel without doing serious damage. On the other hand, the IR 74 troops and supply vehicles were fired upon from houses and trees on the steep slopes to both sides of the road. Several troops were wounded before the shooters were driven away by patrols. Several Belgian civilians were taken prisoner. By 1100, after a 20km march, IR 74 bivouacked in Poulseur. The IR 74 commander convened a field courts martial to try two Belgian civilians accused of firing on the supply wagons. One was released for lack of evidence; the other convicted by eyewitness testimony and ordered to be executed. The conviction was confirmed by the brigade commander, Colonel the Prince of Lippe.

The commander of 43 Brigade, General von Hülsen, took over command of a provisional 'Division' made up of 38 and 43 Brigades. The commander of IR 83, Colonel von Moltke, became commander of 43 Brigade.

The German Uhlans were 'audacious', moving into the operations areas of the forts and trying to push in the Belgian security detachments, which continually had to remain alert.[49] At 0200 a German night cavalry patrol hit a Belgian security detachment south of Boncelles and lost one man. At 0500 a patrol from Uhlan R 5 encountered 3/ I/ 9 L and lost two men while killing a Belgian. At 0800 a German cavalry patrol was wiped out south of Sart-Tilman.

The Belgian 4/ Lancer R 2 had spent the night of 4–5 August bivouacked under the protection of Fort Boncelles and at dawn moved to reconnoitre on the line of the Ourthe, reinforced by twenty-five cyclists. At 1000 they ambushed a German cavalry patrol of about forty men, without adequate security, at Plainevaux. This apparently made the squadron commander overconfident. When at 1150 a column of German infantry was reported approaching from the south, again supposedly without an adequate advance guard (which, given the fight with the German cavalry two hours before, seems unlikely). He deployed his troops on both sides of the road, and when the German rose out of dead ground he opened fire, cutting down the first ranks. The German reaction was immediate: they deployed to both sides of the road and at 'a few hundred metres' range' formed a firing line. The Belgian cavalry squadron commander had made a serious tactical error and was now closely engaged with a superior force of German infantry. Belgian casualties mounted quickly. The squadron commander was killed, the lieutenant severely wounded, and at 1230 the remnants (*débris*) were withdrawn by the senior NCO, the wounded being captured. As is usual with Lombard, no Belgian casualties were given.

German Cavalry Reconnaissance West of the Meuse

Kabisch said that the Greiner composite cavalry division (elements of 2 and 4 KD) was to cross the Meuse to the north of Liège and 9 KD to the south, cut the fortress off from the interior and reconnoitre deep to the west.[50] But the Belgians had destroyed all the Meuse bridges outside Liège. Since the cavalry's artillery could not cross, Greiner did not cross at all, and because it was supposed to be covering the left flank, 9 KD did not cross the Meuse. This should have been foreseen and sounds suspiciously like a rationalisation.

In addition, the Jäger battalions, which gave the cavalry vital infantry support, had been assigned to the attack on Liège. This was another of Moltke's mistakes, because the brigade commanders were unfamiliar with the Jäger battalions' capabilities and generally did not use them properly. Had Greiner had the Jäger, he might have been willing to rely on them for support and cross with his entire division, which would have immediately unsettled Leman and resulted in the complete destruction of the 3 DA.

Therefore, the reconnaissance squadrons went across the Meuse unsupported by the rest of the cavalry division and without the light radio stations.[51] The absence of the radios and the supporting squadrons would be felt severely: messengers from the reconnaissance squadron seldom got through to the KD and the reconnaissance squadrons were completely in the dark concerning the situation at Liège.

At 0500 5 August the cavalry reconnaissance squadrons began to cross using the steel pontoons of the six cavalry regiments, which the official history said was 'completely inadequate.'[52] The infantry gave most of their shelter halves to the engineers to make balls filled with straw. Six such were held together with planks and boards to make small rafts. The pontoons and rafts carried the personnel and horse furniture, the horses swam alongside. The crossing was not easy: the river was 150m wide, the current strong and the bank on the opposite side steep.

In the reconnaissance mission, 2 KD would employ 4/ Hussar R 12 and 3rd Squadron, Dragoon R 2, 4 KD would employ 4t/ Dragoon R 17 and 2/ Dragoon R 18. They crossed at Lixhé near the Dutch border, under some fire from Fort Pontisse. German reconnaissance would initially fall on the cavalry alone: according to the history of Dragoon R 17, there were no reconnaissance aircraft available.

Each reconnaissance squadron sent out patrols, usually ten to twenty troopers strong, subdivided into three sections of three to seven men, the sections well dispersed and moving by bounds from one piece of cover to the next.

Throughout the campaign, fast, long-range movement allowed the German cavalry patrols to appear where it was not expected, leading Belgian and French civilians to think the patrol was British. In addition, civilians had difficulty distinguishing German cavalry uniforms from British. The patrols often used the opportunity to gain information from the inhabitants, as well as food and fodder.

One patrol reported being mistaken for British by the inhabitants, but they soon got wise. The patrol was shadowed by bicyclists and saw patrols of Belgian gendarmes. The patrol secured its bivouac with detachments led by NCOs, one of which was attacked during the night and a trooper wounded. On 6 August another long-range patrol, also shadowed by bicyclists, was ambushed and lost six troopers.

The 4/ Hussar R 12 was given the mission of conducting deep reconnaissance to Antwerp.[53] After crossing the Meuse, it sent out three long-range recon patrols, with their objectives at Diest, Waenrode (not on map, 6km south of Diest) and Tirlemont. In order to advance, 4/ Hussar R 12 had to manoeuvre around Belgian security forces. Its bivouac was fired upon throughout the night, but it lost only a horse. The Belgians withdrew before daylight. Messengers returning with reports had a hard time getting through and several were lost.

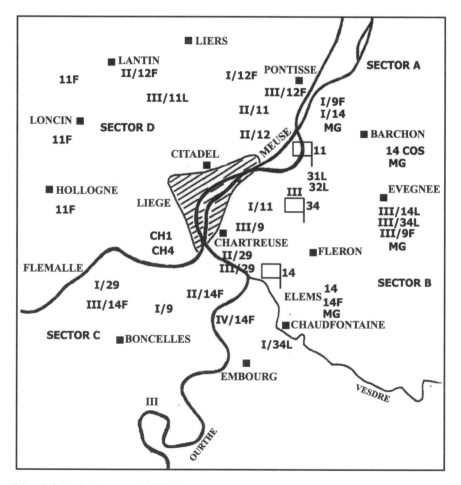

Liège Belgian deployment OPORD, 1600, 4 August.

The 3/ Dragoon R 2 bivouacked in the rain at Glons, (8km east of St Trond).[54]
Three long-range patrols were sent out on 5 August, one of which, with ten dra-
goons, charged a group of thirty Belgians and took them prisoner. A second shot at a
low-flying aircraft and forced it to land, but was prevented from taking the crew prisoner by superior Belgian forces. The patrol established that there were strong Belgian
forces at Waremme, but both of the messengers bringing this report were shot.
Belgian forces were also seen 6km south of Tirlemont. Bicyclists continually shadowed this patrol. On 6 August the squadron reached St Trond and broke up a group of
francs-tireurs. During the entire night a patrol observed Belgian troops marching west
on the Liège–St Trond road.

The 4 KD sent out two reconnaissance squadrons across the Meuse. The
4/ Dragoon R 17 had the mission of reconnoitring towards the Sambre and Charleroi
(off map, west of Namur). The squadron sent out three long-range patrols. Initially
these patrols and two from 2/ Dragoon R 18 moved together for the sake of security.
Civilian bicyclists raced in front, announcing, 'The British are coming!' This allowed
the patrol to advance all the way to the west side of Liège, where the patrols split up.

The 4/ Dragoon R 17, which followed the patrols, was not so lucky: it took fire.
The squadron dismounted, swept through a village, and determined that the shooters
had been civilians, who were captured. The squadron had not taken any casualties,
so the squadron commander only warned the priest that if it happened again the
village would be burned down. The regimental history said that for civilians to fire
on soldiers was 'treacherous murder'. Dragoon R 18 had moved to the sound of
the firing and the two squadrons bivouacked together near a village between Liège
and St Trond.

On 6 August, one of the 4/ Dragoon R 17 long-range patrols infiltrated through
the Belgian security forces and made contact with Belgian troops at a small river
about 40km west of Liège, as did the second patrol somewhat to the north. The horse
of the first patrol leader was killed and he was taken POW; the same fate befell the
officer and NCO of the second patrol and a trooper was wounded. The third patrol,
further to the east, found that all the bridges over another small river, as well as the
crossroads, were guarded. When they passed through a town, the church bells were
rung. The two reconnaissance squadrons sent out two more patrols, which were also
broken up and their leaders captured. A messenger returned to 4 KD with a report
that had found the Liège–Brussels road packed with Belgian troops: the Belgians
were evacuating their field forces from Liège.

Belgian Field Works

The perimeter at Liège was divided into four sectors. Sector A on the north-east
included forts Pontisse and Barchon and half the distance to both sides, B on the

east included Evegnée, Fléron and Chaudefontaine, C on the southern Embourg, Boncelles and Flémalle, D the west and north-west sides Hollogne–Loncin–Lantin– Liers.

A in the north-east and C in the south were considered to be on less likely avenues of enemy approach, in part because of the difficult terrain, and therefore were 'economy of force' sectors which could be held by the minimum number of troops. The field army to the west covered sector D. Sector B on the east was considered the most likely enemy avenue of approach and therefore the most strongly defended. All the Belgian reserves initially were deployed in this sector.

Leman and his staff came up with a plan for three successive lines of field fortifications.[55] The first consisted of field fortifications linking the forts on a circumference of 48km. De Schrÿver said: 'Given the absence of a definitive plan, recourse was made to the draft of a plan drawn up several years ago, for thirteen redoubts and sixty-three trenches to be constructed between the forts, with fifteen redoubts and fifty-two trenches on the east bank of the Meuse'.

The Belgian government and military made no provisions for evacuating or protecting the civilian population. Indeed, they built field fortifications in towns where the civilian population was still present and the fortress artillery would conduct fire missions with heavy artillery into areas inhabited by civilians. There were civilian casualties from Belgian 'friendly fire', but they are mentioned only in the local accounts.

The company-sized redoubts were in the shape of a shallow V, with the point forward and the flanks refused (bent back).[56] The fighting position was a breast-high trench, with a communication trench behind that, and behind that, in theory, a trench with overhead cover.

Work was begun on the morning of 1 August, but only three regiments were available: 34 L was assigned the entire east bank of the Meuse, 32 L from the Ourthe to Loncin, 12 L (two battalions) from Loncin to the Meuse. Instead of concentrating their resources on the most likely enemy avenue of approach, 3 DA spread its effort evenly along the entire perimeter. The troops were divided into three shifts: security, work parties and rest. The security was a further waste of resources. Instead of bivouacking, that evening the infantry marched back to their quarters in the city.

The Belgian redoubt.

On 2 August, 11 and 12 Fortress Regiments and 11 and 31 L became available; all were employed on the west bank of the Meuse, while 32 and 12 L worked on the sector between the Ourthe and the Meuse. Only 34 L continued its work on the east bank of the Meuse: the 3 DA priorities of work had become positively mystifying. The most threatened sector, the east bank of the Meuse, was receiving the fewest resources, one regiment, while the southern avenue of approach, half its size, got two regiments and the western side of the Meuse got four regiments. The only conclusion that can be drawn is that Leman was preparing for Liège to be completely encircled.

By the end the day on 2 August the Belgian troops were exhausted by the heat, the digging, and the necessity of marching from their quarters in the town to the work site and back again. Leman declared that 3 August would be a rest day. The work would be continued by engineers, supported by 500 civilian workers for the intervals between each fort. In total, industrial firms in Liège would supply 20,000 workers.[57]

Then at 0300 3 August, Leman decided that the Germans were attacking through Dutch territory, and alerted the entire garrison, orienting his forces to the north. Occupying a defensive position from Loncin to the Meuse, 11 Brigade (11 and 31 L) and 34 L held the east bank of the Meuse, Lancer R 2 was sent towards the Dutch border. De Schrÿver was unable to explain how Leman had come to this rather unlikely conclusion.[58] Occupying their alarm posts, 12 Brigade (12 and 32 L) were sent back to quarters at 0700, then at noon moved to St Trond to block an German advance through Dutch territory to the north of Liège.

At 0330 3 August the order went out to clear a 600m field of fire around the forts.[59] The forts' wooden peacetime barracks were burned, woods and hedges cut down, as well as civilian houses: at Boncelles 130 houses and a church. On 5 August, that is, before the fighting began, the *Journal de Liège* reported that it was 'deeply moved' by the misery this caused the unlucky families. De Schrÿver put a patriotic spin on the destruction of the houses: '… before the eyes of the weeping inhabitants, who had been forced out of their ancestral homes with heavy heart, but without anger or even a murmur'.

By 1930 3 August the Belgians had identified IR 16 and IR 35 (VII AK) near Aachen, and further south elements of IV AK. The X AK was at the Elsenborn Major Training Area, with strong forces to the south. At 2000 Leman received a report from his 'surveillance service' that the Germans had violated the Belgian border just north of Eupen, on the southern end of the Liège sector.[60] Leman immediately brought Lancer R 2 and 12 Brigade back to Liège. At about 2100 a second report arrived from the same source as the first, announcing that the report that the Germans had crossed the border was a false alarm.

Leman's complete lack of command experience was beginning to show even before the Germans crossed the border. On the shakiest of foundations, or no foundations whatsoever, he would jump to conclusions and order radical actions. Lancer R 2 and 12 Brigade spent 3 August marching and countermarching.

Given five days, 3 DA did not do a very good job of digging in. As De Schrÿver noted, the entrenchments were not deep and had no overhead cover. Reinforcing material, such as wood balks and iron plates, could not be brought forward for lack of transportation. For the same reason, barbed-wire pickets could not be brought forward and the wire obstacles, only 2–3m deep, were poorly strung and obstacles of any sort were few. The fields of fire had been adequately cleared on the west bank of the Meuse and in the sector Barchon–Fléron in the east, but not at all in the other sectors, particularly Embourg–Boncelles in the south.

The second line was supposed to be 2km to the rear of the first. Work was begun by 31 L on the afternoon of 5 August but only a kilometre and a half of it was ever constructed behind the interval between Barchon and Evegnée. The third line was to be an *enceinte* at the east edge of the city. Work was done by the fortress engineers on 5 August and in the early hours of 6 August, and consisted mostly of preparing civilian dwellings for defence. These 'positions' were never occupied.

Leman ordered the first line to be manned at 0530 4 August, three and a half hours before the Germans crossed the border. Keeping the troops at work improving their positions behind a light security screen would have been a far better use of their time, since it was quite clear that whenever the Germans crossed the border it would take them at least a day to reach the east side of the fortress, and that the west side was completely out of their reach. This division order also specified which infantry companies were to guard the eight artillery OPs, which was far too few.

De Schrÿver said that by 4 August the Belgian troops were on edge due to the unusual demands made on them since 31 July.[61] The troops were told that an attack was imminent on the night of 4–5 August and remained tense, on alert, and received no rest. Lombard made the perceptive observation that the Belgian units had five days to try to compensate for their inadequate training and lack of unit cohesion. Instead, they spent that time tiring themselves out digging, and by the night of 5–6 August were completely exhausted.[62]

Leman had also asked that 15 Brigade be moved from Huy to Liège. The General Staff refused, so Leman appealed to the king, who at 0900 5 August ordered the brigade to Liège.

Belgian Demolitions

On the night of 3–4 August, *before the Germans crossed the border at 0800 4 August*, the Belgians executed a series of demolitions. These demolitions were therefore not due to actual hostile acts by Germany, but 'based on news of German preparations around Aachen, Eupen and Malmedy'. They included the rail tunnels leading from Germany at Hombourg (13km south-west of Aachen), Nasproué (25km due east of Liège, on the Vesdre River, north of Verviers), the bridges at Visé and Argenteau, north of Liège, and the road bridges over the Meuse between Liège and Huy, as well as tunnels in the Ardennes,[63] to which Leman later added three more bridges in the Ardennes. The roads to Liège were to be blocked with fallen trees etc. After the Germans crossed the border the Belgians destroyed three more road bridges upstream from Liège.[64] The Chief of the General Staff had attempted to keep these bridges intact, in order to allow the army to cross to the south bank of the Meuse. This made sense only if he expected the German right flank to be south of the Meuse, and once again shows that the Belgian high command was working at cross-purposes.

The destruction of the tunnels was 'very incomplete'.[65] Only the charges on the west side of the Hombourg tunnel fired. The Germans began to clear the tunnel on 7 August and finished work by 18 August. The first attempt to destroy the Visé bridge was a failure and a second charge had to be set off at 0400. The important tunnel at Nasproué near Verviers was equipped with fourteen explosive mines, but only three of them detonated.[66] This may have been the worst possible outcome for the Belgians, because the rubble blocked access to the unexploded munitions (the German engineers pulled out 270 boxes of explosives). The problem was that the tunnel had been provided with electric demolition lines which had not been maintained and had corroded so badly they would not carry an electric charge to the explosives. The Belgians tried to complete the job by ramming seventeen locomotives into each other in the tunnel. The German railway engineers described the damage as 'superficial' and by 11 August had one track in operation, by 15 August both.

According to Leman, the German espionage service had penetrated all of the public services to the extent that it was able do destroy the blasting caps for demolitions soon after they had been installed. It is much more likely that any failure of Belgian demolitions was due to poor equipment and training.

Garde Civique

At 0300 on 3 August the pastors of the churches around Liège were instructed to ring the alarm bells, recalling to duty both the active and inactive *Garde Civique*.[67] A special reporter for the Brussels newspaper *Soir* noted on 3 August that the inactive *Garde Civique* in St Trond assembled in the market square. They were told to arm themselves with whatever came to hand, 'hunting rifles, revolvers, hunting knives, scythes'. 'The *Garde Civique* left in a heroic procession reminiscent of the ancient Euburones.'

The inactive *Garde Civique* had no training whatsoever. As Kabisch noted, this meant that they were completely ignorant of the laws of war, including the requirement to bear arms openly and be recognisable as combatants.[68] The Belgian Interior Minister did not send instructions on the conduct of the *Garde Civique* to the local authorities until 5 August, which was far too late to be effective. On the other hand,

Kabisch said that the German troops had no idea that there even was such a thing as *Garde Civique*, and regarded them as illegal combatants – *francs-tireurs*.

Belgian Panic at Fort Barchon

By 1200 5 August, a platoon (two mortars) from 2/ Foot Artillery 9 moved into position between Dalhem and Mortroux, two from 7/ FAR 4 south of Julémont.[69] The movement was difficult, and in places a new road had to be cut. The positions were in defilade and camouflaged against air reconnaissance, civilians removed from the area. At 1400, 2/ Foot Artillery 9 (-) opened fire against Belgian artillery west of Fort Pontisse, on the orders of Ludendorff, and at 1900 against the fort itself, firing 234 shells in total. At 1440, 2/ FAR 7 (-) opened fire against Fort Barchon at 4,500m range, as well as the towns of Barchon and Communes (near Barchon), where German patrols had taken fire, to conserve ammunition firing only forty-eight rounds. Lombard said that the German bombardment was 'very violent'. Barchon had two excellent OPs in the church towers at Blégny and Heuseux, a small town 2km to the south, which unfortunately were occupied by the Germans.[70] From Blégny the Germans could observe the entire fort clearly, which accounted for the 'disturbing precision' of the 21cm fire. The Belgian FOs had to occupy a fall-back position at the Hospice of Housse, about 800m north of the fort, with a very restricted field of observation. On the afternoon of 5 August the only report the OP made was that it could not observe anything. Nevertheless, Barchon reported 'demolishing' three German batteries (there were never more than five German batteries firing, and none suffered casualties, much less being demolished).[71]

During the morning III/ IR 53 moved forward to find high ground from which it could observe the Meuse. At 1200 it became involved in a firefight with Belgian troops in the town of Housse; the Belgians withdrew to the south, closely followed by III/ 53, which brought the battalion up to Fort Barchon, at which point it stopped, dug-in and asked for artillery support.[72]

At 1315 II/ FAR 43 (light howitzer) was ordered to limber up and move to a firing position south of Ste Rémy to support III/ 53.[73] The section had a hard time finding a suitable firing position in terrain thickly covered with hedges and trees. It finally occupied an open position hidden by bushes about 1.5km east of Housse. Fort Barchon was on a higher location and had good observation into the position, and fields of fire had to be cleared by cutting down fruit trees and lanes through hedges. The FAR 43 history said that all four 21cm mortars had been firing on the turrets at Barchon since 1400, but the infantry positions had not been engaged. At 1600 4/ 43 fired on trenches west of the fort, 6/ 43 fortifications east of the fort and 5/ 43 the fort itself, at 2,100m range. The howitzers quickly adjusted their fire onto the targets and began to fire for effect. The Belgian fire on III/ 53 began to go high and then stopped altogether.

Barchon reported that German MG fire immediately wounded the commanders of three 5.7cm turrets. There is no indication in the IR 53 history that the Machine Gun Korps (MGK) was engaged at all this day, so the turret commanders were wounded by rifle fire. The commander of Barchon was forced to pull his infantry off the parapet and back into the fortress. It is clear that III/ 53 had won its firefight with Fort Barchon. Lombard admits that Barchon lost eight KIA and twenty-seven MIA.[74] The German infantry reported that the German artillery fire was 'excellent' and the howitzers continued their fire until 1900. Throughout the night it conducted harassment fires.

De Schrÿver's description of the fight pulled out all the stops: waves of German troops advanced, only to be mown down by Belgian rifle and fortress artillery fire from Barchon and Evegnée, to be replaced by another wave which was also mown down, until the Germans finally reached the glacis and began throwing hand grenades, after which the Germans withdrew.

Elements of III/ 53 had meanwhile moved through Barchon village and flanked the Belgian 3/ IV/ 34 L, and a platoon of 11 Brigade, which were forced to withdraw, pulling with them 2/ IV/ 34, 1/ IV/ 34 and Artillery Battery No 2. The battalion commander ordered his troops to reoccupy their positions, which was conducted 'very, very slowly: the troops carefully searched every covert, bush and house, because bullets were whizzing everywhere'.

At 1215 the Belgian 11 Brigade was ordered to begin digging the second line of defence, behind the threatened Fléron–Evegnée sector. At 1230 news of the IV/ 34 retreat reached all levels of the Belgian command, spread by 'shady characters' throughout the region, and 'peddled by frightened inhabitants and defeatists': Barchon was being attacked by strong German forces, while other strong forces had broken through at Barchon–Evegnée, where the defenders had fled in panic.

This sent off alarm bells in the entire Belgian chain of command. The 14 L commander (who also commanded the Barchon–Evegnée sector) and the 11 Brigade commander launched separate, unco-ordinated counterattacks. At 1400 the 14 L commander committed 1 and 2/ II/ 14 L, which were constructing the second, fallback position, to Chefneux, about 500m south-west of Barchon. The Belgian 39 Battery shelled Chefneux.

The 11 Brigade commander committed 31 L towards Housse, 700m north of Barchon. At 1240, 31 L marched in order II, III, I. Its advance proceeded very cautiously, under rifle fire from an invisible enemy as well as artillery fire, whose shrapnels generally burst too high. The terrain was difficult, cut up by vegetation and fields enclosed with barbed wire, and German resistance became stronger. The 31 L became involved in a series of small firefights and the regiment dispersed into isolated companies, and finally the attack came to a complete stop. Between 1415 to 1430 the 11 Brigade commander committed his last battalion, I/ 31, in dispersed company penny packets. The 1/ I/ 31 took casualties from German artillery fire. The Germans retreated step by step, offering 'bold' resistance. By 1510 the fighting ended.

The 31 L operation has gone into Belgian history as a successful counterattack, even though the Belgian advance was very hesitant. The IR 53 history does not even mention a Belgian counterattack. After the Belgians around the fort pulled back and the Belgian infantry retreated to the inside of the fort, III/ 53 had nobody to fight and moved back to Housse without incident. Kabisch reported the III/ 53 casualties as 'light'.[75]

That the Belgians counterattacked against an imaginary enemy is confirmed by the fact that the Belgians did not report any casualties on either side. At most the Belgians encountered the occasional stray German trying to rejoin his unit.[76] Lombard said that Pontisse and d'Evegnée conducted fires close to Barchon. Since the III/ 53 history does not mention this, the two forts must have fired after III/ 53 had withdrawn.

Rumours of a setback began to circulate, spread, Lombard said, by German spies.[77] A report reached Leman that 31 L had been stopped and in the sector Barchon–Evegnée there had been a reverse, which had to refer to the retreat of IV/ 34. This caused Leman to overreact, committing 12 Brigade to the east side of the Meuse and Chasseur 1 of 15 Brigade to the area to Jupille, near the Meuse bridge in Liège.

The Belgians had committed eighteen companies from nine different battalions and four regiments, completely intermixed, and as a result there does not appear to have been much command and control above the company level. The senior Belgian officers who had concluded that their army was incapable of conducting offensive operations were proven completely right.

The 11 Brigade commander had also ordered the commander of II/ 12 L to cover the left flank of 31 L. This order was countermanded by Leman, who ordered II/ 12 to Herstal and hold the bridge at Wandre. With only 400 men, the best II/ 12 L could do was construct barricades on the streets and bridges and prepare the houses for defence. The commander of II/ 12 L says he received a telephone message from a German spy to withdraw his battalion from the bridge to Herstal. He called Liège HQ and was told by Leman to remain at Wandre. When he returned to the bridge he found that men were removing the barricade on the bridge, on the order of the commissioner of police. He immediately ordered the barricade replaced and gave instructions for the sentries to fire on anyone trying to remove it.

At 1530 Fort d'Evegnée reported that it was 'completely surrounded' and asked the 11 Brigade artillery to fire on the fort. The fort judged that this fire was 'very effective' and asked that it be continued. In fact, the fort was only being probed by German reconnaissance. Communication with the fort was sporadic, and at 1730 2/ III/ 32 was sent out to make contact. It didn't find any Germans and left at 1920. At 2015 d'Evegnée reported that the Germans were massing to the front. At 2030 the 11 Brigade artillery resumed fire on the fort and the terrain to the front, which it continued all night. At 2200 I and III/ 32 moved out to support the fort. Torrential rain made navigation exceptionally difficult but eventually they arrived at the interval south of the fort. Once again, the Germans consisted only of patrols, which the Belgians fired on all night.

At 1600 the 11 Brigade commander received a report that Barchon was surrounded! He went to the fort personally and found nothing wrong. Even Lombard was forced to give up on the 'German spies' excuse and attributed the bad reporting to 'agitation and nervousness'. He acknowledged that the 'defective command and control system threatened the ability to properly employ the fortress reserves'.

The Germans also sent patrols to the area between Fort Barchon and the Meuse, which the Belgians fired at, although the German field-grey uniforms made them 'invisible'. At 1000 German light artillery fire began to land. At 1315, 2/ I/ 14 F abandoned its position at a redoubt west of Barchon, but was led back to its position by the sector commander. When word of this reached the 11 Brigade commander, it had grown into a complete collapse of the defence in the sector. Firing continued to flare up and die down. During a period of renewed firing 1/ II/ 31 L left its positions and moved in the direction of Fort Barchon. It too was stopped by the sector commander, who held it near his HQ. A subsector commander moved his troops from their trenches to guard the bridge at Wandre, leaving Battery 1 unprotected. The gunners removed the breech blocks and abandoned the guns. All these troops returned to their positions at 1800. When the firing finally ceased, the Belgians in this sector sent out patrols, which found neither dead nor wounded Germans. The defenders suffered one WIA.

At 1930 two batteries of the 9 Brigade artillery were ordered to move to Fléron. When they arrived the fort commander told them they were not needed and sent them back. Soon thereafter, two battalions of 29 L were also ordered to Fléron. After getting lost in the dark, they too were sent back.

At 2015 the commandant of Barchon reported that German engineers were preparing to mine the flanking casemates in the fosse. The sector commander sent a platoon of 9 F, which found nothing. That evening the commander of Fléron said the fort was threatened by German infantry and 9 Brigade was moved in support.

The Belgians reported the Germans recommenced their bombardment of Fléron at 2000, which by 2200 reached an 'uncommon' intensity. This was only harassing and interdiction fire (H and I) from the German field artillery.

The Belgian units in the Evegnée–Meuse sector were close to panic. The two fort commanders had transformed German patrols into major attacks. The troops were conducting uncontrolled firing on imaginary targets and abandoning their positions on the slightest pretence or for no reason at all. A German co-ordinated daylight attack should have had no difficulty in destroying the Belgian units in this sector.

Belgian Estimate of the Situation – 5 August

On 5 August Leman reported that he was opposed by the German VII, IX and X AK, plus an unidentified AK, which amounted to sixteen brigades in total.[78] There is no indication that Leman suspected that the German units were at peacetime strength. In fact, the Germans had a brigade from III AK, one from IV, one from VII, two from IX and one from X, six brigades in total, all at peacetime strength. Leman thought that the Germans were five times as strong as was actually the fact.

At 2100 Leman reported that there had been a serious engagement that afternoon in the area between Fort Barchon and the Meuse, that the Germans had been thrown back and that he expected a night attack near Fort Boncelles. The king instructed Galet to tell Leman to expect a German night attack and to make sure his HQ was secure.

At 0030 6 August Leman issued a bulletin to his troops, which had already been overtaken by events, but which gives an interesting appreciation of his evaluation of the situation.[79] He said that it appeared that the German VII AK had wanted to attack the intervals to the left and right of Fléron. Massed behind this sector to counterattack were 12, 9 and 11 Brigades, plus all the artillery and cavalry of 3 DA. The 15 Brigade had arrived, and the entire Belgian Army was marching from Tirlemont to Liège. A French Army had crossed into Belgium at Virton (east of Montmédy, France) to support Liège. The resistance at Liège would be continued to the last extremity. De Schrÿver says that this bulletin was received with 'delirious, indescribable, enthusiasm' reinforced by the news of the successful counterattack of 11 Brigade, i.e. 31 L.

If this was not sheer theatrical bombast, designed to make the troops fight, then Leman was losing his grip. He had wildly overreacted to a modest operation conducted by a battalion of infantry, twelve light howitzers and four 21cm mortars. It would appear that the capabilities of all three had come as a most unpleasant surprise. Even if a French Army had crossed at Virton (it hadn't), Virton was at the southern end of Belgium and a long way from Liège. But most important, Leman apparently believed that a decisive battle would be fought at Liège, with the garrison holding on to the last ditch and the Belgian Army moving forward to Liège. None of this was even remotely accurate.

De Schrÿver said that by dark on 5 August the Germans had realised all their objectives.[80] German advance guards and reconnaissance elements were in contact with the Belgian positions. On the east bank they had pushed back the Belgian covering forces and OPs.

He also said that the Germans had received information from their 'innumerable' spies: travellers, day labourers, peddlers, harvesters, wagonners, ditch-diggers, priests etc., that were allowed to work and move around freely. A number of spies had been arrested, but 'hundreds' had not.

Lombard said that in Liège the gendarmes were chasing German spies.[81] Several had been arrested, some near the glacis of the forts, but none had been executed, and the impunity with which they operated made them bold. German spies spread false news in order to demoralise the Belgian troops. They even sent telephone messages with incorrect reports, orders and counter-orders to disorient the Belgian units.

Lombard said that as of 2000 the telephone communication between Leman's HQ and Pontisse, Barchon, Evegnée and Fléron no longer functioned, nor did the overhead telephone lines between the forts. During the entire night the forts were 'reduced to impotence'. He says that this was also the work of German spies, which were 'swarming' through the area in the guise of requisitioned civilian labour.

It is highly unlikely that German spies were responsible for any of this confusion. The Belgian rumour mill was just beginning to operate, and would become so active during the night that it would have serious negative tactical and operational consequences. Insufficiently trained unit commanders and staff officers were the source of incorrect reports and bad orders followed by counter-orders. The Belgian spy mania betrays an inability to correctly identify the real problems in the defective Belgian organisation and solve them.

Notes

1. Galet, Albert, 60–1. Kaiser Wilhelm II, the supposed warmonger, on the other hand, was a mere figurehead, the actual orders being issued in his name by the Chief of the German General Staff.
2. On 3 August the Germans told the Dutch that their neutrality would be respected and the Dutch lost interest in consulting with the Belgians.
3. Galet, Albert, 27.
4. Moranville, Babel, 197, 202.
5. Normand, Liége, Namur, 21–2.
6. Galet, Albert, 55–6.
7. Moranville, Babel, 203–4.
8. Galet says that no minutes were kept, and he used notes written by Ryckel.
9. Galet, Albert, 51. In 1940 Manstein developed his famous 'feint in Holland and northern Belgium', which is exactly what Galet was afraid the Germans were trying to do in 1914.
10. Galet, Albert, 63.
11. De Schrÿver, Liège, 14.
12. Galet, Albert, 11.
13. 1912, 4,000; 1911, 7,000; 1910, 9,000; 1906–09, 20,000 per year.
14. Otto Korfes, Das 3. Magdeburgische Infanterie-Regiment Nr. 66 im Weltkrieg (Berlin: Kolk, 1930) 383–4.
15. Galet, Albert, 57.
16. Galet, Albert, 74–6.
17. Paul Doerstling, Kriegsgeschichte des Königlich Preußischen Infanterie-Regiments Graf Tauentzien v. Wittenburg (3. Brandenb.) Nr. 20 (Zeulenroda: Sporn: 1933) 17–18.
18. Offiziers-Verein, Das Fusilier-Regiment Prinz Heinrich von Preußen (Brandenburgisches) Nr. 35 im Weltkrieg (Berlin: Kolk, 1929) 2–3.
19. Kabisch, Lüttich, 69.
20. Kabisch, Lüttich, 63–4, 71.
21. Duvivier/Herbiet, Du Rôle de l'Armée de Campagne et des Fortresses belges, 6. De Schrÿver, Liège, 8–12.
22. Ruther, Loncin, 5.
23. Hollogne, 66. De Schrÿver says that each fort was authorised an eighty-man infantry platoon (Liège, 11). It would appear that some forts were considerably overstrength.

24. Reichsarchiv, Der Weltkrieg I, 109.

25. Generallandsesarchiv (GLA) Karlsruhe, 456/553, Nachrichten #3, 4, 5.

26. Reichsarchiv, Der Weltkrieg I, 108.

27. C. Badinski, Aus Grosser Zeit. Erinnerungsblätter des Jäger-Feld-Battalions Nr. 9 Weltkrieg 1914–18 (Ratzeberg: Lauenburgischer Heimatverlag, 1932) 46–50.

28. Lombard spends four pages describing an epic firefight between five border guards and 'hundreds' of German infantry in grey (Jäger uniforms were quite different). L. Lombard, Face à l'invasion (Stavelot: Vox Patriae, 1939) 37–40.

29. De Schrÿver, Liège, 41–5.

30. Kabisch, Lüttich, 101.

31. Trauwitz-Hellwig, Husaren-Regiment Nr. 15, 29–40.

32. Von Cramm, Geschichte des Ulanen-Regiments Hennings v. Treffenfeld (Altmärkisches) Nr. 16 im Feldzuge 1914–18 (Stendal: Altmärkische Verlagsanstalt, 1921) 6.

33. A. Hüttmann/W. Krüger, Das Infanterie-Regiment von Lützow (1. Rhein.) Nr. 25 im Weltkrieg 1914–1918 (Berlin: Kolk, 1929) 5.

34. Anon, Kriegsgeschichte des Großherzoglich Meckenlenburgischen Fusilier-Regiments Nr. 90 Kaiser Wilhelm 1914–1918 (Stolp: Pommern, 1923–24) 12–15.

35. E. Zipfel, Geschichte des Großherzoglich Mecklenburgischen Grenadier-Regiments Nr. 89 (Schwerin: Barensprung, 1932) 2–3. Zipfel was a Reichsarchiv historian.

36. Hüttmann/Krüger, IR 25, 5–7.

37. H. Maillard, 5. Westf. Infanterie-Regiment Nr. 53 im Weltkrieg (Zeulenroda: Sporn: 1939) 23–30.

38. Offiziers-Verein, Das Königl. Preußische Clevische Feldartillerie-Regiment Nr. 43 1899–1918 (Oldenburg: Stalling, 1932) 23.

39. O. Fleiß/K. Dittmar, 5. Hannoversches Infanterie-Regiment Nr. 165 im Weltkrieg (Oldenburg: Stalling, 1927) 5–7.

40. B. Werner, Das Königlich Preußische Inf.-Rgt. Prinz Louis Ferdinand von Preußen (2. Magdeb.) Nr. 27 im Weltkrieg (Berlin: Bernard und Graefe, 1933) 32–4.

41. A. Benary, Königl. Preuß. Magdeburgisches Husaren-Regiment Nr. 10 im Weltkrieg 1914/18 (Berlin: Bernard und Graefe, 1934) 44–6.

42. 4–2–4: four riders, probably in diamond formation, an interval, then two, a second interval, then four more.

43. Offiziers-Verein, IR 35, 7.

44. Clausius, IR 83, 12.

45. G. Westermann, Die Braunschweiger Husaren im Weltkrieg 1914/1918. Erster Teil 1914 bis Ende 1915 (Berlin/Oldenburg: Stalling:, 1922) 22–3.

46. Gabriel, Hannoversche Infanterie-Regiment 74, 23–5.

47. H. Voigt, Geschichte des Fusilier-Regiments Generalfeldmarschall Prinz Albrecht von Prußen (Hann.) Nr. 73 (Berlin: Bernard und Graefe, 1938).

48. v. der Hude; Klie; Groschupf; Troost, Geschichte des Hannoverschen Feldartillerie-Regiments Nr. 26 während des Weltkriegs 1914–1918 (Lübeck: Colman, 1934) 12.

49. L. Lombard, La Victoire de Sart-Tilman (Verviers: G. Leens, 1934) 13–18.

50. Kabisch, Lüttich, 72.

51. Paul Freiherr von Troschke, Geschichte des 1. Großherzoglich Mecklenburgischen Dragoner-Regiments Nr. 17. Band 2 Der Weltkrieg (Berlin, 1938) 20–1.

52. Weltkrieg I, 110.

53. B. von Studnitz, Geschichte des Thüringischen Husaren-Regiments Nr. 12 und seiner Mobilmachungsformationen im Weltkrieg 1914–1918 (Weimar, 1930).

54. Albrecht Freiherr von Funck, et. al. Das Brandenbergische Dragoner-Regiment Nr. 2 im Weltkrieg 1914 bis 1918 (1933) 6–8.

55. De Schrÿver, Liège, 19–23.

56. Lombard, Sart-Tilman, 27.

57. Kabisch, Lüttich, 54–5.

58. De Schrÿver, Liège, 26.

59. Kabisch, Lüttich, 55–6.

60. De Schrÿver, Liège, 29.

61. De Schrÿver, Liège, 54.

62. Lombard, Face à l'invasion, 66–7.

63. Galet, Albert, 59.

64. Normand, Liége, Namur, 7–8.

65. De Schrÿver, Liège, 18–9.

66. Kabisch, Lüttich, 56–7.

67. Kabisch, Lüttich, 55.

68. Kabisch, Lüttich, 73.

69. Bieberstein, Lüttich-Namur, 19. M. Dobrzynski, Fußartillerie-Regiment Encke (Magdeburgisches) Nr. 4 (Berlin: Kyffhäuser, 1938) 14–16. K. Heydemann, Schleswig-Holsteinisches Fußartillerie-Regiment Nr. 9 (Oldenburg: Stalling, 1921) 17–21. Offiziers-Verein, Das Westfälische Fußartillerie-Regiment Nr. 7 im Weltkrieg 1914–18 (Oldenburg: Stalling, 1932) 293–5. P. Buhle, Erlebnisse der 1. Batterie Schleswig-Holsteinischen Feldartillerie-Regiments Nr. 9 … im 1. Jahr des Weltkriegs (Altdamm in Pommern: Hormann, 1932) 15–22. Foot Artillery Regiment 20 did not write a unit history, nor did any of the 30.5cm or 42cm mortar units. Engineer Battalion 24, which was equipped with heavy trench mortars, also did not produce a unit history.

70. L. Lombard, Sous les Ouragans de Acier (Stavelot: Editions Vox Patriae, 1939) 25–6.

71. De Schrÿver, Liège, 56–7, 75–83.

72. H. Maillard, 5. Westf. Infanterie-Regiment Nr. 53 im Weltkrieg (Zeulenroda: Sporn, 1939) 36–8. This was not an attack on Fort Barchon, as described in Weltkrieg I, 111.

73. Offizier-Vereinigung, Das Königl. Preußische Clevische Feldartillerie-Regiment Nr. 43 1899–1919 (Stalling: Oldenburg i.O., 1932) 29–30.

74. Lombard, Face à l'invasion, 75–80.

75. Kabisch, Lüttich, 81.

76. Somehow the Reichsarchiv got the III/ 53 action entirely wrong, saying that III/ 53 had attacked Barchon and been thrown back by defensive fire (Weltkrieg I, 111). Lombard elaborated on this, saying that III/ 53 had been attempting to storm the fortress, a fools' errand that he attributes to German 'disdain for their opponent'. In the entire action against Barchon and the Belgian troops outside it, III/ 53 lost ten EM KIA, one OFF (the battalion adjutant and author of the regimental history) and twenty-three EM wounded.

77. Lombard, Face à l'invasion, 86–7.

78. Galet, Albert, 56–7, 79–80.

79. De Schrÿver, Liège, 58.

80. De Schrÿver, Liège, 91–2.

81. Lombard, Face à l'invasion, 94–7.

3

Attack

South: 38 and 43 Brigades

The terrain in this sector is heavily wooded, with clearings only around Sart-Tilman, the village of Boncelles and north of Fort Boncelles.

On 1 August, 2,000 employees of the Ougrée-Marihaye steel company, under their normal company supervisors, began work on the interval field fortifications in the southern Ourthe–Meuse sector. Workers and soldiers continued digging in on Sunday, 2 August, reinforced by a detachment from the bridging engineers reinforced with fifty recalled reservists. De Schrÿver was convinced that these men included German spies who 'minutely studied the defensive positions.'[1] At dawn on 3 August the garrison of the redoubts was alerted. Clouds of smoke were visible, as the barracks near the permanent forts were burned down.

Redoubts 1–3 were dug-in on a 600m front along the top of a low ridge (see Sart-Tilman maps, pp. 93 and 103), in an open wheat field, along the road to the hamlet of Sart-Tilman. A sharply V-shaped redan was also dug between Redoubts 1 and 2. The field of fire south of Redoubts 1 and 2 was only 100m deep, and only 50m in front of Redoubt 3. The wheat was still standing, further restricting observation. There was an abatis along the treeline, which probably was a liability because it restricted observation, and a field of wire 2m deep in front of the position, some plain wire, some barbed wire. The positions were not camouflaged and the newly upturned earth stood out clearly. The Germans could establish covered and concealed firing positions 50–100m from the easily-identifiable redoubts, with the Belgian riflemen silhouetted head-and-shoulders on the top of the berm, looking exactly like targets on a German tactical gunnery range. At 50–100m range, the German K98 rifle simply cannot miss (the author owns a K98). To make a 'worst possible case' situation for the Belgian troops, they were opposed in part by Jäger 10, men who prided themselves on their skills as hunters and marksmen. Even if the garrison of Sart-Tilman had communication with the permanent forts (which they didn't) at such close quarters the fort's artillery was as likely to hit the Belgians as the Germans.

The only possible way to defend the open ground around Sart-Tilman would have been to pull the right flank back and dig Redoubt 3 in at the Censé Rouge farm, with Redoubt 1 and 2 in Sart-Tilman village and smaller positions on the north treeline behind them.

Redoubts 1–3 were garrisoned by three companies of II/ Fortress R 14.[2] De Schrÿver said that the battalion had been reduced to 350 men by sickness and desertion, was closer to an armed mob than a military unit, and though capable of heroic conduct, was always on the verge of panic flight. It was solely capable of defending a dug-in position, and had no ability to fight in the open or manoeuvre.

Redoubts 4–6 were dug in the Bois de St Jean (St Jean's Wood) and held by three companies of I/ 9 L, each with 300 men. There was 250m between redoubts, and 650m between Redoubt 4 and Redoubt 3 to its left. Redoubt 5 was built astride the main north–south forest road. Digging the position in the forest had been difficult and time-consuming, the field of fire in the woods had only been cleared to a depth of 50m and the only obstacles were an abatis and a double line of barbed wire. There were two companies in reserve (2 /I/ 9, 4/ II/ 9) with 1 /I/ 29 at the crossroads as the *Grande-Garde*.

The Redoubt 1–6 position suffered from two fatal weaknesses. Redoubts 4, 5 and 6 were pushed too far to the south, and should have been pulled back at least 600m. This created a 650m gap between Redoubt 3 and 4, which could not be covered by fire. Had the Germans conducted a proper doctrinal reconnaissance (which they did not) they could not have failed to have discovered this gap, which would have allowed them to immediately penetrate into the Belgian rear and surrounded the redoubts. The perfect unit to exploit such an opportunity was Jäger 10.

This leads to the second deficiency in the Belgian position, which was the complete lack of any defence in depth. Even if the gap between Redoubts 3 and 4 was not exploited, once one or two redoubts were taken, the rest could be attacked from the rear and the entire position hopelessly compromised.

So, the Belgian leadership failed this tactics problem, 'Establish a defensive position between Fort Boncelles and the Ourthe'. Had the Germans conducted a doctrinal 'reinforced brigade daylight attack on a prepared position', straight out of a tactics problem at the Major Training Area, they would have destroyed the Belgian defences in short order and easily taken their objectives on the Ourthe and Meuse.

On the other hand, the premise underlying the concept of the German attack was that these redoubts did not exist. The Germans expected to march through open ground between the permanent fortifications. Ideally, the Germans would not have encountered any Belgian troops at all. At the worst, the Germans should have encountered Belgian infantry in unprepared positions. But the Belgians were there, dug-in.

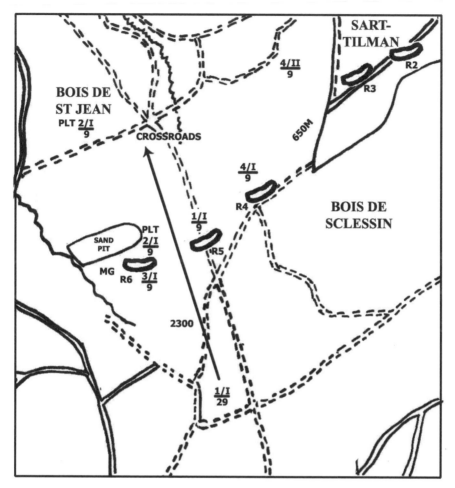

38/ 43 Bde Belgian position 2300 (B).

5 August

At 0400 the commander of II/ Fortress R 14, in Sart-Tilman, went mad, shouting curses.[3] He was disarmed and sent back to Liège in an automobile. Shortly thereafter a soldier accidentally fatally shot himself with his rifle. Fort Boncelles began unobserved area fire against Germans reported near Esneux. When the civilian workers saw the remnants of the Belgian 4/ Lancer 2 arrive, they fled back into Liège, taking some of the II/ 14 F troops with them. The troops were ordered to man their defensive positions.

At 1400 the commander of the German III/ 73 set out on patrol with his adjutant and three hussars on the road from Esneux to Plainevaux. The adjutant reported that as they neared the crossroads south of Plainevaux they noticed movement. The adjutant ordered the three hussars to reconnoitre and they came back at a gallop, reporting that a squadron of enemy lancers held the treeline (it was in fact two platoons of the Belgian Lancer R 2 and twenty-five bicyclists).[4] At 1430 the lead company, 11/73, was immediately brought forward, and deployed towards the woods and opened fire on the withdrawing cavalry, while the next company, 9/73, took heavy fire from the bushes. The left side of the road was blocked by a steep slope and wire, so that it was difficult to deploy the company, but a platoon nevertheless found a way up to the battalion commander, where the visibility was better. The attack gathered steam. The main point of resistance was a blockhouse on high ground, which was taken after a short, intense battle. Three of the 'dead' Belgians were found to be very much alive and were not greeted courteously. A Belgian officer and twelve EM were KIA, another officer and four EM POW. IR 73 lost one EM KIA, six WIA. A cable to Fort de Boncelles was cut, and a large number of weapons and bicycles were captured. The Belgians reported that the officers were almost immediately killed or wounded, and after a 20-minute fight an NCO withdrew the remnants towards Brussels.

Belgian patrols reported contact near the Ourthe and Boncelles town. The advancing German columns were not engaged by the guns at Boncelles or d'Embourg because, as the Belgians admitted, their observation posts had been driven in and they had no way to adjust their fire. D'Embourg was reduced to blasting away at nearby German patrols with its heavy artillery.[5]

On the afternoon of 5 August Jäger 10 sent out two officer patrols.[6] Both patrols were pointless. The mission on the night of 5–6 August was to infiltrate between Fort de Boncelles and the Ourthe River. Neither patrol reconnoitred this area. One patrol reconnoitred towards the Fort Boncelles, which was a waste of effort. The second patrol was to move through Tilff on the road to Liège and determine if at an 'advanced wood' (location not further identified) a dug-in position had been prepared and if so was it occupied. This patrol, however, was well to the right of the brigades' infiltration route. It would appear that the Jäger battalion commander had not been informed of the attack plan and was conducting reconnaissance on what he thought were the two most important avenues of approach. The patrols, however, offer us our first look at Jäger in action.

The Tilff patrol leader, Reserve Lieutenant Finck, noted that finding the objective was going to be difficult, because he didn't have a map, which was going to make it hard to identify one particular copse out of many. The patrol, with three NCOs and twelve EM, set out from Esneux at 1500. They were able to move down the road to the next hamlet, where they were taken under fire by artillery from the forts. Several times they also took isolated small-arms fire, which they assumed came from *franc-tireur*, though they could not be sure. At any rate, they were forced to move through rose and blackberry bushes on the verges of the road. After a couple of wrong turns, at 1830 they reached what the patrol leader took to be their objective. They found some Belgian equipment in what the patrol leader assumed was an abandoned Belgian outpost. He passed through to the other side of the copse and saw a field, a farmhouse and another copse, which also could have been his objective. There was nothing for it but to check it out. Suddenly he saw on the far treeline several Belgians in civilian clothes, who apparently saw the Jäger. The patrol leader waited a bit to see if anything else would happen, then moved forward towards the farmhouse, when four more Belgians in civilian clothes ran out, leaving several Belgian uniforms behind – probably not civilians after all. They pushed on to the second copse, discovered more Belgian equipment and again took artillery fire. Moving further, they came to a cut in the woods, on the far side of which Belgian entrenchments were visible (probably Redoubts 1–3). The patrol leader could not determine if they were occupied. It was now dark, made darker yet by a tremendous thunderstorm; the patrol leader became disoriented, and to reorient himself he moved towards a light, which turned out to be a farmhouse. He surrounded it and entered with two Jäger. The farmer and his family were sitting around the table and tried to make a run for it. The patrol leader stopped him and in sudden inspiration told him in French that his men were British and needed to be led to the road to Esneux. At 2230 they rejoined the battalion, which was moving on Liège.

Ensign Freiherr von Buttlar-Ziegenberg volunteered to accompany Reserve Lieutenant Gebhardt's patrol towards Fort de Boncelles. He wrote:

> Jäger patrol – Jäger mission! Just like hunters at home, we moved towards the fort, between bushes, through small woods and on forest roads. We saw Belgian soldiers (a patrol?) disappear into a hut in the distance to reappear a short time later as harmless civilians, then move off towards the fort. We later determined that the first ditch of the fort was in this woods. We searched the hut and found the uniforms. Suddenly, from the woods 100 metres to our front we heard loud voices and laughing. Lying flat on the ground, we saw, behind barbed wire, trenches filled with Belgian soldiers fortifying themselves with liquid courage (during the night we found beer bottles, etc.). We had completed our mission and withdrew unobserved on the same forest road. We reached the Meuse valley road just in time to meet the battalion, with Finck's patrol in the lead.

At the orders group at 1900, 38 Brigade learned for the first time that it had been given the mission of infiltrating between Fort Boncelles and the Ourthe River and by dawn take the rail junction and rail bridges at the confluence of the Ourthe and Meuse. Following, 43 Brigade was to take the towns of Ougrée and Seraing and the Meuse bridge. Two companies of IR 74 would drop out of the column to conduct a demonstration against Fort Boncelles, I/ 73 would move independently to demonstrate against Fort d'Embourg. The troops would unload their weapons, fix bayonets and put on white armbands.

38 Brigade had been ordered to be on the Esneux road, 4km south of Esneux, in close march column, by 2000, order of march Jäger 10 and 1/ Engineer 10, II/ IR 73,

III/ IR 73, IR 74 (one company), I/ FAR 26 (plus the IR 74 company), 4/ Hussar 17. During the afternoon of 5 August the humidity and crowding in Poulseur had not allowed IR 74 to get much rest.

The approach march from Plainevaux to Beauregard Farm and into the woods was shown exactly on a sketch provided by the guide, the engineer company commander, Captain Schlerau, who as a General Staff captain had in peacetime frequently reconnoitred the route at night, the last time being a week before in just such stormy weather.[7]

Jäger 10 began the march at 2030: the point element was composed of two squads of 3/ Jäger 10 (including the company commander) and two squads of 1/ Engineer 10 armed with hand grenades, a weapon as yet unknown to the Jäger. When the Jäger entered the woods east of Beauregard they dropped their packs. They found bicycles on the side of the trail, probably left there by a Belgian patrol.

The Germans had no way of knowing that they had driven in all of the artillery FOs and that the fortress guns were blind. They had to be concerned that the fortress guns would engage the assault columns. However, the fortress artillery was also the principal defensive firepower of the fort. If the Belgian garrison thought the fort were under attack, they would fire the artillery in self-defence, diverting its fire from the assault column.

To accomplish this, 7 and 8/ IR 74 had been given the mission of demonstrating against Fort Boncelles. They moved forward in the column until they were immediately behind Jäger 10 and in front of IR 73.[8] At 2045 the advance guard reached Plainevaux and turned east, while 7 and 8/ 74 continued to the north to Fort Boncelles. Moving on the right of the Plainevaux road, 8/ 74 went through hedges and bushes until it was 300m from the fort, and 7/ 74 moved through the woods on the left of the road until just south of the fort. At about 2200 (B) both companies were detected by the fort's searchlight and took heavy shrapnel fire, which burst too high over 8/ 74, but caused 7/ 74 serious casualties. When the fire ceased both companies began to dig in, waiting for an opportunity to engage the fort.[9] De Schrÿver was convinced that the Germans had attempted to assault the fort.[10]

At 2100, IR 73 moved out, continually harassed by rifle fire from the woods.[11] By the time IR 73 reached Plainevaux it was pitch-dark and instead of turning east to follow the advance guard, IR 73 followed the two IR 74 companies north. The searchlight did not find IR 73 in the woods, but it did allow the regiment to see that it was on the wrong path. IR 73 and part of 74 countermarched to Plainevaux, which was reached at 0015. Turning the vehicles around was difficult and noisy, and the column had barely cleared the road east of Plainevaux when Fort de Boncelles shelled it. The troops were now dead tired, and the packs of both regiments were dropped before entering the forest. A storm cut loose – thunder, lightning and pouring rain. The troops were soaked through, but were also able to collect water in their canteen cups. Jäger humour was in evidence. 'We've been washed', said one Jäger lieutenant, 'so that we will arrive upstairs clean'. The order of march was now reversed, with IR 74 leading and IR 73 following. The rain had softened the forestry roads, which made the marching even more difficult.

The Jäger point element encountered trees felled by the Belgians, which the engineers had to clear away, the axe blows resounding in the night, but the Belgians for some reason did not hear it. It was pitch-black. The Jäger had to halt for ninety minutes because the following infantry had disappeared (IR 73's wrong turn), in spite of the fact that 3rd Platoon had been dropping off guides along the path to maintain contact. The troops were told to hold onto the mess gear of the man in front. Shells from Fort Boncelles flew overhead. Far to the right flank small-arms fire could be heard; a spent bullet stuck under the epaulette of a Jäger and was passed from hand to hand. The troops staggered on, nearly asleep. At 0045 the lieutenant leading the point reported to the 3/ Jäger 10 commander that they had encountered barbed wire.

The Belgians in Redoubts 4–6 had been on full alert since 1900.[12] At 2200 they heard Boncelles firing and shortly thereafter were soaked by the thunderstorm. When the storm passed, movement was detected to the front and several men fired, which is what the Jäger had heard. The men in Reboubt 5 then heard the Belgian password called out – it was 1/ I/ 29, which had been on outpost duty and had got lost withdrawing in the dark. The 1/ I/ 29 commander reassured the 9 L men that they hadn't hit anyone because they were firing far too high! (Lombard doesn't mention the company again. On his 0130 situation map it is shown withdrawing with the debris of I/ 9.)

A Belgian challenged the Jäger in bad German, the Jäger replied in French, the Belgians answered with a blast of small-arms fire against the Jäger front, left and right. Lombard said it was 2230 (B).[13]

Lombard said that there was no sector commander nor any co-ordination or communication at all between the troops in the field fortifications and the permanent forts. The Liège fortress HQ on the Rue de Sainte Foi made ineffectual attempts to direct the defence: Fort Flémalle was told that 'Belgian troops are counterattacking in the interval Embourg-Boncelles; support them by fire as necessary', which was so vague as to be worthless. Flémalle conducted practically pointless area fire around Boncelles. Boncelles tried to interdict the Tilff–Boncelles and Plainevaux–Seraing roads. Lombard said that the commander of Embourg lived near Tilff and sent patrols to the woods south of Sart-Tilman and that the fort's fire in this area was 'particularly energetic and effective'. Energetic it might have been, but no German unit reported receiving effective Belgian artillery fire.[14]

Lombard says that the odds were one Belgian battalion against two German brigades (thirteen battalions with five MG companies) which conducted repeated 'human wave' attacks, which were shot down in rows and thrown back time and again.[15] In fact, on the 1km front there was physical space adequate to deploy the equivalent of three battalions. Most of the night fighting on the German side was done by Jäger 10, which used the darkness and available cover to quickly close on the Belgian defenders. Captain Wagner, the 3/Jäger 10 company commander, wrote:

> I noticed that, with my two range estimators, we were on the far side of the wire, and that to my left and right the greater part of the company was crawling in my direction. Suddenly, the 'Combat in Woods' chapter of the tactics manual popped into my head: 'narrow front, reduced intervals between men, strong reserves on the flanks!', so I tried to form a short firing line with clumps of troops behind the flanks, as there could be no thought of platoon cohesion. The line bounded forward, fired and bounded forward again. Some even remained standing. In a few minutes the clouds separated and for a good while beautiful moonlight appeared. I used it to assemble the company, standing up with drawn sword and shouting 'Rally!', which they did nicely. I noticed that we were in a clearing, not deep but 80 metres broad, in which stood large old trees. It was lined with underbrush, where dark figures moved, friendly or enemy, it was impossible to tell.
>
> We moved out, and soon recognized that the dark figures were Belgians running for the rear. The *furor Teutonicus* seized the troops, and the company dissolved as leaders gathered five to seven Jäger around them and hunted down the fleeing enemy [...] I did not see a single one escape. I moved forward with 30 to 40 men to the other side of the clearing to get a better idea of the situation. It now appeared to me that we had hit a Belgian forward security position.
>
> I encountered an immense old oak, so large that my range estimator went around one side, I the other. I suddenly heard him call: 'Herr Hauptmann, should I bayonet him?' Followed by 'Please! Don't kill!' in broken German. It was a Belgian captain, quite advanced in years, with a long, gray moustache. He made no attempt to defend himself. I asked him – in full accordance with the regulation – on his word of honour what Belgian forces we were opposed by, and again on his word of honour to promise not to escape. He responded willingly – half-left behind him was his company, left of that his regiment, to the right another regiment. I was able to make out the enemy line by the muzzle flashes. He also followed me like a small dog as we moved forward against his trenches. I assembled 80 Jäger and we charged in double-time against the trench 30–40 paces to our front'.

Officer candidate/Corporal Ludloff continued the tale:

> I crawled forward with a couple Jäger. Captain Wagner saw us, grabbed me on the shoulder and hollered: 'Enemy trench to the right! Take it! Double-time!' I stood up, yelled the same thing, took three steps – and was hung up in barbed

wire. Left and right five paces ahead, muzzle flashes. I felt soft earth under my feet and then slid into the trench, directly onto a Belgian. Dark shadows ran away. I felt my way to the right, as other Jäger jumped into the trench. I entered a smaller trench and stepped on something human. It was two Belgians; they stood up, were unarmed. 'Secure them!' I told several Jäger. Further down the trench I encountered a short Jäger striking a half-sitting Belgian with his rifle butt; the trench did not permit him to put much force behind the blows, but nevertheless they were not so mild that the Belgian could have been indifferent to them; he groaned and howled and attempted to hold his hands up. He was no longer armed. I gave the Jäger to understand that it was past time to take the Belgian prisoner.

The trench was a mess. Lots of civilian clothing lying about. The Belgian troops were partially wearing civilian clothes. Beer bottles and garden tables lying around: it smelled strongly of alcohol.

Jäger notice things out of place, like twine on a rifle trigger. Aha, now it was clear why the Belgian usually shot too high: they didn't stick their heads over the lip of the trench, but fired into the air while sitting in the trench.

1 /Jäger 10 deployed left of 3, with 2 and 4 to the right, and took rifle fire and the first casualties: the commander of 1/ Jäger 10 was killed. The troops quickly calmed down and began firing at the enemy muzzle flashes. The Jäger broke through the first wire obstacle with wire cutters, bayonets and sabres.

The Belgian fire was generally too high, but hit IR 73 and 74 behind the Jäger, who fired back blindly into the Jäger in front. The Jäger yelled the password ('Wörth'), blew horn signals, sang 'The Watch on the Rhine,' 'Deutschland über alles' and well-known Jäger songs. The fire would die down for a second and then a single shot would be fired, beginning another uncontrolled fusillade. Enemy shrapnel shells began to fall, without doing much damage because they burst in the crowns of the big, old trees. Belgian searchlights illuminated the battlefield. The Jäger collected around the nearest officer, who pushed forward on their own initiative: higher command and control was impossible. A group of Belgians tried to escape, but were overtaken by Jäger and, crying 'Don't kill!', threw down their weapons and surrendered. Captain Wagner wrote:

When we entered the first trench, the question was, how to take the next one with the fewest casualties? The trench was shoulder-deep, but there were no sortie steps out of it, as we would build later, so that it was difficult to get out of the deep and narrow trench. Fortunately, I found to the right a long stretch of unoccupied trench, and then the communications trench leading to the rear: bad luck for the Belgians in the second trench! Taking two Jäger, I moved to the second trench and emptied a magazine (five rounds) into their left flank. The Belgian fire ceased and they ducked down into the trench. The Jäger in the first trench responded immediately on their own initiative, since we had no time to prepare a plan. Everyone crawled up out of the trench, over the open ground and onto the heads of the Belgians in the second trench, which was quickly cleared.

They were joined by men from 1/ Jäger 10. Officer candidate/Corporal Behrens reported, 'Suddenly I stood on the lip of a big trench, with most of the Belgians sitting on the bottom, firing in the air. We were about to go at them with the bayonet, when the entire group raised their hands and surrendered.'

At 0130 (B) 4/ I/ 9 in Redoubt 4 was enveloped on the right flank, then attacked from the rear. Part of the company was able to escape, but the company commander was captured.[16]

Redoubt 6, on the Belgian right flank, was held by 3/ I/ 9 L, a platoon of fortress engineers and a platoon of 2/ I/ 9, which had arrived late, did not have time to dig in and deployed to the left of the redoubt.[17] A section of 9 Brigade MGs was emplaced to protect the right flank of the redoubt. There was only a 50m field of fire; on the south-east side of the redoubt the undergrowth had not been cleared at all. There was a large sandpit behind the redoubt; why the redoubt was not sited with the sandpit to the front is unclear. The only obstacle was two lines of normal (not barbed) wire. By 0115 (B) the Germans were pouring in fire from all directions and in particular had occupied the undergrowth to the north and west of the redoubt. Covered by a rear guard of 3 Platoon and the engineers, the garrison of Redoubt 6 retreated across the sandpit, with the rear guard following.

Redoubt 5, held by 1/ I/ 9, was now isolated. Lombard said that it had stood off '15 assaults' but was now being attacked 'from all directions'. The company commander ordered a retreat, which failed to reach a lieutenant and fifty men, who were taken prisoner.

The remaining platoon of 2/ I/ 9 covered the battalion retreat at St Hubert. The battalion pulled back to the north side of the Meuse and attempted to form a line. At 0500 the troops guarding the Ougrée bridge took German fire and several men on both the north and south ends of the bridge were killed, along with a gendarme. At 0615 the commander of 15 Brigade ordered the debris of the battalion to withdraw to Loncin. At the beginning of the fight, it had 1,083 men; it now counted 303. Considering that half of 2/ I/ 9 was not engaged, the garrisons of the three redoubts had been practically annihilated.[18]

Both IR 74 and 73, which were following Jäger 10, initially took rifle and MG fire from the front and in the left flank. The troops threw themselves flat on the ground and then, as the IR 74 history said, some troops began uncontrolled firing, which the officers were unable to stop. The IR 74 and IR 73 men attempted to move forward, while taking fire from the rear. Even infantry from the following 43 Brigade came forward and mixed with 38 Brigade.

The 'division' commander, BG von Hülsen, stopped the forward movement of I/ FAR 26. He was then wounded when a German soldier accidentally stabbed him the back with a bayonet.[19] It was a considerable time until the 38 Brigade commander, Colonel von Oven, took charge.

The leading element of IR 74 was III/ 74, which consisted only of 9 and 11 (10 was clearing obstacles on the road and 12 was artillery protection). The battalion commander deployed to the left side of the road, saying 'Boys, remember Spichern' and led them forward. They encountered barbed wire and, under enemy fire, forced their way through, without wire cutters, along with men from other battalions, and at 0145 took the Belgian trench behind it. They then moved off in the direction of the sound of the Jäger 10 fight.

The next battalion in line was I/ 74, which deployed 2 and 3 and advanced until they hit the barbed wire, which they could not penetrate, and threw themselves flat. Men from other companies joined them or extended left and right. The 2/ 74 commander sat up, shouted 'Bring up the wire cutters' and was killed. Some men began, without orders, to open fire. The commander of 4/ 74, Captain Wersebe, wrote:

We deploy almost automatically to the left of the company in front. The muzzle flashes from hundreds of rifles look like fireworks. Then we run full speed into the barbed wire. No way around it. I yell 'Wire cutters!' and immediately see the troops at work. A blast of fire sweeps over us, everybody takes cover, but some are dead in the wire, many dead next to me. But most of the fire is too high. Left and right we can hear German troops shouting 'Hurrah!' so the Belgians must be running, and we need to move. We wade under fire through the awful wire, but, thank God, the obstacle isn't thick. With a few men I reach a trench and jump down; the defenders have fled, only the dead remain. We move quickly in the moonlight through a heath sprinkled with trees. Suddenly we take heavy fire from German troops in the rear, and everyone falls flat. Fortunately we are on the reverse slope and the rounds generally go over our heads.

Next in column, II/ 74 consisted only of 6/ 74 and half of 5; the battalion also took Belgian fire and 5/ 74 moved to the left. Enemy fire forced 6 to the right, along the line of Belgian trenches, until stopped by barbed wire. The company also took fire from the rear. Part of the company pushed through a gap in the Belgian defences, but was forced by fire from the flank and rear to stop and take cover. More infantry arriving from the rear merely served to add to the confusion, which the leaders could not control in the dark. The MG company commander, Captain Thomsen, a veteran of China and South-West Africa, moved west of the road and stayed there, clear of the chaos in front.

The adjutant of III/ 73 rode forwards to make contact with IR 74. He encountered men from his own regiment who were stopped in front of a wire obstacle, which they were unable to cross because movement drew heavy fire. He and the battalion commander led the troops forward, crawling, but were stopped by renewed fire from German troops in their rear, which not only caused casualties but woke up the Belgians, who were only fifty paces to the front. The adjutant was first wounded in the left arm, then the right.

The IR 74 history said that, given the collapse of command and control in the dark, nothing could be done but wait for daylight. During the night an order went out 'Hold in place. No further advance in the dark'. The Jäger 10 history noted that it was impossible to determine where the order came from, but it was correct under the circumstances.

Leman Commits 15 Brigade to the Boncelles Sector[20]

The 15 Brigade (attached to 4 DA) consisted of Chasseur R 1[21] (three battalions, each with four companies of two platoons), Chasseur R 4 (three battalions, each with four companies of three platoons),[22] an MG company, an artillery group (three four-gun batteries) and a platoon of mounted gendarmes. Neither chasseur regiment had an organic MG company, which put them at a distinct tactical disadvantage. Both chasseur regiments were home-stationed at Charleroi and were unfamiliar with Liège.

On 3 August the brigade had deployed to Huy to guard the bridges. The order to move by rail to Liège had arrived just before noon 5 August and the initial elements arrived in Liège at 1330. Since the population was unfamiliar with the chasseur uniforms, they initially took 15 Brigade to be French. The Liège HQ thought that Fort Barchon was under serious attack and at 1600 sent III/ Chasseur 1 as reinforcements, but it was recalled when halfway there. By 2230 the brigade assembled north of the Meuse, near the confluence of the Meuse and Ourthe. Almost immediately, two officers arrived from Liège HQ with urgent orders, which were issued during a violent thunderstorm:

> Two enemy columns of 1,500 each from the German X Corps have penetrated the Boncelles sector. 15 Brigade will retake the positions occupied by the Germans and hold at all costs the decisive terrain at Sart-Tilman. Chasseur R 1 will throw back the enemy in the Ourthe-Boncelles interval, Chasseur 4 in the Boncelles-Meurthe interval. The two regiments will link up by dawn.

The call for help probably originated from Fort Boncelles, which had telephone communication with Belgian HQ, while 9 L did not. Boncelles, however, did not have communication with 9 L. Whoever sent the report thought that the interval positions had already been overrun. According to De Schrÿver, the Germans had just begun the attack at 2330. De Schrÿver does not explain why 15 Brigade was sent to Boncelles an hour before the Germans attacked.[23]

The order included the requirement to hold Sart-Tilman 'the decisive point, all cost'.[24] This would certainly explain why Leman would eventually commit all his available reserves to this sector. What is unclear is why he decided that Sart-Tilman was the decisive point in Fortress Liège, which it most surely was not.

By 2320 I and II/ Chasseur 1 were moving towards Sart-Tilman, Chasseur 4, under the brigade commander, towards Ougrée. Tired out from marching and counter-marching all afternoon, III/ 1 rested at the assembly area, where the artillery section also remained, as did the MG company, a curious decision indeed: a MG section should have been attached at once to each chasseur regiment. Belgian commanders did not know how to use the MG.

6 August

Belgians at Sart-Tilman

Redoubt 1 on the Belgian left was held by 1/ II/ 14 F. On its right was a redan, then Redoubt 2 held by 2/ II/ 14 F. Redoubt 3, not far from the treeline of the

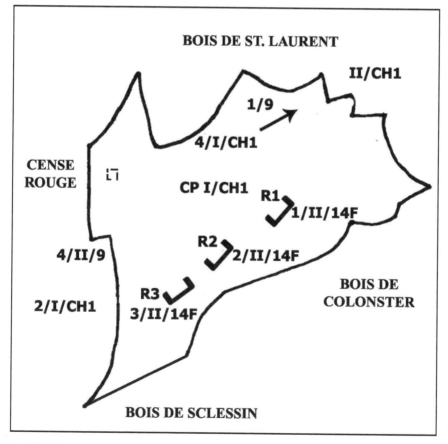

Sart–Tilman 38/ 43 BDE 0100.

Bois de St Jean, was held by 3/ II/ 14 F. There were two sections of 12 Brigade MGs: one between the redan and Redoubt 2, and one at the crossroads north of Sart-Tilman, facing generally south-east. Whoever put the MG there feared that the Germans would turn the Belgian left flank. In the event, they would have done more good in Redoubt 3. The battle in the woods to the west was deafening: two sergeants and a corporal in Redoubt 1 'went mad' and had to be evacuated.

The advance guard company, 2/ I/ Chasseur 1, arrived 300m from Sart-Tilman, guided by two *Gardes Civiques*, who then demanded to be released. At 0100 the advance guard company commander reconnoitred into the town, accompanied by a squad. There he met several men from 9 L, who informed him that Redoubts 4, 5 and 6 had fallen. The I/ Chasseur 1 was ordered to occupy Redoubt 2 – which was by now nearly empty of defenders, 2/ II/ 14 F having apparently fled – as well as the terrain immediately north of Redoubt 3, while II was in reserve north-east of Sart-Tilman.[25]

The chasseur regimental commander ordered the advance guard, 2/ I, to continue the march towards Redoubt 4. At 0120 it moved out, guided by a soldier from 4/ I/ 91. The company entered the Bois de St Jean at 0140, while still in march column, took fire, and fell back to Redoubt 3.

The 1/ I/ Chasseur 1 was sent forward to assist 2/ I but took fire even before entering the woods. 'To avoid an ambush' the 1/ I/ Chasseur 1 company commander sent his 1st Platoon into the woods to reconnoitre: it took fire, disintegrated and ran back to Sart-Tilman, where it reformed and moved towards Censé Rouge farm. The 2nd Platoon, with the 1st Company commander, entered the woods and took fire: the platoon dispersed and ran back to Redoubt 3.

In the woods forty prisoners were being guarded by two Germans. Lombard says that a lieutenant had managed to hide a pistol, and during the firefight he pulled it out, shot the guards and led the breakout back to Liège.

Lombard said that the key terrain at Sart-Tilman was the Censé Rouge farm, which the Germans were able to occupy without difficulty. The Belgian 4/ II/ 9L, 200m east of Censé Rouge, 'withdrew' back to Redoubt 3, except for its 1st Platoon, which was pinned down in the oat field 250m to the east.

Having been on bridge guard, 3/ I/ Chasseur 1 lost contact with the regiment and decided to guard the bridge at Ougrée. 4/ I had scattered. 1 and 3/ II/ Chasseur 1 were moving forward, 2 and 4/ II were in reserve north-east of Sart-Tilman: the Chasseur 1 commander had managed to spread his regiment in penny packets in and around the oat field.

At 0230 the Belgians took heavy MG and rifle fire, which caused 'serious losses' in the redan at Redoubt 1. The commander of Redoubt 1 sent reinforcements through the beaten zone of German fire. After the battle he saw that few had made it 'massacred and torn apart by enemy fire'. The Chasseur 1 commander committed 1/ II between the redan and Redoubt 2, 2 and 3/ II between the redan and Redoubt 1. A platoon from 4/ II was sent to reinforce 1st Platoon 1/ I opposite the west treeline.

Lombard reported the Belgians taking artillery fire; since no German batteries were in action, this must have been friendly fire from Belgian fortress artillery. Lombard says that the protection offered by the Belgian trenches was 'derisory', with fire into the flanks sweeping down the entire trench line. In Redoubt 3 the commander of 3/ II/ 14 F was killed by a bullet in the head, which caused a 'strong impression on the troops'.

The two platoons opposite Censé Rouge took MG fire, which caused heavy casualties, and the survivors crawled back to the redoubts. In addition to fire from the front and flanks, the Belgians took fire in the rear from Censé Rouge.

Dawn began to break. The artillery fire stopped falling. The Belgians were no better able to see the Germans, hidden in the woods, than they had been in the dark, so the Belgian troops fired rapidly but at random. The Belgian positions, however, were easily visible to the Germans, and according to Lombard the Germans MGs at

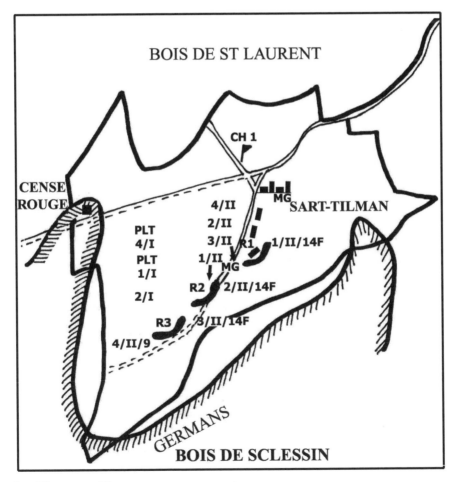

Sart-Tilman 0330 (B).

Censé Rouge, firing into the rear of Redoubts 2 and 3, forced the Belgians to stay below the parapets. De Schrÿver says that the German fire, which to this point had been irregular, now became intense, 'a violent fusillade'. Lying in the open between Redoubts 1 and 2, 1 and 3/ II were particularly hard hit, and ran back to the buildings of Sart-Tilman to try to find cover. The panic spread to the defenders of Redoubts 2 and 3. At this moment 2 and 4/ II appeared on line and 'more or less' turned the fleeing troops around. It was 0330.

The Belgians reoccupied Redoubts 2 and 3 just as the Germans began to advance by bounds. The elements of I/ Chasseur 1 north of Redoubt 3 managed to hold their ground. Redoubt 3 had not been dug deep enough and taller riflemen were forced to kneel. Both Redoubts 3 and 2 were still taking fire from the rear: in Redoubt 2 the troops dropped down from the parapet into the bottom of the trench. Belgian troops fired from the attics of the houses at Sart-Tilman and apparently into the Belgian troops in Redoubts 2 and 3, who thought they were taking German fire. De Schrÿver said that the Belgians fired uncontrollably on each other. Lombard said, 'The disorder was fantastic. Men ran, panic-stricken, hid behind the trees, rushed into the houses'. In an attempt to restore discipline, the regimental commander ordered 'Cease Fire!' sounded, to no effect. It was 0410.

Troops in the open between the redoubts again ran back to the village. At Redoubt 3, Lombard says the Germans were firing at 30m range on three sides. A young German officer crawled up to the parapet and shot the commander of 4/ II/ 9 L in the head; a lieutenant was mortally wounded. The Germans overran Redoubt 3, taking eighty POW.

Lombard said the Germans reorganised quickly and attacked Redoubt 2, and the Belgians withdrew by bounds to Sart-Tilman.[26] Redoubt 1 still held out, and elements of 3/ II/ Chasseur 1 blocked an enveloping movement against the left flank, while other elements of Chasseur 1 protected the right flank. The Germans began to enter the village, but at 0415 the attack there stalled.

At 0215 Leman ordered the 9 Brigade commander to move to Sart-Tilman with III/ 9 L and II and III/ 29 L to 'reoccupy the defences; the enemy had penetrated the interval between the forts'. At 0130 the 15 Brigade commander had ordered III/ Chasseur 1 up to Sart-Tilman, followed – finally – by the 15 Brigade MG Company. Against thirteen half-strength German battalions, Leman had now committed, piecemeal, nine full-strength battalions (Chasseur 1, Chasseur 4, III/ 9, II/ 29, III/29), nearly the entire available Liège reserve force.

Near dawn III/ Chasseur 1 and the MG company were climbing up the road from the Ourthe valley, when they began to meet wounded moving downhill to Liège, who told them that the battle was going badly: I and II/ Chasseur 1 had been driven back to the north of Sart-Tilman, the enemy occupied the west side of the village and was manoeuvring to the south. The road ahead was under MG fire. The advance guard platoon moved forward carefully, using all the cover the terrain provided. When the point left the treeline it was met by fire 'which seemed to come from all directions' as well as a wave of fleeing troops from both the chasseur and line regiments, which ran past them and into the main body of III/ Chasseur 1 'making a disastrous impression', and were stopped by officers brandishing their pistols.

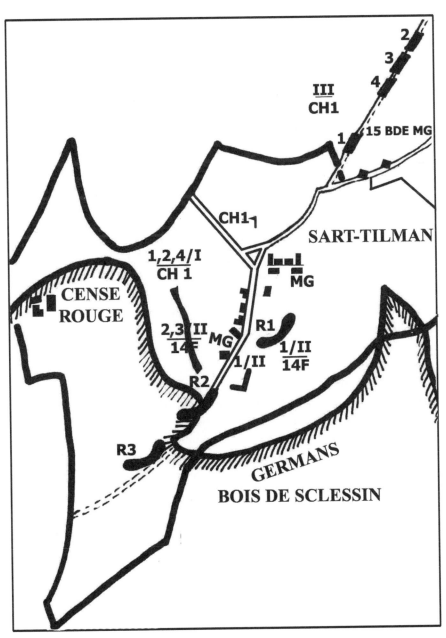

Sart–Tilman 0400 (B).

The Chasseur 1 regimental and battalion commanders conferred, 'the situation was almost desperate'. The village was nearly encircled, and it was unclear if the Belgians still held Redoubt 1. The six MGs were set up where the road entered the woods, 350m north-east of Sart-Tilman, firing south-west, and engaged German infantry at close range – 450m– stopping them, but also firing into Redoubt 1. De Schrÿver said that there were fortunately no Belgian casualties, which on the other hand says a great deal about the lack of accuracy of the Belgian MG fire.

By now I and II/ Chasseur 1 were a disorganised mob, which the officers and NCOs tried to reorganise on the north-east side of the village, with limited success. The lead company of III, followed by two reorganised companies and supported by the 12 and 15 Brigade MG companies, retook Sart-Tilman. The 15 Brigade MG Company bounded forward to set up between Redoubts 2 and 3, oriented south. It was nearly 0430.

The Belgian troops that had withdrawn to the Bois de St-Laurent reorganised, with the remnants of 1, 2 and 4/ I/ Chasseur 1 on the right, 2 and 3/ II / Fortress 14 on the left, 1 and 4/ III/ Chasseur 1 following echeloned behind the flanks, and ran into the clearing north of the village. There was no mention of fire and movement: they conducted a straightforward charge. Had there been significant German resistance, the Belgians would have been mown down in rows. They swung left, between Censé Rouge and Redoubt 2, and retook Redoubts 2 and 3, where the advance stopped. De Schrÿver said that there was 'great confusion' on the plateau. Redoubt 1 was held by 1/ II/ 14 F, with elements of 3/ II/ Chasseur 1 between it and the redan. Redoubt 2 was occupied by 1/ III/ Chasseur 1 and the 'debris' of 2 and 3/ II/ Fortress 14, Redoubt 3 by 3/ III/ Chasseur 1. Right of Redoubt 3, facing the woods, were elements of 2/ I/ Chasseur 1 and 2, 3, and 4/ II/ Chasseur 1. Behind them in reserve was 2/ III/ Chasseur 1.

The Germans re-established themselves on the treelines and once again the Belgians began to take fire from an invisible enemy in the front, flank and in the rear, from the general direction of Censé Rouge, but could not determine the Germans' exact positions. Patrols of volunteers attempted, unsuccessfully, to reach Censé Rouge. An officer crawled to within 50m of the farm, where he found the Belgian's bodies. Belgian troops in the buildings at Sart-Tilman fired on Censé Rouge, which led the Belgian troops to the west of the town to think that the Germans had occupied the houses and were firing on them.

To get the troops under control, the commander of Chasseur 1 ordered the buglers to play 'Cease Fire!' which had no effect whatsoever. According to Lombard, they then played 'Withdraw!' Lombard does not say who ordered this, or why, but for the third time that morning there was a disorganised flight into Sart-Tilman, where a hasty defence was organised, amidst 'a theatre of indescribable disorder'. The first floor of a house was filled with wounded, and there was no one to treat them, 'a horrifying scene'. The commander of the 15 Brigade MG Company was killed. The Germans reoccupied the abandoned redoubts.

The 15 Brigade artillery section arrived: once more the Belgian leadership committed its combat power in driblets, and too late. Lombard said that the artillery commanders had difficulty finding suitable firing positions in the hilly and wooded ground (in other words, the Belgian artillery was capable only of conducting direct fire) and had no means of communicating with the infantry. In 1914, first-rate artillery was capable of indirect fire and was equipped with telephones and wire to send forward observers to the infantry. Meanwhile, the guns were taking small-arms fire. The artillery section commander finally set up one gun at the crossroads to fire blind into the forest to buck up the infantry's morale. Another was set up on the forest road leading to Censé Rouge, 800m from the farm; the first shell set the barn on fire.

At 0515 the point element of III/ 9 L arrived and launched the third Belgian counterattack at Sart-Tilman. If the Germans had reoccupied the redoubts at all, they had done so weakly. With only the point element as reinforcements, the Belgians easily retook the redoubts, only to come under fire once more from three sides, and as De Schrÿver said, 'their morale remained shaky'.[27]

Lombard says that the artillery section commander brought six guns (a section of 61 Battery and 62 Battery) 300m to the north of Redoubt 2. Lombard does not state the direction of fire or the targets, only that 'the effect on morale was immediate and decisive'. It appears that they were firing into the blue, because they failed to suppress Censé Rouge.

Still in Redoubt 1 was 1/ II/ 14 F, with 1/ III/ Chasseur 1 in the redan, 3/ III/ Chasseur 1 in Redoubt 2, 4/ III/ Chasseur 1 and the point element of III/ 9 L in Redoubt 3. A platoon of 2/ III/ Chasseur 1 was north of Redoubt 3 faced the treeline of the Bois de St Jean. It would appear that I and II/ Chasseur 1 and 2, 3, and 4/ Fortress 14 were out of the fight.

Lombard says that forty or fifty Germans moved towards the redan under cover of a white flag. The commander of 2/ I/ Chasseur 1, which had been ordered to reinforce the redan, sent a lieutenant and twenty men to take the Germans prisoner. A German officer came forward, then fell down, yelling out an order. The Germans made 'a sudden movement, the man carrying the white flag stepped aside, unmasking three machine guns, which opened fire. Surprised, the Belgian detachment is cut down without being able to offer any resistance'. Sixteen men were killed, only four survived, including the lieutenant. All this was observed by the companies in Redoubts 1 and 2. The commander of 3/ III/ Chasseur 1 and several men tried to charge the Germans but was hit by several MG rounds and killed. 'A good number' of the Germans were also killed by return fire from 3/ III/ Chasseur 1. If this account were accurate, it would be hard to imagine how any of the fifty Germans, in the open and in close proximity to the Redoubts 1 and 2, could have escaped at all.

Approaching the plateau were II and III/ 29 L and 43 and 44 Battery. The commander of the 12 Brigade artillery reported to the 9 Brigade commander, who asked him only to keep his guns from blocking the roads. The 9 Brigade commander wanted to attack towards Fort Boncelles, which would have cut off the German 38 Brigade. III/ 9 was to lead, with II/ 29 flank guard to the right, III/ 29 in reserve. But both II/ 29 and III/ 29 were delayed by the traffic jam on the road, principally guns and artillery vehicles. At 0530 only III/ 9 was on the plateau, with elements of the point company, 2/III/ 9, already involved in the Chasseur 1 attack.

Any artillery fire was completely at random. One gun from 61 Battery, which had set fire to the Censé Rouge barn, 'fired several shells in the direction of the woods'. De Schrÿver says that German artillery intermittently fired at Sart-Tilman (barely mentioned in the FAR 26 history) while at 'irregular intervals' Boncelles and d'Embourg shelled the north treeline of the Bois de Sclessin.

Once again, the Belgian commanders committed their reserve in driblets: III/ 9 attacked alone, practically without fire support. The 1/ III/ 9 deployed right of 2/ III, 3/ III deployed right of I/ III/ 9 in order to take Censé Rouge, 4/ III in reserve. The battalion would pivot on Redoubt 3 to enter the woods and take the St Hubert crossroads. Taking fire from the treeline, the battalion advanced at the run; no fire and movement, and 2/ III quickly got considerably in front of 3 and 4/ III, and the commander of 2/ III was killed. The battalion entered the woods and was met by a blast of German fire that drove it back into the clearing and all the way to their start line, pursued by the Germans. The battalion commander was seriously wounded, and the battalion had lost one-third of its strength.

The commander of the 3 DA artillery ordered 49 and 51 Batteries to set up on the high ground to the north of the Meuse, directly north of Sart-Tilman. He had no information on the tactical situation on the south side of the river, and the only thing the gunners could make out with their binoculars were black and white figures – stray cattle. But the commander was convinced that the Germans had broken through and ordered the guns to conduct area fire from the Meuse to the redoubts. The troops of 3/ III/ 9 attempted to get the artillery to stop firing on them by waving handkerchiefs on the ends of their bayonets. The artillery group commander soon recognised that the overall situation was so confused that he had to ceasefire.

Going uphill, with great difficulty, were artillery units and II and III/ 29. According to Lombard, the road to Sart-Tilman was in a state of 'indescribable confusion'. Not only were wounded going downhill, but also 'a tumultuous crowd of disorganized units which wanted to reorganize' in the Ourthe valley, which was putting the best possible interpretation of routed troops leaving the battlefield entirely. Wagons blocked the road, which was lined with dead and wounded. This sad spectacle, De Schrÿver said, 'made a profound and negative impression on the troops, robbed them of their courage and contaminated and paralysed their energy. The officers had enormous difficulties getting them to move forward'.[28]

Reaching the top first, III/ 29 entered the woods north of the clearing, where there were several exhausted stragglers. II/ 29 went into the oat field at 0615 in square formation, 2 and 4 leading, 1 and 3/ II 300m behind. Someone's artillery

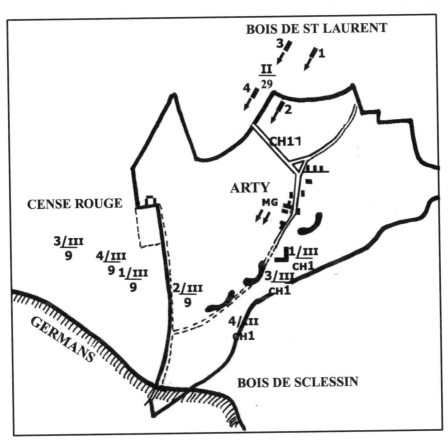

Sart–Tilman 0600 (B).

fire was now landing continually on Sart-Tilman. Then II/ 29 was met by heavy German fire from the Bois de St Jean treeline, which forced the advance to proceed by short rushes or crawling. It encountered the bodies of the 9 Line men, 'many hit in the head'. When they reached the treeline they began to take small-arms fire in the right flank. The battalion commander ordered a withdrawal of 100m to avoid being flanked, and committed 1/ II/ 29 on the left, and 3/ II/ 29 on the right to take Censé Rouge. He was then killed. The Germans reoccupied the treeline. Once again the Belgian troops in the oat field were subjected to fire from the front and into both flanks.

There were only 'weak detachments' left in Redoubts 1–3, and even III/ 29 had already been 'severely reduced' in strength: the German fire had forced the battalion to break up and seek cover in Sart-Tilman. The intensity of the German small-arms fire and the artillery fire of unknown provenance made it appear that the Germans were going to launch a counterattack. The advance on Boncelles was called off and III/ 29 was ordered to reinforce the redoubts with elements of the battalion still under control. At 0700 1/ II/ 14 F was in Redoubt 1, 2/ III/ 29 in the redan, 3/ III/ 29 in

Redoubt 2, 4/ III/ 29 in Redoubt 3. Facing the Bois du St Jean, south to north, was a platoon from 1/ II/ 29, then 2/ II/ 29, 4/ II/ 29. Behind Redoubt 3 was 1/ II/ 29 (-) and 1/ III/ 29 was in reserve south of the village. German fire forced the right flank of 2 and 4/ II/ 29 to fall back 100m. Committed to cover the right, 3/ II/ 29 was forced back 200m by German fire.

Of the seven Belgian battalions that had been committed to the Sart-Tilman plateau, the only combat-effective units were II/ 29 and III/ 29, both under strength, a company of II/ 14 F, and only remnants of 9 L in the woods to the north. There is no trace of the rest of II/ 14 F. At 0715 what was left of Chasseur 1 marched off the Sart-Tilman plateau to reorganise, followed by the 15 Brigade artillery.

The Belgians now committed their tenth infantry battalion from the Liège reserve to this sector, three companies of I/ 12 L, accompanied by the regimental commander. They had been ordered up from Beyne-Heusay at 0355: even though the Belgian situation was critical all along the front, and the German 14 Brigade was breaking the Belgian centre, the Belgian command remained fixated on Sart-Tilman. The 2/ I/ 12 was sent to Redoubt 3 and 1/ I/ 12 to face the treeline to the west, while 4/ I/ 12 went into reserve south-east of Sart-Tilman.

And once again the Belgians in the redoubts were taking fire from the rear, and were still unable to identify exactly where it was coming from. As there had been

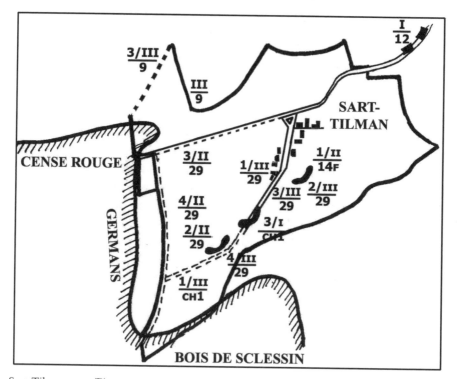

Sart-Tilman 0700 (B).

at 0400, there was uncontrolled firing, which the officers could not stop, and which caused friendly-fire casualties.[29] The Belgians were taking 'terrible' losses.

An officer an NCO and twenty men from 29 L climbed up to the second floor of a house under construction on the west side of the village, from which they could see all of the oat field behind the redoubts, including five German MGs at Censé Rouge. A firefight developed at 400m and Lombard says that the German MGs were reduced to three, then one. Two artillery shells landed near the house. The officer was severely wounded, another man hit in the head; these were the only Belgian casualties mentioned. The Belgians attacked and took the farm, the Germans fled.

Lombard did not explain why it took so long for the Belgians to make use of such a commanding firing position. By the time they did so, the Germans were already withdrawing, and it is far more likely that the five German MGs were not driven out of Censé Rouge by twenty Belgian riflemen, but rather withdrew as ordered, which is further verified by the reduction of the number of German MG to three, then one, and the fact that Lombard did not report the Belgians capturing any MGs.

At 0900 the Belgians were still conducting a firefight with German rear guards. At 0940 III/ 9, 29 L and the 9 Brigade artillery withdrew to Loncin. Remaining at Sart-Tilman were I/ 12, the 12 Brigade MG and fragments of 14 F and Chasseur 1. At 0732 General Leman ordered 3 DA to withdraw from Liège, which did not reach Sart-Tilman until 2315. The only mention Lombard makes of casualties is that there were twenty-six German bodies in front of Redoubt 3.[30]

German Attack North of Boncelles

43 Brigade followed 38 Brigade, with IR 83 in the lead, the order of march III, II, I, MGK, IR 82 following.[31] The IR 83 regimental historian said that it had already marched 60km that day and was at the end of its strength. At 0055 hours IR 83 was ordered by the 43 Brigade commander (actually, its own commander, Colonel Count Moltke) to reinforce the attack of 38 Brigade. It was followed by IR 82.

This was a gross tactical error. Some 3,500 men were engaged in an utterly disorganised night attack on a 1km front. Committing 3,000 more men to this chaos was only going to multiply friendly-fire casualties. Whatever happened on the firing line, 43 Brigade needed to be kept as an intact reserve until daylight. If Jäger 10 and 38 Brigade had penetrated the Belgian line, then 43 Brigade would have been available to take the objectives. If they failed, 43 Brigade could have conducted a deliberate daylight attack.

Colonel Moltke had been presented with an unforeseen tactical situation – dug-in Belgian positions. He lacked the mental flexibility which would have allowed him to re-evaluate the situation. Instead, he bulled forward, following his orders to 'overrun ruthlessly all opposition'. Tactical inflexibility ran in the Moltke family.

The IR 83 forward movement was significantly hindered by guns and troop vehicles stuck on the road. The III/ 83 was committed west of the trail, followed by II.

There was no time for reconnaissance and retreating 38 Brigade troops were taken for enemy, as were German troops to the front, resulting in friendly-fire incidents. The commanders of both III and II were killed, along with several company commanders. The next morning three IR 83 lieutenants were found dead in the Belgian wire obstacles.

German unit cohesion disappeared as units became hopelessly intermixed in the dark and the troops were scattered over several square kilometres of hilly woodland.[32] Men from Jäger 10 and three or four different infantry regiments would follow the nearest officer. The German accounts are therefore fragmentary, and it is often impossible to tell where the German troops were on the battlefield. The German troops generally moved towards one of the two objectives, Sart-Tilman or the Meuse bridges at Ougrée. The IR 73 history said that these groups acted independently, hampered by the fact that only field-grade officers (major and above) knew the actual mission. The Belgian accounts of the fighting are more complete and coherent. The Belgians generally say that the early morning actions took place in the dark, while the Germans generally say they waited for dawn: this discrepancy is probably irreconcilable.

In front of Redoubts 4–6, by 0330 IR 73 had used pauses in the firing to send out patrols to clarify the situation. To its front was a partially completed Belgian trench and wire obstacle. A thin German skirmisher line faced the Belgians, with dense concentrations of German troops behind it. As of 0300 Fort Boncelles and Fort d'Embourg began to shell the woods with heavy and light artillery. At the same time, 43 Brigade came up, which increased the confusion and casualties, requiring yet another reorganisation. At dawn the trench was taken.

On the right, under Major Dewall from IR 74, was a good part of Jäger 10, plus elements of II and III/ IR 74, and later elements of IR 83, including the MG company, which initially assembled in the trenches. At dawn he led the troops forward to put them on line at the edge of the wood, ready to move in the direction of Sart-Tilman and Angleux. Attacking to their right were 6 and 7/ 73 and MGK/ 73.

A patrol from 3/ Jäger 10 was sent out and took enemy fire as it left the woods, advanced by bounds across a meadow and saw entrenched enemy troops 200m to the front, took MG fire and casualties and withdrew. The 3/ Jäger 10 was then ordered to occupy the treeline; the company commander had thirty-five Jäger and three lieutenants. Once in place, the Jäger took lively fire, which went into the crowns of the oak trees, and 800m across slowly rising open terrain saw a heavily occupied trench (probably Redoubt 3). The Jäger advanced 'just like in the local training area at home' by squad bounds, without taking any casualties. At 600m white flags appeared, and the Jäger began advancing at a walk when they took fire again. The Jäger took cover and returned fire, at which point the white flags reappeared, the Jäger advanced and the Belgians again reopened fire. Several Jäger manoeuvred to the flank of a Belgian MG. One took a round through his mess kit, but the Belgian MG was silenced. Captain Wagner said:

We were inexperienced and naive […] the white flags had one positive conse-quence – all forty of us became quite annoyed with these fellows, which made itself noticeable in the manner in which we took the trench. I counted 50–60 Belgians with bullet wounds, 20 head wounds, the result of our marksmanship training. In addition there were 100 unwounded or lightly wounded prisoners. In a similar fashion we took the second trench. According to my notes, during the previous night and on that day we took 300–350 prisoners.

Ensign Haccius assembled a company-strength group from Jäger 10, IR 73 and 74 and attacked a strong Belgian trench, protected with wire, while the Belgian for-tress artillery fired over their heads. The men fired when the Belgians ran to the rear ('like shooting hares', he said), running forward when the Belgians occupied another trench and started firing. When the Germans got close enough to assault, the Belgians ran. While firing offhand from behind a tree at the fleeing Belgians, he took a bullet in the chest that threw him to the ground. He gave his ammunition to a passing Jäger, who tried to reassure him.

Jäger Wolter wrote that the attack advanced by squad bounds, hindered by pit-falls 2m deep armed with sharpened stakes, until they came to the Belgian position, trench lines one behind the other protected by barbed wire. Major Dewall ordered some of the troops to engage the front, while others manoeuvred on both flanks. The Belgians stood up and blasted away without aiming, so that all their rounds went too high. The obstacle was quickly taken, but Wolter received a grazing wound to the head, and when he awoke he was at the aid station.

Officer candidate/Corporal Behrens wrote in a letter home that thirty Belgians tied white flags on their rifles and began to wave them. The Jäger stopped firing and let the Belgians approach. The Belgians then tried to take the Jäger prisoner; the Jäger played dumb, let the Belgians advance and then opened fire at point-blank, mowing the Belgians down. The remainder fled. The Jäger lost three or four men. Behrens was killed a short time later.

Lieutenant Carius, commander of 6/ 74, wrote:

Our dauntless troops formed a skirmisher line in the dark. The platoon leaders organized extemporaneous platoons, the squad leaders likewise and we moved out, driving the enemy from the forest. We were illuminated by a searchlight and tried to remain undetected by lying down, but took shrapnel fire anyway, which caused no casualties because we quickly left the impact area. [All of this was standard German tactical procedure, practised in training.] At dawn we were fired on by a Belgian skirmisher line on high ground behind barbed wire. On Major Dewall's orders we opened fire and advanced up the hill. The outstand-ing fire discipline of our men now showed itself: everyone carefully selected his target, fired slowly and calmly. The Belgians withdrew over the hill, still firing, so that their rounds all went over our heads. Some of our men fired standing or kneeling. We pushed the enemy back into Fort d'Embourg, but had to withdraw because we were out of ammunition and had no reason to expect reinforcements, as the other troops in our brigade had gone in another direction.

Another group, made up of infantry, Jäger and an MG advanced at dawn under Reserve Lieutenant Schneller from 2/ Jäger 10 (probably against Redoubt 6). They took MG fire from some high ground. Covered by their own MG, they stormed the trench and shot the Belgians as they ran down into a quarry, where they later found several wounded and MG ammunition wagons pulled by dogs. Jäger Stotmeister said:

> The flanking fire from our MG had killed several Belgians in the trench and left us a considerable quantity of crackers and canned meat. We had lost contact with battalion, but our group, about two squads strong, advanced deployed, clearing out the terrain as we went, until we reached the outskirts of Liège. There were no enemy troops. The inhabitants, particularly several German-speaking women, gave us plenty of white bread and coffee.

This group moved about to avoid Belgian troops and spent the night in a barn.

Left of Dewall's group, an infantry captain asked for volunteers for a patrol. Officer candidate/Corporal Ludloff wrote that everyone who heard him crawled towards him through the barbed wire until he had to call out, 'Stop! That's plenty!' There were about thirty men, Jäger and infantry. In the dark, they moved in skirmisher order to the treeline, where they lay down opposite an open field. In the distance they could see black objects, between which were fiery-red ones. 'What were they? A riddle', Ludloff said. They moved quietly by individual squads along the treeline, then crawled forward in thick skirmisher line across the field. Three paces from Ludloff was a black object, and he poked at it with the muzzle of his rifle: a mess kit clattered. They stood up at the edge of a Belgian bivouac. The red objects were the remains of bivouac fires, the black objects were Belgian rucksacks, half unpacked. Bread, wurst and such lay around. 'The Belgians had apparently been chased away from their picnic' he said. The troops whispered to each other and packed away something edible, and the captain called for quiet. Suddenly a Belgian searchlight swept through the area. 'Down!' said the captain. The searchlight illuminated the treeline to the rear and the captain ordered 'Follow me!' The searchlight came jerkily behind them and illuminated them again, but they were already down. The searchlight went in front of them, and the patrol followed. It was now possible to see the treeline to the front. The searchlight found them again, but again they were ready.

They reached the treeline and took fire from the right at relatively close range. The troops lay down and some returned fire, but were immediately stopped by the captain. The enemy fire rose to a wild intensity and then died away, but hit no one. The captain instructed the troops not to fire, in order to confuse the enemy, who wasn't going to hit anything in the dark anyway. The patrol moved right along the treeline. Somebody stumbled, others made unavoidable noises. Again they took rifle fire from the right. When it stopped, they moved on, finding a field telephone cable, which they cut, again taking rifle fire: there were clearly a number of Belgian troops in the field to the right. They reached a farmhouse (this may have been Censé Rouge), in which they found a field telephone attached to numerous cables, which was destroyed with a hand axe. There was also military equipment, chests, dress uniforms and underwear. A civilian was found, feigning sleep, another hauled out of a cellar. The captain ordered the patrol to occupy the farmhouse, put out security and sent a report back to Captain Wagner. At daylight the lookout in the attic saw two Belgian platoons approaching in march column at 600–700m range. The captain ordered the patrol to form a line, and said 'Nobody fires until I do – we're going to let them get nice and close!' Cautioning the troops to aim carefully, at 300m range he opened fire at the Belgians, still in march column. The Belgians deployed and attempted to approach by fire and movement. Ludloff says that the Germans were hitting their targets, because the number bounding forward became continually fewer. The Belgians continued to crawl forward until they reached the edge of the wheat field, where they opened a heavy fire, but they were suppressed and fled. Every so often a Belgian would appear, running through the wheat field, but the Germans were eager to hit a target. The only German casualty was the captain, who, according to Ludloff, was doing an excellent job directing fire, but while looking up, supported on his elbow, was hit in both his right upper and lower arm. The patrol returned to the farm.

It was now light. Ludloff was on lookout at a window and saw that the treeline from which they had started out was held by German troops, taking fire from the same area they had been fired on while cutting the telephone cable. He thought he saw upturned earth (probably Redoubt 3), and reported to the captain, who ordered that when the Germans attacked, they should join the left flank and attack, too. The German skirmishers at the treeline made a bound 50m forward and Ludloff cut across the wheat field to join the left flank. The Germans bounded forward by platoons until they reached the upturned earth, and in front of it barbed wire. 'Innumerable' bayonets jutted out from the trench and the Belgians maintained a lively fire, but Ludloff couldn't see the heads of any Belgian soldiers; the Belgians weren't taking the risk of exposing themselves. The Germans approached by individual and squad bounds, firing on the rim of the trench. If a Belgian head was seen, the rim would come alive with the impact of German fire; the Belgians were completely suppressed. At 50m range the Germans started firing standing in order to aim into the trench. As Ludloff said, 'In training we had been taught to think and act in critical situations on our own initiative.' Ludloff, on the far left flank of the line, gathered up a Jäger and two infantrymen, moved thirty paces to the left and a bit forward to be able to fire standing, as fast as they could, directly down the right flank of the trench, which was packed with

Belgians. Many crawled up the backside of the trench, but he saw many others fall. Directly in front of Ludloff the trench bent to the rear and sloped upwards. 'A regular trench exit', Ludloff said:

> The occupants of the trench made for it in crowds; it was soon filled with dead and wounded, whom the following Belgians desperately climbed over with difficulty. Whoever wasn't hit, ran, with one exception, who walked slowly, head held high, with no headgear but a sword in hand – a Belgian officer. Only ten paces away, he threw his arms in the air and collapsed backwards.

There was a second Belgian trench behind the first, but the garrison could not fire for fear of hitting the fleeing men from the first trench. The Germans attacked this trench too, with Ludloff making for the right flank again, but the Belgians ran or were taken prisoner. A third trench was taken.

It is astounding that such diverse groups of soldiers would automatically move in a tactically correct manner under officers they did not know – a tribute to German discipline and training.

Ludloff then single-handedly captured two stray Belgians. The Germans were withdrawing, but he had left his rucksack in the farmhouse, and ran back to get it, meeting the wounded captain on the way, who told him that the Belgian artillery was adjusting its fire onto the farmhouse; he got the rucksack and ran out of the area just as the Belgian artillery began to fire for effect.

Boncelles

The Belgian 3/ I/ Chasseur 1 had been guarding a bridge, was recalled late, and arrived at the regimental assembly area after the regiment had moved out. The company commander could get no solid indications of the regiment's location. He decided to march to Ougrée, but once there found no trace of the regiment, so at 0115 he decided hold the bridge and wait for daylight, as the first wounded came down. Chasseur 4 passed, saying that Chasseur 1 was between Boncelles and the Ourthe. The 3/ I/ Chasseur 1 commander marched his company up the road that led to the east of Fort Boncelles. At the crossroads which led to St Hubert the point element exchanged fire with a dozen Germans, who withdrew. Fort Boncelles was only 400m to the west. At 0325 the company continued the march towards Boncelles town. It was quiet, except for firing in the distance to the east. Almost immediately it was attacked by a 'wave' of Germans which surrounded the company and annihilated it in a half-hour. Some men were able to flee, fifty were POW, the rest dead, including the company commander.[33]

The German account of this fight is more detailed and somewhat different, hardly surprising, given that 3/ I/ Chasseur 1 was destroyed. Colonel Freiherr von Gregory, commander of IR 73, had collected 5 and 8/ 73, as well as elements of II and III/ 74,

MGK 74 and several platoons from 43 Brigade and pursued the fleeing Belgians west, until by dawn they ran straight into 3/ I/ Chasseur 1 in Boncelles town. It would appear that, after the initial contact, the Belgians fell back to the town. The German units were thoroughly intermixed and assaulted without adequate fire preparation, resulting in heavy losses. Nevertheless, progress was made, and, supported by two batteries of FAR 26, from positions near Beauregard, which set the town on fire, plus a platoon (two guns) from IR 74 MG, drawing heavy return artillery fire. Boncelles town was stormed, often only after tough house-to-house fighting. The battle lasted approximately thirty minutes. The German account confirmed that 3/ I/ Chasseur 1 was annihilated, the company commander killed, and only fifty men survived as POW. Some of Colonel von Gregory's force pushed on to the west side of Boncelles town and were surprised to see Fort de Boncelles, which engaged them with canister fire. The infantry of the garrison opened fire from the glacis. An infantry fight with the fort was pointless, and Gregory pulled his troops back.

At dawn, 8/ 74 and 7/ 74 were dug in south of Fort Boncelles and observed movement from the fort, and opened fire on it. Canister fire from the fort caused serious casualties in 7/ 74. Elements of 8/ 74 became involved in the fight for Boncelles town.

The commander of Fort Boncelles had no idea what was going on outside the walls, but German troops were detected to the east and fired on by the four 5.7cm turrets. The parapets extended in a straight line without any traverses to prevent enfilade fire, and the Belgian infantry was swept by rifle and MG fire from the rear (actually 7 and 8/ 74), as well as by artillery high-explosive and shrapnel fire, and took heavy casualties.[34]

The Boncelles garrison saw white flags, and a patrol was sent out to take the prisoners. At the same time, German MG opened fire on the redoubt and the parapets, hitting several infantrymen and the fort commandant, who was in the searchlight tower/observation post. The patrol brought back 100 POWs from IR 74.[35]

Gregory then heard considerable firing to the east and turned his detachment in that direction, slowed considerably by Belgian snipers in the trees and groups of Belgian stragglers that were either captured or driven deeper into the forest. A battery of FAR 26 was encountered, and it did good service. Gregory then turned north-west towards Ougrée, collecting stragglers as he went, to reach the high ground south-east of the town at 0900.

Les Communes

North-west of Fort Boncelles the Belgians had constructed five dug-in positions. South of the village of Les Communes, facing south, were, east to west, Trench C, held by 2/ I/ 29 L, Trench D with 3/ I/ 29 and Redoubt 19, with 3/ III/ 14 F. West of Les Communes, facing west to connect the line of field fortifications to the Meuse, was Redoubt 18 (1/ III/ 14 F) and Redoubt 17 and Trench E (4/ I/ 29). There was also a battery of four US Civil War era 8cm guns, oriented west on the valley of the

Meuse, which constituted all the Belgian artillery in sector. In reserve at the I/ 29 command post (CP) at Les Communes were 2/ III/ 14 F, a company of fortress engineers and two companies of *Garde Civique* artillerymen, apparently without guns. The fields of fire had been cleared to 500–600m in front of the fortifications. During the course of the afternoon of 5 August, German cavalry reconnaissance patrols were seen. The I/ 29 CP had no communications with the forts or its neighbour to the left, and could only listen to the sound of battle to the east. .

Chasseur 4 had left the bivouac shortly after Chasseur 1, at 2345. The objective was designated as the towns of Lize and Les Communes. There was no information available concerning the Belgian defences in the area or the tactical situation. The march proceeded down darkened streets and past houses that were shuttered and seemed deserted. The troops were dead tired from marching and digging the previous day. At 0130 they crossed the bridge at Ougrée and met a number of wounded, who told them that the Germans were very strong and that they had best hurry. When Chasseur 4 reached Lize they could not find anyone, German or Belgian. At the next major crossroads to the south, I/ Chasseur 4 deployed, facing south. The regimental adjutant finally found the commander of I/ 29 in his CP near the church at Les Communes, who was astounded to see Chasseur 4 in his sector, where nothing had happened. He did report furious fighting in the Boncelles–Ourthe interval.[36] Nevertheless, the Chasseur 4 commander decided to bivouac north of Les Communes and wait until more information arrived! Meanwhile, II and III/ Chasseur 4 remained in march column on the road and the troops went to sleep. The civilians began to stir. It was 0400.

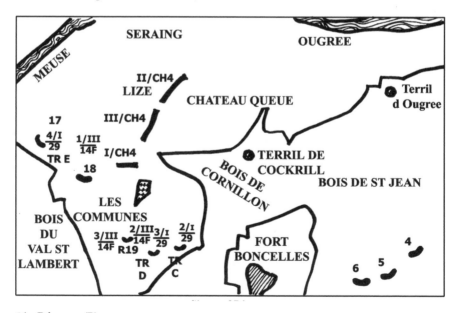

38/43 Bde 0240 (B).

A single MG began to fire on the road and the troops took cover. The fire appeared to come from the high ground to the east, where a civilian reported German troops. Nevertheless, it seemed unlikely that German troops could be so deep in the Belgian rear. From the north end of the column, 3/ II/ Chasseur 4 was sent towards Chateau Queue in reconnaissance. Fort Flémalle also opened fire on these German troops.

The commander of I/ 29 sent 2/ III/ 14 F to occupy a defensive position 400m north of Trench C on his left flank. They did not post adequate security to their front and while digging in they were taken under fire from the treeline, lost twenty men, and fell back 400m to the west. According to Lombard's map, the two *Garde Civique* artillery companies were apparently employed as infantry between 2/ II/ 14 F and Trench C, but he says nothing about them.

At 0555 a messenger from the I/ 29 commander reported to Chasseur 4 that he had just received a report that the interval between Boncelles and Embourg had been broken in and the interval troops forced to withdraw to Seraing. The Germans were in the woods at Bois de Cornillon and Chasseur 4 should occupy Lize.

Chasseur 4 attacked the wooded high ground to the east and took heavy rifle and MG fire. The lack of MGs put Chasseur 4 at a severe disadvantage, as well as the fact that the Belgians frequently had to advance in the open against German troops in a wood line and on high ground. On the left, 1 and 4/ II/ Chasseur 4 moved on a broad front towards Château Queue and Terrill (slag heap) Cockerill. They took very heavy fire, and when they reached the first houses of Château Queue were brought to a halt. There were German snipers in the church tower. Committed on the left to flank the Germans, 3/ II was itself stopped by fire into its own left flank; in fact it was

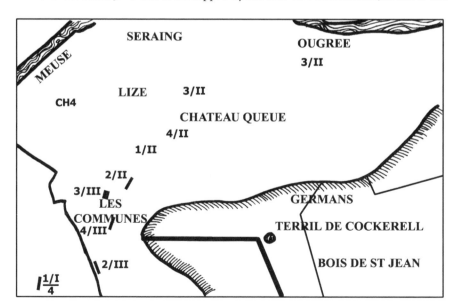

38/43 Bde 0600 (B).

German troops on a slag heap south of Ougrée. The 2/ II was stopped at an open wheat field, then 3/ II was committed on the right.

The next unit right, 2/ III, was stopped by MG fire. 4/ III was sent forward to reinforce (tactically the wrong move, known as 'reinforcing failure') and was quickly stopped in turn. The company commander 'was forced to order soldiers to return fire', proof that the Belgians were normally not supporting their movement by fire. The company commander was shot in the upper arm, the soldier behind him in the heart.

The I/ Chasseur 4 attempted to change front from south to east across a bare hillside and took heavy casualties. According to Lombard's map (but not in his text) only 1/ I/ Chasseur 4 succeeded in facing east and between 0700 and 0800 held the area near the cemetery of Les Communes with difficulty. De Schrÿver says that 'a particularly heavy blast of MG and rifle fire' stopped the battalion cold, and it was all the officers could do to maintain discipline. The Germans in the woods were invisible, while the Belgians stood out like targets on the open field. At 0815 the battalion was forced to retreat and two companies, 'particularly hard hit', withdrew all the way to Redoubt 18.

The IR 74 commander, Colonel Prince Wilhelm of Lippe, had assembled elements of IR 73, 82 and 83 with the intention of marching north-west to Seraing. At 0600 they crossed the Boncelles–Ougrée road, already in contact, and were soon on the outskirts of Ougrée and Seraing, with Fort Boncelles to the rear. They had been preceded by Captain Wersebe and elements of his company, 4/ 74. After German 'friendly' fire into the company rear had died down, Wersebe pushed north-west into the woods, took about thirty Belgian stragglers prisoner and used one of them, who spoke Flemish, as a guide to Ougrée. Wersebe wrote:

> Suddenly a great city lay before us, quiet and illuminated by thousands of lamps, as though no battle was being fought around it. The Meuse swung in a curve to the north, spanned by several brightly lit bridges. We were in the area east of Seraing. What now? In the dark, we dug in along what we thought was the military crest of the hill, hoping that other companies would come up. In the distance, to the left and right, we could just hear combat noise. At dawn I sent patrols to make contact with our units, and make sure we weren't fired on from the rear again, and soon received word that a battalion of a Hessian regiment from 43 Brigade, as well as a MG company from IR 73, was arriving. I had 100 men from our regiment and two battalion standards.
>
> As soon as it was light we began to take fire from houses 200 metres to our left rear. I sent Acting Officer Verclas with a strong patrol to clear the houses. He went out, aided by the low light and bushes, and returned in 30 minutes with 12 *francs-tireurs*, which he had taken prisoner in the houses, some of them while still armed. They were quite a spectacle. Common riff-raff, cowardly and terrified, but they could shoot at us from ambush. They whimpered 'Pardon,

Monsieur' and so on. One of them had 80 rounds of ammunition on him. They had been armed with revolvers. I declared them to be prisoners of war and later attached them to a prisoner column.

Troops from IR 83 arrived, led by their commander, Colonel Count Moltke, who was senior to Colonel Prince Wilhelm of Lippe. By now 400 men and some MGs were assembled, organised by the officers into extemporaneous units and conducting a slow firefight with Belgian troops in the houses to the west, as ammunition began to run out. Around 0900 they detected Belgian detachments south-west of Seraing moving to outflank them and began to pull back to the south-west, with Prince Wilhelm commanding the rear guard. From his position in the skirmisher line he could see with his binoculars Belgian troops on the low ground in front taking cover behind hedges and houses. 'Whoever can't find a target lying down, fires kneeling!' he called out. Inspired by his example, the troops conducted the firefight calmly. The Belgian flanking manoeuvre forced the prince to bend back his left flank. Seeing a small German detachment approaching from the left rear, the prince ordered the flag bearer to raise the flag and attract their attention. The flag bearer was hit, and another man took the flag. Then Lippe was fatally hit in the neck and chest. The rear guard was ordered by Colonel Moltke to withdraw. The Lippe/Moltke group had been in contact with 2/ II and 3/ II. Just after Lippe had been killed, 3/ II was hit hard in the right flank. The company commander was killed and the company forced to withdraw.

Elements of 9/ IR 73 had taken Château Queue in the face of heavy rifle fire, losing the company first sergeant. They were then cut off by Belgian troops and forced to surrender. The Belgians took the company commander, Count von der Schulenberg, and a lieutenant from IR 74 with them into captivity when they retreated; a lieutenant from IR 73 was taken to Fort Loncin and later freed.

One group of Jäger and infantrymen, supported for a time by a gun from FAR 26, was led by Lieutenant Rudolph. They moved through a wood to reach a wheat field at noon, where they shot several Belgians. Lieutenant Rudolph was then hit in the heart; the troops covered his body with pine boughs; Jäger Jensen said, 'I wept like a child'. They avoided heavy fire from a farmhouse on the other end of the field and reached the outskirts of Liège, where they saw a Belgian battalion approaching in march column. They took cover and the Belgians marched past them. The Germans climbed a hill and, as Jäger Bornemann said, 'we had a wonderful panorama of Liège and the main rail station. The roads to the city were full of Belgian troops. If our artillery piece had any shells, there wouldn't have been much left of the Belgian battalion that past us, or the rail station'.

German Withdrawal

At 0630 6 August, Colonel Oertzen gave the order for both brigades to withdraw south past Esneux and out of the range of the fortress guns.[37] The troops were widely scattered and command and control in a further attack into Liège was impossible. He thought it was necessary to pull the troops back in order to get them organised and resupply ammunition. In addition, there was no news from the brigade on the right, where firing had not been heard since morning. To this could be added that Belgian resistance was much more serious than expected, and that the two brigades were in no condition to withstand a strong and well co-ordinated Belgian counterattack, which must be expected from an army that followed French tactical doctrine. Even getting the withdrawal order to the units was slow and some got it very late or not at all. Kabisch says that at 1230 the commanders of 43 Brigade, IR 82 and IR 73 had not received Oertzen's order, but independently decided to withdraw.[38]

By 0915 (B) the battle was over. At 1030 Chasseur 4 was ordered to withdraw to the north bank of the Meuse. The commander of the Boncelles–Meuse interval troops did not get the order until 1330, and did not move out until 1830. One 15 Brigade major did not get this order until 1800. Chasseur 4 said it took 150 prisoners.[39]

Officer candidate/Corporal Ludloff had rejoined 3/Jäger 10 as it withdrew by bounds, taking casualties from rifle and MG fire, which steadily increased in intensity. 'They've got their courage back' he said to an officer candidate/corporal from another company, 'And reinforcements,' just before he was shot in the chest. The Belgians then attacked in thick masses, horns blaring and flags unfurled. The Jäger fired standing behind pine trees. 'Anyone who lay down got a disapproving look from his comrades' said Ludloff. 'Our slow, well-aimed fire tore enormous holes in the Belgian formation. We did not take any more casualties'.

The Jäger 10 historian asked, 'Why the sudden withdrawal? We had taken the enemy trenches with our night attack, in the morning pushed on further, defeated the enemy, threw back his counterattacks and taken several hundred prisoners'. The withdrawal order, according to the Jäger 10 historian, slowly reached one-fifth of the troops, at Sart-Tilman, at 1000.

The IR 74 historian said that morale during the withdrawal was low. The casualties seemed to have been high, the objective had not been taken, night combat and the withdrawal had shaken the troops: the officers had to act forcefully to restore their self-confidence. The regiment bivouacked, with only light local security, east of Poulseur, and on 6 August and during the day and night of 7 August more troops found their way back. Major Dewall, although badly wounded, took over command.

Jäger 10 began to assemble at the battalion aid station, at first only a few officers and squads of Jäger. Rumours began to fly that the rest were casualties and the troops were deeply depressed. Even the MG company was missing. Captain Rauch, the MG company commander, wrote:

At dawn I sent the MG vehicles a distance to the rear and, man-packing the weapons, tried to follow the battalion. We passed over the Belgian trenches but there was no sign of the battalion. I sent two lieutenants out on reconnaissance, and one came back quickly, telling me that the commander of IR 83 wanted to talk to me. He was extremely excited and I understood him to say that the assault had gone badly, with heavy casualties, and that a general retreat had been ordered. I ordered the guns back the way we came, but there was no sign of our vehicles. As compensation, we found several Belgian MG dog carts, the dogs wounded, on which I loaded all our equipment, also taking with us the Belgian MG ammunition, almost the same as ours. After an hour's march we rejoined the battalion, where I found our vehicles. The wildest rumours were circulating concerning the MG Company.

The Jäger marched back to collect their rucksacks. More and more Jäger arrived, including many thought dead; morale rose.

By the evening of 6 August, 38 Brigade had withdrawn to Esneux, 43 Brigade to Sprimont. The rear guard was I/ 73.

Rear Echelon

Corporal Merle, of 1/ Jäger 10, was with the supply vehicles, which initially followed the battalion, then turned back towards Esneux:

In the thickly-wooded valley we were continually harassed by rifle fire; the shooters were not to be seen. Our MG fired into the woods in the direction the shots came from. The rain had let up, but as we approached Esneux it was still pitch dark. The inhabitants had strung cables across the road and built barricades, which had to be removed. The vehicles were pulled off to the right side of the road and the troops deployed left and right of the road to provide security. I put my squad under cover in the roadside ditch when suddenly the inhabitants opened heavy fire.

Corporal Künstel from 4/ Jäger 10 jumped into the ditch in front of me and took a load of buckshot in the back. I treated his wounds as best I could; the buckshot had penetrated his uniform and shirt. Suddenly a building burst into flames and the rifle-fire began in earnest; the inhabitants had set it on fire with petroleum to provide illumination. We fired back as best we could and any civilian we caught was shot. The fight lasted about half an hour; after the building burned down, the firefight died away. At dawn the supply vehicles entered Esneux. The male inhabitants of the town were taken prisoner and brought before courts-martial. There was occasional firing from the woods into the town.

The IR 74 supply vehicles were instructed to wait in the market square at Poulseur; for lack of space some had to park on the road from Poulseur to Esnes. Regimental clerk Helke reported:

> No combat troops were assigned as vehicle guard, so the regimental adjutant ordered me to secure the vehicles with supernumerary personnel, clerks, orderlies and drivers. The guard house was set up in a barn near the market, the rail station was occupied by an outpost and the entrances by double sentries. As I was returning from inspecting the rail station guard I saw a light signal from the fortress ruin. A platoon of Hussar R 11 under an officer had just stopped for a short rest and went out to investigate. I went back to the guard house. Several civilian men who had been lounging around the market place were hastily hauled back home by their women. At 2100 all the houses were locked up and the electric lights went out, and there was terrific fire from almost all the windows in the area of the market place into the vehicles and guard house. At first we could not tell where the fire was coming from, and believed we were dealing with Belgian troops. In addition, a heavy cloudburst made the darkness impenetrable. The dull sound of detonating *franc-tireur* bombs mixed with the rifle fire. We needed to move the vehicles out of the area, which to some degree was successful. The Hussar patrol returned and together with my available men, stormed the houses we were taking fire from, arrested the inhabitants and set the house alight; the firing quickly ceased. Several men and women were put in the middle of the market as hostages. At 0200 a company of IR 83 arrived at double-time. The city was severely punished; only those houses from which we knew we had not taken fire were spared. Numerous inhabitants paid for the cowardly ambush with their lives.

I/ IR 73 and Fort d'Embourg

The I/ IR 73 had the mission of demonstrating against Fort d'Embourg. The battalion bivouacked at the treeline south of Beaufays at 1600. A patrol was sent out to make contact with 11 Brigade 7km to the east; it found neither friend nor foe. Another patrol reconnoitred Beaufays. The town was unoccupied, the main street blocked by fallen trees, but a trafficable side street was clear. The streets leading from the market place were barricaded in the most unusual ways: one by wagons and carts pushed together, a second with stuffed furniture from some wealthy burgher's house, the road to Tilff with flower pots and outdoor furniture from a café. Here the patrol met a Belgian patrol, which withdrew by bounds. Fort d'Embourg and Fort Chaudefontaine were easy to see on their hills, because the surrounding woods had been cut down. The garrison moved freely on the walls. The battalion established a security outpost on the north side of Beaufays. The night was uneventful, although the noise of combat could be easily heard.

There was no contact with either 38 Brigade on the left or 11 Brigade on the right. A patrol established that there were no enemy forces between the fort and the

Ourthe, although the locals maintained that strong Belgian forces were on the move from the north of the Ourthe towards Tilff. There was combat noise in the 38 Brigade sector, but none in the 11 Brigade sector. At noon, all was quiet. The hussars were sent back to Louveigné to find out what had happened and reported back that the assault had failed. The battalion returned to Louveigné late in the evening. The fort did not disturb the movement; the garrison was seen strolling in the sunshine. Wild rumours were circulating, 'Everybody is dead ...' Suddenly the vehicle drivers began a wild firing. The I/ 73 officers and NCOs maintained iron control, holding the troops in company mass formation, singing or practising the manual of arms, while the I/ 73 officers went through the drivers, striking the weapons from their hands.

Both Fort d'Embourg and Boncelles had no means of adjusting their fire: no communications with the infantry and no OPs. Nevertheless, d'Embourg 'participated very energetically' in the fight at the Bois de St Jean and Sart-Tilman, firing in the direction of the 'varying intensity of the echo of the fusillade'[40] (1,000 heavy-calibre shells in twelve hours!)[41] This sort of blind firing would have been as dangerous to the Belgian troops as the German.

Jäger 10 lost six OFF and fifty-two EM, with two officers KIA. IR 74 lost four OFF and fifity-two EM KIA, nine OFF and 201 EM WIA. II/ 74 lost two OFF (including the battalion commander) and five EM KIA, five OFF and seven EM WIA, three OFF and eighty-four EM missing in action (MIA) and probably prisoners of war (POW). According to the present-for-duty strength on the morning of 7 August, IR 73 appears to have lost twenty OFF and 454 EM. This may be too high, as stragglers would surely have come in later. The losses were concentrated in III/ 73, which had only three companies engaged, who started with seventeen OFF and 287 EM and finished with four OFF and eighty-one men. II/ 72 started with fifteen OFF and 517 men and had a present-for-duty strength on 7 August of eleven OFF and 359 men. The MGK lost two OFF and twenty EM. I/ 73 does not seem to have taken any casualties at all. The IR 73 regimental adjutant was wounded. IR 83 lost fifteen OFF and seventy-one EM KIA, twelve OFF and 103 EM WIA, 201 casualties total. On 10 August the regimental strength was forty-four OFF and 2,917 EM. IR 82 lost eight OFF and eighty-three EM KIA,[42] six OFF and 136 EM WIA, 236 casualties. IR 74 lost fifty-six KIA, IR 73 probably around 120 (25 per cent of 475 total casualties). Jäger 10 probably fifteen (25 per cent of fifty-eight), IR 83 lost eighty-six KIA. IR 82 lost ninety-one KIA, 368 total.

Lombard says that the Belgians lost 458 OFF and EM KIA. De Schrÿver says twelve OFF and 416 EM, and that the number of wounded was uncertain, but 'relatively high', and that the Belgians lost more than 100 POW. Belgian casualties were apparently 20 per cent higher than German.

Fort Boncelles had relatively high casualties: fifteen KIA and an unknown number of WIA.[43] These casualties do not seem to have been included in the totals of Lombard and De Schrÿver. The fortress commander was wounded, had to be hospitalised and turned command over to the lieutenant leading the infantry detachment.

38 and 43 Brigades Chew Up Belgian Reserves

Lombard titled his book on this part of the Liège battle *The Victory of Sart-Tilman*. This is patriotic nonsense and misses the tactical and operational point of the battle completely. Leman had ordered the withdrawal of the Belgian troops in the sector before the Germans did, and if there were Belgian troops at the end of the battle, there weren't many, and they would soon leave too.

The operational importance of the fight was that 38 and 43 Brigades fixed Leman's complete attention. He committed to this area all of 15 Brigade and most of 9 and 12 Brigades, eight battalions (plus three that did not engage), practically the entire Belgian reserve, and all eight were used up and rendered combat-ineffective. Instead of a three-brigade reserve standing directly in front of Ludendorff's 14 Brigade, to block further advance or counterattack, there were no Belgian troops there whatsoever.

North: 34 Brigade

Around noon on 5 August the brigade marched to Mouland, on the Meuse.[44] As Captain von Sodenstern noted angrily:

> The inhabitants of the town behaved in an incredible manner. Not only did they refuse to give us water, they would not even sell us food! [...] I observed an incident myself [...] fire from small windows of a house into troops of IR 89 who were resting on the street, arms stacked. This house was immediately searched and two men arrested with Tesching (small-calibre, short-range, rim-fire) rifles and ammunition who did not deny that they had fired on the troops. During the questioning, one tried to seize the battalion adjutant by the neck and was shot by an uhlan [...] There was continual firing, especially from the forested steep slope east of the town, but each time a patrol was sent out, the shooters fled.

The IR 90 was ordered to collect material from the town to construct a temporary bridge, and the troops brought doors, gates, floorboards and window shutters. The German officers apparently regarded such housebreaking as an unavoidable exigency of war, but the Belgians quite naturally did not see it that way.

De Schrÿver said that during the morning fire from Fort Pontisse was quite accurate, but became much less so during the day as German reconnaissance elements crossed to the west bank and pushed back the Belgian OPs. Pontisse was then reduced to a slow rate of ineffective unobserved fire.[45] Fléron, with good OPs, fired on 'main roads, dirt roads, paths', as well as 'villages and hamlets'.[46] Lombard described Fléron's fire with his usual barrage of adjectives, but in fact it was unable to do more than inconvenience German movement.

At 1430, 34 Brigade began crossing on the cavalry steel pontoons, making boats of two connected pontoons. It took three hours for IR 90 to cross. The vehicles had to be left behind; the contents of the company ammunition wagons were distributed to the troops, who now carried 350 rounds. The II/ FAR 60 was also not able to cross, nor was IR 25. Two division bridge trains did not arrive until 1645, too late to assist the crossing.

The terrain on the west bank of the Meuse was open and rolling, with good long-range visibility.[47] The sector Meuse–Pontisse–Liers was under the commander of 11 Brigade. On the right was III/ 12 F, defending Redoubt 2, which was about halfway

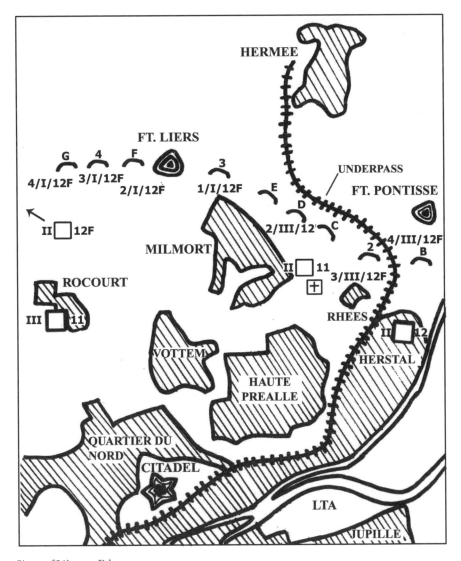

Siege of Liège 34 Bde.

between Pontisse and Herstal, with Trench A (2/ III/ 12 F) and B (4/ III/ 12 F) on the right and Trenches C and D on the left. Stationed between Pontisse and Liers was I/ 12 F, with 2/ 12 F in Trench E, 1/ 12 F in Redoubt 3 to the left of Liers, 3/ 12 F in Redoubt 4 on the left and 4/ 12 F in Trench G to the left of that. The III/ 12 was supposed to have occupied Trench E between I and III/ 12 F, but failed to do so. Unusually, this sector had considerable defence in depth. II/ 12 was in Herstal, and II/ 11 in a bivouac 500m north-east of Rhées, with the cemetery prepared for defence. De Schrÿver said that Pontisse fired all night.

The crossing completed, at 2100 the brigade moved out, IR 89 leading south over Heure-le-Romain. A thunderstorm began, which turned the route to mud. The troops were 'falling-over tired', the march interrupted by stops. The mounted officers walked their horses to stay awake. The brigade reached Hermée at midnight German time (G) and was instantly asleep on the roads and in the gardens.

The IR 90 history says that at 0200 Brigadier General von Kraewel assembled the field-grade officers and informed them, for the first time, that the brigade mission, along with Jäger 7 and 9, was to take the citadel of Liège that night. The order of march was IR 90, IR 89, Jäger Battalions 7 and 9.[48] The II/ 90 was to be advance guard, and Kraewel's order to Major Cleve, the battalion commander, was (more or less), 'Take this road to Liège; overrun everything in the way with the bayonet; don't stop until you reach the citadel'. In other words, the brigade would initially march in column, straight down the road. Weapons were to be unloaded, bayonets fixed. The IR 90 historian then said that, due to the delay in crossing the Meuse, it had not been possible to reconnoitre the route and the terrain was a complete unknown, except the general direction to Liège. A General Staff officer had been attached as a guide, but he had been wounded the previous evening by a *franc-tireur*. What is not usually pointed out is that it is 5km from Hermée to the citadel, which is simply too far for a night attack.

If this had been a peacetime exercise, Brigadier General Kraewel would have just got a 'no-go', followed by a severely critical after-action report from the exercise director and an eventual career-ending efficiency report. Kraewel had been blessed with two Jäger battalions that he should have sent across first, at 1430, reconnoitring the route and enemy positions and securing the attack line of departure. Instead, he sent two infantry regiments stumbling forward en masse in the dark, practically forgetting about the Jäger. The brigade spent two hours in Hermée without sending out any reconnaissance. To make matters worse, Kraewel had detached all the MG companies as his reserve, left them north of Hermée, and they never fired a shot.

The IR 90 moved past IR 89 to take the lead, with 6/ 90 as point. It had barely reached the south end of Hermée when it took shrapnel fire from the left front: the IR 90 historian speculated that the inhabitants of Hermée had informed the fort by telephone of the German's arrival. In fact, the brigade had been seen by an outpost with a bicycle. The Belgian histories do not note that the Belgians had no idea that 34 Brigade had been asleep for two hours in Hermée.

The IR 90 commander ordered the II/ 90 commander to send three companies to take the 'enemy battery'. The The 5, 6 and 8/ 90 deployed, with 7 in reserve, and advanced through high grain towards the muzzle flashes. It soon became clear that the 'enemy battery' was Fort Pontisse itself. Nevertheless, the battalion pushed up as far as the wire obstacles on the glacis. Meanwhile, Fort Pontisse began to shell Hermée. Reservist Karl Otto of 12/ 90 wrote:

A tremendous din filled the air. Stone shattered and pieces flew past our ears. Here and there someone cried out; others fell, hit. Pressed close together we ran down the village street, while over us raged the 'wild hunt'. 'Heads up!' yelled the captain, and ordered us to fix bayonets. When the company reached the church, everyone threw themselves flat on the ground. Shrapnel burst and howled. Shells tore great holes in the church walls. I lifted my head and saw a grenadier (IR 89) company run past us towards the exit from the village; now and again a grenadier was hit and fell. The grenadiers could not get any further forward either and lay down next to us. A young lieutenant stood up on the wall of the church, looked forward and, as a shell tore a corner of the church roof away, with a large block of stone just missing him, called out: 'Boys, they're such terrible shots, they're hitting the church roof!' In front was open space: 'Let's go!' Much back and forth movement in the narrow village street. Finally the order: 'Fusiliers [IR 90], go! Grenadiers [IR 89], stand fast!' spread the troops out.

Fort Liers also opened fire.[49] The talker in the fire direction centre (FDC) who transmitted the fire order to the guns told the FDC chief that they had just fired on his house. The next morning he learned that no one in the house had been injured but that a shell fragment the size of a fist had landed on his brother's bed, which was next to his own. On the other hand, this doesn't say much for the accuracy or effectiveness of Liers' artillery.

As ordered, IR 90 ran past IR 89, down the open road south of the village, the commander of III/ 90 calling to his troops, 'Gentlemen, III Battalion will take the advance guard!' The Fort Pontisse searchlight played continually over the terrain, and every time they threatened to reach the column, the troops threw themselves to the ground, 'just like at the Lockstedt training area': once, twice, a dozen times. The bayonets were getting dangerous and there were some tears in the uniform trousers and flesh wounds. Amazingly, Pontisse continued to shell Hermée but not the road to the south.

Pontisse dominated the Meuse valley, but to the north, south and east was surrounded by ravines which served as avenues of approach for German infantry, which was able to come up to the glacis and open rifle fire on the fort.[50] The fort commandant, fearing an infantry assault, ordered the parapets to be manned. The first men to approach the sally port were stopped dead in their tracks by German fire and the officers had to stand by the door, with a lieutenant shouting at the men and leading them forward personally. The Germans shot out the searchlight. The Germans maintained themselves in close proximity to the fort all night 'monopolising the attention of the defenders'.

The IR 90 history said that it suddenly encountered a rail embankment, which appeared 'like a black wall', with the road entering through an illuminated tunnel. As the advance guard reached the far side, it thought it took MG fire from the rail station; in fact, there were no MGs and this was 2/ III/ 12 F in Trenches C and D. The III/ 90 deployed left and right of the road to climb the railway embankment. The first 2m were vertical stone, the entire embankment 3m high. Men stood on their comrade's backs; the shaft of the I/ 90 standard was leaned on the slope and the men climbed up it. Whoever made it up helped the others; the III/ 90 commander held on to a rifle butt. Deployed to the right of III/ 90 was I/ 90, but the commander of I/ 90 was killed. Then IR 89 caught up with the IR 90 men on the rail embankment or deployed to their right.

The Belgians covered the top of the embankment with fire, but the IR 90 men ran down the other side of the embankment and into a grain field. The commander of III/ 90 called out, 'Boys, get out the umbrellas – it's hailing' and was hit and killed, as was the commander of 6/ 89. The men encountered a wire obstacle and either crawled under it or used wire cutters. A small group of about twenty IR 89 men and a few from IR 90, under the adjutant of III/ 89, used wire cutters to storm Trenches C and D. Only forty men escaped; three officers and 100 men were taken prisoner, and led off to Hermée. The guards used this opportunity to have the prisoners carry the guard's rucksacks. One Belgian complained that he was a nobleman, a count, and that carrying an enlisted man's pack was unworthy. He went on in this vein for some time, until the IR 90 man finally said, in a broad north German dialect, 'No aristocracy here!' (*Ach, wat heeßt hier Graf! – Ach, was heisst hier Graf!*) and loaded a second pack on him.

The Belgian defence was porous, and the Germans said that the trenches were only partially completed. The IR 90 pinned 3/ III/ 12 F in Redoubt 2 and 4/ III/ 12 in Trench B in the Meuse valley. The IR 90 was able to penetrate between I/ and III/ 12 F by destroying 2/ III/ 12 in Trenches C and D and marching through Trench E, which III/ 12 had failed to garrison.[51] At 0200 Belgian time (B), 4/ III/ 12 F retreated from Trench B, leaving behind forty dead and wounded, including the company commander. At 0315 1/ I/ 12 F abandoned Redoubt 3. Normand said, 'blinded by the German searchlights and swept by enemy MG fire, [III/ 12 F] was submerged in their trenches by an enemy bayonet charge'. The Germans did not have any MGs or searchlights; the Belgians had been blinded by the searchlight of the overzealous commander of Pontisse. With daylight the German rifle fire became murderously accurate, forcing 1/ III/ 12 F in Redoubt 2 to surrender at 0600.

The German troops forgot their fatigue and, following the nearest leaders in a display of high morale and aggressiveness, pursued retreating enemy into the pitch-black night, over wire obstacles and trenches, past hedges and barricades, up and down hills. The battle now became a wild free-for-all as independent groups on both sides became completely intermixed. Command and control collapsed in the dark. Not surprisingly, the various accounts of the fight hardly ever agree with each other.

As the IR 89 history said, 'no one knew exactly where Liège was'. This was the consequence of the fact that the brigade commander had issued a vague order at the last minute, and the regimental and battalion commanders were not given time to analyse their mission. Such a procedure was absolutely antithetical to German doctrine and training. The commander of 4/89 said that since they did not know the way to Liège, III/89 and elements of IR 90 just followed the fleeing Belgians.[52] Since Herstal was closest, and the way there was downhill, many Belgians ran in that direction. The mass of I and II/IR 89, mixed in with III/IR 90 men, headed straight south in separate battalion-sized columns

The Belgian II/11 had been preparing the Rhées cemetery for defence and was completely exhausted. The battalion commander feared that his troops had been seen by German aircraft and bivouacked in the open north-east of Rhées, on the soaked ground, and the troops were so tired they actually slept through the noise of the combat about a kilometre to the north. The commander tried to put the battalion on alert, but the men fell asleep again. A group of Belgians were surprised asleep in a barn and 'massacred with the bayonet'. I/89, led by the senior company commander, along with elements of III/90 and several other units, found the sleeping II/11 and opened fire. Completely surprised, the II/11 men fired on each other, then conducted a disorganised retreat to the cemetery. Private Otto wrote:

> The Belgians lay behind the grave mounds and fired. Several Jäger slid off their rucksacks and crawled forward, the long Jäger bayonet in their teeth, rising up suddenly to cut their enemy's throat. We crawled from one grave mound to the next, clearing out the cemetery. After the job was done we took a short breather; exhausted, we lay between the graves or leaned against the crosses. No one paid any attention to the bodies or pools of blood [...] It was once again peaceful in the cemetery.

Elements of I/90 reached a hill east of Fort Liers, with a searchlight shining on their backs. They took heavy fire and the attack stalled 300m from the enemy, who received reinforcements and MGs. Having taken heavy casualties, these troops withdrew.

The IR 89 history said that further advance was impossible without artillery. The regiment could count on a Belgian counterattack, and there were still two forts to their rear. The regiment therefore prepared the rail embankment and the Rhées cemetery for defence.

The scattered Belgian troops tried to reorganise. The 1/12 F was reassembled and sent back north towards Pontisse. It advanced slowly, taking fire from Germans to the north and Belgians to the south, and was stopped in front of Trench E, now occupied by the Germans. Reduced to platoon strength, 2/ 11 moved along towards the Rhées–Milmort road with a group of about a hundred men from all four companies on its left. The II/ 11 men fired into their rear of 3 and 4/ II/ 12 F. The commander of the interval troops, Colonel Dusart, was killed, Major Frère, the commander of II/ 11 L, seriously wounded. The disorganised II/ 11 companies scattered, some to Herstal, others to Liège.[53]

At 0300 1/ 11 tried to make a stand on the Herstal–Milmort road, with 2/ 11 400m to its left. The Germans penetrated between 1 and 2/ 11, turning the 1/ 11 left, and the company was encircled and captured. The 100 men remaining in 2/ 11 fled, and twenty men withdrew to Liège. The commander of 12 F rallied the 'debris' of 3 and 4/ 11 and tried to retake the cemetery. Reluctantly, 4/ 11 moved, but the company commander was killed and it stopped 100m from the cemetery. The Germans turned the two companies' left flank and they withdrew to the Préalle rail station.

A mixed column from IR 90 and III/ 89 under Major Arnim had pushed into Herstal. Arnim did not merely follow the rail line between Rhées and Herstal into Liège, probably because he had not had the time to familiarise himself with the terrain. The II/ 12 L was holding the Herstal and the Wandre bridge, and the streets were barricaded. The IR 90 history says Armin's men took canister and MG fire, which was not true: all the Belgians had were rifles. There were heavy casualties; Armin was killed, the III/ 89 battalion standard lost. As Kabisch noted, the Belgians did not keep it long: it was at Loncin when the fort blew up. The Belgians had to conduct extensive mopping-up operations to clear out German stragglers. The II/ 12, which had been reinforced by men from 12 F and a platoon of 11 L, had been reduced to 450 men. The 14 August 1914 issue of the newspaper *Burgerwelzyn* said that the entire population of Herstal – men, women and children – had fought the Germans, which was praiseworthy.

At dawn, 34 Brigade was spread all over the terrain *behind* Fort Liers and Fort Pontisse. In front, elements of Jäger 9 were in Haute Préalle and Jäger 7 on the north side of Liège. In the middle was II/ 89 with elements of I and III/ 89 at the churchyard of Rhées. About 400 troops from IR 89 and 200 from IR 90, under the brigade commander and the commander of IR 90, collected in a ravine east of Rhées that led to the Meuse. The IR 90 history said that Herstal was taken for Liège. Aware of the fate of Armin's column, the mass of IR 90 pulled back to the high ground north of Rhées, which they reached at 0700 (G). The exhausted troops fell asleep, but the Belgians occupied the surrounding farms and invisible snipers fired from trees and bushes. Bicycle Company/ 7, 3/ Jäger 7 and three MG companies were on the rail embankment.

Belgian units began to move towards Herstal: at 0430, elements of 9 F in company strength, and 2/ I/ 11, now in platoon strength, arrived, joined at 0500 a detachment of 150 men from 9 F, 11/ 1 and 12 F and another made up of elements of 1 and 2/ I/ 12 F and the 'debris' of 3 and 4/ II/ 11. These groups moved out on line at 0630 to retake the cemetery at Rhées.[54] The troops had to be pushed forward 'almost individually'. The lack of officers and NCOs made itself felt. The left flank took fire from Haute Préalle into their rear. The houses were searched, but nothing was found: De Schrÿver blamed *franc-tireur* German mine workers. The fire from the front became more intense, the advance even slower, until the sole officer from 9 F was wounded and the men fled to the rear. At 0830 the right half of the line took fire into its right flank and went to the bottom of the hill. The remaining troops on the left flank held in place.

At 1030 (G) the IR 90 commander observed a Belgian battery going into position near Fort de Pontisse and the Belgian groups marching from Rhées. The IR 90 commander ordered a withdrawal to Hermée. Even before movement was begun, Belgian infantry attacked from three sides, but were driven back in ten minutes. The wounded were left in a house under a Red Cross flag, with medical personnel, and at 1130 (G) the troops began to exfiltrate north in small groups, shelled by the Belgian fortress artillery. The IR 89 history said that the fort's fire caused the retreating Germans 'severe casualties' and disorganised the German units. The IR 90 took heavy fire from Fort Pontisse, the Germans attempting to escape as individuals. The remnants assembled at Lixhé, but still took artillery fire, withdrew to the east side of the Meuse and bivouacked north of Berneau.

A rear guard remained on the hill. At 1230 it took heavy artillery fire from Fort de Pontisse. Retreat was no longer possible. At 1300 a member of the Belgian parliament appeared and demanded that the rear guard surrender. The rear guard refused. During the afternoon renewed artillery and rifle fire caused casualties. Further resistance was senseless; the rear guard surrendered to the Belgian 4/ II/ 32, and was locked in the Liège prison.[55] Another detachment at the churchyard at Rhées was also forced to surrender. The Belgians took 5 OFF and 234 EM POW, but De Schrÿver and Normand neglected to say that most of these were the German wounded.

None of the groups of Belgian troops below the hill at Rhées were aware that the Germans on the hill had withdrawn or surrendered. When II/ 12 withdrew from Herstal, at around 1245, none of these groups were notified. The 1 and 2/ I/ 12 F group on the left flank pulled back at 1100, reached Herstal at 1430 and learned of the retreat order. The other two groups did not recognise that the Germans had withdrawn until 1930. They withdrew to Herstal and bivouacked there. Forgotten, 4/ I/ 32 passed the night near Herstal, and captured three OFF and sixty EM from Jäger 7.

Jäger 7 and 9

In the very early morning of 5 August, Jäger 9 received the order to move through Berneau to Lixhé, cross the Meuse on ferries and pontoons, clear the other side and hold the bridge over the Liège–Maastricht canal.[56] The Jäger moved out at 0330 to avoid observed artillery fire from Fort Pontisse. It occupied an assembly area with the rest of 34 Brigade on the Visé–Berneau road until 0920. Both friendly and enemy aircraft flew overhead. While moving through Berneau, shots were fired on the battalion from several houses and the church tower. Seeing the wounded engineers and cavalrymen enraged the Jäger still further. The Jäger 9 commander (whose father had been killed by a *franc-tireur* in 1870) ordered that any house from which fire was taken to be burned down; the town was soon on fire. The IR 90 historian regarded this as retribution for the night of 4–5 August.

The Jäger 9 historian noted that the Belgians still (in 1932) denied that there had ever once been any such thing as a Belgian *franc-tireur*. The Jäger 9 historian offered as refutation the following examples:

> Five suspicious men were hauled out of a house on the main street in Berneau, from which we had without a shred of doubt taken fire. They vehemently denied doing any such thing. A search of the house produced, from in and under beds, the weapons that must have been used. One of the battalion surgeons caught the priest in the parsonage while in the act of firing on the battalion; he was immediately shot by a Jäger who had accompanied the doctor.

The battalion reached the village of Mouland at 1430. The two infantry regiments crossed first and the Jäger had to wait until 2030 to begin their own crossing. A heavy thunderstorm cut loose and the crossing was not completed until 2330. The MG and the Jäger bicycle companies crossed dead last. The brigade had already moved out, but Jäger 9 and 7 caught up just as it made contact south of Hermée.

When Jäger 7 reached the south side of Hermée, Captain Arnim, commander of 2/ Jäger 7, noticed that 34 Brigade was marching away from Liège and informed General Kraewel, who was in the immediate vicinity.[57] Kraewel ordered Jäger 7 to become the brigade advance guard and continue the march due south to Liège. Had Kraewel made this decision about eighteen hours previously, the 34 Brigade attack would have been even more successful than that of Ludendorff and 14 Brigade. Now, instead of having the entire 34 Brigade behind it, Jäger 7 was followed only by Jäger 9.

Jäger 7 moved along a farm road and slipped into a gap east of 1/ I/ 12 F in Redoubt 3 without making any contact whatsoever. They had broken through and were behind Belgian lines: this was the slickest and most professional work done by any unit this night, and it would pay immense dividends. 'The advance was quite smooth and at a quick tempo'. The principal delay was due to the searchlights from Liers and Pontisse, because when they swung in their direction, everyone had to throw themselves flat on the ground to avoid detection. Jäger 7 somehow gained the impression that other units had already taken Liège and the march was speeded up further. As it became light, the Jäger 7 commander, Major Donalies, discovered that, probably as the result of his fast movement, he had lost contact with Jäger 9 and he only had his own 1, 2 and 4/ 7 with him. The inhabitants told him that he was on the route to Liège, so he speeded up the march even further, to re-establish contact. At dawn, the three companies, dead tired, reached the Quartier du Nord in Liège. There they stopped and rested. Through the fog they were able to see, far below, the Meuse and the houses of Liège. Donalies had been joined by the Jäger 9 commander, Major von der Oelsnitz, who had become separated from his battalion, except for two platoons. Jäger 9 took Haute Préalle after a tough fight, though the battalion history gives no details.

Donalies asked the nearby inhabitants to cook coffee for his troops. They were seen by *Garde Civique*, which sent a report to the fortress HQ, where it was 'badly received'.[58] The messenger was told that if they had similar visions in the future, they could keep them to themselves.

Liège was now quiet, so the commander of Jäger 7 sent 1/ 7 under its commander, Captain Freiherr von Rolshausen, to reconnoitre the city: if it were free of enemy troops, he should find quarters for the battalion. For that reason, 1/ 7 was accompanied by the battalion ration officer. Major von der Oelsnitz, the Jäger 9 commander, went too, expecting to find his battalion. As 1/ 7 marched into Liège it was joined by several civilians who, seeing the green coat and shakoes, took them to be British, cheered and gave them chocolate and cigarettes. The Jäger remained silent and did their best to act British. This, however, led 1/ 7 to march in a column of fours, without security, the officers in front.

The Jäger took on a civilian guide, not knowing that he was a police officer, and told him to take them to the citadel.[59] He used the most roundabout route possible, in the hopes that the Belgian troops there would be warned. The Germans then considered that the citadel was already in German hands, and thought that taking the city hall would be more useful. The police officer unwittingly led them straight to Leman's HQ, a far more valuable target.

Jäger Attack on 3 DA HQ

When the Jäger entered the small square in front of church of Ste Foi, they were still accompanied by cheering Belgian civilians. There are several variations on what transpired next. Kabisch says that a Belgian officer approached the column and asked if they were British or German, and the battalion adjutant said they were German, at which point the Belgian officer opened fire and killed Captain von Rolshausen and Major von der Oelsnitz.[60] The Jäger 7 historian said that the column was recognised and fired on by gendarmes guarding the HQ. They then took fire from the houses: he said it was not clear whether the shooters were Belgian soldiers quartered in the houses or civilians. One case, however, was clear: a civilian stood in a window behind a woman, aimed and fired a weapon, but was shot in the head by a senior NCO.

The company pushed forward towards the church of St Foi and became involved in a firefight with Belgians in the cannon foundry on the opposite side of the square. A high-voltage electric line was cut and fell into the square. Command of the company was assumed by Lieutenant von Dülong, who gave the order to withdraw. There was wild firing from the surrounding houses on the Jäger, which forced them onto a route more to the north-east of the one they had used to come in. It was not possible to carry all the wounded. The Jäger did not know it, but they had attacked the headquarters of the commandant of Liège, General Leman.

The Belgian descriptions of the attack differ considerably. The 9 August 1914 edition of a Liège newspaper, the *Etoile Belge*, described it as an attempted assassination. Leman was working with his staff when firing was heard. His adjutant said: 'This is unacceptable; you can't even work here any more!' went to see what was going on, opened the door, yelled 'The Germans are here!' and was shot dead. A gunfight ensued. The *Etoile Belge* article emphasised: 'The citizens, who were armed with Browning pistols, fired on the German soldiers from their homes.'[61]

Lombard said that Major Marchand, from the HQ staff, was leaning against the entrance doorpost to the HQ, smoking a cigarette. He recognised the Jäger and opened fire, instantly killing Captain von Rolshausen and Major von der Oelsnitz, and was immediately killed, too. During the firefight there were six Belgian and eight German KIA.

Normand said that the Jäger 7 men had been led into Liège by spies (Liège was supposedly 'swarming' with them) up to Leman's headquarters.[62] Two of his General Staff majors were apparently attracted by the noise of the crowd accompanying the Jäger, taking them for British, and at first saw only two officers and three Jäger, whom they took to be parliamentarians, but the Germans opened fired and forced their way into the office. One Belgian major shot a German major with a revolver, and a gendarme captain crushed the skull of the other German officer with a rifle butt. Major Marchand was killed, but the Belgian officers, gendarmes and headquarters personnel shot down fifteen attacking Germans, captured some and forced the rest to flee.

De Schrÿver says that at 0445 a staff officer working on the second floor of the HQ building with the commander of Liège proper, General Janssen, heard civilians yelling happily outside and, leaning out the window, saw 80–100 Germans marching towards him in a column of fours. The staff officer initially thought they were POWs, then yelled out 'Germans!'[63] The HQ guards and gendarmes ran into the road, but froze, even though the staff officer was yelling 'Open fire!' Two German officers approached the door to the HQ and were met by Major Marchand, armed with a pistol. Marchand shot Major von der Oelsnitz, and was killed in turn. This resulted in a gunfight at point-blank range in which eight German soldiers and four Belgian soldiers, a gendarme and three civilians were killed.

Leman, his chief of staff, and two captains initially hid in the cannon foundry next door, then went on foot to the Vivegnis rail station, where they took an automobile to Palace rail station, then to the citadel, where Leman wanted to set up his HQ. It was occupied by the *Garde Civique*, fortress artillery and the two oldest classes of conscripts. Lombard called this the 'dead weight of 3 DA' and 'operetta soldiers, likely to panic', commanded by a colonel who was showing signs of mental instability,[64] and hardly an atmosphere conducive to quiet and calm work. Leman decided to move to Loncin, where he arrived at 0700, joined a short time later by the rest of the staff.

In fact, the entire 3 DA HQ panicked. Leman and his chief of staff had abandoned their posts and left the 3 DA HQ leaderless. The rest of the staff followed their example and fled the HQ. There are well-established methods for displacing a HQ, the most common of which is to send an advanced party, which makes the HQ operational at the new location. Only when that is accomplished does the main body of the HQ move. The 3 DA HQ simply decamped, not even leaving a stay-behind party to man the telephones and inform the rest of the division of what it had done.

At some time in this chaos the order was supposed to be given to blow up the rail bridge, *des arches du pont* (the arches of the bridge) which is not a very precise order in the first place, and was somehow transformed into *Pont des arches*, that is, the old road bridge, which was actually blown up, while the rail bridge was left standing.[65] Indeed, this is the only bridge in Liège that was destroyed.

The Jäger attack had wide-ranging consequences. It took more than two hours to re-establish the HQ at Loncin, during which time command and control was lost completely. Once at Loncin, re-establishing command and control took time. To make matters worse, when Jäger 7 appeared in the town, the central telephone switchboard ceased operations, completely paralysing communications, and did not resume them until 0725. The Jäger attack also convinced Leman that the Germans had penetrated between the forts in strength. This was the first time Leman had been outside his HQ, and he got a good look at the situation in Liège, where a large number of men who had left their units wandered the streets, 'giving the desolate and sad spectacle of disorder and indiscipline'.[66]

Jäger Withdrawal

At 0815 Major Donalies heard firing in the city and sent 4/ 7 to investigate. The company immediately drew fire from Liège and turned back. The city was clearly not in German hands and Major Donalies decided to rejoin 34 Brigade, marching at 0900 towards Vottem. When it reached the town a Belgian column was reported advancing from Fort Liers. This was the Liers–Lantin reserve and 3 and 4/ I/ 12 F, which had withdrawn from Redoubt 4 (west of Liers). The two Jäger companies attacked and threw the Belgians back into the fort, with the Jäger delivering their pursuit fire standing. Taking fire from the direction of Fort Loncin, 4/ 7 swung in that direction and drove back another Belgian column.

Major Donalies decided that the troops desperately needed rest, and at 1500 he moved the two companies to a ravine lined with hedges north-west of Haute Préalle that provided both concealment and shade. While moving there they took heavy shrapnel fire from the forts, which caused no casualties because it burst too high.

Patrols returned saying that they could find no trace of the brigade. This reinforced Major Donalies in the conclusion that the brigade was in Liège. At 1600 he therefore moved the two companies through Haute Préalle towards Liège. As the point entered the main street it encountered a Belgian security post with about ten men, while simultaneously taking fire from all sides. Both company commanders were killed. Major Donalies and the point element broke through, and he ordered them to take cover along a hedge. He became separated from the rest of the point and was surrounded by Belgians. He defended himself with well-aimed fire but had a stoppage while reloading and was bayoneted in the neck and killed.

Command of the two companies, now about 200 men, was taken over by First Lieutenant Weyhe, the battalion adjutant, who decided to defend a quarry; by 1700 the Jäger were in position. Belgian attacks were thrown back. A patrol reported it had found a route not blocked by the Belgians, and at 2030 Lieutenant Weyhe led the remaining men out of the quarry; the wounded and unnecessary equipment had to be left behind. It was clear, but there was no moon. The Jäger marched in single file first west, then north-east around Haute Préalle, then passing over the glacis of Fort Pontisse, whose searchlight continually forced the Jäger to throw themselves prone, at which point several would fall asleep and had to be awakened. It was dawn when the Jäger entered Hermée, where they found a wounded lieutenant colonel and NCO from IR 89. The Jäger bivouacked in a field of rye near the village, wrapping themselves in their ponchos and immediately falling asleep. They were undisturbed and when they awoke the next morning it was raining. At 0830 they set out again and that morning reached Lixhé.

Belgian 11 Brigade Withdrawal

The 31 L, 3/ I/ 11, 3/ III/ 32 and the divisional engineer company crossed from the east bank of the Meuse, under the 11 Brigade commander, and by 1245 (B) had moved through Herstal and continued the retreat west. De Schrÿver says it captured 120 Germans digging in 500m north of the Rhées cemetery. Why these Germans had not either withdrawn or already been captured was not explained. At 1440 it took fire from what the Belgians said were elements of Jäger 7 on the north edge of Vottem: perhaps the Belgian version of the fight described by the 7 Jäger history, or some other Jäger, or other German troops entirely. The advance guard company 1/ III/ 31 pushed the Jäger to the west 'after a hard fight'. It was then supported by 2/ III/ 31, which caused the Jäger 'serious casualties'. The main body stopped to rest at the entrance to

Vottem, and 100 Germans hiding behind a hedge north of Vottem opened fire on the engineer company, killing the company commander and causing heavy casualties. The other units of the main body moved to help the engineers, and the Germans retreated to the cemetery. Then a second German force, in company strength, opened fire from a mill 600m north-east of Vottem. The advance guard turned back and was supported, in typical Belgian fashion, by a mishmash of units: 1/ I/ 31, 3/ III/ 32 and a platoon of 4/ I/ 31. While they attacked frontally, 3 and 4/ II/ 31, and a platoon of 4/ I/ 31, supported by 1/ II/ 12, tried to envelop the Germans from the west, with 3 and 4/ III/ 31 enveloping from the east. The Germans retreated to Rocourt. The 11 Brigade commander turned the column in this direction, and the column broke up, with 4/ I/ 31 and 3 and 4/ III/ 31 continuing on to the west and 3/ III/ 32 south to the citadel. The Belgians pushed the Germans out of Rocourt, but they took up a new position in a sandpit west of the town. Moving north of the town, 3/ II/ 12 took heavy casualties, including the company commander[67] Covered by 3 and 4/ II/ 31 the remainder of the column was able to continue the march to the west.

The MG company, 3/ Jäger 7, and the bicycle company had been stopped by General Kraewel to use as his reserve, and on the morning of 6 August held the rail line Milmort–Haute Préalle, completely isolated. They were joined there by elements of 34 Brigade and Jäger 9. It became clear to General Kraewel that the attack had failed, and at 1030 the group marched back to Hermée. The forts fired on the column in broad daylight but only one shell caused any casualties; again, the bursting point of the Belgian shrapnel was too high. Hermée was burning, but nevertheless the column took fire from civilians. Any armed civilians were taken to Lixhé, where Jäger 7 had the 'awful' mission of providing the firing squad. The remnants of the battalion crossed the Meuse and bivouacked east of Mouland.

General Kraewel ordered the bicycle company to move from the rail line towards Liège and find 1, 2 and 4/ Jäger 7. On the way, it made contact with Belgian infantry and took an officer and fifty EM POW. The bicycle company found 1/ Jäger 7 and at 2200 returned to Lixhé. On the morning of 7 August the bicycle company was again sent on reconnaissance towards Liège, entered the city and bivouacked there.

At about 1900 on 6 August, Jäger 9's reservists met the battalion at Warsage. They were not nearly as enthusiastic as the battalion had been four days previously. They had seen the shot-up elements of IR 25 marching back to Aachen, the convoys of wounded, the destroyed villages and dead *franc-tireur*. Captain Klausa, who was to command 4/ 9, had been shot dead on his horse by a *franc-tireur* using an 11mm (i.e. non-military) weapon. He had just married before deploying, and his body was returned to his wife in Ratzenberg. At 1530 7 August Jäger 9 was returned to the operational control of HKK 2.

The IR 90 lost four OFF (including the commander of I/ 90) and 38 EM KIA, eight OFF (including the commander of III and all four regimental adjutants) and 139 EM WIA, twenty-two MIA. The IR 89 could initially assemble only 663 EM.

This would soon be augmented by returning stragglers and at least 300 prisoners freed in Liège. The regimental history did not give any casualty figures, probably because none were available, and said only that officer losses were 'serious'. The reservists arrived on 8 August, and on 21 August the present-for-duty strength was sixty-eight OFF and 2,795 EM, so losses at Liège were on the order of eighteen OFF and 500 EM. Jäger 9 lost three KIA (including the battalion commander) and 7 MIA. Jäger 7 was scattered all over the north side of Liège and said only that it had 'many casualties'. The Belgians said they took 900 prisoners, but all of these would be released when 14 Brigade entered Liège.

The Belgians lost 165 KIA, including a colonel and two captains. Something like 180 KIA were lost by 34 Brigade.[68] Overall losses were probably about even.

North: 27 Brigade

27 Brigade advanced in two columns, with IR 16 on the left with the mission of penetrating between Fort Barchon and Fort d'Evegnée, IR 53 on the right to move between Fort Barchon and the Meuse. On 5 August, IR 25, which had been unable to cross the Meuse with 34 Brigade, came under the control of 27 Brigade.

IR 16

Fort d'Evegnée was badly sited.[69] It was surrounded by low dead ground which German patrols used to provide cover and concealment in order to harass the garrison. The town of Evegnée was in a valley below the entrance to the fort. The interval from Barchon to Evegnée was held by no less than fourteen companies. In keeping with Belgian practice these were drawn from five different battalions and four different regiments, thoroughly intermixed, practically insuring that command and control above the company level was impossible. Since the frontage here was about 3,500m, this sector was nearly twice as strongly held as the Meuse–Barchon sector. Most of 31 L and 32 L were in reserve for the Meuse–Barchon and Barchon–Evegnée sectors.

At 1020 4 August, IR 16 crossed the border and bivouacked at Julémont.[70] At 0400 on 5 August the regiment resumed the march through Mortier. At 0700 IR 16 was in the area of Blegny, drew artillery fire from Fort Barchon, and pushed its security line west of the village. Moving to within 300m of Fort Barchon, 5 and 7/ 16 dug in. Patrols frequently hit enemy security detachments and pushed them back into the fort, reporting extensive fields of obstacles in the intervals between the forts. At 1400 the two 21cm mortars of 2/ FAR 9 began to shell Barchon, Evegnée and the area in between. At Fort Barchon one 12cm and a 15cm gun had been rendered inoperable.

At 2100 (B), IR 16 moved out to attack into the interval between Barchon and Evegnée in two columns. The approach routes had been carefully reconnoitred and secured with guides. The 12/16 was sent out on reconnaissance and reached a group of houses below Evegnée. The night was pitch-dark and the thunderstorm made the path almost untrafficable. At 2245, fifteen minutes after the Belgians had arrived, IR 16 hit 2/ III/ 32 north of Evegnée. IR 16 said it encountered fallen trees and strong resistance. Although most of the defensive fire was too high, the General Staff officer guide decided that a breakthrough was impossible and the IR 16 commander reluctantly decided only to conduct a feint attack. The Belgians said that the attack between Fort Barchon and Fort d'Evegnée was a feint, 'weak' and 'easily repulsed'.[71]

I/ 16 was also conducting a bitter fight with the inhabitants of Blegny, who were firing from hedges, attics, cellars and even the church, causing considerable casualties. The troops would break into houses from which they were taking fire only to find women and children pleading for mercy. They burned down houses from which they had taken fire. Armed civilians were shot. On the morning of 6 August the battalion bivouacked around Blegny.

The fortress commander spent most of the night convinced that he was under serious attack and demanded artillery fire support and infantry. At 2200 Leman sent I/ 31, I/ 32 and 2 and 3/ II/ 32 to support Evegnée, which they reached at 2330.[72] It must be suspected that, since Evegnée was the fort nearest Germany, the fortress commander had the preconceived idea that he was going to be attacked in force.

At 0100 the Evegnée commander also called for fire from 11 Brigade artillery against German forces that he said were trying to break into the gorge side of the fortress. In turn, this fire made the troops in the Barchon–Evegnée sector uneasy, which was reinforced by the sounds of combat from Rabosée to the north; the Belgian troops thought that the Germans had penetrated as far as the artillery position in their rear. At 0220, stray rounds from the German 27 Brigade at Rabosée to the north landed and 31 and 32 L panicked and began wild firing 'against each other, seeing Germans everywhere'. The units were completely out of control. The 11 Brigade commander was forced to intervene personally, bringing with him a bugler who sounded 'Cease Fire!' and the marches of 11 and 12 Line Regiments, and along with his four gendarme escorts singing well-known songs. By 0300 discipline had been restored and the troops 'reoccupied their positions'.

This firing had important implications for the defence at Rabosée. It was the cause of the panic in 1/ I/ 14. It also diverted the attention of the 11 Brigade commander from Rabosée at a critical point in the battle, assuring that any reinforcements would be too weak and arrive too late.

Under the I/ 165 commander, 1 and 4/ 165 conducted a demonstration against Fort d'Evegnée. They left the bivouac area and by 0200 had closed to within 50m of the fort. At 0200 the two IR 165 companies took and returned fire 'which woke up the fortress [...] every gun spewed fire'. Both companies hunkered down in their holes, 'it was lucky that either the enemy did not know exactly where or shot badly'. Then there was a dull thud to their rear and a hum as something massive pushed through the air; when it was overhead, it sounded like a wagon rattling over the road, followed by a massive explosion in the fort. It was the 21cm mortar of FAR 7. The two companies fell back to dig in 700m from the fort, so as not to be caught in the impact area of the German artillery. The fort's guns immediately fell silent. Lacking any communication with IR 165, the two companies withdrew to Battice.

At 0340 the Barchon–Evegnée commander sent 1/ II/ 14, 3/ IV/ 34 and I/ 31 to d'Evegnée. The guns of the fort and 11 Brigade conducted heavy fire all night on German forces that were thought to be attacking the gorge and Salient III. The German feints had now drawn eleven Belgian companies to support d'Evegnée.

At 0700, 3/ IV/ 34 was pulled out of Tignée, north of d'Evegnée. It had moved about ten minutes and was 300m north of the town, when it came under fire from several MG. Only eighty men were able to fall back to Tignée and all the officers were casualties. An NCO led them to d'Evegnée, which refused to admit them, so they moved to Barchon town.

Stragglers from 14, 31 and 32 L occupied a farm west of Tignée, completely out of control and firing wildly in all directions. Trying to withdraw from Tignée, 3/ II/ 14 took fire from these stragglers, which the company commander took to be Germans. The company withdrew to d'Evegnée but the German artillery resumed firing on the fort, so it withdrew west, eventually meeting up with 2 and 4/ II/ 9 F and reaching 11 Brigade HQ.

At 1200 6 August, the Barchon–Evegnée commander ordered his troops to cross to the west side of the Meuse. The sector commander had no idea where to take his exhausted and discouraged troops, so he marched them towards the citadel, which he found to be under German artillery fire. They finally just bivouacked at a convenient spot near there.

German 27 Brigade at Rabosée

In order to block the high road on the east side of the Meuse the Belgians dug field fortifications on a low ridge north of the town of Rabosée, with the left resting on the Meuse valley, the right was refused (bent back) and supported by the valley of the Julienne stream. On the far left were three trenches: A (3/ I/ 9 F), B (1/ I/ 9 F) and C (2/ I/ 14) then Redoubt D, held by 2/ I/ 9 F with a platoon of engineers. In the centre, Trench F on the west of the road, held by 2nd Platoon of 3/ I/ 14, Trench G on the right of the road with 1st Platoon 3/ I/ 14 and 1st Platoon 1/ I/ 14, Trench H with 2nd Platoon 1/ I/ 14. This comes to eight companies on a 3,300m front. Lombard says the eight companies had a strength of 500 men, De Schrÿver 450, which low number can only be explained if the fortress companies were in fact the size of small platoons and the line companies were nowhere near full-strength. On the far right was I/ III/ 34, 300m south of the road to Barchon, a truly out-of-the-way location. The MG section was also in reserve, a serious misuse of these very important weapons, which should have been sited, dug-in and aimed during daylight. Lombard says that the large brick 'Falla' house was not occupied by the Belgians, which, if true, was a fatal tactical error.[73] The Germans were convinced that the house was fortified and defended. The front was well-covered by barbed wire, the road blocked with abatis, but was not camouflaged and in daylight the newly turned earth was clearly visible. The small villages to the immediate front had been prudently abandoned by their inhabitants.

As elsewhere, the Belgians in this sector developed a spy mania. Several persons travelling near the Rabosée crossroads were arrested and taken back to Liège. The owner of the farm at the crossroads told the troops that many of the civilian workers were Germans, 'probably disguised officers'.

During the morning of 5 August, III/ IR 53 moved south, looking for high ground to use for observation.[74] Shortly after 1200 it said it had a firefight with Belgian infantry holding Housse; the Belgians withdrew to the south. The III/ 53 pursued and came under fire from Fort Barchon, stopped and dug in. At 1330, II/ FAR 43 was ordered to move south of St Rémy to fire in support. The numerous trees and hedges made it difficult to find a suitable firing position, and to clear fields of fire, fruit trees had to be cut down and lanes cut through hedges. On the other hand, the vegetation covered the movement of the section into position and allowed the guns to fire from a well-hidden open position. The 21cm mortars had engaged Fort Barchon since 1400, so at 1600 II/ 43 fired on the Belgian infantry on both sides of the fort.

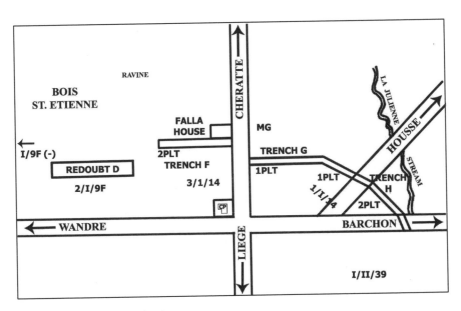

Siege of Liège 27 Bde at Rabosée.

Once the guns had shot in on the target, they fired rapidly for effect, the Belgian fire stopped and III/ 53 broke contact withdrew to Housse.[75] The III/ 53 lost ten EM KIA, one OFF and twenty-three EM WIA.[76]

Lombard said that the right flank of the Rabosée position engaged German troops coming out of Housse at 400m range in an hour-long firefight.[77] It would appear that III/ 53 had also engaged the defensive position at Rabosée without knowing it.

The Belgians said that at 1000, after a 'short and violent' artillery preparation, IR 53 threw back the company of 11 L in front of Fort Barchon, succeeded in reaching the gorge and attempted to attack the fort, throwing hand grenades.[78] They were stopped by intact barbed wire on the glacis and 5.7cm cannon and small-arms fire. Flanking fire from Pontisse and d'Evegnée forced the Germans to withdraw; the last Germans were thrown back by a counterattack by 11 Brigade, but IR 53 did not mention any such engagement. This counterattack pulled 11 Brigade north and weakened the Belgian centre. At 1850 eleven soldiers of 11 Brigade reached the Rabosée trenches, saying that their company had been attacked by surprise 800m east of Barchon. German troops were reported at Housse. A civilian coming from Housse, who had served in the Belgian Army, reported 8,000 German troops near Trembleur, a considerable exaggeration.

At 1700 the 11 Brigade commander stopped at the Rabosée command post. The Rabosée commander complained about the weakness of the garrison and was given 1 / III/ 31 L. Instead of holding it as a reserve, he placed it on his extreme right flank, on the road to Fort Barchon, where it accomplished nothing. At 1700 the garrison was put on 100 per cent alert and ate supper in the positions. Every man had 3–400 rounds of rifle ammunition. At 2000 patrols reported German patrols at Housse and cyclists on the roads to Dalhem and Argenteau. For night security there was only a distinctly non-tactical walking sentry 30m in front of the position. At 2200 there was a soaking thunderstorm. At 2300 the searchlight of Barchon began to play across the terrain.

The IR 53 mission was to attack along the river road from Cheratte to Liège, start time 0030 6 August. The route to Cheratte had been reconnoitred by a patrol on the previous afternoon. However, the patrol did not go up to the Belgian fortifications. The brigade dropped their packs, carrying only *Sturmgepäck* (assault pack), mostly ammunition. The weapons were unloaded and bayonets fixed. IR 53 marched in close column with 20m between the companies. Behind IR 53, IR 25 continued the march in total darkness. At 0130, shortly after leaving Cheratte, the IR 53 point element encountered an abatis, then took rifle and MG fire from the front. De Schrÿver said the range was 30 paces.

Captain Hermann, the commander of the advance guard company, described the initial contact:

4/ 53 marched 30 metres behind the point, 16 men equipped with wire cutters. About level with Fort Barchon, which was 800 metres left of the regiment's route of march, we encountered abatis and wire obstacles, which were cleared. When the company had passed the last abatis, at about 0200, it took heavy rifle and MG fire from a large building west of the road, 60–70 metres to our front [Every command group up to brigade was with the advance guard company and pinned down]. The heavy close-range fire made an assault impossible. There were serious casualties; everyone who wasn't hit deployed east and west of the road and opened fire, particularly against the building. The return fire was delayed somewhat because the troops had been directed by higher orders to unload their weapons. As other companies came forward the units were intermixed. [Captain Hermann survived uninjured, a testimony to the inaccuracy of Belgian fire.]

One of the Belgian MGs was finally moved to the centre of the line, just east of the road, direction of fire north. The other MG was set up in Trench I, 300m south-east of the crossroads, with direction of fire east. The logic behind this location is unclear; Lombard does not even locate the MG on his map and does not mention it again until the end of the fight.

The IR 53 MG Company succeeded in getting two platoons forward, in spite of the confusion caused by retreating German troops, to engage the Falla house. Several Germans forced their way inside and at 0220 (B) took it in hand-to-hand fighting. The IR 53 had already taken 'heavy casualties'. De Schrÿver says that the Germans had used hand grenades, which 'surprised and alarmed' the Belgians.[79] The Belgians concentrated shrapnel, small-arms and MG fire on the Falla house and reinforced their positions opposite it.[80] Lombard and De Schrÿver say the Germans were forced to evacuate the building and the area around it; the Germans say that they steadily reinforced this area, and that the German troops were ordered to hold in place and stop firing until dawn, to prevent friendly-fire casualties. The Belgian fire also died down, but resumed when IR 53 tried to advance. Attempting to move left through the country between the Rabosée position and Fort Barchon, which was 'free of hedges and fences', 7/ 53 was stopped by friendly fire. The IR 53 history made the unlikely assertion that the Belgians tried to envelop both flanks of the IR 53 firing line, but their own right flank was turned and the attack stopped, which shows that IR 53 thought the Belgians were much stronger than was actually the case.

Heavy fire broke out behind the Belgian position, the panic firing by 31 and 32 L, followed by bugle calls for the marches of 11 and 12 Line Regiments and for 'Cease Fire'. This shook the morale of 1/ I/ 14, which abandoned its trenches twice, but was turned back both times by the company commander.

At midnight on 5 August IR 25 was moving behind IR 53 in pitch darkness through Berneau when it took heavy fire from civilians in houses, gardens and behind hedges.[81] There were casualties, the troops began wild return fire, which was stopped only by the signal 'General Halt!' When the regiment had made its way out of Berneau, the weapons were unloaded to prevent uncontrolled firing.[82] 3/ 25 was ordered to return to

Berneau to recover the wounded and protect the movement of the doctors and medical wagons, which were at the other end of the village; thirty wounded were found.

In Cheratte, IR 25 was again fired on by civilians, which caused serious casualties. Lombard says both were cases of German friendly fire, as the citizens of the town had left and no civilian casualties were found.[83] The regiment was also illuminated by the searchlight at Fort Barchon. There was firing and cries of 'Hurra!' from IR 53 to the front. The battalions moved in close column down the village street, while some troops pushed into the gardens to both sides.

By dawn the Germans had re-established order, the Belgian trenches became visible, and the Belgian situation quickly deteriorated. The IR 25 MG Company commander brought three MGs into the Falla house. One gun was able to fire from a small second-floor gable window into 2nd Platoon 3/ I/ 14, while the Belgians were unable to determine the source of the German fire, and the platoon was destroyed: a few survivors were captured, only three escaped.

The brigade commander ordered an envelopment through the woods on the Belgian left, which was conducted by a captain from IR 53 with a small group of fifty to seventy men from several units, evidence of the disorganised state of the two German regiments. The IR 53 captain was killed, but the Germans continued the attack nevertheless. The outpost linking the Rabosée position to the Belgian troops in the Meuse valley was taken. According to Lombard, the Germans fired MG straight into the left flank of Redoubt D, hitting eighty-two men in a dozen minutes, killing both of the 2/ I/ 9 F officers. This fire actually came from the two MGs firing from the Falla house. A German attempt to turn the Belgian right flank was stopped by the MG at the crossroads, which apparently now came into action for the first time. Somebody in 1/ I/ 14 L yelled 'Fall back!' and the company retreated from the trench a third time and was brought by the company commander to a hedge behind the trench. At 0500 they fled again, for good. The Belgians now still held about 200m of trench with the nineteen survivors of 2/ I/ 9 F, 1st Platoon of 3/ I/ 14 and a few men from 1/ I/ 14.

The Germans moved two MGs into Trench F. One gun was put out of action, but the second German MG 'surprised the 1st Platoon of 3/ I/ 14 in Trench G with a terrible enfilade fire. This time it was the end.' The commander of IR 53 had ordered the German troops to crawl up to the Belgian trench; when the Germans reached the trench, the Belgians surrendered.

At 0400 the Rabosée commander again asked for reinforcements so that he could counterattack. The 11 Brigade commander said that no troops were available and sent only ammunition. At 0430 he renewed the request, and 4/ III/ 31 and a platoon of 1/ III/ 31 were sent to Rabosée. The Rabosée commander committed them to counterattack towards Redoubt D. Since the Belgian company outnumbered the IR 53 detachment 3 to 1, the attack should have succeeded. But, as the Rabosée commander noted, 4/ III/ 31 had arrived 'frightened and disorganised' and the company simply disappeared. He tried to commit 1/ II/ 31 from Trench I, but it was too late.

The Rabosée commander ordered the survivors, mostly from 3/ I/ 14, to withdraw to the 11 Brigade HQ, about 2km to the south. German tactical doctrine emphasised pursuit fire against a retreating enemy. One group of five men were all hit; three were killed. Sergeant Lenders tried to get his MG away. Of the team of six dogs pulling the gun cart, only one remained, and it was hit near the crossroads. Two men from the crew tried to carry the gun but were hit after a few paces; Lenders escaped. German MG pursuit fire continued 'for a long distance'. By 0630 the position had fallen. Both MG and ninety POW were taken. The units had been in such close contact that when day broke II/ FAR 43 was not able to provide fire support.

The 27 Brigade commander did not think that an attack through a built-up area into Liège with tired troops was possible. At 0730 the Germans withdrew.[84] The German 27 Brigade marched back to the area between Argenteau and Dalhem, in pouring rain, and bivouacked there, until midday 7 August, frequently forced to move by fort's artillery fire.

This was the last in a series of bad tactical decisions by the 27 Brigade commander, Massow. He could have bivouacked his troops in the Belgian trenches and the built-up area, which would have provided excellent defensive positions and cover and concealment against the fort's low-explosive artillery. By afternoon, patrols would have discovered that there were no Belgian forces on the west side of the Meuse. With a little energy, the conqueror of Liège could have been named Massow, not Ludendorff.

The Belgian 11 Brigade commander gathered up fragments of 31 and 32 L to retake Rabosée, forming two columns, with troops from four different battalions. The left column consisted of an engineer company, 1 and 3/ I/ 31, a platoon from 1/ III/ 31 and one from 4/ II/ 32, with a total strength of four companies. The right column was formed from 4/ II/ 32, a platoon from 1/ II/ 32 and one from 4/ I/ 32, with a strength of two companies. The 11 Brigade commander led the left column personally, mounted on his horse.[85] De Schrÿver says that the Belgians took fire from German patrols at Rabosée; these were almost certainly only stragglers. The Belgian morale had been badly shaken and the two columns now began firing on each other, causing a half-dozen casualties. Discipline was re-established only with difficulty, but the Rabosée position was retaken without opposition at 0740.

At the sound of renewed firing near Rabosée, units near the 11 Brigade HQ began to drift to the west side of the Meuse, beginning with the 11 Brigade artillery, 48 Battery and the 14 Brigade MG section, followed by the 'debris' of 1 and 3/ I/ 32 and 2/ III/ 32. When the 11 Brigade commander returned to his HQ he was therefore unable to find his brigade artillery. At 1145 the 11 Brigade commander received the order to withdraw to the west side of the fortress.

Lacking both communications and well-placed OPs, Barchon had been unable to fire. The fort had its own problems. During the thunderstorm that night, water streamed into Fort Barchon through the cracks in the armour. Mud made the barracks uninhabitable and the troops had to sleep in the central gallery. The water became so deep in the machine room that it threatened to short out the electrical system and had to be pumped out by hand. A trench was dug to empty the water into the fosse. The mortuary was located next to the hospital, a severe violation of standard military hygiene. In the heat the bodies had already begun to decompose, and had to be moved. At dawn they were given to the Mayor of Barchon for burial. On the morning of 6 August the commander of Barchon learned that the infantry company protecting the OP had withdrawn and the telephone line had been cut. It would appear that the fort had run out of telephone line, for the OP had to be re-established 500m south-west of the fort. It was able to see scattered groups of German troops and direct 21cm fire onto them. At dawn the German artillery resumed fire, less regularly and less violently, but just as accurately. Through breaks in the firing the wounded were evacuated.[86]

The German IR 53 lost seven OFF (a major, three captains and three lieutenants) and 128 EM KIA, twelve OFF (including all four adjutants) and 271 EM WIA. German IR 25 lost five OFF and seventy-eight EM KIA, nine OFF (including the regimental commander and a battalion commander) and 313 EM wounded. Total German losses were twelve OFF and 206 EM KIA, twenty-one OFF and 584 EM WIA, 823 total casualties.

Belgian casualties were 133 KIA, 150 WIA, 90 POW, 373 total casualties, 80 per cent of the Belgian defenders, with an unusually high proportion of KIA.

On the Belgian side, the three companies in the Rabosée position had literally fought to the last man, inflicting disproportionate casualties and rendering the two attacking German regiments incapable of further offensive action. But while the Belgians were effective in the defence, the 4/ III/ 31 counterattack was a fiasco, and Forts Barchon and Pontisse took no part in the battle, not even in daylight.

The German General Staff attack plan was an abysmal failure. It did not provide for effective reconnaissance. Marching two regiments in close column on a single road in the dark (with the tiny point element only 30m in front of the tightly packed main body) was senseless unless the brigade gained complete surprise, which by this time the German commanders had to know was not going to happen.

The IR 53 history implicitly criticised the plan for the high casualties, saying that the General Staff had dictated the 'form and execution' of the attack. It said that the attack demonstrated that deployment in depth was necessary if heavy casualties were to be avoided, and that victory was certain only if the infantry had artillery support. The commander of 10/ 53 wrote:

There were piles of dead, shot in the head, which lay where there were caught by MG fire [actually rifle fire] while still in march column. I recognized many good comrades and a fierce rage seized me, and I asked myself – was this necessary? But we had won nevertheless, and that gave us confidence.

The decisive factor was the aggressive German use of their MGs, which first wiped out the centre Belgian platoon, allowing more MGs to be brought forward to point-blank range to annihilate the company in Redoubt D on the left and finally the remainder of the centre company. In contrast, the Belgians had only two MGs, neither of which were properly employed.

If a night attack was required, there was room for a one-battalion attack, prepared with careful reconnaissance. A deliberate daylight attack conducted by a single battalion promised the greatest chances of success, demonstrated by the fact that the brigade commander quickly ordered the troops to break off the night attack and wait for daylight. The Germans had covered and concealed avenues of approach to within a few hundred metres of the easily-identifiable Belgian position. The terrain also allowed the establishment of MGs in offensive strongpoints. The brigade had three batteries of light howitzers for fire support, and could have called on II/ FAR 60. The two 21cm mortars were capable of suppressing Fort Barchon; if they fired on the trenches they would probably have cleared the Rabosée position themselves.

Notes

1. De Schrÿver, Liège, 104
2. De Schrÿver, Liège, 108–9.
3. Lombard, Sart-Tilman, 31–3
4. Normand, Liège, Namur, 30–1.
5. De Schrÿver, Liège, 61–2.
6. Jung, Goslarer Jäger, 22–53.
7. Lombard says that five Belgian civilians had been forced to act as guides, which does not make much sense. Lombard, Sart-Tilman, 51. Lombard also says that the German force numbered 12,000 men, and continually emphasised this to show how outnumbered the Belgians were. This would have been true if the units were at full strength. In fact, they were slightly above half strength and the two brigades, plus the Jäger, probably numbered about 7,500.
8. Gabriel, IR 74, 27–41.
9. Lombard devotes no less than ten pages (Sart-Tilman, 41–50) to the diversionary attack on Boncelles, inflating it into a full-fledged attempt to storm the fort. No credence was given to German sources or even simple common sense. Lombard also says the two German companies had MG, which they did not. If it concerns the Germans, instead of sober military history, Lombard presents pages of purple prose. (The Feldgrauen, cut down, flattened, crushed, quickly realized the inanity of their enterprise', 49). The German attack is often compared to 'a giant octopus' (82).
10. De Schrÿver, Liège, 105.
11. H. Voigt, Geschichte des Fusilier-Regiments Generalfeldmarschall Prinz Albrecht von Preussen (Hann.) Nr 73 (Bernard und Graefe: Berlin, 1938) 81–8.
12. Lombard, Sart-Tilman, 55–60. Lombard says (61) that 'in order to revive their flagging energy and inspire a spirit of victory' the approaching German 38 Brigade sang 'Westphalen (Westphalia) über alles', which, he says, corresponded to the behaviour of the ancient Germans as recounted in Tacitus. There is no mention of any such thing

in the German regimental histories. In any case, IR 73 and 74 were from Hanover, a principality which dates back to the end of the seventeenth century, and which had practically no connection to Westphalia. The Duchy of Westphalia was associated with the Prince-Bishop of Cologne until 1802, when it became part of the Grand Duchy of Hessia, then in 1807 a kingdom under Jerome Bonaparte, which incorporated Hanover in 1810. In 1813 the kingdom was overrun by the Russians and dissolved. In 1815 Westphalia was annexed into Prussia and Hanover re-established. Hanover became a Prussian Province in 1867. In 1946 Westphalia became part of the State of Nordrhein-Westphalen, Hanover of Niedersachsen. There is little possibility that Hanover regiments would sing 'Westphalia über alles', in the unlikely event that such a song actually existed. Once again, Lombard's knowledge of German actions is unreliable.

13. De Schrÿver says that the Jäger advanced chanting 'Westphalien [sic] über alles'. The battalion's unofficial name was the 'Goslarer Jäger', after their garrison city, Goslar, which is not in Westphalia but Hannover, as the official title, Das Hannoversche Jägerbataillon Nr. 10' clearly shows. The battalion was created in 1803 as the Hannover Guard Jäger Battalion.

14. Lombard says that fire from Embourg produced a 'disastrous moral effect' on 43 Brigade, which was reduced to a 'disorganized mob'. (Sart-Tilman, 79), which, with a singular lack of consistency, he later recounts conducting determined attacks and storming Redoubts 2 and 3.

15. Lombard, Sart-Tilman, 63–74. Purple prose.

16. De Schrÿver, Liège, 106–8.

17. Lombard, Sart-Tilman, 75–86.

18. De Schrÿver, Liège, 108.

19. Buhle, Erlebnisse der 1. Batterie Schleswig-Holsteinischen Feldartillerie-Regiments Nr 9 … im 1. Jahr des Weltkriegs (Altdamm in Pommern: Hormann, 1932) 19.

20. Leman, Sart-Tilman, 88–99.

21. In The Forts of the Meuse in World War I, Donnell uses the cavalry symbol to designate Chasseur R 4 (43). This is incorrect. Chasseur R 1 and 4 were Chasseurs à Pied (on foot), and not Chasseurs à Cheval (mounted). The distinction goes back to the army of Napoleon I. Chasseurs were hunters, and the foot chasseur regiments were similar in concept to German Jäger battalions, even having distinct black uniforms and shakoes.

22. There may not have been a difference in rifle strength, but in the cadres available to form platoons.

23. De Schrÿver, Liège, 94–109.

24. De Schrÿver, Liège, 109.

25. De Schrÿver, Liège, 109–20. The Belgian accounts do not always agree with one another, which is a reflection of the lack of command and control at Sart-Tilman.

26. Lombard says that the Germans used men from 4/ I/ 9 'who they had captured several hours previously' as human shields. It is highly unlikely that the Germans would have been able to move a group of prisoners forward across the battlefield. Lombard does not mention the reaction of the Belgians in Redoubt 2 or what, if anything, happened to the 'human shields'. If any Belgians were moving from Redoubt 3 to 2, they were certainly men from 4/ II/ 9 escaping. Redoubt 2, according to Lombard, was 'no more than a frail reef in a living sea of assailants that threatened from one moment to the next to submerge it', 124.

27. De Schrÿver, Liège, 114.

28. De Schrÿver, Liège, 117.

29. De Schrÿver, Liège, 118–9.

30. Lombard says that the withdrawing Germans were horrified to see 700 German bodies piled next to the road in front of Redoubt 5. There is no possibility that the Germans could have found and moved 700 corpses by 0900, 6 August.

31. Clausius, IR 83, 15–17.

32. Lombard said that Colonel Oertzen was fully in control of both 38 and 43 Brigades and minutely directed the fight at Sart-Tilman, an assumption that finds no confirmation in the German accounts of the battle, which show that the German units were completely intermixed and that the fight was conducted by the German unit leaders on the front, with little or no higher control. The only effective order Oertzen issued was the one to withdraw, and that was only partially effective.

33. De Schrÿver, Liège, 120–1.

34. De Schrÿver, Liège, 121–2.

35. Since this took place in front of salient II, the point of the fort's triangle, these were probably troops from 7 and 8/ 74. The IR 74 history does not mention such an incident.

36. De Schrÿver, Liège, 122–8.

37. Gabriel, IR 74, 37; Bieberstein, Lüttich-Namur, 48–9.

38. Kabisch, Lüttich, 86.

39. Normand, Liège, Namur, 38. Normand says the battalion attacked the German right flank, the German regimental histories say the left.

40. De Schrÿver, Liège, 132.

41. Lombard, Sous les Ouragans d'Acier, 106.

42. G. Schmidt/E. Ahlhorn, 2. Kurhessisches Infanterie-Regiment Nr. 82 (Berlin: Stalling, 1922) 14–15.

43. L. Lombard, Ceux de Liège: Chocs de Feu dans la Nuit (Verviers: G. Leens, 1937) 138.

44. Anon, IR 90, 15–25.

45. De Schrÿver, Liège, 91.

46. Lombard, Face à l'invasion, 92.

47. De Schrÿver, Liège, 184–93.

48. Zipfel, IR 89, 36–41.

49. Lombard, Face à l'invasion, 112–3.

50. Lombard, Face à l'invasion, 114–6.

51. Lombard, Face à l'invasion, 115–26.

52. Kabisch, Lüttich, 89.

53. Normand, Liège, Namur, 31.

54. De Schrÿver, Liège, 192–3.

55. Normand, Liège, Namur, 32.

56. Badinski, Jäger 9, 50–65.

57. Verein der Offiziere, Das. Kgl. Preußische (Westfälische) Jäger-Battalion Nr. 7 (Feldbattalion) im Weltkrieg 1914–1918 (Oldenburg: Stalling. 1929) 18–26.

58. Lombard, Face à l'invasion, 140.

59. Lombard, Face à l'invasion, 141–5.

60. Kabisch, Lüttich, 93.

61. Jäger 7, 21.

62. Normand, Liège, Namur, 32–3.

63. De Schrÿver, Liège, 197–8.

64. Lombard, Chocs de Feu dans la Nuit, 150.

65. Kabisch, Lüttich, 163.

66. De Schrÿver, Liège, 199–200.

67. De Schrÿver says the Germans drew the entire Belgian company forward by waving a white flag and then opened fire. De Schrÿver, Liège, 196.

68. IR 90, 42; IR 89, 125 (25 per cent of 500 casualties); Jäger 9, 3; Jäger 7, perhaps 10.

69. Lombard, Face à l'invasion, 97–8.

70. Rinck von Baldenstein et al., Das Infanterie-Regiment Freiherr von Sparr (3. Westfälisches) Nr. 16 im Weltkrieg 1914–18 (Oldenburg: Stalling, 1927) 18–19.

71. Normand, Liège, Namur, 34.
72. Lombard, Chocs de Feu dans la Nuit, 45–7.
73. L. Lombard, Chocs de Feu dans la Nuit, 13–47.
74. Maillard, IR 53, 36–44.
75. Offiziers-Verein, FAR 43, 29–31.
76. This was not an assault on Barchon as described in the Reichsarchiv official history.
77. Lombard, Chocs de Feu dans la Nuit, 16.
78. Normand, Liège, Namur, 28–9.
79. De Schrÿver, Liège, 169–74.
80. Bieberstein, Lüttich-Namur, 30–1.
81. Lombard says this was a friendly-fire incident; Chocs de Feu dans la Nuit, 24.
82. Firing was conducted in Germany under the control of squad and platoon leaders.
83. Lombard, Chocs de Feu dans la Nuit, 27.
84. Normand, Liège, Namur, 31–2.
85. De Schrÿver, Liège, 177–8.
86. Lombard, Sous les Ouragans d'Acier, 27–8.

4

14 Brigade Breakthrough

The German 14 Brigade moved from Herve at 0245, 5 August. As the last combat elements of IR 27, III/ 27 and the MG company, left Herve, they took fire from the town, which led to confused street fighting. It was not possible to re-establish order until daylight. At 0500, IR 27 reached Micheroux and sent 4/ 27 to Ayeneux to make contact with 11 Brigade.[1] As it approached the town it was taken for an enemy unit by 11 Brigade artillery. Three shells landed in the march column, killing an officer and thirteen EM, with the company commander, another officer and nineteen EM WIA. The company scattered and had sixteen MIA; the remnants were led by the first sergeant back to the regiment. During the afternoon the regiment continually took fire from Fort Fléron and had to move the bivouac to an orchard east of Micheroux. It would appear that Fléron had got lucky: the IR 165 history said that the fort was firing at random. IR 27 took fire from the inhabitants of the village. Some of them were disarmed, arrested and tried by courts martial. Several MGs fired at the houses. Finally, the houses from which fire was being taken were burned down, which stopped the firing. The troops remained on the alert in a thunderstorm throughout the night.

The corps attack order arrived shortly before midnight. The 14 Brigade order said:

1. The Corps will conduct a surprise attack to take the Fortress of Liège by dawn, 6 August.
2. All 14 Brigade units will be in position to storm Liège by 0400.
3. The centre of Liège will be bombarded by Zeppelin between 0000 and 0300, 6 August.
4. Order of march:
   Assault column a) advance guard: 5/ 27, two platoons Engineer Bn 24
   b) main body: II/ 27 (-), 1/2 platoon Hussar 10, [MGK], III/ 27, platoon Engineer 24 (with ladders, ropes and hand grenades), II/ FAR 4, I/ 27.

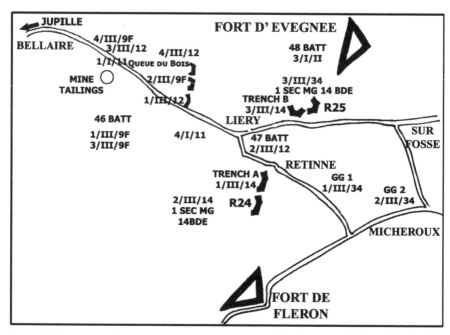

Siege of Liège, Queue du Bois, 14 Bde.

Detached on independent mission: two companies from I/ 165 and II/ 165 each.

Reserve: Colonel von Oven with IR 165 (-), Jäger 4, 1/ Hussar 10 (-).

5. Advance Guard will cross Line of Departure Queue du Bois–Bellaire at 0130.
6. Main body follows 100 metres behind.
7. Reserve follows assault column 200 metres behind.
8. During the night weapons are to be kept unloaded; resistance will be broken with the bayonet. Troops will fire only on the orders of an officer. All leaders are responsible for assuring that they have tight control of their units and maintain contact between units. White armbands. Password: 'Der Kaiser'. Field artillery fires only during periods of daylight. Foot artillery fires between 2200 5 August and 0400 6 August. All units must take their assigned objectives; do not become involved in secondary operations.
9. After Jupille has been taken, the artillery will occupy an assembly area south of Jupille; artillery will be prepared to conduct fire support against the Chartreuse. IR 165 will signal the capture of the Chartreuse with a black-white flag.
10. Field trains remain in bivouac area.

The commander of IR 27 requested permission to delay conducting the attack until what would now be called BMNT (beginning of morning nautical twilight), around

0230, to avoid conducting a night attack, the smartest recommendation made by any German commander that night. Permission was denied.

Ludendorff said that the troops were uneasy; the officers he spoke with had little confidence that the operation would succeed. This from the originator of the concept of the Liège operation![2]

General von Emmich, the corps commander, would accompany 14 Brigade, and at 0400 his CP would be on the route of the march near Jupille. Emmich was accompanied by the OHL LNOs, Captains Harbou and Brinckmann.

Belgian Position

The commander at Queue-du-Bois sector was the commander of 34 L, Colonel Lambert. He was given the mission of defending the town on the morning of 4 August, with twelve companies drawn from four different regiments, the worst possible conditions for command and control. Since then, the troops had not dug in properly due to a lack of time and equipment.

Security was provided by 2/ III/ 34 *Grande-Garde* 2 near Sur Fosse and 1/ III/ 34 at *Grande-Garde* 1 at Retinne. In the first line, 2/ III/ 14 was in Redoubt 24 with a MG section from 14 Brigade, north of which was 1/ III/ 14 in Trench A. In Redoubt 25 were 3/ III/ 34 with another 14 Brigade MG section, with 1/ III/ 14 in Trench B to its right. At the Liéry crossroads were 47 Battery and 2/ III/ 12, with 48 Battery left of Fort d'Evegnée, guarded by 3/ I/ 11, and 46 Battery, guarded by 4/ I/ 11, in an open field south of Queue-du-Bois. The III/ 12 was at Queue-du-Bois. The sector was divided into northern and southern subsectors, the HQ for the latter being at Retinne. It is evident that there was no unit cohesion above company level. The troops were alerted several times early on the night of 5–6 August and there was some isolated firing.

German Franc-tireurs

A rumour spread that German miners lived in the town and that they had been seen firing on the Belgian troops. The Belgian troops became jumpy. Just after dark there was some firing in Liéry and serious firing 'in all directions' in Queue-du-Bois. The troops there began to panic, but the officers and NCOs re-established discipline. Patrols found no trace of the enemy. De Schrÿver said, 'These cowardly and disgraceful attacks, designed to spread terror and horror in our ranks, and which were renewed again during the German attack, were all perpetuated by German coal miners who remained in Belgium and by spies who circulated with complete impunity.'[3] De Schrÿver said that at Bellaire and Jupille Germans also fired into the backs of the Belgian defenders in order to panic them.[4] Once again, the Belgian troops were not able to determine where this fire was coming from.

In other words, De Schrÿver said there were large numbers of German *franc-tireurs*. It is probable that this was friendly fire from Belgian *franc-tireurs* who didn't recognise the Belgian troops at night.

14 Brigade Advance

The IR 27 advance guard moved out from the bivouac area, a kilometre south of Micheroux, towards Sur Fosse, at 0100. First Lieutenant von Nida from IR 25 was the guide. It was pitch-dark. As soon as the advance guard, II/ 27, began to move, it took fire from Micheroux. The regimental history said that 'thanks to the outstanding training in night operations that the regiment had recently conducted, the troops remained under the control of their officers and the march went forward'.

Lombard says that the Germans wiped out a four-man Belgian patrol.[5] De Schrÿver says that the Germans had come in contact with Outposts 1 and 2 from *Grande-Garde* 2, which then withdrew not on 2/ III/ 34, but to Redoubt 25.[6] At 0200, 2/ III/ 34 heard German troops moving on its left and withdrew to the south side of Fort d'Evegnée, apparently without making contact. On outpost duty at Retinne, 1/ III/ 34 also reported being attacked. None of these three engagements are mentioned in the IR 27 history.[7]

While IR 165 assembled immediately south of Micheroux in several columns, (infantry, artillery, ammunition vehicles, combat trains) with elements already moving into the town to form march columns, it took intense fire from the houses.[8] The muzzle flashes in the pitch-dark night were easy to see. The first houses were stormed and the civilians hauled out, most of them armed. It was then necessary to clear out the next layer of houses. In the meantime the horses had bolted and there was general chaos. The order to advance with unloaded weapons had now been overtaken by events. The rattle of Belgian weapons was mixed with the resonant crack of the German infantry rifle. Actually aiming their weapons didn't seem to be a priority for the Belgians, who apparently laid more emphasis on volume of fire than accuracy. Captured weapons went from excellent rifles recently manufactured in Liège to ones that were positively ancient. IR 165 losses were relatively light.

Lombard would have us believe that 14 Brigade did not take fire from civilians in Micheroux, rather this was wild firing by Belgian troops at Liéry which flew over the houses and landed in the 14 Brigade units behind Micheroux.[9] This interpretation is directly contradicted by all three German infantry unit histories, which make it clear that the firing from Micheroux preceded the contact at Liéry. Micheroux is about a kilometre from Liéry. Any rounds that were fired so high that they would clear the houses of Micheroux would continue to sail off to the maximum range of the weapon – about 2km – and not drop immediately onto IR 165.

Ludendorff pointed out that the forts had not fired, 'which was a wonder'. Lombard said that the telephone lines had been cut and the observation posts withdrawn, so that Evegnée and Fléron were reduced to firing canister around the forts at random.[10] Since the Germans had not sent any patrols into this area, how the telephone lines had been cut and why the OPs had been withdrawn is unexplained.

Liéry

The Belgian position at Liéry had a fatal flaw: neither Redoubt 25 north of the road nor Redoubt 24 to the south of it could put fire on the Liéry road. Redoubt 25 had its field of fire blocked by houses; Lombard speculates that the position was chosen before the houses were built.[11] A trench was added to the right of Redoubt 25 which nevertheless failed to correct this deficiency. In Liéry, 2/ III/ 12 deployed a platoon directly north of Queue-du-Bois road, one 100m north of the road, and a platoon at two farm buildings 150m north of the Liéry crossroad.

There was apparently a road barricade at Sur Fosse, which the Germans quickly cleared. Nevertheless, local security in Liéry was completely inadequate – a single sentry on standing guard watch 40m to the front of the battery. The Germans could approach unhindered immediately in front of the two 7.5cm field guns of 47 Battery stationed directly at the Liéry crossroad. Lombard says that the sentry was surprised to see an automobile slowly approach his guard mount. He challenged it three times, at which point it turned around and returned in the direction of Sur Fosse. He walked back to the battery position and reported this occurrence to the battery commander, who told him that after three challenges he should have opened fire. It is clear that Belgian peacetime tactical training in night local security was in need of considerable improvement. He returned to his post and in a quarter-hour the vehicle returned and one of the occupants shot the sentry dead with a pistol.[12] Lombard does not say who related this incredible story.

Be this as it may, there was no longer a sentry to the front. Lombard says that the gunners could hear men approaching, which had to be military because they were marching in step. It was felt that these were unlikely to be German; firing had been heard to the front, but not much. In any case the battery had not been informed of the location of the other Belgian defensive positions. When the advancing troops were 40m to the front the battery commander yelled out 'Halt, or I fire!' which was met with rifle fire which hit three men who were not behind the gun shield, killing one. Only at this point did the battery commander order the guns loaded! The lieutenant leading the two-gun section issued another challenge, which resulted in further gunfire. He issued another challenge, fired his pistol, and took more return fire. He then commanded 'Three rounds rapid fire': the target was at 30m range, the first of thirty rounds that each gun would fire. It was 0100 (B).

The IR 27 advance guard deployed but could not advance and took heavy casualties. Both the brigade commander, Wussow, and the IR 27 commander, were apparently still mounted on their horses, with the forward elements. The umpires in peacetime training would never allow such non-tactical behaviour. Both were immediately killed. At the same time, the IR 27 history says that the inhabitants of the town began a murderous fire on all sides from houses, ditches and gardens, and the units became intermixed. Command and control was nearly impossible in the winding streets and maze of farms, gardens and bushes, the pitch-dark night and the noise of small-arms and artillery fire. De Schrÿver says that the Germans jumped into the roadside ditch and replied with 'extremely violent' rifle and MG fire.

The two OHL Liaison Officers (LNOs), Captains Brinckmann and Harbou, moved forward and entered the village, until they were 300m from the Belgian cannon, which Brinckmann said were located near walls and hedges. Brinckmann said that his first thought was to report to General von Emmich, but immediately reproached himself for merely wanting to get out of the line of fire. Brinckmann saw that the troops around him wouldn't advance. He recognised that the solution to this tactical problem was a double envelopment of the guns: he would take a group through the meadows and hedges to the left, Harbou to the right.

Harbou's group ran into the 2/ III/ 12 platoon in the two farmhouses, each enclosed by a wall, whose fire forced Harbou to swing right around them. Harbou says he then encountered three more Belgian platoons in a trench: in fact, he was still opposed by only one Belgian platoon. Harbou was steadily reinforced as other groups from Jäger 4 and IR 27 moved forward on their own initiative.

The platoon in the farmhouses was under serious pressure. The 2/ III/ 12 commander believed it was 'encircled', and attempted to relieve it, but was stopped by wire fences and hedges. The subsector commander sent an order to the platoon to retire to Queue-du-Bois, but it never arrived. The Belgians took rifle fire from German troops in houses and behind walls. De Schrÿver says that the Germans brought an MG up to the second floor of a house and swept the Belgian trenches with it, aided by the illumination of German searchlights; the Germans, however, did not have any searchlights, so this must have been illumination from d'Evegnée.

In Liéry, the German fire was causing serious casualties, while unwounded men moved to the rear under the pretence of evacuating the wounded. By 0200, 2/ III/ 12 had been reduced to forty men. The leader of the platoon at the two farms was wounded for the third time and rendered unconscious. His men thought him dead and the platoon dissolved and fled to the rear. This exposed the left flank of 2/ III/ 12, whose remnants withdrew.

Harbou said that one of the Belgian platoons withdrew to the north. The other two fell back to Queue-du-Bois, along with the platoon in the two houses. At the crossroads the Belgians brought a third gun into position to fire on Harbou's men, but took German fire, which killed a Belgian captain.

The subsector commander had asked the sector commander for reinforcements, but was told none were available. The 2/ III/ 12 commander moved with eight men, which he thought were all that remained, to Queue-du-Bois, where the sector commander told him that he could not move 1/ III/ 12 forward and that the 2/ III/ 12 commander was to return to Liéry. Halfway back, accompanied by a corporal as point man and two soldiers, the 2/ III/ 12 commander met the subsector commander moving back to Queue-du-Bois, who told him that the Germans were overrunning the position. The point man then reported that the Germans had captured 47 Battery. The fight for Liéry had lasted two hours.

The Belgian sector commander had displayed a stunning lack of tactical ability. He had five line companies (the battalion of fortress infantry was of no use) which he could have committed to Liéry. Had he done so, he almost surely would have stopped the 14 Brigade attack, at least until Ludendorff brought up the German howitzers.

Jäger 4 had immediately and independently begun a double envelopment of the Belgian Liéry position, 3/ Jäger 4 moving through the gardens, farms and hedges north of the road, 4/ Jäger 4 south of it. Five squads of 4/ Jäger 4 under the company commander, Captain von Hausse, along with Brinckmann, encountered no opposition at all, reached a road behind the Belgian guns, took the munitions wagons and horse teams and attacked the artillery's right flank while more German infantry attacked frontally. Meanwhile Harbou attacked from the north and captured the two Belgian guns at the crossroads, the first guns taken by the German Army. Several Belgian officers and 100 men retreated straight into the arms of 3/ Jäger 4 and were captured, including the artillery section and battery commanders. The Jäger then took heavy fire from the houses, returned the fire and cleared several houses.[13]

As II/ FAR 4 approached Retinne, the horses of the lead team were shot, blocking the road and causing a break in the column. The I/ 27 pushed past the artillery. Ludendorff was with General von Emmich at the back of the column. He went forward into Retinne and found that the halt was 'unnecessary, in fact, it was the result of an evaluation of the situation that was completely incorrect'. Given the hasty instructions the officers had received in the middle of the night, and the lack of reconnaissance and preparation, this was hardly a surprising state of affairs. Contact with the forward elements lost, Ludendorff, who admitted he had no command authority, put himself at the head of a unit (probably I/ 27) and led it out the wrong side of Retinne, took fire and had to retreat, which he found 'painful'. Ludendorff passed Wussow's body, which he said had been hit by canister fire.

The IR 165 had finally been able to begin movement, continually taking fire from hedges along the road. Shortly before Retinne, the regiment had to pass a block of houses on the rail line and once again took very heavy fire which this time brought more serious casualties. Contact with IR 27 was lost. The battle dissolved into numerous small-unit fights. The IR 165 historians said: 'It stands to reason that we were not gentle when we hauled out of houses civilians who had acted as combatants.'

Redoubt 25

Redoubt 25 was about 700m north-east of Liéry, held by the 3/ III/ 34 under Major Jean Simonis, with 3/ III/ 14 in Trench B to the right. It was protected by two belts of barbed wire, where a sentry was posted.[14] First, firing was heard at Retinne, then troops in Trench B heard the noise of movement on the Liéry road and opened blind fire. Heavy firing was then heard at Liéry, followed by Belgian fire from Liéry, which eventually forced the abandonment of Trench B. The sentry reported a column marching towards the redoubt on the road from Sur Fosse. When it reached the level of the barbed wire obstacle the Belgians opened fire. The Belgians only had 120 rounds per man and quickly began to run out of ammunition.

2/ Jäger 4 moved from Sur Fosse on the road leading north from Liéry and ran straight into Redoubt 25.[15] The Jäger were outnumbered nearly three to one, but the Belgians were convinced the Jäger were turning both flanks and getting into the Redoubt 25 rear. Lombard thought that the Redoubt 25 was being attacked by a battalion of IR 165, reinforced with MGs. Two Belgian MGs stationed in an orchard to the left of Redoubt 25 opened fire, drawing German counterfire.

The Belgian account of the fight now takes some strange turns. Both Lombard and De Schrÿver say that Redoubt 25 was illuminated by three searchlights located 100m away; Belgian fire put two of them out. Then three or four artillery pieces opened fire at the same range. To the left the fire passed 50cm too high, but on the right it hit the top of the parapet. The problem arises in that the Germans didn't have any searchlights and the FAR 4 regimental history does not mention any of its guns engaged in this direction. The only possible explanation is that this was friendly fire from Fort d'Evegnée.

After a long firefight, 2/ Jäger 4 sent a member of parliament to demand that the Belgians surrender; Major Simonis refused, but asked for ten minutes to consult with his officers, who told him that most of their troops were out of ammunition: a few had 5–10 rounds left. Simonis therefore proposed to the 2/ Jäger commander that he would withdraw if the Jäger would not advance for fifteen minutes: the Jäger officer agreed. It is unusual that Simonis made no mention of the Jäger shako.[16]

Back in Retinne, a sergeant from IR 27 jumped out of the bushes onto the road and asked the Jäger 4 MG Company for help. The MGs moved to the north of the Liéry road, west of Redoubt 25. The terrain rose gently to the west covered with orchards and cut up by thick hedges. After six minutes of movement, Simonis' two companies ran straight into MGK/ Jäger 4, which knew nothing of his deal with 2/ Jäger 4, and pinned the Belgians down behind a house with heavy MG fire.

Simonis, together with a bugler, advanced towards the Jäger MG, which ceased fire. Simonis then returned to his troops and found them surrounded by German troops and made prisoner. Again, Simonis doesn't mention shakoes. Simonis was outraged and explained to the Jäger MGK officers that he had just made a deal with another German officer for fifteen minutes' safe passage. There was no possibility that the MGK officers could give credence to such a story, and if they did they would have found themselves fighting these two Belgian companies in ten minutes.

Queue-du-Bois[17]

Queue-du-Bois was an industrial town of 1,900 inhabitants, dominated by a hill of mine tailings called Quatre-Jean. The broad road, which descended west to the town of Bellaire, was lined by modest brick houses. From Bellaire the road descended rapidly to Jupille.

At 2400, Colonel Lambert, at his HQ on the slag heap, was informed that *Grande-Garde 2* had been attacked. Only at this point did he deploy his troops to their positions. At 0100, cannon fire was heard at Liéry.

The countryside was covered with meadows and orchards separated by hedges, which provided the Germans with concealed avenues of approach. The Germans made contact with the Belgian defenders north of the town, then at 0230 (B) with 1/ III/ 12 L, which occupied an isolated position at the east edge of the town, north of the road.

At about 0300 (B) the Germans attacked almost simultaneously against the east edge of Queue-du-Bois as well as the north-east and west sides. The initial German fire from a nearby house killed the commander of 1/ III/ 12. A platoon of 4/ III/ 12 quickly took serious casualties from Germans firing from the second floor of a house. German infantry also attacked 1/ I/ 11 on the Saint-Jean slag heap.

Lombard also said that bullets ricocheting off the walls led the Belgian troops to think that they were taking fire from the 'German miners' in houses to their rear, and the Belgian troops panicked and began firing at windows where they supposed the fire had originated. De Schrÿver said that this attack was co-ordinated with fire from windows in houses in the interior of the town, with many of the Belgians fleeing in disorder from the west side of the town all the way to Bellaire.[18]

De Schrÿver mentions several incidents where the Belgian troops took fire in the rear from 'German miners' and 'German spies', even when there was no other firing going on, which invalidates Lombard's 'ricochet' explanation. Once again, it is much more likely that this was friendly fire from Belgian *franc-tireurs* who did not recognise the Belgian troops because of poor visibility. The IR 165 historian said that the civilians resisted here, but 'we had gotten a lot better at street fighting'. In Queue-du-Bois, both sides were being fired on by civilians.

Brinckmann says that the sky had begun to lighten and that they were taking fire from all the houses, which stopped further forward movement. A platoon of the IR 27 MG Company went into action and at 0330 (G) Ludendorff called forward two howitzers of II/ FAR 4, and then a third gun.[19] The artillery platoon leader, Lieutenant Neide, said that his guns had moved through Micheroux under fire, then across a field to Liéry, where they again took fire, to Queue-du-Bois. There he unlimbered his guns, manhandled them forward and engaged each house at ranges of twenty to thirty paces. All three howitzers opened rapid fire and the effect was 'terrible'. The III/ 12 battalion commander and a lieutenant were killed, a major wounded. At about the same time the Belgian 46 and 48 Batteries pulled out on their own initiative. Finally Neide put a shell in a house full of Belgian infantry (2/ III/ 9 F) who fled 'in masses', pulling the troops on the west side of Queue-du-Bois with them, pushed along by howitzer shells and rifle fire, particularly into their left flank. Lieutenant Kybitz of Jäger 4 described the attack:

> I saw an unlimbered gun and ammunition wagon being pushed forward behind the armoured shields by about 20 men, infantry, Jäger and artillery. Only one man walked in the open between the two, an older, tall officer in a coat and field cap, and I noticed by the red braid on his belt and coat that he was a general officer. In his right hand he carried a rifle with fixed bayonet. He did not yell commands, but his voice was calming and fatherly 'Forwards, always forwards, children! Come along, don't let me go alone!' The enemy rounds hit the armoured shields like a drum and hammered off the street. The general would point at a house from which we were taking fire and command 'Fire!' The walls and roof would collapse, smoke would boil up and then – silence. The gun would move forward 50 metres until the enemy fire rose again. Now, I said, he is going to be hit. But it didn't happen. He turned halfway around and commanded 'Fire!'

Ludendorff was with the howitzers the entire time and told Lieutenant Neide that without his guns 14 Brigade never would have made it through the town. By 0540 (B) Queue-du-Bois was in German hands.

The Jäger MGK continued the march from north of Liéry to the north of Queue-du-Bois accompanied by half of 2/ Jäger 4, through hedges and wire fences. Belgian fire was intense, and the Jäger expected heavy casualties, but fortunately the Belgians fired too high. Several MG men were wounded, but others took their places. North of Bellaire the MG went into position 150m from the line of Belgian infantry, which was mown down. Distinguishing friend from enemy was difficult, so German troops shouted the password, 'Der Kaiser', used horn signals and fired flares. The MG continued forward with elements of IR 27, pursuing the Belgians through a wood, then uphill on a narrow path to a group of houses, which were taken. A stray platoon of hussars rode past. Beyond Bellaire the MG company reached high ground where it could orient itself. The MG company had taken 600 Belgian POW and became a rallying point for disoriented German infantry and even medical officers. The MG continued their advance until, a considerable time later, they rejoined the battalion at Jupille.

Bellaire

It was 0530 (B) and daylight and the mass of the Belgian troops in the sector retreated in disorder through Bellaire:[20] the Germans reported that the road to Bellaire was strewn with Belgian packs and weapons. The III/ 9 F (-), which had not been seriously engaged, deployed on the west side of Bellaire to try to stop the Germans. Their morale was immediately shaken by German howitzer fire that Lombard said 'was so precise that it paralysed the defenders'. To this was added MG fire from a house. III/ 9 F 'believed itself to be isolated and not seeing any reinforcements' fell back to Jupille, where it was 'reconstituted'.

The II/ 32 L was diverted from Sart-Tilman to Bellaire. At 0730 the advance guard company entered Bellaire and took fire from the houses; the company was forced to move in two files on each side of the road, firing at the windows on the opposite side, but could not suppress the fire. The company commander said that a bugler was killed by a grenade thrown out of a partially opened door. The Belgians were then stopped by heavy small-arms, MG and howitzer fire. Once again, the troops had the impression that they were being enveloped on both flanks. Two or three howitzer shells then hit the lead company, which fell back to Jupille. By 0800 the elements of the battalion that had deployed to the north of the advance guard company were also forced to withdraw, followed by the stragglers from Bellaire. A Belgian major commanding a detachment said that in Jupille his men took fire from German miners. He stopped his troops and threatened to fire at any house where the windows were open, at which point the fire stopped. At 0930 the troops at Jupille received the order for the general withdrawal of 3 DA.

Lombard said that Queue-du-Bois was the principal redoubt between Forts Fléron and Evegnée. When the Germans took Queue-du-Bois, they had both penetrated between the forts and were in a dead zone that the forts' fire could not reach. Leman had already committed all his reserves to Sart-Tilman. When Leman heard that the Germans were at Queue-du-Bois, he immediately ordered the troops in this sector to withdraw. This threatened the rear of the Belgian troops at Sart-Tilman, who would be forced to withdraw also.

At 1100, IR 27 continued the attack along the road to Jupille; the Belgians withdrew to Liège without offering much resistance. At 1400, IR 27 reached the south side of Jupille and bivouacked.

Patrols were sent out to find German troops but didn't, encountering resistance at Wandre and Beyne-Heusay (where 27 and 11 Brigades should have been), but finding the route to the east end of Liège and the Meuse free. It became clear that 14 Brigade was the only one to establish itself behind the Belgian fortress line. During the afternoon a white flag was seen over Liège. General von Emmich sent a parliamentarian to demand the city surrender, under pain of bombardment by artillery. The military commandant of Liège was no longer in the city, and the mayor refused to surrender, saying that the white flag was a mistake. In fact, the Citadel commandant had 'gone mad' and had to be arrested. Emmich ordered 14 Brigade to take up a position on the high ground south of Jupille to Chênée, facing the town, IR 27 on the right, IR 165 on the left. The II/ FAR 4 fired on the citadel at ten-minute intervals, all that was possible given the quantity of shells available. The III/ 165 was instructed to set up the Chartreuse as a POW camp for the 1,500 prisoners the brigade had taken. The city was completely lit, especially the rail station, and there was lively rail traffic; the locals said that two French divisions had arrived, which was not out of the realm of possibility. At 2200, 2 and 3/ Jäger 4 were sent forward to occupy four of the bridges over the Meuse and Ourthe, where they arrived at 0100, 7 August. They did not encounter any resistance, but the brigade also lost contact with them.

Casualties

IR 27 lost 8 OFF and 40 EM KIA (plus one died of wounds – DOW), 11 OFF and 187 EM WIA, 246 total. On the morning of 6 August there were 97 EM MIA. The regimental historian said that most of the casualties were due to artillery fire; the Belgian infantryman was not a good shot, usually firing too high.

IR 165 lost 1 OFF and 34 EM KIA, an OFF DOW, 5 OFF and 89 EM WIA, 377 total.

The Jäger 4 took 18 KIA. Total German casualties in this sector were approximately 103 KIA, an estimated 471 total.

Lombard said that the Belgians in this sector lost 76 KIA: 22 at Retinne, 40 at Liéry and Queue-du-Bois, 7 at Bellaire and 7 at Jupille. There are usually 3–4 WIA for every KIA, so conservatively (at 3 WIA per KIA) 228 WIA, 304 total. The point of contention was the number of POW: Major Simonis says 400–500 Belgian POW. The IR 165, which guarded the prisoners, says there were 1,500 Belgian POW in the Chartreuse.

At the most conservative estimate (76 KIA, 228 WIA, 400 POW), the Belgians in this sector lost 704 casualties. The Germans lost approximately 471. By this measure Belgian casualties were about 50 per cent higher than the German. Given that the Germans say they had 1,500 Belgian POW, the more likely figure is 1,804 Belgian casualties to 471 German, nearly 4:1.

Lombard said that there were 200 dead Belgian civilians in this sector, from Battice and Herve to Retinne, men women and children 'exterminated' by German troops.[21] This leads to the question as to why there were any Belgian civilians in the sector at all. The Belgian defence was based on holding Retinne and Queue-du-Bois, but the civilians had not been evacuated.

Centre: 11 Brigade

At 0315 on 5 August, 11 Brigade moved out with the mission of occupying a security line south from Ayeneux, push back the Belgian security outposts and conduct reconnaissance for the attack to penetrate between Fort de Fléron and Fort de Chaudefontaine. Since the area west of Olne was visible from the line of forts 5–7km to the front, II/ FAR 39 went into battery west of Olne, while IR 20 deployed on the left of the Olnye–St Hadelin road, IR 35 on the right

The IR 20 deployed I and II/ 20 on the first line, behind an open-order skirmisher line, III/ 20 following echeloned left.[22] The objective was the village and castle of Forêt. The regiment had to pass over steep slopes, ravines, hedges and, above all, barbed-wire fences, which took considerable time and energy. Enemy infantry was visible in the far distance, and at 0700 the enemy artillery opened fire, without doing any damage or having any effect on the troops. The German artillery conducted a counter-battery duel while displacing forward. The IR 20 attacked Forêt, which was defended by border security troops and *Garde Civique* and at 1000 took the town. The houses were searched and any armed civilians were shot. The fire from Chaudefontaine was becoming stronger, so IR 20 took cover in a ravine south of the castle park and fed lunch from the field kitchens. At 1400, I/ 20 was ordered to advance a short distance; a shell hit the column resulting in six KIA and fourteen WIA, including the battalion commander. At 2000, 3 and 4/ 20 were ordered to demonstrate against Fort Chaudefontaine. Total losses for IR 20 on 5 August were 11 KIA, 32 WIA, 16 MIA.

The IR 35 advanced with I/ 35 towards Ayeneux, followed by II on the right, III on the left, keeping contact with IR 20.[23] Movement was sometimes in waves of skirmishers, sometimes in column according to the terrain, 'just like at the training area at Jüterbog'. Between 1000 and 1100, I and II/ 35 reached Ayeneux, without contact, and continued the march to St Hadelin. Meanwhile III was involved in house-to-house fighting against armed civilians. Brand-new Belgian uniforms and pieces of equipment were found in the village. The IR 35 moved to the brigade assembly area at St Hadelin, where the troops rested on the streets, in gardens and the larger farm buildings. The surrounding buildings were evacuated and hostages taken. At 2200 IR 20 arrived.

At 1700 the brigade commander assembled the officers to discuss the coming night's operation. Each battalion of IR 35 sent out an officer's patrol to reconnoitre

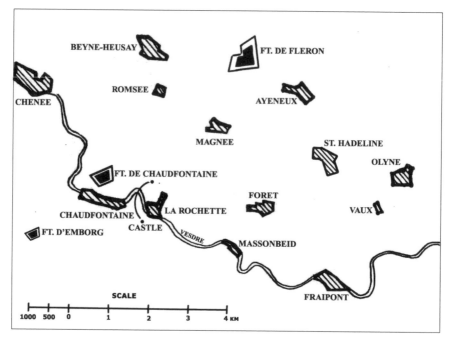

Siege of Liège 11 Bde (1).

the enemy position on the high ground between Chaudefontaine and Fléron; the trenches and firing ports in the hedges were easily visible. All three took lively rifle fire and one patrol leader was killed.

At 2350 the brigade moved out, first the point element, 100m behind that 5/ 35, then 6/35, 50m behind a squad of engineers with hand grenades, 50m separation, then 7 and 8/ 35, followed 100m behind by 9 and 10/ 35, I/ 35, IR 20 and Jäger 3. This was the wrong formation, since the Jäger should have been leading. The 11 Brigade commander was obviously unfamiliar with the capabilities of Jäger battalions.

The objective was the town of Magnée. As a guide, the General Staff had attached an officer from FAR 4. He lead them down a footpath and then cross-country over a meadow. The brigade was soon in single file; there were halts in movement, then the guide lost his orientation, backtracked, changed direction and returned to the foot-path. Since these manoeuvres were executed soundlessly and in the dark, the result was disorder and an intermixing of the units. Finally, II/ 35 resumed the lead, now followed by IR 20.

The regimental command group with six companies, I/ 35 and 9 and 10/ 35, were now at the end of the column, became separated from the brigade and had to climb the steep sides of a quarry and then back out of it to the quarry entrance. The vehicles – artillery, MGs and horses – had taken the road to Magnée, and near dawn patrols reported that this column was visible on the road only 500m away; the six companies joined the end of the vehicle column. The brigade reassembled east of Magnée.

In order to cover the 11 Brigade night attack, 3 and 4/ IR 20 were to demonstrate against Chaudefontaine. They marched off at 2000 from St Hadelin towards Chaudefontaine. At 0115 they encountered barricades which they thought were defended by the inhabitants; in fact, it was the *Grande-Garde* held by 3/ II/ 34. The Belgians withdrew while Germans backed off to try another avenue of approach. They took fire in a village and had to shoot their way through. They missed the turn they wanted to take towards Forêt and re-entered St Hadelin, where they again took fire from the inhabitants and had to shoot their way out. The troops were now exhausted and the companies bivouacked at a farm south of St Hadelin, rejoining the regiment at Magnée late the next morning. The Belgians were sure that the two companies had been guided by German spies and workers who had been in place for years and knew the country like the backs of their hands.[24]

The towns from Magnée to Romsée to Beyne-Heusay rest on a low, gently rolling ridge. The Chaudefontaine – Fléron sector, under the 14 Brigade commander, a major general, was divided in half, each under a major, with the southern half centred on Chaudefontaine and a northern sector centred on Romsée. From Fort Chaudefontaine north to Romsée, there were Trenches 8, 9, (1/ III/ 14) and 10, 11 (3/ I/ 14 F). Trench Number 12 was 400m north of the church, held by 2/ IV/ 14. There was a barricade 400m to the south of the town held by elements of 3/ I/ 14 F. Redoubt 23 on the Belgian left was held by 1/ 4/ 14. The redoubt was poorly sited and prepared. There was also Battery 60 as well as a number of obsolete artillery batteries that never fired. The placement of the Belgian MG was mystifying: instead of being located on the forward positions they were placed far to the rear, and never got into action.

De Schrÿver says that at 0130, 3/ IV/ 14, guarding the Fléron OP east of Magnée, was engaged with 11 Brigade, which resulted in house-to-house fighting in the town and heavy German losses. Lombard acknowledging that Fléron shelled the town.[25] The artillery at Fléron then supposedly shelled the column on the road to Romsée. Neither the IR 20 nor the IR 35 histories, which are quite detailed, mention any of this. At 0230 a MG section from Belgian 9 Brigade, which had recently occupied a position 300m south-east of the Romsée church tower, came under fire from houses in the village, which were searched to no result. De Schrÿver says that this was a frequent tactic practised by German spies and miners to spread panic by firing at Belgian troops from behind. A far more likely explanation was that the movement of the 9 Brigade MG into the 14 Brigade sector had been poorly co-ordinated and the MG took friendly fire.

The Belgian and German accounts of the fight do not agree. The IR 35 and IR 20 histories say that the engagement began at 0500 (0400 B), the Belgians at 0130 (0230 G). In the German accounts the fight lasted a little longer than an hour: in the Belgian accounts five and a half hours. Since the Germans had got lost and wandered around all night, the German time-line is the more plausible.

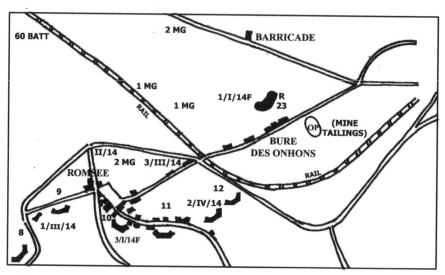

11 Bde/Romsée

The point element was approaching Romsée while the advance guard had just cleared Magnée, when both came under heavy fire from Romsée. The commanders of IR 20 and II/ 35, as well as two IR 35 captains, were killed.[26] In addition to getting himself killed, the II/ 35 commander had allowed his battalion to enter a sunken road lined with houses and hedges, where it provided a fine target while being unable to disperse or deploy. A platoon of six ran forward with 5/ 35 on the road in a mass. The IR 35 historian said:

> The troops in the brigade main body were tired and hungry and strung out along the road. When they took fire from Romsée, as well as from numerous snipers, squads and platoons scattered in all directions. Visibility was 50 to 100 metres, restricted by houses, fruit trees, hedges and fences, and the brigade became completely confused. To restore order, the brigade commander instructed 'General Halt' sounded [the signal to end a peacetime exercise – TZ]. After this was repeated several times, not only did the Germans cease firing, the Belgians did, too!

The Belgians had built a barricade across the road with tables, chairs, benches, window shutters and an iron garden gate, defended by ten men under a corporal, who held their improvised position for three hours, reinforced by some men from 3/ I/ 14.

In Trench 12, 400m east of Romsée, was 2/ IV/ 14, and they were involved in terrific fight which became hand-to-hand combat. The 2/ III/ 14 commander was killed, the company demoralised and only twenty men escaped to join 3/ IV/ 14. The Germans began to infiltrate in twos and threes along the rail line and slag heaps to the north of Romsée. The Germans were soon engaging both the barricade and Redoubt 23.

According to both German and Belgian accounts, it was now daylight. The German
11 Brigade commander received a report that there was a white flag in Romsée and
sent Lieutenant d'Heureuse forward to tell the Belgians to surrender. The Belgian
leader was not so minded, and replied that the white flag was a Red Cross flag and
that the German troops had been waving handkerchiefs. Events then unrolled as if it
were an eighteenth-century battlefield. After discussion back and forth thirty-minute
ceasefire was arranged for the Belgians to recover the German wounded, two OFF
and thirty EM. Three German lieutenants and twenty-nine EM that had penetrated
to the Belgian position were now presented with the alternative of surrender or
renewing the fight. Lieutenant Rittershaus said:

> Because of the negotiations, we were now completely without cover in front of
> the Belgian barricade. We three officers, after consulting with Lt. d'Heureuse,
> decided to surrender, thinking that the other attack brigades had already entered
> Liège or were about to do so, and we would be freed in a matter of hours. The
> Belgian commander shared our opinion, telling Lt. Zelter 'Gentlemen, keep
> your swords; in a few hours we are going to be your prisoners!'

During the ceasefire the Germans reorganised their units and artillery was brought
forward. When it terminated, the howitzer section opened fire on the town and the
barricade; a platoon of 6/ FAR 39 moved forward to fire close support, destroyed the
barricade, blowing away benches, chairs and tables as though they had been struck by
a hurricane, and scored multiple direct hits on the surrounding houses.[27] The Belgians
said that Trenches 8, 9, 10, and 11 came under especially effective fire. The Belgian
commander found the artillery fire too hot and ordered a withdrawal, back to the
houses of Romsée. Fléron's OP at Magnée had fallen back to the slag heap at Bure
des Onhons, where they were surprised by the Germans, with two KIA and two
WIA. Further German advance was stopped by Redoubt 23.

The 11 Brigade troops were so tired that the brigade commander ordered them back
to Magnée to rest and be fed. Ironically, the Belgians were also withdrawing by individual companies. At 1100 (G) the 11 Brigade advance was resumed towards Romsée.
Howitzers from 4/ 39 and 6/ 39 were attached by individual guns to infantry platoons and companies to provide fire support at point-blank range. In conjunction with
long-range support from 5/ 39 the town was taken. The IR 35 history says that every
house had to be stormed and fire from Fléron and Chaudefontaine avoided. In fact,
the Belgians had left the town two hours previously and the Belgian positions were
probably empty save for stragglers. Withdrawing to the west side of the Meuse, 2/ II/ 34
could not gain admittance to the citadel, and was fired on by German Jäger, panicked
and dissolved. The company in Trench 15 on the main road was cut off and captured.[28]

At this point, 11 Brigade had broken through and was behind the line of forts. But
the 11 Brigade troops had to manoeuvre to avoid the artillery fire from Fléron and

Chaudefontaine, and although by 1400 I/ 35 had already entered Beyne-Heusay, the troops were exhausted and the brigade had before it the built-up area east of Liège. The brigade commander therefore withdrew the brigade to the west of Magnée. At 1800, artillery fire from Fort Fléron forced the brigade to move to a ravine south-east of Magnée. The brigade commander and staff and the artillery couldn't follow the troops cross-country and bivouacked at a small town practically next door to Fort Fléron. the 5 and 7/ 20, with the supply vehicles and field kitchens, got separated from the regiment and did not rejoin it until 11 August, in Liège. The commander of IR 35, who was the senior officer actually with the two infantry regiments, was determined to renew the breakthrough attempt the following morning.

The 11 Brigade commander's argument that he had to withdraw because the troops were tired does not hold water. As in the 27 Brigade, the decisive factor was the 11 Brigade commander's lack of aggressiveness and loss of nerve. Had he continued the advance, at the least he would have moved his troops out of the fire fan of the fortress guns. By withdrawing, he only ensured that they would have to pass between the forts again and be shelled for the rest of the day. Had the 11 Brigade commander any willingness to take risks, he would have entered Liège that afternoon.

The IR 35 lost three OFF and thirty-two EM KIA, thirty-one EM WIA, three OFF and twenty-one EM MIA (POW). During the entire Liège operation IR 35 suffered a total of five OFF (a major, threecaptains and a first lieutenant) and forty-eight EM KIA, 187 WIA, forty MIA and probably KIA.

The IR 20 lost two OFF and twenty-one EM KIA, including the regimental commander and the first sergeant of 11/ 20, three OFF and fifty-seven EM WIA, including the regimental adjutant. Jäger 3 had four WIA.

Belgian Command Chaos

Leman remained fixated on Sart-Tilman. At 0320 Leman ordered the 14 Brigade commander to send I/ 12 to Sart-Tilman. At 0300 Leman ordered the 12 Brigade commander to send 'all available troops' to Sart-Tilman. He sent II/ 32, 1 and 4/ III/ 32 and the artillery of 12 Brigade. For some reason these troops moved out slowly and arrived at the foot of the Sart-Tilman plateau just in time to meet I/ 12 coming down the hill, and never reached Sart-Tilman. The 12 Brigade commander was left with three companies of II/ 32. At 0345 the 14 Brigade commander learned that III/ 9, II/ 29 and III/ 29, (9 Brigade) which had been in reserve directly to the 14 Brigade rear, had been ordered to Sart-Tilman at 0230.

By 0300 the entire Belgian situation appeared grim. In the south, the Germans had reached the high ground above the Meuse, while in the north they had penetrated between Pontisse and Liers. They were exerting pressure all along the front on the east side of the Meuse, and had made 'notable progress' at Queue-du-Bois.[29] 'The most pessimistic reports continually arrived at the sector HQ, spread who knows how.' Belgian morale, already shaken by fatigue and the effect of the night battle, was collapsing.

Belgian command and control began to unravel. At 0405 the 14 Brigade commander personally received a telephone order to retreat, an order that Leman and his staff deny having given. De Schrÿver saw German spies at work. In fact, the Belgian commanders thought they were losing the battle. At 0450 the 14 Brigade commander ordered a 'methodical' withdrawal. This order never reached the two subsector commanders, but they pulled back anyway. Instead of stopping at the '3rd position' on the east edge of Liège, they moved over the Meuse to the centre of the city. The 14 Brigade commander then began to have second thoughts about the withdrawal order he had just issued, and called Leman's HQ, which didn't answer. By this time Jäger 7 had chased Leman out of his HQ, and as De Schrÿver ruefully noted, no one had the wit to leave a stay-behind party to answer the phone. The Jäger 7 attack added to wild rumours circulating through the Belgian chain of command: that Leman had been gravely wounded; that the Germans were entering Liège along the west bank of the Meuse; that the Belgian troops at Sart-Tilman were in retreat. The Belgian rumour mill was working far faster than the chain of command. At 0540 the 14 Brigade commander left his HQ with his entire staff to look for Leman. He did not inform his subordinates and he abdicated his responsibility to supervise the withdrawal of his brigade. In most armies, this sort of thing would have resulted in the 14 Brigade commander's court martial.

At 0450, 48 Battery and a section of 14 Brigade MG arrived at Belgian 11 Brigade HQ (north-east sector) and reported that the Evegnée–Fléron sector had been penetrated and the Queue-du-Bois was under attack. He sent 4/ III/ 31, which was dubious assistance, as the company had just failed to execute the counterattack at Rabosée, and kept the artillery and MG under his own control with his last reserves, a platoon of I/ III/ 31 and 3 and 4/ II/ 31.

At 0600, I/ 31, I/ 32 and 3/ II/ 32 were withdrawn from Fort d'Evegnée back to 11 Brigade HQ, except for 2/ I/ 32, which never received the order and stood fast. Their movement was detected by II/ FAR 4 at Queue-du-Bois, heavily shelled and the column dispersed but eventually rejoined 11 Brigade.

The Belgian 11 Brigade commander then learned that the Germans were advancing on Bellaire. He decided to send all the elements 31 and 32 L available in that direction. But under the effects of the shelling they had recently endured, plus the horrifying stories told by the survivors of Rabosée, their march slowed, and when they were shelled again their morale broke and they fled back to 11 Brigade HQ.

Fort Fléron

Fort Fléron lay between the axis of advance of 14 Brigade to its north and 11 Brigade to its south. It was built on the east side of the town. There were buildings up to the glacis on the gorge side and the remainder of the terrain was covered with orchards and hedges, which considerably limited visibility.[30] The garrison consisted of 300 artillery and eighty infantry, commanded by Captain Mozin.

OPs were essential to the effectiveness of the fort's fire. The distance between Fléron and Evegnée to the north was 3,445m and to Chaudefontaine to the south 4,650m, so that Fléron's portion of this sector was about 4,000m. Without OPs the fort's fire could only be directed from the fort itself, which had observation in daylight out to about 600–700m, and at night practically no observation at all. On 1 August Fléron laid telephone lines to OPs at Micheroux and the church tower at Magnée. This was ineffective and amateurish. Even in daylight, two OP were inadequate to observe such a broad built-up sector. At night two OPs were even less adequate. Putting the OP in the obvious place in Magnée church tower was dangerous during the daytime and both dangerous and ineffective at night. Mozin needed to put out more OPs, OPs in depth and specific OPs for day and night operations. There is no evidence that Mozin analysed the enemy's most likely courses of action for day and night attacks and determined preplanned targets that he could fire unobserved.

Mozin said that he laid telephone lines to the infantry positions at Romsée and Retinne. There is no evidence that he did any such thing. The infantry did not mention having communication with the fort. There were no calls for fire from the infantry during the night of 5–6 August and Fléron did not provide any artillery fire for the infantry. At best, this shows Mozin's recognition of the fact that he should have laid a telephone line to the infantry, but didn't.

Mozin had a curious concept of both his fort's mission and his responsibilities. Fléron was an artillery base. The job of artillery is to support the infantry, period. The infantry positions were about 2km – twenty minutes' brisk walk – north and south of his fort. His reconnaissance teams should have had no difficulty finding the infantry, at which point he needed to get over to the infantry and co-ordinate fire support. His presence was not needed at the fort to supervise stringing barbed wire or clearing fields of fire – that's what sergeants are for. Instead, Mozin stayed in Fléron and didn't leave it to co-ordinate with anybody, or even send his officers out to do so. As a consequence, he knew practically nothing concerning the other Belgian forces in his immediate vicinity.

On 2 August the fort was ordered to clear the fields of fire, but not to demolish houses. On 3 and 4 August several hundred coal miners assisted with the work on the exterior of the fort. The Bureau of Telegraphs and Telephones installed requisitioned telephones to link the fire direction centre with the turrets, flanking positions and searchlight, where the commander established his own OP. The garrison was divided into three watches of eight hours: guard (turret crew, external security); work party (flanking battery crew, internal security, work parties); reserve (resting). Local security was placed 600–700m from the fort.

Mozin said that in 1912 and 1913 the General Staff of the fortress and the fort commanders had developed a plan for the positions in the intervals that would be covered by flanking fire from the forts. He does not say where these positions should have been or what units had been planned to garrison them. He now knew that the infantry was digging in the intervals but nothing more, which worried him, but though he did not say so, he obviously did not take the initiative to find out exactly what was going on. This is hard to square with Mozin's assertion that he laid telephone lines to the infantry on 1 August. On 3 August an infantry lieutenant appeared at Fléron to point out the infantry positions on a map, which had no resemblance to the positions decided on in 1913. There was no time to change them.

As far as command and control were concerned, Mozin says that he knew that there were two sector commanders behind him, one for sector Chaudefontaine–Fléron and one for Fléron–Evegnée, as well as the HQ of the governor of Liège. Communication with them was by civilian overhead telephone line through the switchboard in Liège, which Mozin says, with considerable understatement, was 'precarious'. In fact, it could be relied on to fail immediately. The information he received from higher HQ was 'vague' and there was no general defensive fire plan whatsoever.

Mozin did form his own reconnaissance teams from intelligent, self-sufficient, reliable professional soldiers native to the area, who knew the terrain in the fort's area of operations. They knew how to read a map, make a sketch, evaluate forces, give a report. They operated in pairs on bicycles or motorcycles. There is no reason to believe they operated in uniform (he does not call them OPs or patrols, but 'lookouts').

As of the afternoon of 3 August, reconnaissance teams were sent out in the direction of Aachen and Eupen, maintaining contact with the fort by telephone and carrier pigeon. On the night of 3–4 August they were set up at Herve and Verviers, in contact with the cavalry. They reported sundry noises, but could not discover their origin. At midnight an exterior guard fired on an automobile coming from the east, which did not heed his repeated orders to stop and in which he could see uniformed personnel. It contained *Garde Civique* from Verviers, two of whom were wounded and brought to the fort aid station.

At 2200 on 3 August, the governor ordered the destruction of houses in the fort's field of fire. After giving the inhabitants a few hours to clear out their belongings, the work began on 4 August. The fort had a 'derisory' quantity of explosives to do so, but were assisted by a local explosives factory and the engineers of the neighbouring coal mines. Twenty houses were demolished, but the rubble could not be cleared away and provided excellent cover and concealment at the foot of the glacis. Nothing could be done about the 'hundreds' of structures in Fléron town, immediately behind the fort.

A bit before 1000 on 4 August, the fort was informed by the governor (and not by Mozin's 'lookouts') that the Germans had crossed the border at 0800. The lookouts were then able to keep track of the Germans, and when the Germans reached the Fléron zone of fire the fort engaged them. At 2100, the OPs at Micheroux and Magnée reported contact and the artillery fired in support. The OPs were pushed to the next fall-back position but at 0020 were able to reoccupy the primary positions. This was almost surely a false alarm; it is unlikely that any German troops were in the area. That night two artillerymen went out to relieve the men on local security and fell into the fosse, which was full of water; one drowned.

Beginning at 0430 on 5 August, as it had just become light, Fléron conducted an all-day series of fire missions against sundry artillery and infantry targets. In spite of optimistic reports of conducting 'precision fire with remarkable effectiveness', inflicting 'frightful' casualties on the Germans, it appears that the Germans suffered few losses. For their part, the German field artillery fired on the fort, which had no effect at all. The OPs and the company-sized security outpost at Retinne also took artillery fire, which means that the Germans had located them. At 1100, the OP at Micheroux was forced to withdraw, as had, at 0920, the Chaudefontaine OP.[31]

Even if Mozin's rosy estimate of the German casualties inflicted were true, Fort Fléron had failed to accomplish its mission. With the only Belgian artillery in its 4,000m sector, Fléron's mission was to stop German forward movement. The conditions for doing so could not have been better: daylight, good visibility, and the Germans had no siege artillery, which could have disturbed the Belgian fire. But the best Fléron could accomplish was insignificant harassment of the German advance: both German brigades reached their jump-off positions in good time. In addition to the insufficiency and poor placement of the OPs, the armament of the fort was just not up to the job. Two 15cm and four 12cm cannon and only two 21cm howitzers, in five turrets, with a low rate of fire and low-velocity (inaccurate), low-explosive shells were not going to put up the kind of barrages necessary for Fléron to accomplish its mission.

At 1425 the commander of the Chaudefontaine–Fléron sector judged that an attack was imminent and issued his operations order. The mission of the interval troops in sector was to hold their position 'to the last man' while under attack for four hours, which would allow 12 Brigade, which had moved to support 11 Brigade, time to withdraw. The troops ceased work and occupied the trenches.[32]

Towards the afternoon the commander of the Belgian 9 Brigade asked if Fléron needed any support. The fort asked for two companies to watch Fléron town. That afternoon, two battalions appeared, accompanied by an artillery battery. Shortly after 2000 the fort's local security was driven in by German patrols. Fort d'Evegnée requested a fire mission on its own gorge side. The lookouts who had left that afternoon did not return. Then the telephone line went dead: Fléron no longer had communications with the governor, the sector commander, the other forts or its own

OP to the north. An attempt to re-establish communications with this OP immediately took German fire. The fort could hear the firing at Retinne, but lacking fire direction and was helpless to intervene.

'By a miracle, our OP in the church tower at Magnée continued to function'. At 0200 it observed German troops in the town and immediately had to leave Magnée for the fall-back OP at Romsée. The fort put unobserved fire on the crossroads in Magnée. From here the OP was able to adjust fire on the Germans as they advanced towards Romsée. Then the OP was overrun. The OP commander reported in two days later, saying that two men had been killed, one POW. Fléron was now blind and unable to fire.

The 11 and 12/ 35 demonstrated against Fléron. The regimental history doesn't mention this further, but De Schrÿver says that the two companies succeeded in making a concealed approach to within 100m of Salient III, reaching and cutting the barbed wire, before being driven off by 5.7cm fire. Naturally, De Schrÿver believed that a German attempt to storm the fort had been driven off with heavy casualties.

Under the II/ 165 commander, 6 and 8/ 165 also demonstrated against Fort Fléron. It took them until 0300 to disengage from the street fighting in Micheroux. They approached to within 150m of the fort, became involved in an infantry firefight with the garrison until two of the fort's artillery pieces began firing, at which point they withdrew to Micheroux. The Belgian troops south of the fort thought that their flank had been turned and withdrew to Battice. Lombard acknowledged that the Germans succeeded in 'reducing the fort to impotence during the night'.[33]

At around 0400 on 6 August a group of German troops in open order retreated through the interval between Fléron and Evegnée. The infantry manned the parapet and engaged them. Almost immediately the commander of III/ 14 appeared with two officers and some MGs, giving a vague report concerning events that evening in the Fléron–Evegnée interval and then saying that he was withdrawing through Beyne-Heusay to Liège. The OP from the north came in, saying that the Belgian troops in the Fléron–Evegnée interval were in retreat. A gap in the houses near the church at Magnée allowed Fort Fléron to see German troops moving on Romsée, and the fort's guns fired in this direction. When the Germans marched back from Magnée to Romsée, Fléron continued to fire.

German troops now appeared in the demolished houses and then moved up the glacis, cutting the barbed wire. Belgian infantry occupied the parapet, the 5.7cm turret at Salient III fired, and the Germans withdrew. Two Belgian artillerymen were KIA. The lack of OPs and the resulting ineffectiveness of Fléron's artillery fire meant that German infantry was now appearing without warning within rifle range of the fort, ranges so short that the artillery could not engage them.

Patrols established that the enemy was at Retinne to the north, and to the south and south-west. There were no Belgian troops to the west: the two Belgian battalions in the town had left without telling Mozin. Fléron was cut off.

Fléron's fire marginally inconvenienced the forward movement of two German brigades advancing in solid march columns that were kilometres long. It is a startling demonstration of the ineffectiveness of the fort's fire that they did not inflict massive casualties on targets like these. But the real demonstration of the ineptitude of Mozin's defensive preparations is shown by the fact that there were no preplanned targets directly in front of the infantry defensive positions, where artillery support surely would have been decisive – as the German field artillery was.

Belgian Field Forces Withdraw from Liège

The German attack on the night of 5–6 August was a complete fiasco; five of the six German brigades were no longer combat-effective and even Ludendorff himself admitted that 14 Brigade, which he had led past the ring of forts, was in a parlous position. Nevertheless, the Belgian 3rd Division withdrew from Liège.

The reports that reached the Belgian HQ prior to the Jäger attack at 0445 were grim.[34] De Schrÿver says that they were 'strangely exaggerated, being spread and arriving who knows how.' The Belgian headquarters was, however, convinced that the Germans had penetrated the intervals at Boncelles and that the troops at Sart-Tilman had fled.

By 0700 Leman had finally settled his HQ at Loncin. At 0715 the Chaudefontaine–Fléron commander found Leman and reported that the Germans had broken his position and that his troops had been forced to withdraw.[35] Leman had also received alarming reports of German success south of Barchon and Pontisse and at Sart-Tilman. The 34 Brigade attack had been transformed into a Prussian army crossing the Meuse, which had penetrated to Vottem: in fact it was really just the Jäger again. Reports of the Jäger at Vottem continued through the morning. Further reports led Leman to conclude that his troops were in a 'lamentable state'. Lombard said that the Belgian troops were in 'bad shape'.[36] Some simply fell asleep on the side of the road. The 3 DA was 'used up'. De Schrÿver said that Leman had been informed of 'the extreme lassitude of the men and the disorganization, even dissolution, of certain units'. One thing was certain: as of about 0100 (B) German howitzers had begun shelling the city, spreading panic.[37]

At 0732 Leman ordered a general withdrawal of all his field forces to the west side of Liège, between Hollogne and Lantin. The exhausted troops dragged themselves forward rather than marched, and they were in no condition for another fight.

At 0750 Leman reported to the army HQ that he had decided to pull 3 DA, 15 Brigade, and even the four fortress regiments back to Waremme. Leman is surprisingly uninformative concerning the most important command decision he made during his entire military career. He says only that many of the reservists were old, had been tired out by digging defensive positions, and had reached the limits of their endurance fighting a superior enemy, an appreciation supported by the brigade and regimental commanders.[38] Leman also said that the Germans had penetrated the Belgian line, threatened to take the Belgian forces in the rear, and he had no reserve to close this penetration. Galet said that Leman reported that 'after the fighting of the 4th, 5th and 6th August the troops not actually manning the permanent forts were completely exhausted.'[39]

Lombard said that the Belgian 3 DA was 'exhausted, disorganised, dispersed and in no condition to withstand another such violent shock such as the one that it had just victoriously survived' and that 'its routes of retreat could be cut off at any time'.[40]

Duvivier and Herbiet make the strongest case for explaining 'this paradoxical situation' (failure of German attack and Belgian withdrawal).[41] Leman thought he was faced by four corps, but to this point only two had been engaged. His communications with his troops were bad and reports were slow in arriving and contradictory. This was aggravated by the fact that the Jäger 7 attack had forced him to move his HQ to Fort Loncin. According to reports, the front had been penetrated in multiple places. The situation was worst in the south where the German penetration threatened the line of retreat from Liège, in spite of the fact that Leman had committed his entire reserve in this sector. Leman felt that he was threatened with imminent catastrophe. They note that Leman intended to resume the defence on the line of the western forts, but when the troops arrived he saw that given their fatigue and disorganisation, this was not possible.

It appeared to the young Belgian General Staff officers, then and later, that Leman had a golden opportunity to counterattack and destroy the German 14 Brigade and thereby seal a glorious Belgian victory. This included De Schrÿver, who maintains that, had the troops been told of their successes, their morale would have immediately recovered and they would have been capable of 'a new and vigorous effort'.[42]

The Jäger 7 attack on the 3 DA HQ was the decisive point in the battle. Galet said that the attack 'disorganized the command at a critical moment and was largely responsible for the order to retreat given to the 3rd Division'.[43] This is an understatement. The Jäger attack broke Leman's nerve. Within thirty minutes of re-establishing his HQ at Loncin he decided to pull the division back to the west side of the fortress. In fact, Leman probably would have issued the order immediately, but the telephone net was non-operational until 0725. Twenty minutes after that he decided to leave the fortress altogether.

The Belgians had also received reports that strong German cavalry – the estimates varied from seven regiments to two divisions – were across the Meuse.[44] Lombard said that the area near Waremme was 'infested' with German cavalry.[45] At 0750 Leman reported that there were 5,000 German cavalry at Waremme.[46] The commandant of the province of Limbourg reported that the Germans had already occupied Tongres. This was, in fact, only the 3rd Squadron Dragoon R 2. The German cavalry was operating behind Liège in an area 30km broad and 20km deep; each time German cavalry entered a town, its presence had surely been reported. When the Germans cut the telephone and telegraph lines they added to the confusion. The Belgians reported the German cavalry activity to the British and French, and the report reached the personal attention of the President of France.

It appeared to the Belgians that German cavalry not only threatened to cut off the reinforced 3 DA in Liège, but that the left flank of the main army, assembling behind the Gette, was also in danger. This caused the Belgians to withdraw all their field troops from Liège on 6 August while they still could, leaving only the garrisons of the permanent fortifications. Belgian sensitivity to the threat posed by the German cavalry is shown by De Schrÿver's criticism of Marwitz's failure to push his two cavalry divisions across the Meuse, which would have 'gravely compromised' the 3 DA retreat.[47]

There would be no counterattack against Ludendorff's isolated brigade. Credit for taking Liège has been given to Ludendorff. That his bold action succeeded was due in great part to the work of the German HKK 2 cavalry reconnaissance squadrons.

The attack on Liège had taken the Belgians by surprise: they had expected that the Germans would wait to complete their deployment before attacking, and had not anticipated an *attaque brusquée*.[48] Galet wrote:

> During the night various telephone reports enabled us to follow the course of the fighting which was especially violent round Boncelles. At 4.45 a.m. on the 6th telephone communication with Liège ceased, with the words, 'The Germans are here'. Towards 7 o'clock a wireless and a telephone message from Fort Loncin stated that the division was falling back from Liège, that it had withstood the whole VIIth Corps, that the Xth Corps had advanced by Ougrée on the left bank of the river, that our troops were decimated, entire regiments having been destroyed, and that the attacks had been delivered by a force four times as strong as that of the defenders.[49]

Galet said that the Germans had driven back:

> the 40,000 men of the 3rd Division supported by the line of forts. This could have only been done by a powerful force 'four times as strong as ourselves' according to the message from the division. Was this force all, or only a portion of the four corps mentioned by Leman? We knew the Germans to be methodical; and we believed that they had secretly massed certain corps as an advanced guard in order at once to gain a base in Belgium ...

At 1600 a report from Leman reached Belgian HQ via Namur, saying that 3 DA had successfully resisted attacks from the entire German VII and X AK, but 3 DA was completely exhausted and retreating out of Liège from the west side of the fortress. 'The mere fact that a man like General Leman should have made up his mind to retreat, in the face of imperative orders he had received from the King, was conceivable only on the supposition that he had found himself facing overwhelming odds.' And the Germans could be reinforced easily. Later messages said that 5 regiments of German cavalry and 150 lorries had crossed the Meuse at Lixhé and that 3 DA was used up and feared being 'sabred'. The cavalry division was ordered to move from Hannut to Waremme to cover the 3 DA withdrawal.

Leman reported that he had been attacked by four times the strength of his division; a wild estimate. In fact, the odds were, for all practical purposes, even. The German infantry had hit Liège so hard Leman was seeing not double, but quadruple.

De Schrÿver said that the 3 DA march column during the withdrawal from Liège was 'heterogeneous', which was a considerable understatement.[50] Belgian command and control had collapsed. There was no brigade or regimental integrity: the largest cohesive unit was the battalion, there were several companies marching independently, and 'fragments of 14 L, 34 L, 9 L and 29 L'. The column moved out from Loncin at 1300 6 August. The garrison of Fort Hollogne helped 3 DA officers disguise themselves as enlisted men. The retreat resembled flight.[51]

At 1800 there were still fragments of units from battalion size down to an isolated company scattered at nine different locations in Liège. During the night of 6–7 August Liège was in chaos.[52] While the 'majority' of the troops marched out of the fort, groups of troops bivouacked everywhere from the citadel to the area around Loncin, without bothering to put out security.

By 0700 on 7 August, a large number of troops still had not moved out. At the citadel there was the fortress artillery, stragglers from several regiments, the oldest two classes of reservists and the 14 Brigade MG section, at Herstal 2 and 4/ II/ 9 F, a platoon of 2/ I/ 11 and stragglers from 11 L, 12 F and 9 F, and at Ans 1 and 3/ II/ 9 F and 3/ II/ 14.

Collapse of German Command and Control

Emmich, the commander of X AK and overall commander of the Liège attack units, had accompanied the 14 Brigade attack. The only possible explanation for such a decision was that he was convinced that all six brigades would break through into Liège. This is further proven by the fact that he did not leave a deputy commander outside Liège to control any units that did not break through. This left Marwitz, the cavalry commander, completely on his own without instructions. The 2nd Army commander, Bülow, was still in Hanover.

This led, on 6 August, to the worst-case scenario for German command and control. Emmich was with 14 Brigade, where he was supernumerary. He had no way to communicate with the other five brigades and three cavalry divisions, who spent most of the day with no idea of what had happened or what they were to do, so, with the exception of 11 Brigade and IR 16, they did nothing.

Nor could Emmich communicate with 2nd Army HQ. The Armeeoberkommando 2 (AOK 2) LNO to Emmich was no longer with the X AK HQ, and could only report to AOK 2, in Hanover, that as of the morning of 6 August the attack had not succeeded.[53] The routes to Liège were barricaded, there was resistance from civilians and the German units had taken relatively heavy casualties. The LNO expected that the attack would be renewed on the night of 6–7 August. At 0900 6 August, AOK 2 sent a second LNO forward to get a report from Emmich. At 1045 the first LNO reported that 14, 27 and 34 Brigades were still outside the fortress ring, which in the case of 14 Brigade was wrong. He knew nothing of Emmich's location but assumed he was continuing the attack. AOK 2 instructed the HQ at Aachen to require a report from HKK 2. At 1230 the first LNO reported that Liège had not fallen. Both 2nd Army and Oberste Heeresleitung (OHL – German HQ) thought the attack had failed. The second LNO reported that he had arrived at Aachen and asked what he was supposed to do. He was sent to join 27 Brigade at Battice. At 1802 the first LNO reported that HQ X AK had ceased to exist. Three minutes later a transportation corps (!) officer reported to Aachen HQ that Emmich had penetrated into Liège. At 1815 the second LNO reported that Emmich was negotiating with the mayor of Liège. Emmich sent a private telegram to his wife saying 'Hurrah! In Liège!', a double violation of operations security: his wife should not have known what he was doing in the first place, and secondly such a message should not have been sent clear text to her at all. Not to mention that Emmich had not reported to AOK 2. On the night of 6–7 August OHL ordered IR 39 and IR 56 to move to Liège without completing their mobilisation, but didn't bother to inform AOK 2.[54]

Kabisch's Conclusions

The attack on Liège on 4 August put 'military necessity' before politics. This had serious negative repercussions on German policy, including the requirement to declare war on Russia and the fact that Germany was the first to take aggressive military action – against a neutral country.

Kabisch said that Bismarck would never have allowed the elder Moltke to dictate policy to him, and cited 1866 as proof. This was a very perceptive observation, which has passed unnoticed because 'common knowledge' holds that Bismarck and Moltke synchronised their plans perfectly.

In fact, in 1866 Moltke thought he had a window of opportunity from about the twenty-fifth to the forty-fifth day of mobilisation, in which Prussia's faster rail mobilisation gave Prussia a significant numerical superiority.[55] In order to exploit this, Moltke wanted to attack as soon as the Prussian army had deployed.

Bismarck paid no attention to Moltke's planning. After the Prussian army deployed, Bismarck refused to let it invade Bohemia, pending the outcome of several of his political initiatives. Moltke didn't advance into Bohemia until long after his twenty-fourth to forty-fifth day window of opportunity had long passed. Moltke was now forced to concoct a war play on the fly.

Both the elder and younger Moltke cited 'military necessity'. Bismarck upheld the primacy of national political policy: Bethmann-Hollweg, Chancellor of Germany in 1914, didn't.

Kabisch made some very perceptive observations concerning the attack itself. He said that had the 14 Brigade attack failed, the repercussions for the German Army and German morale would have been serious. The success of the 14 Brigade attack was due to Ludendorff's determination, personal example, tactical ability and use of artillery. But the other brigades, while they did not penetrate into Liège, played an important role in the 14 Brigade success. The brigades which did the toughest work were 38 and 43, drawing the mass of the Belgian reserves away from the 14 Brigade sector. Pressure from 27 and 34 Brigades (and 11, though Kabisch does not mention it) led Leman to believe that his front had been penetrated at multiple places and that his troops were no longer combat-effective. But the palm went to 1/ Jäger 7, the importance of whose attack on the Belgian HQ 'cannot be rated too highly, for at the decisive moment it paralysed the Belgian command and control'.

Kabisch points out that Ludendorff had a decisive advantage over the other commanders: he knew of the attack years in advance, had the opportunity to analyse it and recognised the necessity that the attack succeed. The other brigade commanders learned of the concept of the operation only hours before they had to execute it and had no opportunity to conduct a thorough mission analysis. In fact, 38/43, 11 and 27 Brigade had all driven off the Belgian defenders in the sector. The 11 Brigade had no enemy between it and the centre of Liège, 27 Brigade had only weak Belgian forces (and could have drawn on an unengaged IR 16) and 38/43 Brigades could have at the minimum held a line at Redoubts 4, 5 and 6. In each case, lacking an understanding of the necessity of penetrating into Liège at any cost, they withdrew.

Moranville's Conclusions

Moranville concluded that it would have been preferable to have not attempted to defend the intervals between the permanent forts at Liège and Namur.[56] Both divisions should have remained with the field army and fallen back to Fortress Antwerp, requiring the Germans to detach another (third) corps to blockade them.

In the event, Moranville said that committing 3 DA to the defence of the intervals at Liège accomplished nothing. The division was not able to defend the intervals for as long as the individual forts could hold out, and could not aid in the defence of the individual forts themselves. Moranville says that 3 DA (and later 4 DA) returned to the army 'reduced in numbers, equipment and combat power, and incapable of performing the same missions as the other four divisions of the army.' In fact, all five Belgian brigades committed to a defence of Liège that lasted for precisely one night of combat were wrecked, reducing the combat power of the Belgian field army by a quarter.

Moranville said that it was the duty of the Belgian High Command to consider the very real possibility that the entire country would be occupied by the enemy, a situation that, in the event, came to pass. In that case, the army was the sole tangible representation of the Belgian state. Preserving the army intact was a political necessity of the first order.

De Schrÿver concluded that the night operations favoured the Germans, who were guided by a 'swarm' of spies who knew the terrain down to the last detail.[57] He explains Belgian friendly-fire incidents 'which it was not always possible to stop quickly' by saying that to some degree they were due to spies firing into the backs of the defenders.

Lombard's Conclusions

Lombard said that the Belgian units were made up of different reservist year groups and lacked cadres, cohesion and the ability to manoeuvre.[58] In the days preceding the attack they had been overworked. Then there were errors in organising the defence. Instead of employing entire battalions and regiments as a unit, with their own reserves, they were intermixed. Most of the forts had been reduced to impotence by poor communications, which also made co-ordination between the units themselves impossible. Then communications between Leman's HQ and the units broke down.

As a result, reserves were committed not on the basis of accurate reports but on 'alarmist rumours spread by enemy agents or deserters'. This began on the evening of 5 August, when 15 Brigade was sent to the Ourthe–Meuse sector. Lombard says that Leman remained 'obsessed' by the fear of German infiltration from the south. This was motivated by his knowledge of the cut-up and forested terrain, which made defensive observation difficult. At 0215 he received an inaccurate report that the sector had been broken in and sent four battalions there, the reserves of the Evegnée–Fléron and Fléron–Chaudefontaine sectors. These troops arrived 'in a pitiful state' after a long march. The 12 Brigade artillery, which accompanied them, never managed to get into action because of blocked roads. At 0310 Leman added the 3rd Artillery group.

The reserve of the Evegnée–Barchon and Barchon–Meuse sectors, 31 L and the 11 Brigade artillery, could have been committed against the German 14 Brigade at Queue-du-Bois, but the Belgian 11 Brigade sector commander had no idea what was going on in the sector to the south. These units remained south of Rabosée, doing nothing.

Leman's Leadership

There were no pre-war plans or preparations to defend the intervals at Liège with manoeuvre units. Leman succeeded in convincing the king to do so, over the head of the Belgian Chief of Staff, just days before the war broke out. He gave no indication of what he intended to accomplish. He seriously overestimated the combat power of both the fortress and 3 DA. During the battle his sole means of influencing the situation was by committing his reserves. He sent them to the wrong place, the Boncelles–Ourthe sector, and committed them piecemeal. While the German 14 Brigade was breaking his centre, Leman was still sending that sector's reserves to Sart-Tilman, with the result that they arrived too late and didn't fight at all. When his HQ was attacked, Leman panicked, abandoning his HQ and then, two hours later, ordering his division first to break off the battle and then to leave the fortress altogether. All of this can easily be explained by the fact that Leman was a desk soldier with no troop-leading experience whatsoever.

Moltke's Planning

The same can be said for Moltke, who spent the better part of his career as the elder Moltke's aide and as adjutant to the kaiser. The premise of the attack on Liège was that the German troops would be able to march unopposed into the undefended intervals between the forts. By 31 July, even before the Germans began mobilisation, German intelligence reported that the intervals would be defended and the Belgians were ready for the German attack. Even though the assumption on which the attack was predicated was known to be invalid, Moltke ordered the attack to proceed unchanged.

Moltke's plan, a night attack in brigade march column, straight down the most likely avenue of approach, a road, no less, is the concept of a tactical incompetent. Optimistically, the lead battalion was going to be able to fight: the rest of the mass accomplished worse than nothing. It is a practical certainty that the Belgian infantry, which consistently fired too high, caused very few German casualties, most of which were friendly-fire casualties as German troops in the rear fired into German troops ahead of them.

It had to be assumed that the columns were going to meet some kind of resistance. Even in the most optimistic case the advance had to be preceded by extensive patrolling, led by a point element and well-spaced advance guard and one lead battalion. The other two battalions had to be a terrain feature (hill, town) to the rear, so as to be kept under control, and not immediately get involved in the lead elements' fight. In the case of the 38/43 Brigade attack, 43 Brigade should have been kept well to the rear and not committed until daylight.

Moltke had only three realistic options. The first was a doctrinal German night attack, with adequate reconnaissance and preparation, on the night of 6–7 August. The inept mass night attack of 5–6 August destroyed the Belgian 3 DA; a well-prepared night attack would have done far better. Second was a doctrinal daylight attack on a narrow front Fléron–Evegnée–Barchon on 7 August, supported by four 21cm mortars, sixteen 10.5cm howitzers, and eight 7.7cm field guns, against inadequate Belgian field fortifications. Third was a much stronger daylight attack on 12 August, by which time the German heavy artillery and another ten light artillery pieces had arrived, the German infantry regiments would have been at full-strength, and the German cavalry would have crossed the Meuse in strength. There is no possibility that, even if the Belgians had another six days to improve their field fortifications, they could have withstood the fire of thirty-two 21cm mortars and sixteen 15cm howitzers. The third option was by far the best, as it would have kept the Anglo-French guessing concerning German intentions.

Notes

1. There are six principal histories of the Belgian and 14 Brigade fight on the night of 5–6 August: IR 27, IR 165, Jäger 4 Lüttich-Namur, and Lombard's Ludendorff and Chocs de Feu dans la Nuit, and they hardly ever agree with each other. This reflects the confused night fighting in built-up areas. The IR 27 was the lead unit and its history seems to be the most reliable German source: it was written in 1933 with the help of numerous officers. It describes fights in Retinne, Liéry, and Queue-du-Bois. Even so, the narrative is not always chronological and requires careful attention. The IR 165 does not describe a fight in Queue-du-Bois at all. The Jäger 4 history is a mess. It describes two fights for Queue-du-Bois in succession. The sketch map does not agree with the text. Lüttich-Namur was written in haste in 1918. Werner, IR 27, 36–44, 51–3. Bieberstein, Lüttich-Namur, 33–40.
2. Ludendorff, Kriegserinnerungen, 25–30.
3. De Schrÿver, Liège, 72.
4. De Schrÿver, Liège, 151.
5. Lombard, Chocs de Feu dans la Nuit, 51–2.
6. De Schrÿver, Liège, 150.
7. L. Lombard, Ludendorff à Liège (Stavelot: Editions Vox Patriae, 1937) 52–65.
8. Fließ/Dittmar, IR 165, 8–14.
9. Lombard, Chocs de Feu dans la Nuit, 55.
10. Lombard, Chocs de Feu dans la Nuit, 51.
11. Lombard, Chocs de Feu dans la Nuit, 57, 69.
12. Lombard, Chocs de Feu dans la Nuit, 57–8.
13. Normand, Liège, Namur, 34–6.
14. Lombard, Chocs de Feu dans la Nuit, 69–82.
15. E. Neumann, Das Magdeburgische Jäger-Battalion Nr. 4 im Weltkrieg 1914–18 (Zeulenroda: Sporn, 1935) 14–33. The Jäger 4 history says there was opposition in Sur Fosse, not mentioned by IR 27 or IR 165. The Jäger 4 map does not show Sur Fosse, which is odd, and mislabels Liéry as Retinne.
16. On 7 August Simonis saw the 2/ Jäger 4 commander as his company guarded the Meuse bridge in Liège.

17. Lombard, Chocs de Feu dans la Nuit, 83–93.

18. De Schrÿver, Liège, 158–61.

19. F. W. Rübesamen, Feldartillerie-Regiment Prinzregent Luitpold von Bayern (Magdeburgisches) Nr. 4 Teil I (1 August 1914 bis 31 Juli 1916) (Magdeburg: Faber, 1927) 36–7, 46–7.

20. Lombard, Chocs de Feu dans la Nuit, 94–8.

21. Lombard, Chocs de Feu dans la Nuit, 97.

22. Doerstling, IR 20, 24–28.

23. Offiziers-Verein, IR 35, 7–12.

24. De Schrÿver, Liège, 136–43.

25. Lombard, Chocs de Feu dans la Nuit, 110.

26. Officers can get away with this on badly-conducted training exercises, where being with the point element looks dashing. In combat, only the squad leader has any business being with the point element. When the point takes fire – and it will – any officer that far forward will get pinned down at best.

27. H. Rosenthal, Kurmärkisches Feldartillerie-Regiment Nr. 39 (Oldenburg/Berlin: Stalling 1923) 14.

28. Duvivier/Herbiet, Du Rôle de l'Armée de Campagne et des Fortresses belges, 42.

29. De Schrÿver, Liège, 96–7.

30. Mozin, 'La défence du fort de Fléron' in: Bulliten d'Information des Officiers de Réserve, 1er Trimestre 1937, 9–30, 2me Trimestre, 111–33.

31. De Schrÿver, Liège, 63–6.

32. De Schrÿver, Liège, 67–8.

33. Lombard, Chocs de Feu dans la Nuit, 119. Lombard attributes this action to Jäger 3, which is incorrect.

34. De Schrÿver, Liège, 197.

35. De Schrÿver, Liège, 98.

36. Lombard, Chocs de Feu dans la Nuit, 147, 153.

37. Ludendorff, Erinnerungen, 28. Lombard, Chocs de Feu dans la Nuit, 153.

38. Leman, Liège, 102–3.

39. Galet, Albert, 57.

40. Lombard, Ludendorff, 75.

41. Duvivier/Herbiet, Du Rôle de l'Armée de Campagne et des Fortresses belges, 30–40.

42. De Schrÿver, Liège, 98.

43. Galet, Albert, 80.

44. Troschke, Dragoner-Regiment 17, 26–31.

45. Lombard, Chocs de Feu dans la Nuit, 154.

46. De Schrÿver, Liège, 200.

47. De Schrÿver, Liège, 211.

48. Weltkrieg I, 100.

49. Galet, Albert, 80–2.

50. De Schrÿver, Liège, 200–1.

51. Lombard, Sous les Ouragans de Acier, 150.

52. De Schrÿver, Liège, 100.

53. Bülow, Mein Bericht zur Marneschlecht (Berlin: Scherl, 1919) 5–9.

54. Reichsarchiv, Der Weltkrieg I, 117–8.

55. T. Zuber, The Moltke Myth (Lanham: University Press of America, 2008) 113–123, 129–32.

56. Moranville, Babel, 235–8.

57. De Schrÿver, Liège, 95.

58. Lombard, Chocs de Feu dans la Nuit, 147–57.

5

7 August

Belgian HQ

The 3 DA reached Hannut on 7 August 'completely exhausted'. The division (four brigades) and 15 Brigade were reorganised into three brigades. Galet said that 9 and 12 IR and Lancer R 2 had taken the worst losses 'but they were by no means destroyed'. He does not give the casualties suffered at Liège.

The 3 DA was in such bad shape that an accurate assessment of its strength was impossible. The division, one of the two strongest in the Belgian Army, with four brigades, and including artillery, cavalry and service support, and elements of four fortress infantry regiments attached, started the battle with 23,000 troops. Moranville said that 3 DA had been reduced to 10,000 troops, a vague enough number.[1] The division did not take anywhere near 13,000 combat casualties. But the combat on the night of 5–6 August had shattered its morale and since many of the personnel came from Liège and the surrounding area, it can be safely assumed that much of the division simply went home. Duvivier and Herbiet said that the ten regiments of 3 DA and 15 Brigade had suffered 40 per cent casualties and were reorganised into six regiments.[2] This would mean 10,000 infantry casualties. A report on 14 August said that the 3 DA retreat from Liège had been 'lamentable' and conducted 'in panic'. The division had only 7,500 infantry remaining (of about 19,000, or 12,500 casualties), which meant that mass desertion continued for the next week.[3]

Belgian HQ learned that the forts still held out and that Leman was at Loncin. Contact with elements of the German IX, VII, X, IV and XI AK was reported by 3 DA, a sobering fact indeed. 'Numerous detachments' of German cavalry were reported west of Liège and east of Namur. The king, who had considered moving the army east to block the Germans closer to the Meuse, decided to remain behind the Gette.[4]

At 1500 an aviator brought a report from Leman. He said he had withdrawn the 'debris' of 3 DA from Liège because his reserves had been committed, the troops were exhausted and would not get any rest in the trenches, 'and to have kept them there would have been to make a gift to the Germans'. As governor, he had decided to remain in the fortress. None of the forts had surrendered. The Germans had attacked Pontisse on the night of 6–7 August and 'were repulsed with great loss.' The Germans had only a brigade in Liège.[5]

Collapse of Belgian Command and Control at Liège

General Leman had withdrawn to Fort Loncin on 6 August, a quixotic decision. When the Germans entered Liège on 7 August he was for all intents and purposes cut off from the other eleven forts and was only *de jure*, but not de facto, the commandant of Liège. Leman said that after he arrived at Fort Loncin on 6 August he remained in communication with the other forts until 13 August.[6] Since the Germans took control of, or cut, the telephone lines almost immediately, communication was by couriers ('*des hommes*') sent to and from Loncin, probably in civilian clothes.

At Fort Loncin he was supernumerary: the fort already had a commander, a major, and did not need a lieutenant general in addition. The most likely outcome of his decision to stay at Loncin was that the Germans would take a senior Belgian general officer prisoner, which is exactly what happened. Leman was also the commander of 3 DA. By locking himself up in Loncin, he surrendered command of his division. He was therefore unable to exercise command over either 3 DA or Liège. By withdrawing to Waremme with 3 DA, he could have retained command over 3 DA and still send messengers to the forts.

On 8 August Leman signalled the Belgian HQ that the 3 DA could 'easily reenter Liège'. If he had still been in command of 3 DA, he would have been in position to execute that manoeuvre; in Loncin all he could do was make suggestions that were never carried out. Belgian HQ, on the other hand, had identified German cavalry west of the fortress and elements of six corps in the vicinity. The 3 DA continued its withdrawal.

Joffre's Plan

The Belgian LNO to the French army arrived at Belgian HQ with a verbal communication from Joffre. Sordet's cavalry corps would cross the Semois (in the Ardennes, just east of the Belgian border) on 7 August and move through Neufchâteau towards Liège to prevent or delay the German investment of the fortress. An infantry brigade would defend the Meuse bridges south of Namur. The French deployment would be completed on 11 August. Then, four French corps (I, II, X and XI) would march north towards Namur.

Joffre wanted the Belgian Army to march on Liège to co-operate with Sordet. If the Belgians could not march on Liège, Joffre proposed that when the German right flank advanced through the Ardennes, masking or investing Liège and Namur, so as to cross the Meuse south of Namur, the French would attack the Germans in front while the Belgians attacked from Namur into the German right flank.

Galet said that the Belgians were hardly in agreement. They had just decided not to advance towards Liège. They were convinced that the Germans would advance both north and south of the Meuse. They wanted to fall back on Antwerp, not Namur. And Joffre contemplated an immediate general offensive, while the Belgians thought time was on the Entente side, allowing the Russians and British to bring forward their entire strength; until that occurred, the Entente should stay on the defensive.

A French LNO then arrived, with essentially the same message, and reported to Joffre that the Belgians intended to withdraw to Antwerp, which would prevent them from co-operating in the French offensive.

Galet said that it was clear that the French were not going to provide the Belgians with direct assistance, but intended to attack south of the Meuse in the near future. The Belgians knew nothing at all of the British. For their part, the Belgians 'could only subject our Army to risks compatible with the defence of our independence' which did not include taking the offensive against the German Army.

At 1840 the king informed Joffre by telephone that Liège was capable of holding out for a considerable period.

Belgian Strategy

Galet saw that it was necessary to explain why he and the king wanted on 1 August to deploy the Belgian Army on the Meuse and why on 7 August they did not. He makes the not unreasonable argument that, had the Belgians begun moving to the Meuse on 2 August they would have arrived on 5 August, preceding the Germans, and been able to organise a defence of the river that could not have been flanked and would have compensated for the Belgian's inferior numbers (and combat power). If they had begun to move on 7 August they would only have got involved in a manoeuvre battle in the open country west of the Meuse, which would have resulted in the certain destruction of the Belgian Army.

On the other hand, Liège was a day's march from a major German city and rail centre, Aachen. Had the Belgians attempted on 5 August to hold the Meuse, the Germans would quickly have brought up enough heavy artillery (which the Belgians did not have) and engineers to conduct an opposed river crossing. Once the Germans were across the river, it is hard to see how the Belgians could have broken contact and successfully conducted a withdrawal to Antwerp against the far more mobile German Army.

Had the Belgians really intended to hold the Meuse on 5 August, they would have had to begin co-ordination with the French much earlier: French troops, and in particular French artillery, were absolutely essential, and even rail movement would have taken days to plan and conduct. But co-ordinating with the French before 4 August would have violated Belgian neutrality. In any case, the Belgians soon learned that the French weren't coming. Defence on the Meuse was completely unworkable.

While there is some truth in Galet's argument, it avoids other possibilities. There was no reason for the Belgian Army to have remained near Louvain. The Gette is not a particularly strong position, and the army could easily have occupied an assembly area near Tirlemont, a day's march from Liège. Germans would have had to cross the Meuse, which could not be hidden and was a slow process, providing the Belgians plenty of time to withdraw. Alternatively, if they saw an opportunity, as they had on 7 August, to crush an isolated German brigade in Liège and at the same time occupy the river line, they would have been a position to quickly do so.

By 5 August the king had seen first hand the low state of Belgian discipline, leadership and training. This was confirmed when the Germans smashed the Belgian 3 DA at Liège on the night of 5–6 August. Initially, the Belgians thought that they had been outnumbered four to one. Nevertheless, they were defending a fortified position, which the Germans had overrun in the initial attack. Moreover, it is likely that the Belgians soon began to recognise that they had been attacked by only the elements of four corps, and not four entire corps: the Germans had not defeated 3 DA through sheer numbers, but with superior combat power.

Between Namur and Antwerp there was only a 40km gap not covered by the fire fans of the guns of the fortresses. On the left was water and neutral Holland, on the right the Meuse and the French border fortifications. This seemed to be the place, said Galet, for the Entente to defend while waiting for the Russian steamroller to get under way. The Germans were of the same opinion, and the initial objective for the right wing 1st and 2nd Armies was to open this gap. Two German cavalry divisions would soon direct their principal reconnaissance effort in this direction.

On 8 August the king decided that the Belgian strategy was to hold the line of the Gette and wait for the Entente to arrive. This would also allow the Belgian Army to protect the greater part of the country, including the capital.

Adoption of this strategy was not a foregone conclusion. The Belgian HQ established itself at the Louvain Town Hall, with the king in the mayor's office. Galet was now in effect the king's LNO to the General Staff, particularly the 1st (operations) and 2nd (intelligence) sections. He said:

> The atmosphere was not harmonious, and the General Staff had before long split up into three factions […]
>
> The first, represented by the Chief of the General Staff and one or two other officers, was inclined to think that it had done its duty in having assembled the

Army on the Gette. The second favoured a retreat to Antwerp at the first threat of the enemy. This faction had as its head General de Ryckel who, knowing well the weak spots of the place – of which he had been the Chief of Staff – emphasized the necessity for keeping our field army intact to insure the defence of the national keep. The third, consisting of the great majority, dreamt of a war of manoeuvre and the offensive. Between these parties there quickly arose an animosity which grew into deep mutual distrust. It was obvious that the 2nd Section placed an interpretation on the intelligence it received, which differed sensibly from our own [...] to avoid controversy, we refrained from comment.

On the other hand, the King exercised a strict supervision of the orders emanating from the 1st Section, and nothing concerning the employment of the troops could go out from General Headquarters without His Majesty's approval.

14 Brigade

At 0600 7 August, the commander of IR 165, his General Staff officer and a squad from 12/ 165 marched towards Liège, accompanied by 300 Belgian POWs – a German agent said that the Belgians had planned to blow up the Meuse bridge with the Germans on it. German engineers cut every wire on the bridge that could serve to detonate explosives. Once IR 165 was across, the Belgian POWs were moved to the rear of the column. The III/ 165 was detailed to guard the other 1,200 Belgian prisoners in the Chartreuse.

It was not clear if the Belgians would offer any resistance, but the Germans had orders to fire only if it was unavoidable. Numerous Belgian troops came out of the houses and surrendered. Captain Brinckmann, mounted on a horse, entered Liège with the lead German troops. To the front 100m a Belgian platoon entered the main road from a side street from the north, turned right and marched in front of the German troops. Brinckmann said he felt like an umpire on a field training exercise: he galloped up to the Belgian column and demanded they surrender, which they promptly did.[7]

Immediately on crossing the bridge, at the Place St-Lambert in front of the main rail station, IR 165 captured 3/ III/ 32, which was preparing to move out.[8] A column under the 14 L commander, with 2/ IV/ 14 in the lead, followed by 1 and 2/ II/ 14, 1 and 2/ II/ 34 and IV/ 34 (with three companies), was moving south about 500m west of the rail station. It then turned west, directly in front of IR 165. Colonel von Oven said, 'I am the lead element of 30,000 men: resistance is pointless' and the entire column, excepting only 2/ IV/ 34, was captured: 625 more Belgian POWs were led to the Chartreuse; 1, and 3/ II/ 9 F and 3/ II/ 14 were captured at the Ans city hall. The fragments of units that had been collected at Herstal (elements of 9 F in company strength, a platoon of 2/ I/ 11 and about 150 men from 9 F, 12 F and 11 L) surrendered at Ste Walburge, about 1,200m north of the rail station. That afternoon, 2 and 4/ II/ 9 F and 4/ I/ 32 were captured while trying to flee the city. In all the Germans captured sixteen Belgian companies in Liège.

A German General Staff officer appeared at the St Leonard prison, where the German POWs were being held, and announced that Liège was in German hands. The German prisoners were freed, the Belgian guards made prisoner, disarmed and led by their former captives to the citadel.

The IR 165 marched to the west side of the town and organised the area opposite Forts Loncin and Lantin for defence. Aside from some shrapnel bursting 'extremely high', the forts were inactive. Ludendorff said that there were rumours that the French were approaching from Namur. The IR 165 historians noted that the civilian population was 'completely quiet and didn't try anything. The news that the German troops would without fail punish [hostile actions] by the civilian population had obviously reached the city.'

Thinking that IR 165 had already taken the citadel, Ludendorff drove up to the gate in a requisitioned vehicle and banged on the door, which opened and 'a couple hundred' Belgians surrendered. On 7 August the Germans took about 1,800 Belgians prisoner.

The IR 27 followed IR 165 and marched through the gates of the citadel in *Paradeschritt* ('goose step'), passing in review before General von Emmich and Ludendorff. The regiment garrisoned the citadel and individual companies pulled guard duty: 3/ 27 the citadel, 5 the rail stations, 6 the Chartreuse. The 2/ 27 moved to the Palais de Justice. 'They must have left in a hurry' said the diary of an IR 27 ensign, 'The morning papers lay on the tables, there was coffee in the cups. Masses of people began to assemble in the square and we were ordered to prepare the Palais for defence.'

11 Brigade

In the absence of the brigade commander, the IR 35 commander decided to continue the attack into Liège. The brigade commander soon arrived and confirmed this decision. At 0900, 11 Brigade left its bivouac east of Magnée and resumed the advance on Liège, IR 35 in the lead, order of march III, I, II, MGK, followed by II/ FAR 39 and then IR 20, through Romsée and the previous day's battlefield.[9] This time the brigade passed through the town without a shot being fired: white flags hung from houses, indeed from all the houses on the road to Liège. As the brigade left Romsée on the road to Chênée it recieved heavy artillery fire from Fort Chaudefontaine and took cover. While moving through Romsée 5/ FAR 39 lost a gun to a direct hit, but nevertheless went into action on the west side of the town and diverted the attention of the fort. When the fort ceased fire, the brigade continued the march. IR 35 casualties were not serious, but included one OFF DOW, one WIA.

Halfway between Romsée and Chênée the brigade halted to send out reconnaissance, except for the lead battalion III/ 35, which continued the march and entered Liège shortly after noon. It was greeted by 2 and 3/ Jäger 4, who were able to turn over eighty POWs, including twenty officers, and III/ 35 took quarters in the citadel. The I and II entered Liège at 1600 in pouring rain, II taking quarters west of the citadel, I and the MGK in a school in the parish of Ste Walburge near the citadel. At 1830, IR 20 entered the city in pouring rain, following the regimental band, and moved north-west of the citadel, sending out patrols on bicycles to Hermée and Haute Préalle, which found nothing. Fléron shelled the 11 Brigade movement from Magnée to Romsée without being able to stop it.[10]

The German regiments had deployed without their medical units. The IR 20 regimental surgeon did the best he could:

> When the brigade moved out on 7 August, I was ordered to follow with the wounded at the end of the column. We loaded 55 wounded onto seven wagons. For protection I was assigned a squad from 11/ 20. After a long march we encountered a steep hill, which the wagons could climb only slowly and by doubling up the horse teams; by the time we got to the top, the brigade had gone. We reached Magnée, where I decided to stop. The wounded were unloaded and put on straw in the church. With the help of the mayor, the curé and several women we fed the men a bit from a local restaurant. In an hour the women made a Red Cross and it was hung from the church tower. At about 1800 a General Staff auto informed me that the German troops were in Liège and the way there was free. I immediately had the wounded into the wagons and at dark set out for Liège. We arrived at about midnight and by 0600 8 August it was possible to deliver all the wounded to the local hospitals.

German Command and Control

Emmich gave Lieutenant Nida the mission of finding 38 and 43 Brigades.[11] Nida was at a loss as to where to start. His *Belgian* driver said that there had been fighting west of the Ourthe, so he set off in that direction, with a soldier from Jäger 4 as a guard. They could see a Belgian fort in an artillery duel with the Germans, but passed through the fort line without difficulty. He encountered 11 Brigade outposts, which were surprised to see a German officer come out of Liège. When he reached the brigade HQ he was arrested as a spy. He had to 'recite half the officer's roster, the operations order for the attack, and finally produce the secret map he had used to guide his brigade'. After an hour he was released, rejoined his car only to be arrested again. The brigade commander's aide secured his release. 11 Brigade knew nothing of

38 and 43 Brigades. By now soaking wet, he set off again, with the car breaking down frequently in the hilly terrain. He returned to Liège, got a more powerful vehicle and passed through the fort line a third time, towards Plainevaux. He had told the Belgian driver he was looking for wounded: initially the Belgian believed him, later probably not. Every time he stopped he excited the curiosity of Belgian civilians, but much to his surprise nothing untoward happened. They were overtaken by a Belgian car and led to the next village, where they found the body of the IR 74 commander, the Prince of Lippe, in the city hall. Nida took an inventory of the Prince's belongings. They drove without difficulty through the market square 'black with people'. They then encountered a barricade across the road. His driver conducted a conversation including 'lively arm movements' with a man who wore a brassard in the Belgian national colours, and established that he was on the best road to reach Fort Boncelles. Nida was astonished when the brassarded Belgian climbed on a motorcycle and 'led us in a endless curve through the woods south-east of Liège, past a complete net of barricades.' When they approached German-held territory, the Belgian left them, and they found an isolated forest inn. They ate lunch while the 'quite attractive' owner and the guests told him that his brigades had retreated past here twenty-four hours ago, while in revenge he related that the Germans had entered Liège. He drove east across the Ourthe and found some wounded from IR 73. He drove upstream along the Ourthe and at dusk found an outpost from 3/ Uhlan R 5. When he said that Liège had fallen, everywhere the troops cheered. First he found the HQ of 9 KD, and at 0100 the two brigade HQs. After an hour he drove back through the fort line for the fourth time, with the LNOs from the two brigades, along the 14 Brigade attack route through Micheroux and Retinne, and after a 24-hour trip reported to General von Emmich.

Soon after 11 Brigade, IR 16 entered the city. By the end of the day on 7 August the Germans had in Liège two shot-up brigade battle groups and an infantry regiment that had seen little combat, and had effectively secured the centre of the city.

Just before AOK 2 was to leave for Aachen at 2000 7 August, the first LNO reported that Emmich had entered Liège at 0745 on 7 August, the Belgian commandant had fled, the bishop was a prisoner, there were no Belgian troops in Liège, the citadel was in German hands, but he did not know how many of the forts had fallen.

At 1900 Ludendorff left Liège to report to the 2nd Army commander, von Bülow. A Belgian *Garde Civique* offered to be his driver, which Ludendorff accepted.[12] The Belgian recommended using a particular vehicle, but Ludendorff picked another one, which broke down even before it left the citadel; as Ludendorff noted, he had no choice but to trust the Belgian's judgement. When they reached German terrain, the Belgian said that he could no longer drive. Using 'various means of transportation' Ludendorff arrived in Aachen, still accompanied by 'my Belgian soldier', spoke with the 1st LNO, ate supper, then drove back west again to get reinforcements moving to Liège.

Jäger 4 Attacks Fort Fléron

Early on 7 August, Jäger 4 (minus 2 and 3 on the bridges) was ordered to form a task force with a platoon from, FAR 4 and a few engineers and attack Fort Fléron.[13] The idea was that a howitzer would fire on the entrance at the gorge of the fort. When the turrets would raise to return fire, they would be suppressed by MG fire. Covered by the howitzer and MG fire, and supported by the engineers, the Jäger would storm through the entrance and take the fort. This was pretty clearly an experiment to determine if there was any way for the Germans to take a fort with the limited resources available.

As befits a Jäger battalion, the approach march was concealed by the town of Fléron, the battalion stopped at the east end, facing the fort, and then conducted hours of careful reconnaissance. There was a rail line in front of the fort with a large number of boxcars full of Belgian military equipment. Using the boxcars for cover and concealment, the MGs were brought forward to high hedges at the glacis of the fort. Firing lanes for the MGs were cut through the hedges and each gun given an armoured turret as a target. A cold rain was falling. It was not possible to find artillery firing positions because of the buildings of Fléron town, and the battery left that afternoon to help attack Fort Pontisse.[14]

At 1400 (B) the fort was surprised to take MG fire from the town, aimed at turrets, searchlight OP and the sentinels on the ramparts. MG rounds ricocheted off the observer openings into the turrets, causing casualties. The left-hand 12cm fired at the MG but the Jäger were only 200m from the guns, which could not depress enough to engage them, the shells going over the Jäger's heads (and probably into the town). Why the Jäger did not take fire from the 5.7cm guns is not clear. It could well be that the garrison of Fléron could not even see the Jäger, given the bad visibility, the hedges and poor observation from the fort's defensive positions. The sole positive effect all this German fire had was to keep the Belgians off the open positions on the parapet, where they should have actually been able to engage the Jäger. A Jäger lieutenant reconnoitred up to the ditch and found it to be 5–6m deep with wire obstacles: an assault was impossible. This should hardly have come as a surprise. The fort had several casualties from MG rounds and ricochets: the gunner in the 5.7cm at Salient III was hit in the chest by a round that bounced off the gunbarrel.

At 1700 the Jäger 4 commander, Major Marquard, went forward under a flag of truce to demand the fort's surrender, and was admitted inside the fort. According to Mozin, Marquard said that Liège was in German hands, several forts had already fallen and German siege artillery was approaching: further resistance would result in the destruction of the town. Mozin said that he was 'particularly struck' by the news concerning Liège and the forts, and wanted confirmation, hoping to get some information concerning the situation of the Belgian troops, having received none since the morning of 6 August.

In return for the right to send an officer to Liège, the commandant of Fléron would permit the Germans free use of the main east–west road to Liège until 1000, 8 August. Marquard agreed. (Mozin said that the fort reserved the right to fire on any German movement it observed in its radius of action. In the event, the Germans were able to resupply and reinforce 14 Brigade). Mozin said he needed to rest his troops, who had been going non-stop for six days, including three days of combat, as well as conduct maintenance on the fort. Mozin sent a lieutenant to Liège, which he found completely occupied by the Germans, though he could get no information concerning the Belgian troops. Leaving a security screen outside Fléron, the Jäger 4 task force returned to Liège.

27 Brigade

On 7 August IR 25 held Mortroux with IR 53 behind it at Neufchâteau. Reservists from IR 25 arrived that day, and the brigade received word that 14 Brigade had entered Liège.[15]

38 and 43 Brigades

The two brigades initially had no contact with the rest of the German units. The 38 Brigade commander, Colonel von Örtzen, ordered the two brigades to march to the right to close with 11 Brigade. The 38 Brigade would move to Louveigné. At noon IR 74 bivouacked in villages between Sprimont and Louveigné. Given past experience, the houses were searched for weapons and an exterior guard posted.

In the evening a report from 9 KD said that strong French forces were approaching, which was false, but Örtzen ordered the two brigades to move to Theux, a day's march to the east, where they could also join the reservists arriving from garrison and resupply ammunition. At 2030, I/ 74 led off in pouring rain and bivouacked near midnight. In the meantime, Lieutenant Nida had arrived from General von Emmich, saying that Liège had been taken and ordering the two brigades into the town, but it was felt that issuing a counter-order was impractical and movement into the city was delayed until 8 August.

Belgian Forts

The forts fired at anything they could see, which was not much.[16] Pontisse fired on three small groups of Germans. Barchon tried to engage IR 16 as it moved to Liège. Evegnée engaged a 'small column', Embourg a reconnaissance patrol, Boncelles 'small groups', Hollogne 'two strong reconnaissance patrols that approached to within 1,100 metres of the fort', Lantin a cavalry patrol. Loncin claimed to have inflicted 'severe casualties' on IR 165 and an artillery battery near Ans, on the west side of Liège, which was not mentioned in German histories. At Chaudefontaine a lucky hit by a field artillery piece into the 15cm turret embrasure destroyed the gun and wounded three men.

Notes

1. Moranville, Babel, 234.
2. Duvivier/Herbiet, Du Rôle de l'Armée de Campagne et des Fortresses belges, 39.
3. Galet, Albert, 102.
4. Galet, Albert, 82–91.
5. De Schrÿver, Liège, 212–3.
6. Leman, Liège, 106.
7. Kabisch, Lüttich, 123–4.
8. De Schrÿver, Liège, 204–8.
9. Offiziers-Verein, IR 35, 12–13. Doerstling, IR 20, 28–30.
10. Mozin, Fléron, 28–30.
11. Kabisch, Lüttich, 129–35.
12. Ludendorff, Kriegserinnerungen, 30–1.
13. Neumann, Jäger 4, 31–3.
14. Offizier-Vereinigung, FAR 43, 34.
15. Hüttmann/Krüger, IR 25, 7–8. Offiziers-Vereinigung, FAR 43, 31–2.
16. De Schrÿver, Liège, 207–8.

6

The German Artillery Takes Liège

The Liège Myth

Any history of the Battle of Liège attributes the fall of the fortress almost exclusively to the effect of the super-heavy German 42cm guns, an explanation that the Germans fostered themselves, since it emphasised the effectiveness of a German 'wonder weapon,' which would presumably demoralise the enemy. This is clearly the intent of the German official history *Der Weltkrieg* I, which emphasises the 42cm to the exclusion of the rest of the German siege artillery.[1] The Belgians, Moranville in the lead, attributed the fall of Liège entirely to the German super-heavy artillery, which excused the rapid surrender of the Belgian forts. These monster guns continue to fascinate historians of the Marne campaign and their readers.

Barbara Tuchman's Pulitzer Prize-winning *The Guns of August* combines 'common knowledge' with dramatic prose and is therefore the most popular book on the Marne campaign. She gives her imagination free rein: for example, according to Tuchman the Austrian Skoda 30.5cm mortars were employed at Liège (they weren't), and the destruction of Liège was caused solely by super-heavy artillery; the German 21cm mortars are not mentioned.[2]

John Keegan's *The First World War,* an exceptionally popular and influential military history, repeats the Liège 'common knowledge' verbatim: according to Keegan, the destruction of the Liège forts was due solely to the German 42cm guns.[3] Keegan dutifully footnotes his sole source concerning Liège, Christopher Duffy's 'The Liège Forts' in *Purnell's History of the First World War,* I, 131–8. This is a useful demonstration of how 'common knowledge' becomes entrenched. *Purnell's* was a populist weekly magazine, first published in 1970, which had 128 issues. Each magazine was about thirty pages long and covered perhaps four different topics. Each article was heavily illustrated with drawings and photos: Duffy's had four fully illustrated pages, two half-illustrated and only two of text. Duffy cited eight sources, only two of which had specific information about the siege of Liège.[4] This is not a well-researched article, which would explain why the 21cm are mentioned once. For good measure, Duffy throws in the participation of the Austrian 30.5cm, which never fired at Liège. The strongest part of the article are drawings of the 30.5cm and 42cm. But the 42cm get credit for everything.

In fact, nine of the twelve Liège forts were destroyed by just thirty-two German 21cm mortars, exactly the gun calibre that Liège was designed to defeat. Only one fort, Loncin, fell to the 42cm gun fire – Pontisse had been wrecked by 21cm fire before the 42cm arrived – and even here the 42cm fire was supplemented by the fire of other weapons. The last two forts surrendered, one while under a short period of 21cm fire, the other while not under fire at all.

And Liège fell with dizzying speed. Fort Barchon was reduced on 8 August by the fire of six 21cm mortars, d'Evegnée on 11 August by four 21cm mortars in two days of bombardment. The mass of the siege artillery, almost exclusively 21cm mortars, arrived on 12 August. Three forts fell on 13 August, two on 14 August, three on 15 August and the remaining two on the morning of 16 August. The German siege artillery, and principally the four battalions (thirty-two guns total) of the hard-hitting, mobile 21cm mortar of FAR 4 and 9, had reduced Liège in less than four days.

Development of German Siege Artillery

Armies fight the way they have trained to fight. Behind the brilliant successes of the German heavy artillery at Liège, then Namur, Maubeuge and Antwerp, lay nearly twenty years' worth of work in developing doctrine, equipment, and good, hard training, especially the live-fire shoots at the artillery MTA and the fortress General Staff exercises. Lombard reported that from the very start German artillery fire was 'devastatingly accurate'.[5]

By 1883 the German siege artillery faced the daunting prospect of massive French fortifications from Verdun to Belfort, and Antwerp, which led the Chief of the General Staff, Schlieffen, and the General Inspector of the Artillery, to develop the 'Heavy Artillery of the Field Army' (*schwere Artillerie des Feldheeres*), which would consist of a battalion of 15cm guns at the corps level and 21cm guns at the army level.[6]

In 1902 the corps batteries began to receive the new 15cm *schwere Feldhaubitze 02* (sFH 02). This was a revolutionary new design, with a recoil brake which kept the gun stable in position and allowed a far more accurate and higher rate of fire. The steel gun tube reduced weight and increased mobility. Maximum effective range went from 6,000m to 7,400m. A battery consisted of four guns and two munitions wagons, a battalion of four batteries and a light munitions column. The mission of the howitzers was to provide corps general support artillery, conducting counter-battery fire against field artillery equipped with armoured shields, and against dug-in infantry. It was not a siege weapon.

The German 21cm mortar in the 1890s was 'extremely unwieldy'. In 1909 the army-level artillery received the new 21cm mortar, which also had a recoil brake, an armoured gun shield, weighed about 9000kg and fired a 100kg shell 9,400m. It was broken down to three pieces for movement. A particular innovation was the *Radgürtel*: a wheel with flexible rectangular wooden plates affixed. One plate was always in contact with the ground, and significantly reduced the ground pressure generated by firing the weapon, and therefore no longer required a special base plate. A battery included six OFF, thirty-five NCOs, 218 EM and 150 horses. Each mortar battalion had two batteries, each with four guns, and a light munitions column. The mission of the 21cm mortars was to engage French border fortifications, especially the *Sperrforts* located between the four main fortresses. There was also a 13cm flat-trajectory gun with a range of 15km, which in siege operations would allow rear-area lines of communications to be engaged in depth.

For a considerable period the largest German siege weapon was an older-type 30.5cm mortar which had been introduced in 1893. It had a maximum effective range of 7km and a shell weighing 400kg. Its official designation was a 'heavy coastal mortar' and its code name was 'β-*Gerät*' – 'β apparatus'. Initially it was moved on narrow-gauge field railways, later on tractor-pulled trailers. Only nine were purchased. It was followed in 1909 by 'β-*Gerät* 09', which was also pulled by tractors and trailers. Only two of these were acquired.

In 1909 the heavy artillery also acquired a 42cm 'short naval mortar' (*kurze Marinekanone*) with a range of 14km and a 930kg shell. Its code name was γ-*Gerät*. It needed to be moved by regular rail line into the firing position. Firing tests showed that the weapon had outstanding accuracy as well as a very effective shell, so that in 1913–14 four more were delivered. The disadvantage of the mortar was its great weight and consequent dependence on rail mobility.

The success of the *Radgürtel* for the 21cm mortar led the artillery commission to use it for heavier weapons. To test this, in 1910 Krupp developed a 28cm howitzer on a wheeled *Radgürtel* chassis, in 1911 a 30.5cm howitzer.

In 1914 the German field army had 408 15cm howitzers, 112 21cm mortars, sixteen 10cm guns, one 28cm howitzer on a wheeled carriage, twelve 30cm mortars and seven 42cm mortars. The reserve foot artillery units included 400 15cm howitzers, 176 10cm guns and thirty-two 13cm guns. There were 420 pieces of heavy artillery without horse teams and 834 pieces of heavy fortress artillery.

21cm mortar

'Big Bertha' – The 42cm Mortar and Short Naval Cannon Battery 3[7]

In 1913 Krupp produced a 42cm howitzer on a *Radgürtel* wheeled chassis under the code name 'M-*Gerät*'. It had an 800kg shell, with 150kg of explosive filler, and a 9,300m range.

It was road-transportable in five sections, although each of the five pieces weighed between 16–21 metric tons (16,000–21,000kg). Each prime mover was 5m long, the entire vehicle 12m. In total the mortar weighed 70 metric tons (70,000kg). The mortar could be reassembled using a crane in four hours, but six to eight hours of hard work was necessary to prepare the entire mortar position. It is easy to see the mobility advantage possessed by the 21cm howitzer, which weighed about an eighth as much.

The availability of high-capacity mechanical prime movers was the prerequisite for the towed 42cm mortar. Even heavy draft horses were limited to loads of 6,000kg, and only for a limited time. In the absence of mechanical prime movers, heavy guns and mortars could only be moved by rail and fired from on or next to the tracks. The first experiments with mechanical prime movers were conducted in exercises at Metz in 1908.

Short Naval Cannon Battery 3 was pulled by requisitioned agricultural steam ploughs and locomotives. Although they weighed 2,000kg, they had never been designed as artillery prime movers and therefore were of limited tactical usefulness, as they could not pull such colossal loads for long distances. They also varied considerably in size and manufacturer. They required large quantities of coal and water and gave off clouds of black smoke. The crews were their usual farm drivers. Nevertheless, this field-expedient mobility for the 42cm was a resounding success. Due to Belgian demolitions the rail-mobile guns would never have got near Liège in time to affect the outcome of the battle.

All this made the choice of a firing position difficult. In addition, once the mortar was emplaced, the barrel could move left and right only as much as necessary to adjust fire. Shifting targets required a prime mover to haul the trail of the mortar around, necessitating an even larger gun position.

Ten to fifteen 900kg shells were brought forward on each rail wagon to be offloaded at a rail siding about 15km from the battery position, onto lorries, three to a vehicle. Unloaded near the gun position, each shell and powder charge were put onto a shell carrier and pushed by three men along a plank road to the gun position. They were hauled up to the loading tray by the ammunition crane on the mortar. The range was regulated in part by the size of the powder charge, in part by the elevation of the mortar

The first test-firing of two M-*Gerät* mortars took place at Krupp's private firing range at Meppen in February 1914, followed by more test-firing at the artillery MTA at Kummersdorf. These required 'certain improvements' on the mortars. Mobility exercises were conducted using the steam agricultural tractors near the Krupp works at Essen. Large farms were given subsidies to have the tractors on hand when needed.

A total of four batteries with seven 42cm mortars were on hand in 1914: three rail batteries with five mortars and one battery with two wheel-mobile mortars.

The development of the mobile, fast-firing, highly accurate 21cm mortar, directed by FOs with telephones, led the German siege artillery to develop a new form of siege

42cm mortar M-*Gerät*

warfare, the *verkürztes Verfahren*, a hasty attack. Where normal siege doctrine required a laborious and methodical deployment and advance, in the *verkürztes Verfahren* the 21cm would rapidly occupy a defilade position, followed by an immediate, intense bombardment and, if necessary, quick assault by infantry and combat engineers. At Liège the Germans employed the *verkürztes Verfahren*, and not the conventional siege doctrine, with devastating effectiveness, and which caught the Belgians and French completely by surprise.

German Artillery Order of Battle at Liège

None of the accounts of Liège give the order of battle for the German siege artillery, nor note the laughably small number of siege guns that the Germans employed – with breathtaking effectiveness.[8]

Short Naval Cannon Battery 3	Two 42cm mortars
II and III/ FAR 4	Sixteen 21cm mortars
I and II /FAR 9	Sixteen 21cm mortars
Total	Thirty-two 21cm mortars
II/ Reserve FAR 7[9]	Eight 13cm guns
4/ Fortress Combat Engineer Battalion 24	Four heavy trench mortars

The siege of Liège was a stand-up fight. The burden of the German attack would be carried by thirty-two pieces of the principal German siege artillery, the 21cm mortar, against a fortress than had been designed to defeat 21cm mortar fire. What Brialmont could not have foreseen in the late 1880s was the mobility of the German guns and the high rate of fire and accuracy provided by the recoil brakes and FOs equipped with telephones. This combination provided combat power which allowed the German siege artillery to demolish the Belgian forts in short order. The intensity of the German attack also revealed significant deficiencies in Brialmont's forts, further exacerbated by the Belgian high command's unwillingness to seriously defend Liège.

Artillery 6–7 August

On 6 August, 2/ FAR 9 (-) pulled back to Aachen with elements of 27 Brigade. The 2/ Foot Artillery 4 (-) held in place, was joined by the second two-gun platoon, and fired ninety-eight shells.

42cm mortar M-*Gerät*

Due to a lack of shells, 2/ Foot Artillery 4 could not fire on 7 August. At 2100, 2/ FAR 9 (-) left Aachen for Liège, having been resupplied with ammunition.

8 August

Fort Barchon Falls

Barchon had already been sorely tried by the III/ IR 53 attack on 5 August, which caused serious casualties. On the afternoon of 6 August Barchon was completely cut off. It had no telephone communications and could not see any Belgian units. Morale dropped. The commandant sent out several men by different routes to make contact.[10] On 7 August the garrison heard rumours from the local civilians that 3 DA had withdrawn, there were no Belgian troops on the east bank of the Meuse and Liège was occupied by the Germans. The commander sent out another messenger. Then one of his original messengers returned saying that he had talked with General Leman at Loncin and that orders would arrive soon. He also reported that 3 DA had withdrawn and the Germans were in Liège: morale in the garrison dropped further.

On 8 August, 2/ FAR 9 (-) was delayed by *francs-tireurs* in Moresnet and reached Julémont at 0900. Together with 2/ Foot Artillery 4, it engaged Fort Barchon, while field artillery fired on the gorge. Barchon lost communication with the OP and the Belgians abandoned it. Lombard admitted that the German artillery was invisible.

The IR 16 took up a position at the rear of the fort, in low ground on the Wandre–Blegny road and shortly after 1100 the IR 16 commander sent a parliamentarian under a white flag to the fort with a letter demanding the fort's surrender. After a quarter of an hour, the commandant refused, and at 1130 the German artillery reopened fire. Lombard said that the Germans rained shells on the fort, often firing four-gun 21cm salvoes, which shook the fort. Gas from the explosions entered the fort, and the latrines, which could not be emptied, overflowed. At 1500 it was determined that none of the turrets were operational and they were evacuated. Pieces of concrete began to fall on the garrison. The right-hand 21cm turret took a direct hit, wrecking the gun and projecting flames into the fort. The gunner in the 5.7cm turret at Salient I was severely wounded. At 1700 Barchon surrendered to IR 16. The 2/ Foot Artillery 4 had expended 180 shells, the number fired by 2/ Foot Artillery 9 (-) was not given, but was probably fewer than 90. The 2/ FAR 9 munitions column returned to Aachen at 2030, while 2/ FAR 9 (-) began reconnaissance against Fort Pontisse.

The fall of Barchon, on 8 August and after just one day's serious bombardment by six 21cm mortars, was a major embarrassment to the Belgians and compromised the effectiveness of the entire fortress. The Germans now had a free line of communication into Liège, and on the most direct route to Germany. Siege artillery, troops and supplies would pour into the city.

After the war Leman conducted a thorough analysis of the damage each fort had sustained and the degree of resistance they offered. He physically inspected the forts, interviewed the NCOs and enlisted specialists (mechanics, electricians) and read the General Staff reports. His own report was detailed and highly critical of the performance of the garrison of Barchon, and he clearly felt that the fort could have held out longer.[11] Leman said that Barchon had taken a few shells at 1130 4 August, was bombarded for a short time on 5, 6 and 7 August, and then more heavily shelled on 8 August. When it surrendered it still had munitions in the magazines. One gun in the right-hand 12cm turret was out of action, the 15cm turret was difficult to turn, the left-hand 21cm and right-hand 12cm turrets had been hit, the 15cm hit four times, in each case without doing serious damage. One 5.7cm turret had been obliterated. The flanking batteries in the ditch were intact, that is, an infantry assault was impossible. There was no problem with the ration and water supply, but ventilation was bad and oxygen bottles had to be used. The fort surrendered because one shell had penetrated the central gallery in the citadel, killing twelve infantrymen and wounding twenty; morale collapsed, the troops were near to mutiny and a Belgian doctor said the troops threatened the fortress commander.

In Liège

In Liège, Emmich's 8 August order gave the mission as, 'holding the city and bridges under all circumstances and reducing the fortresses, beginning with the east front'. The enemy situation was described as:

The Belgian Army [probably meaning 3 DA] is in retreat to Tirlemont. The troops unloaded at the rail station at Waremme are not advancing. French troops, at most two infantry divisions with an advance guard of cavalry and bicyclists, which were reported on 6 August to be in rail movement to Namur, have not been observed advancing. Belgian troops are digging in at Loncin [in fact, the Belgians had withdrawn]. The east and south fronts of Liège are free of enemy forces. The forts are combat-ready except for Fort de Barchon, which fell today.

The inability of the Liège forts to block the roads into the city became glaringly evident on 8 August, as German messengers, LNOs, units and supplies poured in unhindered. A much-needed munitions column arrived, as did the reservists from both 11 and 14 Brigades. In effect, both brigades completed their mobilisation in Liège. At 0800, IR 165 moved from the citadel and reached Ans.[12] The IR 165 commander took over command of 14 Brigade from Ludendorff.

The reservists from I and III/ 165 were led by two captains. The leader of the I/ 165 group, Captain Gruson, said that they arrived at the Aachen rail station at 0300, 7 August. He learned from the rail station commandant that the Wolff press agency had reported that IR 165 had been destroyed. Then he received a note from an IR 165 officer saying that IR 165 urgently needed reinforcements. Where the note originated was not stated (the officer was actually in hospital in Aachen). He moved the detachment towards the border at 0345, but instead of bivouacking there as his instructions from OHL required, he continued the march. Just across the border he encountered a messenger in an automobile saying that the regiment's situation was serious. It had been reduced to four companies, the brigade and regimental commander had been killed (untrue, although the commander of IR 27 had been) and the X AK HQ destroyed. No one knew what was going on. There were *francs-tireurs* everywhere and ammunition was running out. The messenger wanted to know when artillery support was coming. He also said that the wells in Belgium had been poisoned with cholera bacillus, along with what Gruson said were other ridiculous rumours. The messenger directed him to march to Battice. Gruson passed this message on to the IR 27 reservist detachment, which had already bivouacked. Gruson then rode ahead and reached Battice at 1100, where he encountered half of IR 165, led by a lieutenant colonel, who believed that the other half of the regiment had been destroyed and the regimental commander killed. At 1500 a General Staff officer appeared, saying that the regimental commander was alive and the other half of the regiment was in Liège. The IR 165 troops moved out in pouring rain, which allowed them to infiltrate between the forts without taking any fire. They arrived at the citadel at 2200 and were told to bivouac. The inhabitants took pains to show they were friendly. The IR 165 *reservists* had marched 51km in eighteen hours.

In Liège, IR 27 enjoyed a rest and some troops were quartered in private houses. Initially the regiment was formed into two battalions, Battalion Petiscus with 2, 3, the remnants of 4 and 7; Battalion von Blanckensee with 8, 9, 11, and MGK. The 10 and 12/27 received the mission of transporting the Belgian prisoners to Germany. Then 1,000 reservists arrived.[13] The 11/27 protected some 21cm mortars.

14 Brigade was given a defensive sector on the north-east quadrant of the city; from the Meuse to St Nicholas. The IR 27 had the right half. This did not mean that the regiment prepared Liège for defence, but rather that the roads were blocked, security established and the companies took up alarm quarters nearby.

According to the IR 16 history, the time the regiment spent in Liège was positively pleasant: the troops got along well with the population, the city was beautiful and wealthy and the summer weather wonderful. The regiment was also able to get in considerable training to bring the reservists up to standard.

After much confused back-and-forth movement, the 1/Hussar R 10 supply vehicles entered Liège at 0900.[14] The NCO in charge passed out the oats and then followed the squadron as it marched to Ans, but not until he had purchased some picture postcards of Belgium. The next day he was ordered back into Liège, where his fourteen-man supply column bivouacked alone, surrounded by 'hundreds of civilians'. Nevertheless, he went out with another NCO to drink a glass of German beer and eat white bread and a green salad; 'I still to this day have no idea what it was made out of.' The next day he found a courtyard to stable the horses in. The owner had a four-storey porcelain warehouse and was happy that nothing had been damaged. Initially the ration situation was not good, but the order came down to requisition, paying with quartermaster receipts: a German-speaking civilian helped him. The populace had to turn in their weapons, and there were piles of them. One day he ate in the same hotel that General von Emmich was quartered in. The soup, roast and potatoes were paid for with quartermaster receipts, but the troops had to pay for their own beer, 50 pfennig. 'The days we spent in Liège were very pleasant.'

The 1/Hussar 10 reservists (three OFF, twenty-one EM) were not so lucky. On 8 August at the east side of Herve they took fire 'apparently from civilians in the houses'. The field kitchens and supply vehicles fled in panic to the rear. Two hussar lieutenants gathered up some infantry and with the dismounted hussars stopped the hostile fire after a half-hour engagement. One hussar was hit in the leg, which had to be amputated. Another was lightly wounded by buckshot. Since the *franc-tireurs* made a further advance dangerous, the reservists waited for the rest of the regiment to arrive.

The IR 20 was on the west side of Liège. The 'defensive position' again consisted of observation posts at the crossroads and road patrols. In case of attack the regiment would defend the houses. At 2200 the field trains arrived, with some of the field kitchens and ammunition wagons.

Outside Liège

On the morning of 8 August, as the AOK 2 HQ was still moving by rail, the first LNO reported by telephone that he had spoken with Ludendorff, and received an accurate situation report, with the exception of the fact that he reported Fléron had fallen.[15]

When the AOK 2 HQ arrived west of Aachen at 2200 the second LNO reported that OHL had ordered the arriving corps to send units forward to support the Liège attack. The first LNO therefore had ordered IX AK to send a brigade, or a regiment at the minimum, plus artillery, to Visé, VII AK was to send a similar force to the south-east of Liège and X AK south of Liège. There was still no communication with Emmich and the AOK learned that Fléron was still in enemy hands.

Ludendorff had been unable to return to Liège and reported personally to Bülow. Communication with Emmich in Liège was impossible. He said it had to be assumed that the Belgians, reinforced by the French, had defeated the German troops in Liège.

The three brigades outside Liège were still uncertain as to the situation inside the city.

In the 34 Brigade sector, IR 89 stayed in bivouac on the Dutch border between Mouland and Fouron until 12 August. Initially, the regiment was reorganised into four companies: 1 and 2/ 89 became 1/ 89, with 149 EM, 3 and 4 became 2/ 89, with 185 EM, II/ 89 became 3/ 89, with 199 men, II/ 89 became 4/ 89, with 130 EM. The IR 89 started the attack with 1,631 EM; it now had 663. The regiment quickly recovered its strength. Stragglers returned. On the evening of 8 August the reservists arrived and on 9 and 10 August conducted training. On 11 August the troops that had been captured returned to the regiment – from 7 to 11 August these troops, armed with Belgian weapons, had helped garrison the Liège citadel. On 13 August they received German weapons again.[16] The IR 90 was in much better condition, having taken only 199 EM casualties.

The bridge across the Meuse at Lixhé was completed on 8 August, and at 1700 8/ 90 crossed to hold the bridgehead, followed by 2 and 4 KD, which continued the march and bivouacked halfway to St Trond. On the next day their orders were to reconnoitre towards Brussels.

On 7 August, Jäger 7, which consisted of 3/ Jäger 7, the MGK and parts of 1, had been attached to 4 KD and did some pointless marching to Aubel, halfway back to Aachen. While it was still dark on 8 August it was ordered to move through Battice to Hervé. Vehicles were requisitioned to carry the packs of the exhausted Jäger. A Belgian priest then arrived in an automobile with a German soldier as driver, with an order to march through Queue-du-Bois to Liège, which the battalion found 'curious'. At almost the same time a bicyclist from Jäger 4 arrived with instructions that all troops marching into Liège were to be regarded as neutral; each march column was to carry a white flag (a measure straight out of a peacetime exercise, and probably the truce with Fort Fléron at work).[17] The houses all displayed white flags. At 1200 the battalion took quarters at the Chartreuse. Elements of 2 and 4/ Jäger 7, about 200 men, including stragglers and men who had been released from Belgian captivity, were at the citadel. A sergeant had become separated from the battalion.

He had walked towards Liège until he was taken in by a German woman, who fed him breakfast and let him rest a bit. A young boy led him into the city. He arrived at the citadel shortly after Ludendorff, receiving the proper military greeting from the Belgian on guard duty. The main body of the battalion remained at the Chartreuse until 11 August, when it moved to join HKK 2. Duty time was used for maintenance and training. Off-duty the Jäger were allowed to go shopping in the city. There was a carrier pigeon station in the Chartreuse, and every hour a bird would fly in with a message, which the Germans intercepted, showing that the Belgians had absolutely no idea what the situation was.

On the morning of 8 August IR 25 again set out to attack Cheratte, but took only fire from Fort Pontisse, which forced it to leave the road. Reconnoitring to the front, 2/ Uhlan R 16 continually took scattered small-arms fire from soldiers and civilians in houses, hedges and vineyards: 100 were taken prisoner and turned over to the infantry.[18] The brigade entered Liège at 2300, 2/ Uhlan R 16 took quarters in the Belgian Lancer R 2 barracks, IR 25 in the barricaded houses near the Meuse bridges, followed by IR 53.

The IR 53 was reorganised into two battalions, each with four companies, probably principally because of officer casualties. On 16 August, 344 replacements arrived and the regiment was reorganised into three battalions; on 18 August more replacements arrived and the regiment was near full-strength.[19] It spent 9–15 August in training and guard duties.

Fort d'Evegnée had an OP in the church tower of the small village of Tignée, between Evegnée and Barchon, which provided observation over Micheroux, Herve and Battice.[20] The OP was connected to the fort by telephone and adjusted fire using prearranged points. It said it engaged a supply column, then infantry. At 1215 a German 10.5cm ammunition supply column with six caissons marched right down the road to the fort and was destroyed by 5.7cm fire.[21]

Brigades 38 and 43 were on a line, Olne–Louveigné, with 9 KD on the flank at Sprimont. Deploying early, 28 Brigade was formed out of IR 39 and 56, and crossed the border on 8 August. In a strange mission, I/ 56 was instructed to reconnoitre towards d'Evegnée and occupy the fort 'if it was in German hands'.[22] The I/ 56 carefully approached using farm paths, hedges and bushes to within 800m of the fort, the battalion fully deployed, 1/ 56 leading. A patrol reached the fosse, when it took rifle fire, with an officer candidate being wounded. The fort was surrounded by dead ground which provided cover and concealment for German infantry, which allowed them to severely wound several defenders. One had both arms nearly blown off and he died several hours later; the fort commander had a bullet pass through his cap. The I/ 56 commander pulled his unit back to a flat depression near the town of Mélen under artillery fire. It was then ordered to withdraw, followed by ineffective artillery fire. Both II and III/ 56 took artillery fire and suffered casualties, including a corporal KIA. The IR 39 history said that it tried to close off Fléron, but took artillery fire and, lacking artillery support, and because it had already taken casualties, backed away.[23] The 28 Brigade bivouacked at Soumagne. Lombard says that during the night, Fléron engaged infantry detachments, cavalry patrols, artillery batteries and the towns where 28 Brigade units were bivouacked. The IR 39 history mentions only that it got a friendly reception from the town's Flemish inhabitants. Lombard claims that the forts stopped 28 Brigade from entering Liège, but their actual mission was not to go to the city at all, but to close off the eastern forts.

That evening the senior AOK 2 General Staff officer went to VII AK HQ to get oriented on the situation. The VII AK was no wiser, having no communication with Emmich.

General von Bülow put the commander of VII AK, General von Einem, who arrived at Eupen at 2200, in charge of the siege of Liège. As they arrived, the heavy artillery and elements of IX, VII and X AK would be at his disposal. After being briefed by Ludendorff at the Eupen rail station, von Einem decided to leave 11, 14 and 27 Brigades to hold Liège city under General von Emmich. The 34 Brigade would continue to hold near Visé in the north, while 28 Brigade was to move towards Fort Fléron and d'Evegnée. On its left, 38 Brigade would secure to the north of Fraipont on the Vesdre, 43 Brigade to the south of it. To their rear, 40 Brigade of X AK was to move on Pepinster. The IX AK would unload at Aachen, VII at Eupen, X at Malmedy.[24]

At 2200 the Belgian cavalry division commander said that 1,500 German cavalry, with MGs had been reported near St Trond and he requested permission to attack them.[25] The king quickly replied that seven German cavalry regiments had been reported west of the Meuse and that the Belgian cavalry division would continue to screen in place; the German cavalry had nearly got exactly what they wanted, a battle with the Belgian cavalry division.

9 August

The I and II/ IR 90, along with a battery from II/ FAR 60 and 5/ Dragoon R 16, crossed the pontoon bridge over the Meuse at Lixhé and secured the bridgehead. While on reconnaissance the commander of 10/ 90 was wounded by a civilian.[26] On 11 August 150 men who had been captured on the night of 5–6 August returned to the regiment.

On 9 August, IR 25 enjoyed a rest day and the field kitchens were brought up. Two companies of IR 25 and two of 53 policed up the Cheratte battlefield and buried the dead.

From a position south-west of St Remy, 2/ Foot Artillery 9 (-) opened fire against Fort Pontisse. In order to engage Fort Fléron it ceased fire and marched during the afternoon through Jupille to a position at Wandre, west of Fort Barchon, where it arrived at 2045. Ammunition resupply arrived in six lorries.

The fall of Barchon demoralised the garrison of Pontisse. In order to impress on his troops the seriousness of their mission, the fortress commander, Speesen, had the ladders of the exits into the fosse destroyed. The infantry lieutenant put guards on the exits to prevent desertion.[27] The armour was cracked so severely that rain-water got into the magazines and the shells had to be moved to the galleries.[28] Any member of the garrison who showed himself drew MG fire and, after 1900, light artillery fire. One of the 15cm guns had the end of the barrel blown off, the other immobilised, and the crew was burned by the flames from the exploding shells and had to be replaced completely. So much of the glacis and scarp had been blown into the fosse between Salients I and II that the 5.7cm flanking guns had to be moved to the upper floor.

The 2/ Foot Artillery 9 (-) consisted of one platoon – two 21cm mortars. They made quite an impression on the garrison of Pontisse, creating an 'infernal concert' which shook the entire fort. The garrison was 'on edge, numbed, physically ill'. Since Pontisse no longer had any OPs, Speesen sent out men on bicycles, presumably in civilian clothing, to acquire targets.

The mass of I/ FAR 9 began rail movement from Cologne late that evening. Having intended to engage Fort Fléron, 2/ Foot Artillery 4 was moved on 9 August to attack Fort d'Evegnée. Until 9 August Evegnée had an OP in the church tower at Tignée, but at 1645 it was chased out by German infantry.

In Liège

The IR 20 was redeployed to the south-west sector opposite Fort de Flémalle, backed up by 5/ FAR 39. Trenches were dug, wire obstacles laid, the streets barricaded. The quarters for the officers and men were 'excellent', the food from the field kitch-ens 'very good'. The regiment remained here until 14 August. Fort de Flémalle and Boncelles fired a few rounds, two of which hit the parsonage occupied by 11/ 20, but there were no casualties.

On 9 August, IR 165 was pulled back from Ans to Liège, ostensibly to occupy a defensive position. In fact, the regiment conducted training for the reservists. On 10 August, II/ 165 (- 7/ 165, guarding the corps HQ at the citadel) was sent to Rocourt with the mission of harassing Forts Liers and Loncin. During the afternoon 8/ 165 went to the north-east side of Liers and shot at the Belgian security posi-tions, then pulled back when the fort began to fire its artillery. That evening, 6/ 165 approached Lantin, but could not find anyone to shoot at. The III/ 165 moved back to Ans to harass Loncin: 12/ 165 occupied the airfield. On 11 August the two bat-talions again sent harassment patrols to the forts: their return fire was practically at random and did little harm. On 12 August they were relieved and given a rest, on 13 August sent back again. To the right was IR 27.

To the left was 11 Brigade, with the mission of holding from the Brussels rail line south to the Meuse, opposite Fort Hollogne. It deployed IR 35 from right to left II, I, III/ 35, each battalion getting a platoon of MGs. The Belgians shelled III/ 35 positions a few times, without effect. The regiment held these positions until 14 August. Patrolling was continual. One patrol from 9/ 35 was sent out to reconnoitre Fort Hollogne. The lieutenant reported:

I took three squads, all men I had trained as recruits. I wore the same uniform as the men: field cap without brim, rifle and ammunition pouches, no packs. We moved through a factory district. In front of us, not a soul to be seen, behind us large groups of civilians, including young military-age men. Since I feared an ambush by the civilians, especially in St. Nicholas, where their attitude was particularly hostile, I took four hostages, including the mayor. On the way we were shadowed by bicyclists, who moved to the fort. In a few hours we reached the area of the fort; I left the hostages behind, guarded by two men. The civil population nearby fled into the fort. There was a copse about 1,000 metres from the fort, in which men could be seen working; on our approach they too fled to the fort. One remained, then finally ran; he was ordered three times to stop, and when he did not my range estimators and I each fired a shot, one of which hit him in the head. On the body we found a notebook with the plan of the fort and the obstacles. From this we decided that the men were reinforcing the abatis with high-voltage electric power lines.

When we reached the abatis we took fire from troops on the crown work of the wall; the troops, about two companies, evenly spaced, were easy to see. When we closed in to 500 metres we took shrapnel and canister fire from two guns. Big lead balls about 2 centimetres around sailed lazily in our direction. One hit a man in his bread case and stayed there. Another fusilier was immobilized by a leg wound. We reached the edge of the copse, about 200 metres from the fort. Immediately to our front was a ditch with vertical walls. The draw bridge [*sic*] on the gorge raised close behind a mob of civilians, which pushed panic-stricken inside. The enemy fired far too high, probably because of our calm return fire, and we didn't take any casualties. Since further advance was pointless, we withdrew to the rally point at the abatis. The return trip, on the same route we came, was slowed by the need to carry the wounded man. The expected pursuit from the fort did not materialize, but the road was black with civilians. The patrol returned to the battalion several hours after dark.

That day the reservists arrived, as well as the combat and field trains, which had been believed lost. The march column commander, the senior captain, had received no intelligence concerning the situation. He established that without previous reconnaissance it was impossible to infiltrate between Fort Evegnée and Fort Fléron, and he marched back through Herve to bivouac at Battice. He decided to go through Soumagne, moved out at 0400 and stopped in Soumagne to reconnoitre. For this, he had only the three mounted captains and his personal bicycle, nothing else. At noon he resumed the march to Ayeneux. The last two squads were leaving Soumagne when they were hit by shells from Fléron: there were fifteen KIA and twenty-six WIA. The column continued the march through deep watercourses, which provided conceal-ment from observation by Fort Fléron.

The men had no first-aid dressings, and the only doctor had only one aid man and no medical equipment. Fortunately he was able to obtain assistance from the doctor and pharmacy in Soumagne, as well as an aid man from IR 20. The wounded were brought to the Catholic nuns that ran the school, as well as several German-speaking women.

The Belgians had identified IX, VII, X, AK near Liège, which was correct, but also III, IV, and XI. III and IV did not finish rail deployment until 11 August, XI prob-ably not until 12 August. The XII and XIX were identified near Houffalize in the Ardennes – they were also not complete until 12 August. The VIII AK, identified at Bastogne, was ready on 10 August. From their location south of the Meuse it should have appeared probable to the Belgians that XI, XII, XIX and VIII AK were not going to be their problem. The Belgians also identified the two German cavalry divi-sions approaching St Trond, which caused the Belgian cavalry division to fall back behind the Gette and screen the army left flank, crippling Belgian cavalry reconnais-sance. There was also a report that 20,000 German troops had crossed the Meuse on newly constructed pontoon bridges at Lixhé. No such German movement actually took place. In sum, Galet said 'we felt that the German sweep north of the Meuse was beginning'. He was nine days too early: the German right wing advance did not begin until 18 August.

The king summoned the French and British military attachés and told them:

> If we are faced by very superior forces we think it might be necessary, in order to avoid the destruction of the Belgian Army, to withdraw temporarily under the protection of the Antwerp forts, with the intention of resuming the offen-sive when the approach of the Allied armies makes itself felt.'

10 August

The IX AK (General von Quast) had been assigned the northern and eastern fronts of Liège: Forts Liers, Pontisse and Fléron. In addition to his corps' organic I/ FAR 20 (sFH), he was given operational control over Short Naval Cannon Battery 3 (42cm mortar), Heavy Coastal Mortar Battery 5 (30cm mortar), a 21cm mortar regiment consisting of II and III/ FAR 4, and II/ Reserve FAR 9 (flat-trajectory 13cm guns).

On the south and east fronts (Forts Chaudefontaine and d'Embourg) was 13 ID of VII AK (General von dem Borne) with I/ FAR 7 (sFH) and operational control of Coastal Mortar Battery 1 (30cm) and a 21cm mortar regiment composed of I and II/ FAR 9.

The Belgians had blocked the Aachen–Liège rail line by driving seventeen locomotives together in the Nasproué tunnel: the Germans had to offload from the railcars at Herbesthal on the border. This is probably the reason why the 30cm mortars did not participate in the siege.

Priority was given to blinding the forts' artillery by denying them external observation posts; special attention was made to clearing and securing nearby church towers. De Schrÿver acknowledged that this was completely effective, and that counter-battery fire became 'impossible'.[29]

The 19 ID would cover the army left flank and establish contact with 9 KD.

On 10, 11 and 12 August, 4 and 6/ FAR 43 (light howitzers) went into a covered position west of Wandre and engaged Pontisse.[30] Firing on the fort's armour was pointless, so the howitzers engaged the observation towers and claimed to have destroyed two. They also repeatedly fired on Belgian troops in a ditch behind the fort. On 10 August, Pontisse returned the batteries' fire, but the shrapnel burst too high to do any damage. On 11 August, Pontisse's fire was accurate, but still caused no damage. The only casualty was the artillery section commander, who was hit by a flying piece of a wall.

On 10 August the two 21cm mortars of 2/ Foot Artillery 9 (-) once again engaged Fort Pontisse, this time from a position west of Fort Barchon. In spite of optimistic Belgians claims, Belgian counter-battery fire was ineffective. The two mortars, however, were taking Pontisse apart.[31] One ditch was filled in with debris and some of the barbed wire had disappeared. A majority of the turrets were jammed by concrete debris and could not turn. Concrete fragments in the barrels of the artillery caused the shells to detonate prematurely. Service in a turret 'was like torture'. The seams in the turret armour split, allowing flames from the explosions to enter, burning the gunners. The 12cm and 15cm turrets had been shaken out of their mounts and would not aim properly. The 21cm turrets offered less protection than the howitzers. The shock of the explosions would cut the heads off the bolts in the armour and send them into the turret like bullets. Turrets became untenable and were evacuated. The only food available was biscuits, 'monkey meat' – canned corned beef – and muddy water. As the German infantry closed in on Pontisse, the fort's patrols could only move at night and became less effective.

De Schrÿver also says that at Loncin the German artillery tried to lay down a smoke screen in front of the observation posts, but were suppressed by the fort's counter-battery fire.[32] No German artillery unit mentioned even having smoke shells, and it is not clear what they would have accomplished by firing them at Loncin now. Lantin fired on German patrols trying to attack the fort's observation posts, and at cavalry patrols. Liers scattered German troops marching on St Trond, and Hollogne fired on German patrols. The only real success was when d'Embourg engaged a German supply column which had got lost, inflicting six KIA, eight WIA and taking three POW with numerous horses killed or injured.

The I/ Foot Artillery 9 unloaded at Aachen and bivouacked near Eupen.

The IR 35 continued to reconnoitre and harass Fort Hollogne. On 10 August, 2/ 27 was given the mission of annoying Fort Pontisse. It went to the south-east of Rhées, sighted some Belgians digging in, and fired several salvoes, returning that night. On the night of 10–11 August IR 25 conducted a demonstration with three companies and an artillery battery, without taking any casualties.

The 2/ Foot Artillery 4 fired at Fort d'Evegnée. At 0800 an eight-man patrol left the fort, equipped with carrier pigeons, for the church tower at Tignée, in order to try to locate the German artillery positions, but were 'unable to find any indication whatsoever of a battery in action'.[33] Finally they thought they saw a German battery and Evegnée opened fire with the two remaining operational guns, a 15cm and a 21cm. Lombard says that the Germans were silenced for fifteen minutes. The observers then gave a location where there appeared to be German batteries. This time the German fire did not slow at all. Finally the fort fired on suspected enemy locations. The 15cm gun was put out of action, along with the 5.7cm at Salient III. After a break in the fire from 1230–1300, the German bombardment was 'more violent and more accurate than before'. The fort fired on enemy troops and a battery with the one remaining gun. A German patrol found the d'Evegnée OP and at 1910 a stronger German force chased it off for good. The 2/ Foot Artillery 4 history does not mention any Belgian counterfire.

Evegnée was masked by I/ IR 25. It found a hollow road near Retinne that was good protection from both the Belgian artillery and the occasional German 21cm shell falling short. The battalion commander, a captain, reconnoitred the fort and found a 20m deep wire obstacle and the concrete ditch, which he could not overcome with field-expedient materials. He also requisitioned a motor vehicle and made his way to 2/ Foot Artillery 4, which was surprised to hear that a German infantry battalion was in the immediate vicinity. The artillery commander informed the infantryman of his fire plan, which would become very important in the near future. After dark, the battalion moved to the village of Evegnée, which was only 600m from the fort, and locked the male inhabitants in a barn as hostages, threatening them with death if they betrayed the Germans. The fort was now closed off on two of three sides.

The Belgians continually overestimated the intensity of the German fire. De Schrÿver says that Pontisse counted 3,000 21cm shells on 10 August, Evegnée 2,500,[34] which was off by a factor of twenty. He also said Fléron's counter-battery fire silenced three German batteries (Lombard says two). The IR 25 history reported counter-battery fire from Forts Pontisse and Fléron, but the German artillery histories do not.

11 August

Fort d'Evegnée Falls

Near dawn on 11 August, I/ IR 25 began an assault on the infantry defensive positions of Evegnée and moved up to the edge of the wire obstacle, about 300m from the fort. They were greeted by lively small-arms and 5.7cm fire. The Belgians were visibly taking casualties. The 2/ Foot Artillery 4, which could know nothing of the I/ 25 attack, reopened fire on the fort. The infantry was soon endangered by pieces of the German shells and chunks of Belgian concrete, so withdrew first to Retinne and, finding the town too exposed, back to the sunken road, leaving an observer in the Retinne church tower. The Belgians made one more attempt to reoccupy the Tignée OP. They were able to remain there for twenty minutes before being chased back. Another attempt was stopped when the first man through the fort sally port was killed. The last operational 15cm gun fired blind until it too was no longer operational. Repair crews were chased out of the turrets by spalling from the turrets and flames from exploding shells. The 2/ Foot Artillery 4 was firing four-gun salvoes. The garrison withdrew to the central gallery, which filled with gas from exploding shells.

The I/ 25 commander drew up a demand for the fort's capitulation – in French – and during a break in the 21cm fire from 1545 to 1630, sent an officer, a French-speaking NCO, the battalion drummer and a Belgian prisoner, in the requisitioned automobile and under flag of truce, to demand the fort's surrender. The 2/ Foot Artillery 4 had no knowledge of this. The interruption of the fire was almost over when the officer returned, waving his helmet, and accompanied by the commander of the Evegnée infantry company: the fort had surrendered and raised the white flag on the ramparts. The garrison was allowed to march out with military honours, the officers kept their swords. The senior German officer saluted the commander of Evegnée, shook his hand and praised him as a 'brave soldier'.

Evegnée had been reduced to a smoking, defenceless ruin by four 21cm mortars. Even before the arrival of the main body of the German siege artillery, six 21cm mortars had taken two forts, creating a 3km gap that no Belgian artillery could reach.

The 2/ Foot Artillery 4 had expended 224 shells. De Schrÿver said that the Germans had been firing 250–275 shells an hour.[35] Leman reported that the fort had been bombarded on 5, 6, 8, 10 and 11 August. The concrete of the citadel had been severely damaged. By the time the fort fell none of the artillery turrets could turn. The armoured embrasure plates on the 12cm turrets had been blown off and when the guns fired the smoke was drawn back into the turret. Bursting rivets in the 15cm turret had wounded several of the gun crew. The 15cm turret had taken two direct hits, a 12cm turret one. All the 5.7cm turrets were inoperable. One incident of unsteadiness among the garrison had been quashed by the fort commander, and morale remained 'good'. The kitchen was destroyed, the troops ate whatever they could scrounge, and only unleavened bread could be baked. There was still water and electricity, but the ventilation was inadequate and the garrison had been forced to surrender due to effect of the gas caused by the exploding shells and the pestilential odour from the latrines.

The I/ 25 commander immediately drove to 2/ Foot Artillery 4 to prevent it from reopening fire. Here he learned that the commander of 18 ID was at Herve. He drove off to report and was ordered by the division commander to try to get Fort Fléron to surrender, too. He returned to the sunken road, which now held the garrison of Evegnée, 5 OFF and 407 EM, whom he marched as POW to Herve. The I/ 25 commander then rode off to Fléron, where, after long negotiations, he was unable to convince the commander of Fléron to surrender, a decision that the IR 25 historian characterised as 'soldierly and correct'.

Crossing the border at 0830, I/ FAR 20 moved through Pepinster and Louveigné and went into position at 2010, with the forward observer on the north side of Beaufays, prepared to engage Fort d'Embourg the next day. On the evening of 11 August, II/ Foot Artillery 4 and I/ Foot Artillery 20 went in position against Fort Fléron, III/ Foot Artillery 4 (-7, which moved to Liège) took position immediately east of Fort Barchon. The two-mortar platoon of 2/ Foot Artillery 9 did not fire on 11 August due to lack of ammunition, but was resupplied that evening by a truck column originally intended to motorise the Jäger. At 1900 the platoon moved to rejoin the regiment. Pontisse therefore enjoyed a quiet day on 11 August, with the exception of some light howitzer fire

The I/ Foot Artillery 4, the second company of III, and the regimental staff made a 30–33km march to their firing positions near Fort Barchon. The regimental staff and the other three platoons of I/ FAR 9 marched through Eupen to Verviers. The Jäger battalions were detached to return to HKK 2. General von Hülsen, who had received a bayonet wound on the night of 5–6 August, was able to resume command of 43 Brigade.

Combat Effectiveness of the Belgian Army[36]

Galet wrote:

> On the 11th August I accompanied him [the King] to a review of the 2nd Mixed Brigade [...] There was certainly some improvement, although the units were not yet reliable. He also made a point of questioning the officers of the 3rd Division as to the conduct of the men under fire. General Bertrand, who had distinguished himself at the head of the 11th Brigade, submitted a report which contained the following sound appreciation:
>
> 'The offensive value of the troops is poor. They are bad at manoeuvring, owing to the lack of officers who are known to the men. The conclusion is unavoidable that in its present state the Army should be employed defensively, without attempting counter-attacks or *retours-offensifs* on any scale'

Certain junior officers also, whose enthusiasm was beyond question, declared that their men were unreliable, unhandy and jumpy at night, and that the old soldiers inspired no confidence.

At 0900 the division commanders were confidentially instructed to reconnoitre routes of withdrawal to Antwerp. At 1300 the three forward divisions were ordered to organise a defensive position on the Gette.

12 August

Haelen[37]

On 11 August, HKK 2 identified the Belgian forces on the line Tirlemont–Huy, with the Belgian cavalry division on the left flank. Marwitz, the commander of HKK 2, decided to conduct a reconnaissance in force on 12 August to turn the Belgian left and penetrate their line.

The Belgian cavalry division was defending dismounted to the west of Haelen. Marwitz launched a series of mounted cavalry charges without proper prior reconnaissance. His cavalry encountered wire fences around factory buildings and pastures and were turned back with serious loss, having accomplished nothing. Towards the end of the engagement the Belgian 4 Brigade attacked and ran squarely into Jäger Battalion 9 and, although the Belgian brigade had the support of three artillery batteries and outnumbered the Jäger four to one, the 4 Brigade attack came to a screeching halt and the Jäger counterattacked. The 4 Brigade lost three of four majors, nine of twenty-seven company-grade OFF and 399 EM. Initially, the Belgian cavalry division commander reported that his entire force had lost three KIA and 200 WIA, which bore no relation to reality. 'This fight' said Galet, 'was a fresh test of the real value of our troops':

> The cavalry had come up to our expectations, but our doubts as to the lack of manoeuvring power of the infantry had been confirmed. It appeared next day that the 4th Brigade was shaken, and at most was only capable of 'holding on'. Its commander bewailed the dearth of officers, especially of platoon leaders, the inexperience of the non-commissioned officers, and the untrained condition of the men recalled to the colours.

Haelen raised high hopes among the officers who wanted the Belgian Army to go over to the offensive, now supported by the French LNOs. They assumed that the Germans had given up the attack north of the Meuse and would advance south of it. Galet said:

The First [Operations] Section began to work out in detail plans for a general advance to the Meuse […]

It was principally in Brussels that public opinion showed impatience at the inaction of the Army. At the instigation, or at all events, with the approval, of the Minister, the Press, thinking that it was performing a patriotic task, circulated the wildest reports and promoted an insensate atmosphere of optimism. If the newspapers were to be believed, the Germans were already becoming demoralized by the blows dealt them by the Belgian troops, their cavalry was useless; their horses were so starved that our men refused to ride the animals that they captured; their soldiers were so famished that they surrendered for a crust of bread […] the German Army was no more than a mob of beggars and cowards […] Every report of the surrender of the Liège forts was characterized as propaganda and false, at a time when two of them had already surrendered and the fall of the others could only be a matter of days.

Liège

During the afternoon of 12 August, a platoon of two guns from I/ FAR 9 went into position in the Vesdre valley south of Forêt and opened fire on Fort Chaudefontaine at 1810, receiving ineffective counter-battery fire. The battalion's fire was directed by a lieutenant FO connected to the guns by telephone.

Remunitioned, the two-gun platoon of 2/ Foot Artillery 9 was already in position, reopened fire on Pontisse and claimed to have destroyed two turrets with 109 shells, while receiving effective counter-battery fire which caused casualties. De Schrÿver said that the intensity of the German fire rose from 80–100 shells an hour to 150 and occasionally 250, which, if accurate, included light field artillery. The fort was poorly sited, and the terrain allowed the German infantry covered and concealed close-range MG positions, which fired on the turrets. The garrison was 'visibly at the end of their rope' and the guns were so badly damaged that they could be fired 'only with extreme difficulty'.[38] Fire against the rear of the fort broke open the armoured blinds on the windows and cracked the concrete, allowing the gas from the explosions into the fort, in spite of attempts to close them up with mattresses. The latrines in the scarp were rendered unusable and 'there were 380 men in the fort'. A shell hit the latrine sewer line, spreading human waste down the corridors and creating an 'indescribable stench'. A short time thereafter the cistern was hit, filling the neighbouring rooms with water. In the aid station, there was water up to the calf. The garrison was now without water. The electrical system failed; illumination was by hurricane lamp.[39]

'Short Naval Cannon Battery 3': Mobilisation and Deployment[40]

The battery had been ordered to begin mobilisation on 2 August 1914. The cadre (two OFF, five NCO, seventy EM) from the active-duty personnel of the Experimental

Battery at the *Artillerie-Prüf-Kommission*, the German Army's artillery testing agency at the artillery MTA at Kummersdorf, arrived at Essen on 5 August. It was followed on 8 August by the battery commander and reservists – ten NCOs and 175 EM. The reservists, although artillerymen, had no training on the 42cm mortars. Eight different types of agricultural tractors were requisitioned to move the battery. The Krupp fire department provided heavy draft horses and drivers for the supply wagons, which came from the Krupp grocery store and museum(!). Herr von Bohlken, the Krupp director, provided riding horses from his own stable, as well as automobiles with drivers and assistants. On the evening of 10 August the battery began rail movement to Aachen. Since the Aachen–Liège rail line was unserviceable, on the morning of 11 August the battery unloaded at Herbesthal on the border and by 2200 had road-marched 15km. The prime movers frequently broke down and the passing troop units and supply columns were pressed into service to pull the mortars. The battery spent an unquiet night at the Franciscan monastery at Henri-Chapelle due to firing from *francs-tireurs*.

From Trench Mortars to Super-heavy Mortars

On 12 August, the 42cm battery went into an open firing position on the high ground 500m north-east of Mortier. The observation post was set up at Fort Barchon. After forty shells had been brought up, the first 42cm shell was fired at 1840. When the battery ceased fire at 2010, it had fired eight shells.

The fort's infantry commander, Lieutenant Couvreur, was on watch when he saw a huge detonation to the east, followed by an immense column of black smoke. Fifteen minutes later there was a second volcanic explosion on the slope leading to the Meuse, closer to the fort, followed by a third and a fourth. Couvreur reported his observations to Speesen, who replied that it was 'Quite simple; they're mining us. There is an old coal mine in that direction and the Germans are using the galleries to blow us up.' The lieutenant had hardly returned to his OP when there was another explosion, more violent this time, and the black geyser seemed to have come closer. Three further explosions followed, and the fort shook 'like a boat that had hit a reef'. The black clouds were now quite close, just beyond the glacis that faced the Meuse. The Germans had fired short, and then walked the rounds up to the target.

In the fort, the critical problem was the complete lack of water. The aid station was filled with wounded and sick. Fort Liers attempted to assist Pontisse by 'firing on locations which seemed suitable as infantry assault positions',[41] but the Germans intended to do no such thing and the shells hit empty land.

The Germans also employed, for the first time, 'heavy trench mortars' (*schwere Minenwerfer*), operated by combat engineers, intended expressly for fortress and trench warfare. These were simple and highly effective weapons, with a short barrel, affixed almost vertically to a baseplate. This allowed them to fire from a completely defilade and protected position, such as a trench. It had a range of only 800m, and since the range was

Heavy trench mortar (*schwere Minenwerfer*)

so short, aiming was simple. It fired a shell with a very thin casing and 100kg of explosives: the detonation was terrific. Fort Pontisse was therefore the first target of two new generations of modern siege weapons, 'heavy trench mortars' and the 42cm 'M-*Gerät*'.

13 August

Pontisse Falls

II/ IR 90 had moved to Hermée at 1800 on 12 August in case Fort Pontisse surrendered. It spent the night shivering in a large oat field. The next morning it moved to Oupeye, north of Pontisse, cooked coffee and bought what it could to eat. A patrol from 5/ 90 was sent to reconnoitre and was shot down by civilians in Oupeye, retribution coming from a platoon of 5/ 90.

Due to the fog, the German siege artillery resumed fire at 0900. The 42cm fired at 0930. As the FAR 43 history said:[42]

> The 42cm shell sounded like an express train approaching from a distance [...] the howling gradually became a deafening roar and struck the armour of the fort with a thunderous crack and a house-high pillar of smoke. When the air cleared a crater became visible, surrounded by a ring of debris. The bombardment was organised so that after every 42cm shell, first the 21cm mortars and then the light howitzers would blast away these debris to create the best possible surface conditions for the next 42cm shell.

The effect on those in the fort was terrific – 'a long howling dominated the noise of the bombardment, followed by a shock so powerful that nothing could approximately describe it, shook the fort to its foundations, threw the men against each other, overturned the cases of ammunition in the corridors, emptied the contents of all the shelves onto the ground'. A tremendous blast of air blew out all the hurricane lamps, plunging the fort into darkness. The lamps were relit. In the central gallery, Speesen discussed the possible causes of this explosion with his officers when a second massive tremor shook the fort. An EM reported that a room in the scarpe had been destroyed with such violence that the floor had been pushed up to the ceiling. The garrison was 'in mortal agony': it was clear that the Germans had a weapon capable of utterly destroying the fort. A third shell hit. An EM brought in the base of a shell casing so large and heavy he could barely carry it, measuring 38cm in diameter: the gunnery officer added 2cm for the casing itself and came to the conclusion that the shell was at least 42cm. The bombardment had now reached a 'dreadful intensity' of shells small, medium and large. A fourth 42cm shell landed between the two 5.7cm turrets, throwing them into the air 'like cardboard', reducing the guns to debris. When the gun crews were found, it was discovered that their bones had been crushed. The ready ammunition in the stairway to the 5.7cm guns exploded, injuring and burning men nearby. A fifth round landed in the fosse of the gorge, blowing out the window armour and lifting the floor of the barracks rooms. Soon thereafter, the roof of the coal storage was caved in, sending coal dust throughout the fort. At 1120, a 42cm shell hit directly over the central gallery, which gave the impression that it would collapse, and Speesen decided to surrender. The Germans again granted the garrison the honours of war and the officers kept their swords.

The 42cm had fired forty-three rounds, with the eight from the previous day, fifty-one in total. The number of shells fired by Foot Artillery 4 or heavy trench mortar bombs by the engineers is unknown.

There were several breaches in the counterscarp, one 60m long. A metre of concrete protection had been torn from the entire citadel. One 42cm shell had cratered the concrete between two turrets, another had collapsed a gallery. The armoured door and grill of the citadel infantry sally port had been torn off. The left-hand 21cm turret was unserviceable, the right-hand turret damaged, the 15cm turret immobilised, the 12cm turrets unserviceable, the four 5.7cm turrets were out of action. Some of the armoured shutters for the windows had been blasted into the interior of the citadel. Large chunks of concrete had been blown off the ceiling in the infantry ready room. The effect of the 42cm shells had impacted the nerves of the garrison. There were three dead and thirty wounded.[43]

The 42cm battery was ordered to break down the mortars and move to a firing position against Fort Liers. The gun crews were exhausted, and 12/ IR 31, 4/ IR 85 and 1/ Engineer 9 were assigned to help. Security had to be provided against friend and foe alike, because everybody wanted to see 'Big Bertha'.

The usual accounts of the siege of Liège would have it that the destruction of Pontisse was due solely to the 42cm guns. This was clearly not the case. By the time the 42cm arrived, two 21cm mortars had reduced the Pontisse to the point where none of the main guns were functional, there was no electrical power or water, and the air was pestilential. The 42cm merely delivered the *coup de grace*.

The 42cm battery had just been thrown together, even the personnel from the Artillery Testing Agency had little experience with the 42cm, the mass of the gun crews had none whatsoever, and it showed. The performance of the battery looked like an initial practice shoot at Kummersdorf: adjustment of fire on 12 August was slow and laborious, and even when the guns were adjusted onto the target on 13 August, they were not particularly accurate. From the Belgian account, it would appear that at most six of the fifty-one rounds were direct hits, and the accompanying sketch shows only four. But the effects of this gunnery practice at Pontisse would show good results at Loncin.

Chaudefontaine Falls

The I/ Foot Artillery 9 opened fire on Fort Chaudefontaine at 1800, 12 August, with the battery commanders observing from the park of Roche Castle. The first shell was a direct hit on the citadel. As the historian of 1/ Foot Artillery 9 wrote, 'Foot Artillery, you've trained well!' 'Precision fire by individual mortars against armoured cupolas – not an easy first combat mission!'[44] The crews sweated in the August heat, as the sound of 21cm mortars firing echoed through the Vesdre valley. The detached platoon of 2/ Foot Artillery 9 rejoined the battalion after an all-night march. Now eight mortars engaged Fort Chaudefontaine, and continued to fire throughout the night. Concrete blocked the air supply for the electric generator and the lights went out and were not restored until 0200, 13 August. The fort filled with fumes. The 5.7cm turret at Salient II was put out of action. As Leman noted, the Germans fired a shell every six to ten minutes all night to keep the garrison on edge, what we would now call H and I (harassment and interdiction) fire.

Chaudefontaine occupied a hilltop, but observation was poor, due to low ground to the south, east and west, and wooded terrain to the north. The fort was therefore reduced to firing at suspected enemy positions. German fire adjustment was difficult because 'a few batteries' of 15cm howitzers began firing and kicked up smoke and dust. This was I/ Reserve FAR 7, four batteries of 15cm howitzers (sixteen guns).[45] After a 45km approach march on 12 August, the battalion chose a firing position on the east side of the village of Forêt with the OP on the park wall on the west side of the château. It did not open fire until 2025 against the 5.7cm turrets and field artillery identified on the north-east side of the fort, at a range of 4km. De Schrÿver reported that the Germans fired 200–300 shells an hour: again, if true, overwhelmingly field artillery.[46] That night a single round from Chaudefontaine hit the roof of the château, where the battalion staff was quartered, leading to a mass exodus. After an hour and no second shell landing, the staff reoccupied the château. All night the battalion conducted harassing fire.

On 13 August, 13 ID assault team closed in on the fort, and with them went the 21cm battalion FO with his telephone; as the bursting shells made observation from the battery command posts more difficult, he assumed the fire direction. The 13 ID wanted to assault at 1100. The 1/ Foot Artillery 9 historian said that by 1030, the fort had been hit by 300 21cm shells 'that is, 135 tons of steel and high-explosive melinite'. 'Unlucky, brave garrison, hammered by a 15-hour hurricane of fire'. The left-hand 12cm turret had been dismounted, the 15cm turret had taken a hit on the embrasure, one of the 5.7cm turrets had been destroyed.

At 1025 the FO, immediately next to the fort, reported, 'Number 4 Mortar 1/ 9, two clicks to the left and it's a direct hit on the damaged turret!' The battery commander personally got on the telephone to the gun commander, 'Number 4! 2 clicks left: be exact! Shoot!' The battery counted off the time of flight, and then observed as the shell scored a direct hit and the delayed time-fuse exploded inside the 21cm turret, which set off the powder charges. 'A massive, thunderous explosion, fire, steam and smoke', followed by a string of secondary explosions, and then a raging fire, killed ninety men outright and thirty others were burned or asphyxiated.

A German infantry patrol observed the destruction and signalled the FOs to ceasefire. Unwounded Belgians attempted to aid their wounded and trapped comrades, and were soon assisted by 4/ IR 158, work which went on for several hours. Several men were lifted out through the 21cm turret, which no longer had a top. Only seventy-six effectives remained when the fort surrendered, some of the unwounded having fled. The I/ Foot Artillery 9 history said the battalion expended 457 shells.

The mortar battalion immediately began preparations to engage Fort d'Embourg, but the terrain made it difficult to find an observation post and the wire team spent hours marching up and downhill to lay a telephone line. Fort d'Embourg fell before the battalion was ready to fire.

The I/ FAR 9 historian pointed out an aspect of operating an artillery battery that is seldom mentioned, 'The newly-assembled horse teams were outstanding. They were our pride and joy. The horse-care was exemplary.' The battery first sergeant had supervised their selection on mobilisation. The battery was supported by an excellent veterinarian and a skilled farrier.

The I/ FAR 9 had put on a convincing demonstration of the hitting power of its 21cm mortars, and of the highest level of training and fire control. The first round fired was a hit, which for any indirect-fire unit is a real accomplishment. The telephone-equipped forward observer and the guns crews accurately made the most exacting corrections in their fire. In fairness to Brialmont, when he built Chaudefontaine, this degree of accuracy was unthinkable.

d'Embourg Falls

According to Lombard, from 6 to 12 August d'Embourg conducted almost continual fire missions. What their targets were is hard to say: there were probably only German patrols in the area, as the experience of I/ 34 and IV/ 14 F (below) shows.[47]

On 12 August, IR 82 closed off the fort to the north, I/ IR 57 to the south. On the night of 12–13 August II / FAR 43 occupied firing positions near Beaufays.[48] During movement they took fire from d'Embourg, which went too high and landed in the meadows next to the road. At 0500 the section fired for a short time, and took ineffective counterfire from d'Embourg and Chaudefontaine. During the day two horses were wounded. In the afternoon the section fired to cut the wire obstacles around the fort.

At 0515 13 August, II/ FAR 9 opened fire on Fort d'Embourg. The fort was unable to locate the German guns and conducted a rather pointless area counter-battery fire.[49] At 1000 an officer was sent as parliamentarian, accompanied by an NCO and trumpeter, to demand the fort surrender. The commandant refused, and on the return trip the group was fired on.

By now there was no return fire from the fort (the crews had abandoned the turrets), which was obviously heavily damaged, and the commander of 14 ID resolved to carry it by assault at 2000. The I and II/ IR 57 would attack on the east side.[50] To provide close support, 1/ FAR 43 was moved to a covered position 700m from the fort. It adjusted fire against the empty infantry positions on the glacis, and then waited to support the assault.[51]

To prepare the assault, Foot Artillery 9 opened rapid fire – 3/ II/ Foot Artillery 9 firing 120 rounds in twenty-seven minutes. The garrison had withdrawn to the central gallery, the intense bombardment caused chunks of concrete to fall on them, it appeared the entire vault would collapse, and at 1930 d'Embourg surrendered. Total II/ FAR 9 ammunition expenditure was 431 shells.

The citadel had been penetrated to nearly a metre. There were breaches in the concrete around all of the turrets. Only one 21cm turret was operational, the other turrets had been dismounted and one 15cm turret split open. One 5.7cm turret had been broken free of the mount and only one was operational. The flanking positions in the ditches were intact. The water supply was clearly designed for peacetime convenience and to save money: water came by a pipe from Beaufays, which was cut, and the cisterns were broken open and drained, so lack of water became critical. Morale remained good until blocks of concrete began falling from the roof into the central gallery. Leman said that the fort surrendered due to the danger of asphyxiation from gas. Four officers and 360 EM were taken prisoner and the Germans found a plan showing the layout of Fort Boncelles, which proved useful. The Germans also found four Belgian artillery pieces in the interval with Boncelles.

Along with 7/ FAR 4, III/ FAR 4 went into position near the churchyard in the Quartier du Nord in Liège and fired on Fort Liers.

On 8 August, II/ Reserve FAR 7 (eight 13cm guns) received orders to accelerate its mobilisation in order to move to Liège. The battalion was transported by rail from Cologne to Herbesthal, but apparently the accelerated mobilisation had created problems, for it remained at Herbesthal from 10 to 13 August to organise the equipment and train the crews. On 13 August it moved to a bivouac at 2200, 2km east of Fort Barchon, after a march of 29km. The IR 25 marched towards Aachen to rejoin its parent unit, VIII AK. On the sunny afternoon of 13 August it entered the city, greeted by flags and cheering crowds.

Flémalle, Hollogne, Loncin and Lantin fired on small groups of infantry and cavalry.[52]

Left Behind: Belgian I/ 34 and IV/ 14 F

The Belgian I/ 34 L was stationed between Chaudefontaine and d'Embourg, IV/ 14 F between d'Embourg and the Ourthe. Neither received the order to withdraw. Until 7 August they were not in contact with each other.[53] The Germans had no idea the two battalions were there, but patrols sent out by the two Belgian battalions made contact with Germans, so they knew they were cut off. The 1/ I/ 34 dug in to protect the battalion rear. On 8 August civilians told I/ 34 that the Belgians were retreating to Waremme: it was now clear that they had not received the withdrawal order. They did not know that General Leman had transferred his HQ to Fort de Loncin. The troops obtained food from the surrounding villages, but from 7 to 10 August these were occupied by the Germans. The troops of IV/ 14 F shot at any vehicles on the Ourthe river road and on 10 August killed a German officer and a female passenger. German vehicles on the road to Liège between Chaudefontaine and Embourg were stopped and the occupants taken prisoner. On 11 August the I/ 34 commander learned from a civilian that Leman had withdrawn to Loncin and sent two messengers in civilian clothes requesting orders, and Leman told them to withdraw to Awans, south of Loncin, but the returning messengers were arrested and held at Fort Boncelles on the suspicion that they were spies and did not return until 13 August.[54]

On 12 August the Germans began to bombard Chaudefontaine and Embourg, and patrols immediately made contact with German forces. At 0830 13 August, survivors from Chaudefontaine arrived. Withdrawal was now an absolute necessity, but involved crossing both the Ourthe and Meuse. It was not possible to wait for darkness, and the I/ 34 commander told each company to march independently. 2/ I/ 34 was captured immediately. Before they met up at the village of Embourg, 1/ I/ 34 and 3/ I/ 34 both had firefights with German troops, then they were joined by IV/ 14 F and the crews of two fortress mobile artillery batteries that had been emplaced outside of Embourg, about 800 men. At a ford, I/ 34 crossed the Ourthe. The IV/ 14 F tried to move independently, ran into German forces and followed I/ 34. The two battalions moved up to Sart-Tilman. It was 1600 and the heat was terrific. The two battalions reached Boncelles village, avoiding German sentries near the fort. Information from the locals allowed them to avoid or chase off German sentries and they crossed the Meuse at an unguarded railway bridge, but were then fired upon by Boncelles, which did not cause any casualties. The entire group reached Awans at 0300 14 August, with 604 men, leaving 200 stragglers on the road.

At 0600 the two battalions learned from the locals that there were Germans in all the neighbouring villages and they were surrounded again, but, as the commander of 1/ I/ 34 said, 'much more effectively than at Chaudefontaine'. A serious firefight ensued when a Belgian platoon moved to stop advancing German troops. During the morning the two battalion commanders went to Loncin to inform Leman of their arrival. At 1300 he ordered them to drive back German forces west of Loncin. 2/ IV/ 14 F attempted to do so but was stopped cold. At 1500 the bombardment of Loncin resumed, cutting off communication with Leman. It was decided to retreat that night. Hollogne was informed, but the patrol sent to Flémalle was broken up. Nevertheless, the two battalions were able to pass through the zone of the fort's searchlights. They scattered some German cavalry, but this forced them to give up the idea of going into bivouac. The two battalions continued the march to Huy, which was not occupied by either side, but where they were able to board a train to Namur.

14 August

Flémalle engaged several small German detachments. Then the Germans drove in the observers for Flémalle and Lantin, blinding both forts. The German 17 ID moved to a position west of the remaining Belgian forts.

Fléron Falls

By 8 August Fléron had lost all its OPs and was blind. It attempted to occupy a building in front of the fort with infantry and FOs, but 'they didn't get far', as the Germans occupied the house. The fort commandant then had the building destroyed with artillery fire. 'Flying patrols', presumably on bicycles and in civilian clothes, were sent out to acquire targets.[55] When Fléron heard on 9 August that Barchon had fallen it lobbed a few shells in that general direction.[56] The lookouts reported German troops in the town of Soumagne, so it was shelled, too. The garrison was convinced that during the night the Germans were sneaking around outside the fort; if a suspicious noise was heard one of the main guns would fire canister, which surely served only to ruin the garrison's sleep. On 10 August Fléron conducted counter-battery fire against Germans guns near Barchon that were shelling d'Evegnée. A courier, dressed in shabby civilian clothing, arrived from Loncin with a comforting message from Leman. On 11 August, Fléron conducted counter-battery fire in support of d'Evegnée and harassment and interdiction fire on the roads to Liège. Two separate German emissaries, the second accompanied by the commander of d'Evegnée, which had just surrendered, demanded Fléron surrender. During the night Fléron was able to send a message using the searchlight, asking for news of the Allied troops, but the reply could not be deciphered.

On 12 August, II/ FAR 4 (eight 21cm) and I/ FAR 20 (eighteen 15cm sFH) engaged Fort Fléron. The 15cm were heavy field artillery and would have had no effect on permanent fortifications. They were covered by IR 13 in a position from 2km east of the fort, with IR 158 to its left.[57] IR 13 sent patrols towards the fort and Magnée. At 1900 both regiments were ordered to march to Fort Chaudefontaine.

A hit on the embrasure of the left-hand 12cm put the left gun out of action and wounded the gun commander and the assistant turret commander. By 1200 there was already serious damage to the citadel. The turrets were filling with gas from the German explosions and the Belgian black powder charges, which the hand-powered ventilators could not expel.

The I/ FAR 9 was ordered to prevent the garrison from using breaks in the foot artillery fire to move on top of the fortress and clear away debris that was jamming the turrets, as well as suppress the turret's fire.[58] The I/ 9 command group and the 3/ 9 commander conducted a leader's reconnaissance on the morning of 12 August, crawling forward until the could get a good look at the fort and the surrounding terrain. Observation would have been better from a nearby slag heap, but they wanted to use that as a battery CP the next day and did not want to draw attention to it. The section commander found a firing position 300m further to the rear, but took rifle fire, from civilians in the houses further to the rear, they assumed. A second firing position 700m further to the rear was chosen at the major cross-roads between Queue-du-Bois, Evegnée and Micheroux. This was prudent, for just as the four 7.7cm guns guns of 1 and 2 Platoons were moved into the second firing position that evening, shells landed in the first. The Belgians never found the actual battery position. The battery commander established his CP on the slag heap, but halfway up, not at the top. The Belgians heavily shelled the top, far less effectively the rest. Almost immediately, two Belgians moved to the top of the fort, the Germans thought to clear debris away from a turret, but were swept into the fosse by fire from 1/ 9, though neither was actually hit. In fact, this was Mozin himself and a senior NCO. The Belgians reported that at 1915 the Germans opened fire with field artillery and succeeded in driving the OPs underground. During the night 1/ 9 conducted harassment and interdiction fire.

On the surface, the infantry parapet no longer existed. There were craters 3m, 4m, even 5m deep in the earth of the terreplein between the redoubt and the fosse. The right-hand flanking battery in the gorge was blocked with earth and concrete. Mozin said that on 12 August Fléron had been hit by 1,000 shells. There is no possibility that eight 21cm mortars could have fired so many shells, so if Mozin's count is not mere exaggeration, he included field artillery shells landing on the fort.

The 28 Brigade marched around for several days until on 13 August it was ordered to seal off Fléron, IR 56 to the north of the fort, II/39 to the south and I/ 39 west, with a loose skirmisher line pushed up to the glacis.[59] The III/ 39 was ordered to garrison Liège, and was able to infiltrate between the forts without loss.

The bombardment began on 13 August when four heavy trench mortars (*schwere Minenwerfer*) of 4/ Fortress Combat Engineer R 24 opened fire. Mozin testified to the effectiveness of the *Minenwerfer*. He says that the fort began to take fire from guns not far from the fort, located in full defilade, firing on the gorge. These produced powerful explosions, which sent flames and fumes into the gun turrets. At 0400 a large-calibre shell, probably a heavy mortar, landed in the fosse, blew in the armoured door there, sending shrapnel into the central gallery, which caused several casualties, followed by heavy and acrid yellowish gas, followed by the gas of subsequent shells. The interior of the fort went nearly dark and breathing became difficult. The armoured covers were ripped from the windows and blown completely out of the fort. The aid station, which had been evacuated, was hit and the contents caught fire. The kitchen was hit, leaving only a water boiler for coffee that had been hauled laboriously into the scarp corridor. The bakery was hit and burned, leaving the garrison with only biscuits to eat. Since midnight the latrines had not been useable; the garrison henceforth used pails, which had to be carried downstairs to be emptied. Water had to be hauled day and night from a well with a winch and poured into a cistern by two-man teams, in a room that it was impossible to ventilate, 'you would think they were convicts at work'. At 0800 the right-hand gun in the left 12cm turret was inoperable when the hydraulic recoil brake failed, but was repaired that afternoon. The right-hand 5.7cm gun covering the gorge was blocked by debris.

At 1140 the German heavy weapons ceased firing and the Germans opened up with MG and field guns on fronts II–III and the gorge in order to make the Belgians take cover, preparatory to Mozin's *idée fixe*, a German infantry assault. Mozin says that the two 5.7cm and the right-hand 15cm prevented the Germans from crossing the glacis. In fact, there had been no German assault.

At noon a German aircraft was seen flying over the fort, which the Belgians thought was marking targets by dropping the equivalent of a smoke grenade. German sources deny that they had any method at this time of directing artillery fire from aircraft.

The 1/9 said that the Belgians had cleared the debris away from the turrets, which moved actively. The battery concentrated its fire on one turret, which turned towards 1/9. The German 7.7cm scored several direct hits on the embrasure; the turret depressed and did not rise again.[60] It appeared to 1/9 that Fléron was firing blind; in any case its fire did no damage.

At 1445 on 13 August I/ Reserve Foot Artillery 7 (15cm) began suppressive fire on Fléron's turrets. Three times the Belgians raised and turned a main gun turret, only to draw a rolling salvo from sixteen howitzers, forcing the Belgians to depress the turrets and close the ventilation shafts. At 1700 the battalion ceased fire in order to allow the mortars to fire for effect.

Mozin said that at 1250 13 August, the bombardment by German heavy artillery resumed, apparently with more guns, because there were salvoes of fifteen, twenty and even twenty-four shells landing simultaneously. Fléron fired at 'suspected' German gun positions, as well as harassment and interdiction against the lines of communication. The heat in the turrets was such that the gunners worked bare-chested, with wet rags over the nose and mouth due to the gas. Several gunners had to be evacuated, hit by fragments of armour blown off the turrets, or unable to breathe. But there was little breathable air anywhere in the fort.

At 1500, the 5.7cm at Salient II was out of action, the top of the turret carried away. At 1600, all four 12cm were unserviceable and the 5.7cm turret at Salient III had literally disappeared. The aid station, which had moved from Salient III to Salient I, now had to be moved to the citadel, in a dark and humid room opposite the powder magazine.

At 1700 the Germans opened fire with a MG hidden in a rail goods wagon and firing past two demolished houses. The fire must have been effective, because it had to be 'dislodged' by fire from a 15cm gun. Then the 15cm turret reported that it was inoperable: one gun was no longer functional and the armour on the embrasure of the second was damaged.

Throughout the fort it became more and more difficult to breathe. Smoke and gas were everywhere. The turret ventilators were 'completely inoperable'. The electric ventilator in the machine room had been destroyed, in the fire control room it had been torn from its support by an exploding shell and now vented outside the fort.

In some places the concrete of the citadel had craters 1–1.5m deep. The scarp at Salient III had been destroyed and an ascent was possible from the fosse, nearly so at Salient II. On the two forward faces of the fort the ramparts had fallen into the fosse, restricting the effectiveness of the flanking batteries. In the rules of fortress warfare going back as far as the early modern period and Middle Ages, a 'practicable breach' in the wall permitted the fortress commander to surrender honourably.

During the morning of 13 August someone in the German command decided that Fléron was *sturmreif* – that it could be successfully assaulted by infantry.[61] How they came to this conclusion is hard to say: the barbed-wire obstacle was still intact and several guns, including two 5.7cm turrets, still functional. A daylight attack with MGs and close-support 7.7cm artillery fire might have had some chance of success, but the German leadership decided for an unsupported night attack. This attack would appear to be an experiment and not a well-thought-out operation. The II and III/ 56 moved to an assembly area west of the villages of Micheroux and Soumagne, 6, 5, 11 and 12 in the first line, 7, 8, 9, and 10 in the second. Patrols were able to come 'quite close' to the fort. The IR 56 history said that during the day the fort was bombarded, but its return fire was weak and ineffective.

After dark, 11 and 12 moved forward to dig an assault position and patrols began to clear lanes through the thick wire obstacle.

Near midnight, the garrison heard sounds of digging, which to Mozin meant that the Germans were trying to dig a mine under the fort or were preparing an infantry assault. At 0100 the 'bombardment' (actually German harassing fire) ceased, which Mozin took to mean that the Germans were going to conduct an assault, and he deployed his infantry across the field of shell craters to where the parapet used to be. The two remaining 5.7cm turrets and the infantry opened fire, which, he said, 'completely surprised' the attackers.

The Belgian firing caught the IR 56 patrols attempting to cut the wire, killing one man and severely wounding many others. The assault position could not be held and 11 and 12 returned to the assembly area. The patrols reported that an assault would have failed, because the wire obstacle was completely intact.

Mozin said that the Germans fired red star clusters, which he took to be an SOS call from the infantry for artillery support. The German artillery resumed fire, catching the Belgian infantry first completely in the open, then in movement at night back to the fort across the cratered ground. The Belgians were lucky: only nine wounded, none seriously, including two that had to remain outside until dawn. Nevertheless, this constituted a loss of 10 per cent of the infantry. The sole main gun capable of firing, a 15cm, conducted unaimed flat-trajectory fire into the night – until all of its ammunition was expended!

On the west side of the fort I/ 39 had moved up to the gorge-side glacis and dug an assault position, while the four heavy mortars threw 'shell after shell' into the gorge ditch.[62] The II/ 39 closed up on the south and west sides and the regiment waited for the signal to conduct a dawn assault. At midnight it was, however, withdrawn 3km to allow the heavy artillery to fire freely. The IR 39 history did not report taking any fire from the fort.

At 0400 Mozin says that Fléron began to receive fire from especially heavy shells, which shook the entire fort. Mozin says that he surrendered when he realised that the super-heavy would destroy the fortress. This was an *ex post facto* excuse for his decision to surrender. On the morning of 14 August he could have known nothing of the employment of the 42cm at Pontisse. He notes that the *Ehrenbuch der Deutschen Schweren Artillerie* (Book of Honour of the German Heavy Artillery) is quite specific concerning the employment of the German 42cm at Liège, and it does not mention them firing at Fléron. As a fallback position, he speculated that the fire might have come from the Austrian 30.5cm, which, however, did not fire at Liège at all. In fact, super-heavy artillery notwithstanding, Mozin and his garrison had held out as long as they could, and the fort was no longer defensible. The IR 56 history said that the assault was scheduled to take place as a daylight attack at 1200, had the fort not surrendered.

The IR 31 had returned from Chaudefontaine and on 14 August was ordered to occupy a security line with six companies from Magnée to Romsée, with IR 39 to its right. In a wood 4km south of the fort a platoon found eight abandoned undamaged Belgian artillery pieces complete with caissons. At 0800, regimental HQ sent Oberleutnant von Beerfelde and a platoon from 7/13 towards the rear of the fort. During the pauses in the German bombardment, the lieutenant and his platoon slipped over the lowered drawbridge across the gorge and up to the fort gate, from which point he yelled to the fort to surrender. After repeating this several times, a pole with a piece of sackcloth was thrust through a firing port next to the gate. Von Beerfelde demanded that a white flag be raised from the citadel, and this was done at around 1015 (B). He then accepted Mozin's surrender, including the keys to the fort and Mozin's sword.

Mozin said that the bombardment included an extraordinary 5,000 German shells in fifty hours, which if allowance is made for fourteen hours of low-intensity German night harassment fire is made, would mean about 135 German shells an hour. Even if this were true, very few of these shells were dangerous 21cm or heavy mortar.

II/ FAR 4, IR 13 and IR 39 moved to Liège.

Liers Falls

After the German night attack on 5–6 August, Liers lost its FOs and could only fire blind, or on the information provided by its 'spies'.[63] The II/ Reserve FAR 7 (13cm cannon) moved into position 2km east of Fort Barchon at 0500 on 13 August, and opened fire at 1000, along with III/ Foot Artillery 4 and 7/ FAR 4. The fort sat on an open plain and 'offered a magnificent target for the German artillery' which was able to direct fire from the gun positions, without a forward observer. The III/ IR 90 moved to Fexhé-les-Slins on 13 August to close off Fort Liers from the north. On 14 August the battalion lay in the hot sand of a reverse-slope position. On the night of 13–14 August, 3/ FAR 9 fired shrapnel to keep the Belgians from doing any repair work. The German fire was so accurate that the fort's guns were completely suppressed.[64] In fortress warfare, suppression of the fort's guns takes place when the besieger's fire is so intense and accurate that the guns crews have to abandon the turrets and move deeper into the fort. The fort surrendered at 1430 on 14 August.[65]

The counterscarp had a 65m long breach and in other places had been reduced to half its original height. The fort's fire direction centre and one of the flanking casemates had been destroyed. The citadel had been cratered a metre deep in three places, 8m, 14m and 35m in length. The infantry sally port had been blown open and one of the flanking casemates had been destroyed. All the turrets were operable except one 12cm which was jammed by blocks of concrete. One of the turret mounts was cracked open. Leman said that the rations were 'good': during the bombardment there was no fresh food and at the end the garrison was eating biscuits and canned food. Four-fifths of the garrison, including the doctor, had been incapacitated by gases. Leman says that the morale of the garrison was 'good enough' until forced to surrender by the stench from the overflowing latrines.

Fire was shifted to Fort Lantin. The II/ FAR 4 set up in the suburb of Ans at 1600, while II/ Reserve FAR 7 took up a position 1km east of Lantin, with an observation post at the Liers rail station.

The 42cm battery moved out on the morning of 14 August through Blegny to Barchon. The march was difficult because of the steep road into the new position. It was able to take canned goods and medical supplies from the fort and the gun tractor crews armed themselves with Belgian carbines and ammunition. By the time the battery had arrived, Fort Liers had already fallen and the battery was ordered to move to another position to fire on Fort Loncin. After a difficult up and downhill march on roads packed with supply vehicles it reached the Liège local training area north of the Chartreuse and bivouacked.

Belgian Army[66]

The king instructed his secretary, who was still in Brussels, to brief the minister of war on the true state of the army. There were five divisions on the Gette, with 67,000 infantry. Companies had only a single officer.

There is no discipline (The soldiers do not even salute their officers, not from any ill-will, but from the lack of military spirit). There is no liaison, no training, no power of resistance. The troops are not capable of marching. At the end of ten kilometres they are done. All the reservists complain of sore feet. The casualties caused by marching are shocking.

A march of 15km in five hours, without packs, reduced one division to an 'unhappy condition'. The commander said that 'it is impossible to attack'.

The 3 DA had not recovered from the fight at Liège and was immobile. In his report, General Bertand told of the panic during the retreat from Liège.

> He declares that our troops are only fit to fight in the trenches. As soon as they are turned they retire in confusion [...] The strength of the division is now about 7,500 infantry. If the losses of the cavalry, the field artillery and the fortress troops be added this brings the deficiency to 12,000 men.

The Belgian HQ now knew that they were on their own: the British would come with only two corps, begin movement on 15 August and would assemble at Maubeuge on 22 August. The Belgian LNO at the French Grand Quartier Général (General Headquarters – GQG) reported that the lead two corps of French left wing 5th Army were barely across the Belgian border, south of Givet, with two corps still in France at Rethel and Busancy.

The king concluded that the defence of Antwerp was the first priority and required the entire field army. The army would remain on the Gette as long as it could, but it was 'quite possible that the Germans [...] will overrun Central Belgium and occupy Brussels'.

Galet listed just nine (!) intelligence reports received at Belgian HQ on 14 August. All but one were from civilians, the sole exception being an officer's patrol to the north-east corner of Belgium, where the officer apparently got his information from the Dutch. This was the most accurate report, stating that the Germans had put four bridges across the Meuse, that 150,000 to 200,000 Germans had crossed and that a reserve corps was assembling at Wesel. Belgian reconnaissance was non-existent. The civilian reports made it clear that large numbers of German infantry and artillery had crossed the Meuse at Lixhé. Civilians also reported the Germans crossing the Meuse east of Huy.

At Loncin, Leman says that 'several times' he sent situation reports to Huy for transmission to the army HQ.[67] He said that he learned (without specifying when) that Barchon had fallen on 8 August, that Pontisse, Evegnée and Fléron were under fire on 10 August, that Evegnée fell on 11 August, Chaudefontaine and Pontisse on 13 August, Liers on 14 August. He asked for situation reports from the army HQ but never received any. On 14 August he sent his last situation report: he did not know whether it got through because the messenger did not return. Galet did not report receiving it. On 14 August Loncin was sealed off from further contact. It is clear that Leman had no radio or telephone communications.

15 August

Boncelles Falls

After the night of 5–6 August, Boncelles was completely isolated: no friendly forces far and wide, no contact with Belgian headquarters, no reports and no news.[68] The sense of isolation was reinforced by the fact that the fort was located in the middle of a vast wood. Patrols either returned without seeing anything or were captured.

Early on 14 August, I and II/ FAR 9 moved to engage Fort Boncelles. The II/ FAR 9 set up at 1100 at Sart-Tilman but did not open fire, perhaps because an intermediate Belgian position was reported to be in the area. On the road to Boncelles village, I/ FAR 9 crossed the Ourthe bridge. The battalion commander and the commander of 2/ 9 went forward in a passenger vehicle to reconnoitre, leaving the 1/ 9 commander to move the column into firing position in a very restricted space. This, the 1/ Foot Artillery 9 commander said, was not easy. Two 21cm batteries had twenty-four vehicles drawn by six-horse teams, followed by a munitions column with even more. It required the supervision of the first sergeant, his deputy, and eight mounted senior NCOs. He said that the vehicle drivers were 'capital fellows' who learned to manage their 'wonderful cold-blooded horses' and drive their vehicles in the most difficult situations. These were older, grey-haired men. One, a Bavarian who worked at a coal mine in Cologne, had even served with the German Expeditionary Force during the Boxer Rebellion.

During the afternoon, I/ 9 set up north-west of Tilff and began firing at 1830, with an FO in the church tower of Boncelles village, 400m from the fort. One of the first casualties was a latrine. At 2000, after I/ 9 had fired 'a couple hundred' shells, the battalion adjutant rode forward with two men under a flag of truce to demand that the fort surrender. The commandant refused and the withdrawing artillerymen were fired upon. The bombardment continued during the night. The II/ 9 moved at 0230 to a position 1.5km north of Tilff and was ready to fire at dawn, with an FO north of Boncelles village. Boncelles surrendered at 0930. FAR 9 had expended 750 shells in fifteen and a half hours' firing.

Deprived of its detached OPs, the best Boncelles could do was fire blind. The counterscarp had three breaches, 9m, 12m and 63m long. The wall of the left-hand flanking battery in the ditch had been destroyed, the infantry sally port blocked. All the turrets, large and small, were immobilised and the armour had been penetrated. There were breaches in the concrete around the 15cm turret as well as between the searchlight and both of the 12cm turrets. Late on 14 August the pipes in the water supply were destroyed and thereafter there was no water. The electricity failed and with it the ventilators. There was one KIA, fifteen WIA. The fort was forced to surrender by gases from exploding shells, which penetrated from the sally port and the armoured windows in the escarpment, in spite of attempts to block them up with mattresses.

The II/ FAR 9 moved to a position south of Les Communes and at 1940 opened fire against Fort Flémalle. the II and III/ IR 90 marched through Othée to Odeur (off map, north-west of Loncin) to bivouac in the pastures. Large placards demanded that the populace turn in all weapons. To avoid difficulties, the fusiliers were forbidden to enter the town.

Lantin Falls

When the war began, Lantin was being repaired and upgraded. As a consequence, the fort was not combat-ready.[70] Tools and supplies had been hastily stored in the galleries. The magazines were being reinforced, so 7.5cm ammunition in caissons sat in fosses I–II and II–III, many of the hydraulics in the turrets and recoil brakes for the guns were out of service. The repairs had to be made in haste, but were completed.

On 14 August, II and III/ 165 were moved towards Lantin, I/ 165 and engineers to Ans. If the fort did not surrender by evening, IR 165 was to take it by assault. It surrendered at noon. Foot Artillery 4 fired 619 shells. Again, the fall of the fort was due to the high rate of accurate 21cm mortar fire. The counterscarp had been breached in several places, one being 45m long. The citadel had been cratered everywhere a metre deep. Two of the exterior armoured plates of the 21cm turret had been blown off; only the left-hand 12cm turret was intact. The proximate cause of the surrender of the fort was asphyxiation. The latrines were pestilential, the number of sick increased continually, and the air was so thick that the petrol lamps did not burn properly.[71] Four OFF and 450 EM were POW.

Loncin Falls

Loncin had been under the command of Captain Nassens since July 1907. The wartime strength of the garrison was 530, of which 350 were artillerymen, the majority of the rest infantry.[72] Most of the troops were from the immediate area. The fort dominated the rail line to Brussels.

On 29 July, artillery OPs were established at the Château de Waroux and in the church towers at Alleur and Loncin. It appears that the only church towers in the vicinity were at Alleur and Loncin, so that's where the OPs went, whether it made tactical sense or not. Only the OP at Waroux, in a park just across the road to the south-west of the fort, could have been tactically useful. Alleur is well to the southeast of the fort, Loncin even further to the south. They could have seen virtually nothing from the most likely enemy avenue of approach, to the north-east. If the enemy approached from behind the fort (to the south-east), as was actually the case, it was certain that these church towers would quickly become German OPs. Beginning on 1 August, the day before the German ultimatum arrived, the fields of fire were cleared to a distance of 600m from the fort: houses demolished, trees and hedges cut down, crops brought in, a hollow road filled in.

At the same time, the fort was to be provisioned by means of local requisitions. Since there was a lack of potatoes, 12,000kg of tubers and 3,000kg of vegetables were seized from a train destined for Germany 'to the great joy of the entire garrison'.

There was plenty of grain for bread, but immediately after the start of the war the bakery ran out of leavening. An attempt was made at sourdough bread (which does not use leavening, but fermented milk), but it was declared to be inedible by both the doctor and Nassens. Nassens sent a vehicle to pull out of bed a baker who was reputed to make good sourdough. Once at the fort, the baker was told that he could leave only when the fort's bakers learned how to make sourdough bread. The slap-dash provisioning of the fort does not speak well of Belgian preparations.

The infantry company attached to Loncin had been moved out of the fort and was engaged on the night of 5–6 August, where and how is not stated, but it returned on 6 August under the command of a sergeant, the commander having been killed, and the company had taken 50 per cent casualties. Leman arrived at the fort. For the rest of the day the garrison watched the 'debris' of 3 DA pass by in the rain. Loncin was on its own.

Nassens was convinced that Belgium was crawling with German spies, and that the German battery positions had been reconnoitred, even prepared, in peacetime. Several Germans were arrested near the fort, some even before the declaration of war. One was 'in the process of' making a sketch of the field fortifications. How Nassens came by this information, and what happened to these supposed German spies, was not stated. A German was arrested who had documents proving that he belonged to 'every sport and social club in the town [Liège]' which Nassens thought suspicious because he did not know the man. Nassens threatened to have him shot by firing squad, at which point the man fell weeping to his knees, which Nassens character-ised as cowardice. Nassens was forced to admit that 'the man did not have a single compromising paper in his possession', so he had him thrown into the potato cellar for twenty-four hours. Another man, a homeowner near the fort, was employed in the German headquarters in Liège. Nassens sent a patrol in automobiles to capture him, but failed. Nassens said that, had they caught him, he would have had him shot. Nassens said his telephone operated until 6 August, and during that time he received several false reports. He wondered where they came from, but implied it was the work of German spies – and not poorly-trained Belgian personnel. The telephone lines between the fort and the OPs were frequently cut, which Nassens attributed to sabotage, and he had the lines patrolled, with orders to shoot saboteurs. He doesn't mention any actually being shot.

The prevalence of German espionage, Nassens said, led him to organise his own intelligence agency: troops from the garrison who would circulate through the area in civilian clothes on bicycles or motorcycles. They were also given false identity papers. Nassens recognised fully that if the German caught them they would be shot as spies. Several were caught, but never held for long, some were chased and fired upon but escaped. Nassens used them every day as couriers to the other forts. They were often stopped and thoroughly searched by the Germans. Two set up in St Trond and noted the German units passing by, with one returning each day with a report hidden in the bicycle tyre. Two others gathered intelligence in Liège, and on their way through were stopped and interrogated by German sentries every day.

Nassens said that he gave men money so that they could drink with the German troops. One reported that a German officer told him, 'We've been eight days in front of this damned fort de Loncin and haven't been able to move a single foot forward. It shoots well. This is the most powerful of the forts at Liège', which, if true, proves only that this was a German officer who didn't know what he was talking about.

Nassens also put troops in automobiles to conduct long-range reconnaissance, attack German cavalry and isolated groups of Germans. Nassens reports that they captured three horses and enemy equipment, but only one specific serious engagement, when they killed one German cavalryman and captured an officer. When the fort was destroyed on 15 August, a half-dozen men were out with their automobile. They put on civilian clothes in order to rejoin the Belgian Army, and were captured by the Germans, who accused them of being soldiers. In spite of their denials they were lined up against a wall to be shot. One of them was dressed in a slovenly fashion, and was berated by a comrade: 'In the name of God, man, straighten yourself out! Die properly!' The Germans laughed, and released the men, who were thus able to rejoin the Belgian Army.

Nassens says that his infantry conducted several 'operations', which today we would call 'patrolling'. His description of these patrols on 9 and 10 August is impressive, but woefully and suspiciously short on details; the actions described are unlikely to say the least, and therefore not credible. He says a patrol 'attacked and put to flight a detachments of cyclists', apparently without casualties on either side; 'reconnoitred two villages; attacked and put to flight 350 cavalry; "exterminated" [?] a cavalry patrol; conducted an ambush in the direction of Liège'.

Nassens praised the work of his FOs in reconnaissance and adjusting fire. One FO was nearly encircled, but stayed at his post until dark, when he was able to put on civilian clothes and slip through the German lines.

Nassens finds the propensity of Belgian soldiers to wear civilian clothing – a violation of the laws of war – to be admirable. Indeed, he commands his own soldiers to do so. The Germans suspect the Belgians of this practice, and stop and search the Belgian soldiers in civilian clothing, but unable to find solid evidence, let them go: Nassens is proud that the Belgians could pull the wool over the eyes of the gullible Germans. Nassens did not cite a single incidence of Germans shooting his soldiers in civilian clothing. This hardly squares with the usual Belgian accounts of German troops indiscriminately shooting civilians.

Nassens then spins a completely unbelievable tale of the effectiveness of his black powder artillery over the next seven days, destroying German infantry columns and artillery batteries in job lots, beginning on 7 August. On that day he says his bicycle reconnaissance confirmed that he had forced away two German field artillery batteries, leaving behind three destroyed guns and twelve bodies. However, all the German forces in Liège at this time were concentrated at the citadel, including the only artillery, II/ FAR 4, which did not report any casualties until 23 August at Mons.

On 7 August, two German parliamentarians appeared. When they were leaving the fort and outside the citadel, the Belgian officer accompanying them said that one officer furtively lifted his blindfold. Informed of this, Nassens said that further parliamentarians would be given three summations to turn around, after which they would be shot.

On 8 August, Nassens said that Loncin successfully engaged a German column at Ans. At the end of the day a German aircraft landed at the airfield at Ans. Several officers went out in automobiles to meet it and were fired on by Loncin with a six-gun salvo that resulted in perfect first-round hits: given Loncin's antiquated black powder artillery, a practical impossibility. The Loncin artillery officer maintained that General von Emmich told him later that one of his 'most brilliant' lieutenant colonels had been killed. On 9 August, Loncin shelled German troops at the Ans rail station. One would think the Germans would have learned to stay away from Ans.

Nassens decided that the Germans had an OP in the church tower at Ans. He fired several 12cm shells at it on 12 August. On 13 August 'in order to avoid a massacre of the inhabitants' he sent one of his best reconnaissance men with petrol to set fire to the church. The man returned, unable to penetrate the German outposts. So Nassens fired on the town anyway, but Belgian gunnery was brilliant, twelve of fourteen shells were direct hits on the tower, which was destroyed.

On 11 August, one of Nassens runners, in civilian clothes, was caught by the Germans. The Belgian said that he was a Luxembourger trying to get home, and the Germans released him. He returned to Loncin and informed Nassens of the Germans' location.

According to Nassens, the German bombardment began on 10 August, after a four-hour battle the German artillery was suppressed by Loncin's counter-battery fire. Leman says that Loncin was bombarded on 11 August by 10.5cm howitzers, which not surprisingly had no effect, and again on 13 August by 10.5cm (and 21cm, which was wrong), with no effect.[73] The German battery was supposedly suppressed. On the morning of 14 August, preparatory to opening fire by siege guns on Loncin, the German infantry entered Alleur and flushed out the OP there. Nassens made no mention of the FO at Loncin, which had probably been pulled in long since. When the men of 34 L and 14 F infiltrated from d'Embourg to Loncin, Nassens thought that he had received a reinforcement of 850 men, and he was clearly disappointed to find that they had 'continued their retreat'. That evening the German infantry put an end to Nassen's patrolling and the infantry of Loncin was forced to remain in the immediate vicinity of the fort.

On 14 August II/ Reserve Foot Artillery 7 was able to fire on Loncin without shifting battery positions; only the FO was moved, to the Liers village church tower. The III/ FAR 4 then shifted front to fire onto Loncin at about 1600 on 14 August. The I/ FAR 20 (sFH) also fired on Loncin.

At 1645 on 14 August a German approached to within 200m of the fort carrying a white flag, when he was stopped by a sentinel. Leman says that at this point the German artillery opened fire and the sentinel shot the German, an artillery lieutenant. Leman says that his mission was to act as a forward observer: how he was to accomplish this Leman did not say. What is evident is that the Belgians shot an officer carrying a white flag, and Leman's excuses for this are threadbare.

Nassens tell the story differently. When the German officer continued to advance, although the Belgian sentries called out 'Halt!' and 'Go back!' five times, pursuant to Nassens orders a sergeant shot him in the chest, with the officer rolling into the fosse. He was brought into the fort, seriously wounded, but survived its destruction. He and Nassens were sent to the same hospital at Magdeburg, where the officer accused Nassens of having committed a war crime 'which at the beginning of my captivity caused me serious difficulties: there was even talk of having me shot'.

Nassens says that the bombardment on 14 August cut all the telephone lines and threw up so much dust and smoke that observation was no longer possible. He finally acknowledges that his counter-battery fire was ineffective. Nassens was convinced Loncin was taking fire from all directions, even the north and west. Shells landing on the scarp and in the fosse had generated gases, which penetrated through the damaged areas into the rooms behind the scarp, forcing the garrison to abandon them. The garrison was forced to pack itself in the citadel, but the gases began to penetrate there, too. The 5.7cm crews remained at their posts; throughout the entire siege-gun bombardment, Nassens remained convinced that at any moment the Germans were going to conduct an infantry assault. The German fire continued until 1830 'with great precision'. During the night the Germans conducted harassing fire every ten minutes.

At 0100 15 August, a shell hit the left-hand flanking battery in the gorge, turning the gunner into 'mush' and set off most of the ammunition. At 0130, earth and blocks of concrete blocked the airshaft for the electric generator, which shut down, turning off the fort's lights and ventilation system. It took two hours to clear the obstruction.

Leman says that on the morning of 15 August it was discovered that considerable damage had been done. The Germans were firing from near Liège to the east into the rear of the fort. The scarp in front of the gorge had taken considerable damage and the concrete of the left-hand flanking battery had been blown away. Several armoured shutters in the rooms on the scarp had been blown in, along with large breaches in the wall. Leman said that the bombardment recommenced with 21cm fire at 0530, 15 August. The German fire was 'very violent' and 'well-aimed'. A 'great number' of shells hit the citadel, the entrance and the scarp. The fire direction centre,

where Leman was located, received 'terrible impacts: the fort shook on its foundations several times'. Shells landing near the airshaft forced suffocating gases into the
fort. At 1000 the electricity failed completely, and along with it the ventilation, except
for the hand ventilators in the turrets. Illumination was by three acetylene lamps,
which went out every time a heavy shell landed. A hit on the left-hand 21cm turret,
and subsequent fire, threatened to set off the ready ammunition. After the fire was
put out, the ammunition was withdrawn from the turrets and Loncin ceased fire. The
German 21cm were firing four-gun salvoes. Dust from the vault of the central gallery began to fall on the garrison, then cracks appeared. Between 1430 and 1500 the
German fire slackened and Leman went into the gallery of the scarp to inspect the
damage. He found 'a disaster', the gorge front 'completely ruined'. There was so much
rubble in the fosse that a flanking 5.7cm had to be moved up to the second storey.

The 42cm battery began to set up at the Liège local training area at 0630 15 August,
which became a public spectacle as crowds of Belgians gathered to watch, requiring
that heavy guards be posted. The NCO in charge of the 1/ Hussar 10 supply vehicles
says that he 'absolutely had to see; such a thing could not exist.' It was necessary to
lay an 8km long telephone line through Liège to the FO at the Year 1830 Monument
in the Walzburg suburb. The hussar NCO found the guns by following the telephone line. He got quite close, and the crew explained everything to him. Fire was
opened at 1415 (G).

Leman arrived at the left corner of the gorge, near the flanking battery, at 1600
when the bombardment resumed 'with more violence than one could imagine'. To
Leman, it seemed like the German siege artillery was firing salvoes. In fact, what he
was hearing was the 42cm shells descending: a howling like an approaching express
train that got progressively louder, ending in a massive explosion which shook the
ground and threw up clouds of dust. The first round landed several hundred metres
from the fort. The fourth was a direct hit.

At 1710 the nineteenth 42cm shell, with a delayed-action fuse, penetrated the concrete and exploded in a magazine containing 12 metric tons (12,000kg) of powder,
creating a fireball 60m high, and a crater 30m in diameter and 6m deep. The blast
destroyed all the main gun turrets. The 39-ton 21cm turret was blown into the air,
inverted, and fell straight back down. The roof of the central gallery, 4m thick, was
lifted up and fell back down on the garrison assembled there. The walls, 2m thick,
were pushed into the fosse. Men in the corridor from the entrance to the central
gallery were killed by the shock of the explosion or by cases of ammunition blown
down it. The gallery filled with fumes. Most of the 100 survivors were in in the fire
direction centre (including Nassens, two officers and the senior NCO), the flanking
5.7cm batteries and the 5.7cm batteries at Salients I and III. They were burned or
injured by rubble and lost consciousness. Two hundred and fifty men were killed.

The artillerymen behind the 15cm cupola were the first to see daylight. Some
began to climb out of the rubble. Initially, the German artillery continued to fire, and

two of the first out were killed. Then the dust cleared and the German FOs saw what had happened and ordered a ceasefire. The Germans immediately began to try to dig out any survivors and treat the injured. Some forty were able to escape, as were later many of the wounded, especially NCOs.

Leman had just begun to return to the fire direction centre when a blast of air pushed down the corridor, spinning him, a staff officer and his batman, around and throwing them to the ground. He got back up and tried to move forward when a flash set fire to the barracks' rooms in the area, followed by a wave of exhaust gas from a massive explosion. Leman and his companions were once again thrown backwards into the room they had just left. They would have been asphyxiated had the staff officer not been able to pry open the armoured covering from a window. Leman fell into the fosse, and was stupefied to see that it was filled with debris from top to bottom, like a dike, on which he saw soldiers walking. Taking them to be Belgian gendarmes (they were actually German), he called out to them, but then was overcome by the gas and fell unconscious. He woke up at 1830 to find the staff officer and his batman trying to revive him, but also a German captain who offered him a glass of water. Leman was taken to the palace of the Belgian provincial governor as a POW.

The author of the IR 39 history, Lieutenant Colonel (then Captain) Rudorff was detailed to watch over Leman in the Palace of Justice. Rudorff said that Leman watched the German troops march past, saying several times '*Quelle belle armée!*' (What a fine army!)[74]

Belgian Army[75]

The German cavalry had shut down Belgian reconnaissance. The Belgian cavalry division was able to report only that it could not penetrate the German counter-reconnaissance screen. Reports from Belgian civilians, principally gendarmes, of German troops crossing the Meuse north of Liège were again localised, impressionistic and vague (no unit designations). One report said that Barchon and Pontisse were still in Belgian hands: Barchon had fallen on 8 August, Pontisse on 13 August.

16 August

Flémalle and Hollogne Fall

On 3 August the garrison of Hollogne caught a man they identified as a German spy and sent him 'to the General Staff'.[76] On 9 August Flémalle caught a man with a shaven head who spoke French with an accent. He admitted to being a German spy. Instead of interrogating him, which might have revealed useful information (such as the identity of his controller) or, more likely, have shown he was mentally deranged, the man was given a drumhead court martial by the officers of the fort, and shot, one of two 'spies' executed at Liège.

The artillery officer at Flémalle wanted to bombard the Liège–Brussels rail line as well as two nearby rail stations. He was forbidden to do so by Leman, who wanted them intact to assist the expected counteroffensive.

Bad news reached the fort every day, as one fort after the other fell, and the expected relief by French and British troops failed to appear. On 15 August the observers at Hollogne saw Loncin blow up, 'a spectacle that would have impressed even the bravest'.

German parliamentarians offered to allow an officer from Hollogne to see the ruins of Loncin, and the fort commander sent his artilleryman, with the doctor as interpreter. The citadel was now a huge crater and there were ongoing attempts by German soldiers and Belgian Red Cross to find survivors. The Belgian lieutenant's version of events diverges from the German one. The Belgian officer said that the Germans offered to bring him to General Leman, not the other way around. The Germans maintain that the lieutenant asked if Hollogne could surrender; the Belgian lieutenant said he asked Leman for orders. Leman's aide, however, thought that the lieutenant was asking for permission to surrender the fort, and Leman said that the fort had to have been bombarded first.

On hearing the lieutenant's report – the Germans had captured all the forts but Flémalle and Hollogne, and had a monster gun that had reduced Loncin to rubble – the commander of Hollogne decided to evacuate the fort and blow it up. He sent two NCOs to see if the route followed by I/ 34 and IV/ 14 F was still open. They came back at 0300 to say that the fort was completely encircled.

Except for the FAR 9 history, which says that II/ 9 was engaged, and a reference to II/ Foot Artillery 20 (sFH) firing, the German sources have almost no specific information concerning the bombardment of Flémalle, beyond that the bombardment began at 0600. Flémalle surrendered at 0900, with four OFF and 450 EM POW. Normand says that only one turret was seriously damaged and only six shells had hit the citadel. Leman said that the fortress armour had sustained 'minor damage'. There was a crack in the concrete over the central gallery and one in the fire direction centre. An infantry sally port was destroyed. The bakery was partly destroyed. There was minor damage to the concrete in the ditch and the armour over the windows. In the citadel there was a breach in the concrete between the left-hand 21cm and 12cm turrets. The 21cm and 15cm turrets turned with difficulty, the left-hand 12cm didn't turn at all. Three of the 5.7cm turrets were also difficult to turn. The latrines were full and 'disgorged a veritable stench', which, along with gas, overcame a great many men and forced the garrison to surrender.

On 15 August, I/ FAR 9 moved towards Fort Hollogne and at 2000 bivouacked in houses at St Nicholas on the west side of Liège. The battalion was going to go into position at 0730 the next morning in a cabbage field north of the town, and the I/ 9 battery commander warned the women of the surrounding working-class houses to gather in the cabbages beforehand, which they did. It was now a question of finding a battery command post on top of one of the numerous mining slag heaps that dotted the area. The wire teams laboriously hauled the telephone line uphill. Somebody even brought coffee and the battery command post enjoyed a sunny Sunday morning cup on top of the slag heap. Just as I/ 9 was ready to fire, one of the officers from Hollogne that had visited Loncin the previous day came out to negotiate, and at 0930 (G) the fort surrendered, the fort commander saying that his decision to do so 'was dictated by reasons of humanity and his conscience': he saw no reason to get the garrison of the fort killed for nothing.

Leman said that from 0400 to 0700 on 16 August the German shells landed outside the fort. By 0710 the Germans gunners had adjusted their fire onto Hollogne and at 0720 the fort surrendered. Part of the counterscarp had been damaged in an area 3–4m long and half as high. Otherwise, the fort was completely intact. The morale of both the garrison and the fortress commander had been crushed by the destruction of Loncin, and this led to the capitulation of the fort. On the other hand, further resistance by the last remaining fort was going to be a minor inconvenience to the Germans, but would probably have got the garrison killed.

Liège had fallen. Of 5,000 defenders, there were 600 KIA, 1,000 WIA, and most of the remaining 3,400 POW.[77] There were practically no German casualties.

August 16 was a rest day for II and III/ IR 90, and was used to maintain equipment and hold inspections. Bivouac fires were lit and the officers and men sang 'songs of home and of war.'

Diverging Belgian and French Enemy Estimates[78]

The Belgians had practically no hard intelligence. The Belgian cavalry reconnaissance was still unable to penetrate the German counter-reconnaissance screen; there is no evidence to this point of Belgian air reconnaissance. The Belgians believed that 'very large bodies of troops of all arms had crossed the Meuse, part near Visé, part between Liège and Huy'. They had identified 2 KD and IR 34 and 42 (3 ID) of II AK on the German right flank at Hasselt, with the forward line of German troops to the south, while strong forces were preparing to cross the Meuse at Huy. IR 92 had been identified at Huy. That was the sum of Belgian knowledge of the German order of battle; the Belgian estimate of German forces north of the Meuse was so vague as to be practically useless.

The French had a much more detailed order of battle, but most of it was wrong. The 2 and 9 KD were supposed to be east of Huy, but 2 KD was actually near Hasselt, 4 KD and 9 KD at Tirlemont.[79] The IX, X and VII AK were supposed to be south of the Meuse, north of Marche: X was actually at Huy, but IX was north of the Meuse, south of St Trond, with VII behind it. The German 2nd Army, with XI, III, IV and VI AK were supposed to be 'in front of Dinant'. In fact, III and IV were 1st Army units, north of the Meuse between Hasselt and St Trond; VI AK was a 4th Army unit and north of Metz. The Guard KD and 5 KD were in front of Dinant, as the French thought, but they had also identified 6 KD there, which in fact was north of Metz. The Guard, XIX and XII AK were identified in the Ardennes; all were actually south of the Meuse. Supposed to be in the Ardennes, 8 KD was in Lorraine.

Galet summarised the French intelligence estimate given to the Belgians: north of the Meuse there was only German cavalry, screening the Belgian Army; the German right wing was south of the Meuse, right flank 15km south of the river. How the French came by this information is something of a mystery, since Sordet's cavalry corps had crossed back over the Meuse, was on the Sambre and had provided little useful information. There is no evidence of effective French air reconnaissance at such long range and in heavily-forested terrain. The optimistic French assessment was adopted by the Belgian General Staff intelligence section and encouraged the operations section to re-establish the Gette bridges at Tirlemont, preparatory to an advance. The king would only allow the cavalry division to reconnoitre west of St Trond.

In fact, the Germans had six corps north of the Meuse and west of Liège, with three more following and X, Guard and Guard Reserve Corps crossing the Meuse at Huy, plus the XI, XII, XIX AK heading for Dinant. The Germans had nine corps north of the Meuse to oppose three weak Belgian corps and at most four from the French 5th Army, and the Belgians and French were operating in diverging directions.

The only information Belgian HQ was getting concerning the French came from the Belgian 4 DA at Namur. One French corps was east of Givet on 14 August, while the advance guard of a second was approaching Namur on the 15 August. The French 5th Army was oriented on the Meuse, facing east, with Sordet on the left flank. At 1130 the Belgian LNO at 5th Army HQ reported that Sordet would attempt on 17 August to link up the Belgian and French armies, and the French 5th Army would defend on the Meuse south of Namur.

Joffre transmitted his estimate to the British Expeditionary Force – but not to the Belgians until 2200, 18 August. 'The enemy seems to be making his main effort on his right and centre, on the one side to the north of Givet, on the other against the front Sedan–Montmédy–Damvillers. South of Metz he appears to be maintaining a defensive attitude.' Joffre expected that the German right flank was well south of the Meuse. The French 5th Army was assembling south of Namur, in depth on a line Dinant–Philippeville–Beaumont. The Franco-British left wing would be ready to move on 21 August. The BEF would cross the Sambre east of Mons, marching north towards Nivelles on the left flank of the French 5th Army or echeloned behind it. The Belgians were to attack or envelop the German far right flank.

17 August

The German cavalry had created an 'impenetrable veil'. Galet said that officer's reconnaissance, the gendarmerie, the railway and telegraph staffs and civil functionaries 'did their best to keep the Army Command informed'. The emphasis on non-military sources is indicative of the difficulty Belgian intelligence was experiencing. The Belgian General Staff intelligence section was only able to identify German cavalry and a German brigade which had crossed the Meuse at Lixhé.[80] The Belgian LNO at 5th Army HQ said that the French still thought that the German X, IX and VII AK were on the Ourthe south of Liège and 'that only columns of not more than one or two kilometres in length, therefore of no great strength, have been observed beyond the Ourthe.'

The king decided to move the government and royal family from Brussels to Antwerp.

Sordet's cavalry corps reported that on 18 August it would advance north-east on an axis Sombresse–Gembloux, halfway between Wavre and Namur. A force of 2,000 German infantry was supposed to be in a wood 5km north-east of Gembloux, and a brigade of 6 DA was ordered to take this force in the rear at 0900.

Did Liège Delay the German Army and Give the Entente Time to Meet the German Right Wing?

It is 'common knowledge' that the defence of Liège delayed the German attack through Belgium and that this delay significantly aided the Allied defence. In *Forts of the Meuse in World War I*, Clayton Donnell gives the delay at 'between two and 14 days according to Allied reports' (Donnell does not use German sources).[81] This 'gave the Allies the opportunity to make some strategic shifts that absolutely affected the outcome and success of the German invasion'. (Donnell does not explain why some sources say fourteen and some say two.)

Donnell gives an entire long paragraph to Leon van der Essen's *The Invasion and the War in Belgium*, which said that the German armies 'sat on the Meuse for 12 days'. The book was published in 1917, so van der Essen had no idea what the German war plan was (this information was not available until after 1920): he merely assumed the German armies had mobilised and deployed and were ready to move on 6 August.

In the same vein, he cites Leman, who maintained that, except for the defence of Liège, the Germans would have entered Brussels on 10 or 11 August and Tournai–Lille on 13 or 14 August. Leman wrote his report between December 1918 and his death on 17 October 1920, so he too did not have any knowledge of the real German deployment plan. It is striking that Leman assumed that the German Army was ready to move on 6 August: there was a fundamental failure in Belgium to form a clear appreciation of German capabilities and actions.

Donnell also cites Barbara Tuchman's opinion that 'the march [of the German right wing] had not been scheduled to begin before August 15; Liège had held up the

German offensive by two days, not two weeks as the world then believed'.[82] There is no footnote for the 15 August date, which Tuchman clearly made up.

Donnell says that Ludendorff's assertion that Liège did not delay German movement is 'ridiculous'. Unfortunately for Donnell's thesis, the Belgian Chief of Staff, Moranville, reached the same conclusion as Ludendorff.[83]

> The delay imposed by Liège, once estimated at 14 days, has been successively reduced as, after the war, we received more and more precise information concerning the enemy plan and initial operations. Three officers of the French Army, friends and allies of Belgium, General Dupont,[84] Colonel in the General Staff Bujac and Lieutenant-Colonel Corda,[85] have concluded that 'contrary to the legend, the resistance of Liège did not delay the beginning of the German advance by a single day'.

Moranville explained why this was so with a detailed description of the German 1st Army deployment and approach march.[86] He said that the combat elements of the active-army corps would disembark on 12 August, but the supply units would not complete deployment until 15 August. The combat elements of III Reserve Corps (RK) would debark 14 August, IV RK 14 August, the RK of the armies further south not until 17 August. Klück, the 1st Army commander, had intended to begin forward movement on 14 August, when the RK had finished deploying, but was ordered to begin movement on 13 August. Unfortunately, Moranville said, the fall of Forts d'Evegnée and Barchon had opened a gap for the 1st Army, which reached the Meuse on 14 August. The fall of Fort Pontisse allowed the Germans to put two pontoon bridges across the Meuse north of Liège. The fall of Liers on 14 August and Loncin at 0830 15 August allowed the 1st Army to cross the Meuse on 15 August on the two pontoon bridges and the undamaged permanent bridge at Herstal and march forward to the area of St Trond. The 1st Army was a day ahead of schedule, so it could use 16 August to complete the Meuse crossing and recall 11 and 14 Brigades, which had participated in the attack of 5–6 August. By 17 August the concentration of the 1st Army was complete.

Moranville said that, in summation, the German armies needed sixteen days (2 to 17 August) to mobilise and deploy.[87] The general advance was begun on the seventeenth day of mobilisation (18 August) when the right wing had finished concentration. The centre and pivot of the German right wing had still not finished concentration, which required short marches on the following days.

'The campaign began in the most favourable auspices for the Germans' Moranville said, 'for the day the German advanced commenced, 18 August, was that provided for in the German plan, which was exactly realized without the slightest delay, in spite of the valiant but ineffective resistance of the Liège forts'.

The French drew no operational conclusions from the German attack on Liège. Joffre began the war determined to conduct an all-out joint offensive, in conjunction with the Russians, and that is exactly what the French army did.

But for the sake of argument, let's assume that Liège delayed the German right wing two to four days. What good did it do the French and British? None whatsoever. In fact, any delay in the initial contact had only negative consequences. The Anglo-French were advancing against an enemy that was far superior in strength and intended to turn their left flank: they were rushing towards their own destruction. If there really had been a two-to-four-day delay, it merely would have allowed the French 3rd and 4th Armies to push further into the Ardennes and to get smashed by the German 4th and 5th Armies.

In the event, Joffre put the French 5th Army and the British Expeditionary Force in a potentially catastrophic position in the corner of the Sambre-Meuse. Only gross operational errors by all three right wing German Army commanders prevented their encirclement and destruction. The Battle of the Frontiers in the Ardennes and on the Sambre was an unmitigated disaster for the French: the French were not able to re-establish a cohesive defence for more than two weeks, and only then at the gates of Paris.

In fact, the Germans would have been better off had the Battle of the Frontiers been delayed even further: the German 5th Army should not have attacked on 22 August, but waited until 23 or even 24 August, allowing the French 4th Army to advance further into the Ardennes and giving the German 4th and 5th Armies time to bring up three more corps, the German 5th Army two more days of pursuit to the Meuse, and the German 2nd Army a day or two more to sweep into the French rear. The German 2nd Army should not have attacked on 21 August, but 23 August, when it would have done so in conjunction with the 1st Army attack on the BEF.

Liège: Evaluation

Barchon fell to the fire of six 21cm mortars on 8 August, d'Evegnée to the fire of four 21cm on 11 August. The mass of the German 21cm siege mortars opened fire on 12 August, and by 16 August, after five days of fire, all eleven remaining forts had been reduced. The 21cm mortars were solely responsible for the surrender of nine of the twelve Liège forts. In total, I/ FAR 9 had fired 1,500 shells at Liège, II fired 1,007. Short Marine Cannon Battery 3 (42cm) fired 70 shells, and participated in the destruction of only 2 forts. Belgian counter-battery fire was negligible: there were two EM WIA in I/ 9. The I/ FAR 9 historian said that the heavy artillery, once the wallflower of the German Army, was now queen of the ball.

The Germans killed or captured almost the entire garrisons of all twelve forts, about 5,000 men. Together with the 13,000–14,000 killed, wounded, captured or

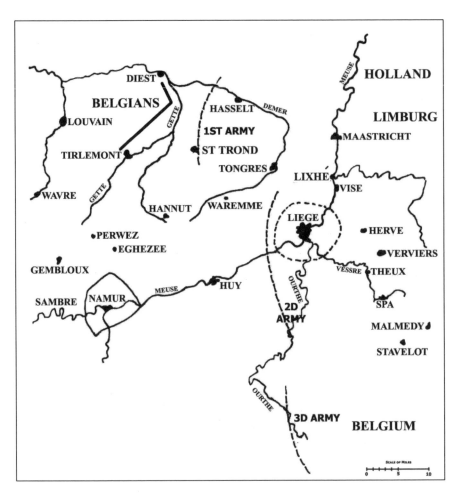

Siege of Liège situation, 17 August.

deserted from 3 DA and the fortress regiments, and probably another 1,000 casualties in 15 Brigade (4 DA), total Belgian casualties were about 19,000. The Belgians lost at least seventeen field guns. German casualties from the night of 5–6 August were about 4,000. The Belgian:German casualty ratio was 4.5:1

Leman said that the principal cause for the fall of eight of the twelve forts, often decisive in itself, was the danger that the garrison would be asphyxiated, arising from the gas of the exploding shells and the pestilential odours rising from the latrines.[88]

He did not mention that once the bombardment began the kitchens were almost always immediately destroyed and the troops lived off biscuits and whatever they could scrounge. In three forts the water supply immediately failed. Since the forts usually surrendered in two days or less, the lack of proper nutrition and water was not a problem, but if the forts had tried to hold out for a month, the garrison would have been quickly debilitated to the point of ineffectiveness.

The fact that in peacetime the troops lived in barracks outside the forts should have been a dead giveaway that the forts were uninhabitable. Nor is there any indication that the Belgians ever held a long-term exercise to see if the forts were habitable. The first and last to fall suffered from 'the low morale of both the garrison and the commander.' Nevertheless, Leman concluded that the defence of Liège was 'honourable' and 'heroic'.

As Normand noted, the forts on the north, east and south sides of Liège fell 'extraordinarily quickly' and that the individual Liège fortresses resisted, on average, forty-eight hours under fire.[89] The Belgians thought that Liège would block the German route of march and supply lines for a month: it fell after five days of bombardment.

Manonviller

At roughly the same time that the artillery attack on Liège began (7 August), OHL ordered preparations begun by the 6th Army in Alsace-Lorraine to take the isolated French *Sperrfort* at Manonviller, on the Franco-German border in central Lorraine. For this purpose OHL allocated:[90]

Heavy Naval Cannon Battery 1	Two 42cm mortars
Heavy Coastal Mortar Battery 2	Two 30.5cm mortars
II/ Bavarian FAR 3	Eight 21cm mortars
II/ FAR 13	Eight 21cm mortars
III/ FAR 13	Eight 21cm mortars Twenty-four 21cm mortars

The 21cm mortars opened fire on Manonviller on 25 August, the super-heavy 30.5cm and 42cm on 26 August. There was no effective French counter-battery fire. At 1635 on 27 August the fort surrendered. The German siege artillery had fired 4,596 21cm rounds, 134 30.5cm and 159 42cm (293 super-heavy shells, total).

Six super-heavy guns were assigned to Liège, four to Manonviller, however the 30.5cm did not arrive at Liège in time to fire, so in fact Manonviller was engaged by twice as many super-heavy guns as Liège. At Manonviller 24 21cm mortars were engaged, at Liège 32. The German siege artillery expended far more shells, especially super-heavy, at Manonviller than at Liège.

It is therefore highly significant that the German siege artillery commander rated the capabilities of the twelve forts at Liège not much higher than that of one French

Sperrfort and allocated his forces accordingly. If he had thought that Liège was a greater threat to the free movement of the right wing, he would have allocated more guns from the attack on Manonviller, which was in a secondary theatre. He did not. In the event, his estimate of Liège proved to be correct.

The professionalism and good judgement of the German siege artillery commander stands in stark contrast with Moltke's amateurish insistence that Liège be taken by a risky and politically and militarily foolish *coup de main*.

Liège: A Failure of Doctrine and Design

Liège was built according to the principles of late nineteenth-century fortress warfare, which required infantry and heavy artillery to defend the intervals between the detached forts. Aside from some overage reservists and museum-grade field guns, neither were ever provided. Nor was a serious attempt made to resolve this contradiction between design requirements and the failure to meet them.

At the last minute (31 July or 1 August) it was decided to keep first four, then five, brigades in Liège to defend the intervals: the defence was therefore unprepared and unco-ordinated. The five Belgian brigades, one-quarter of the Belgian field army, were shattered in less than twelve hours of combat, at the eventual cost of some 13,000 Belgian casualties, for little or no military return.

There was no provision for communication between the troops in the intervals, the twelve forts or the fortress commander, so the infantry received no artillery support. The forts were therefore unable to intervene decisively in the battle.

There was no effective provision for artillery FOs: the gunners of the individual forts could do no more against distant targets than fire blind. It appears that the Belgian Army thought that this would suffice to block the German lines of communication, which, if true, is absurd. In any case, the forts never had enough ammunition to conduct such fire for more than a few hours. In the event, the lack of observation and weak firepower of the guns meant that the forts, Fléron is a good example, were unable to prevent entire German brigades from marching past in broad daylight.

German infantry, MGs and field artillery were able to find covered and concealed positions right up to the glacis, from which they could inflict casualties on the defending infantry, 5.7cm gun crews and sometimes even suppress the observers and main guns.

When bombarded by as few as two 21cm mortars, the main guns were soon rendered unserviceable, the scarp and counterscarp destroyed, armour breached, the fort rendered uninhabitable and the garrison demoralised. The fort's capacity for resistance under fire could be measured in hours.

Liège was one of the least effective fortresses in European history.

Notes

1. Reichsarchiv, Der Weltkrieg I, 119–20, which even mentions the presence of a German 38cm battery at Liège, which never happened.
2. B. Tuchman, The Guns of August (New York: Macmillan, 1962) 166–8, 191–3.
3. J. Keegan, The First World War, (New York: Knopf, 1999), 86–7.
4. Hautecler, La Rapport du General Leman and Wesener, Eine 42cm Batterie. Duffy used Tuchman's August 1914, which is as non-serious as you can get.
5. Lombard, Face à l'invasion, 71.
6. C. Jany, Geschichte der Preußischen Armee vom 15. Jahrhundert bis 1914 IV 2nd ed., (Osnabrück: Biblio Verlag, 1967) 314–5. F. Kaiser, Das Ehrenbuch der Deutschen Schweren Artillerie (Berlin: Kolk, 1931) 21–8.
7. R. Schindler (ed.), Eine 42cm Mörser-Batterie im Weltkrieg (Hans Hoffmann: Breslau, 1934).
8. The German divisional artillery – 7.7cm guns and 10.5cm howitzers – were nearly worthless against heavily armoured fortresses.
9. Engaged Liers for five hours on 14 August, Lantin (misspelled Lautin in the regimental history) on 15 August, Loncin (misspelled Loucin) on 16 August. The 13cm guns were long-range cannon whose function in siege warfare was not to engage the forts but reach deep into the fortress to strike logistics and lines of communication. Their usefulness at Liège was limited.
10. Lombard, Sous les Ouragans de Acier, 28–32.
11. Leman, Liège, 110–13.
12. Fließ/Dittmar, IR 165, 14–18.
13. Werner, IR 27, 47–50.
14. Benary, Hussar R 10, 54–6.
15. Bülow, Mein Bericht, 8.
16. Zipfel, IR 89, 43–4.
17. Offiziers-Verein, Jäger 7, 26–9. As though they were making an administrative move during a manoeuvre.
18. Von Cramm, Geschichte des Ulanen-Regiments Hennings von Treffenfeld (Altmärkisches) Nr. 16 im Feldzuge 1914–1918 (Altmärkische: Stendal, 1921) 6–7.
19. Maillard, IR 53, 49–50.
20. Lombard, Sous les Ouragans de Acier, 20.
21. Lombard, Sous les Ouragans de Acier, 20.
22. M. Schültz, Das Infanterie-Regiment Vogel von Falckenstein (7. Westfälisches) Nr. 56 im Großen Kriege 1914–18 (Berlin: Blau, 1926) 18–19.
23. F. von Rudorff, Das Fusilier-Regiment General Ludendorff (Niederrheinisches Nr. 39 im Weltkrieg 1914–1918 (Berlin: Reinhold Kuhn, 1925) 15–20. Lombard, Sous les Ouragans de Acier, 20.
24. Bieberstein Lüttich, 42–4.
25. Galet, Albert, 85.
26. Anon, IR 90, 27–8.
27. Anon, 'Marcel Speesen' in: Collection Nationale Civisme No. 8, Octobre 1953.
28. De Schrÿver, Liège, 219–20, 231–2.
29.
30. De Schrÿver, Liège, 231.
31. Offizier-Vereinigung, FAR 43, 34–5.
32. 'Marcel Speesen', 10. Lombard, Sous les Ouragans de Acier, 45–6.
33. De Schrÿver, Liège, 224–5.

34. Lombard, Sous les Ouragans de Acier, 51–5.

35. De Schrÿver, Liège, 223.

36. De Schrÿver, Liège, 228.

37. Galet, Albert, 90–1, 97.

38. Galet, Albert, 98–101. Zuber, Mons 97–101.

39. De Schrÿver, Liège, 232.

40. On the early morning of 12 August, a platoon of Medical Company 2 (VII AK), with an escort of a platoon of 1/ IR 13 got lost and approached to within 400m of d'Embourg. The column tried to turn around but took canister fire. The platoon lost twelve men, including three wounded and two captured, who were freed and returned to the company on 17 August.

41. Schindler, 42cm Batterie, 83–5.

42. De Schrÿver, Liège, 232.

43. Offiziers-Vereinigung, FAR 43, 35.

44. Leman said that the fort had been forced to surrender because the air had become pestilential from the gas of exploding shells and the stench from the overflowing latrines; the account above makes it clear that Speesen surrendered because the 42cm threatened to completely destroy the fort.

45. P. Buhle, Geschichte der 1. Batterie Schleswig-Holsteinischen Fußartillerie_Regiments Nr. 9 (Altdamm im Pommern: Hormann, 1932) 15–21.

46. Offiziersverein, Das Westfälische Fußartillerie-Regiment Nr. 7, 218.

47. De Schrÿver, Liège, 233.

48. Lombard, Sous les Ouragans de Acier, 106–11.

49. Offiziers-Verein, FAR 43, 36–7.

50. Bieberstein Lüttich, 53.

51. H. Castendyk, Das Kgl. Preuß. Infanterie-Regiment 'Herzog Ferdinand von Braunschweig' (8. Westfälisches Nr. 57) im Weltkrieg 1914–1918, 15.

52. Offiziers-Vereinigung, FAR 43, 38.

53. De Schrÿver, Liège, 233–4.

54. Lombard, Chocs de Feu dans la Nuit, 124–141. Normand, Liège, Namur, 37. Normand says a battalion of 8 F, but there is no other evidence of this regiment being at Liège.

55. Leman, Liège, 179–80. The Belgians were still gripped by a spy mania. Leman's editor, Hauteclair, lists several false orders to withdraw which he says originated from a certain enemy agent named Troupin, who pretended to be working for the Belgian government at the rail station hotel. Hauteclair admits that Troupin was discharged from the Belgian Army in 1893[!] due to mental instability. Nevertheless, he was arrested and shot as a spy. Hauteclair also says that Troupin was 'probably the author of the panic at the telephone exchange, when the headquarters at the Rue Saint-Foi was attacked and the orders given for the units to retreat from Liège'. It seems more likely that the Belgians issued their own orders to withdraw and found Troupin to be a convenient excuse for the panic.

56. Lombard, Sous les Ouragans de Acier, 19.

57. Morin, Fléron, 111–33.

58. C. Gross/ W. Rudolff (eds.) Infanterie-Regiment Herwarth von Bittenfeld (1. Westfälisches) Nr. 13 im Weltkrieg 1914–1918 (Berlin, 1927) 16–7.

59. Hans-Erich Henning, Feldartillerie-Regiment Generalfeldmarschall Graf Waldersee (Schleswigsches) Nr. 9 (Oldenburg: Stalling, 1934) 20–3.

60. Rudorff, IR 39 im Weltkrieg, 15–20.

61. The German foot artillery was convinced that the Belgians had turrets which could depress, which was incorrect.

62. Schültz, IR 56, 21–2.

63. Rudorff, IR 39, 19–20.

64. Lombard, Sous les Ouragans de Acier, 133–6.
65. De Schrÿver, Liège, 245.
66. Leman said that the fort was bombarded all day on 13 August, and again from 0300, 14 August, and it surrendered at 0930.
67. Galet, Albert, 101–4, 324–5
68. Leman, Liège, 146–7.
69. Lombard, Sous les Ouragans de Acier, 138–40.
70. Lombard, Sous les Ouragans de Acier, 140–2.
71. Lombard, Sous les Ouragans de Acier, 142.
72. L. Lombard, L'Epopée de Loncin (Verviers: Leens, 1933). Colonel Nassens/ L. Lombard, Loncin, (Verviers: Leens, 1937). Colonel Nassens, Les Derniers Jours de du Fort de Loncin. Only identification number D/2009/11.688/2. Nassens wrote 'La defense du fort de Loncin' in: Le Courrieur de l'armée No. 694, 21 mars 1920 and 699, 25 avril 1920. An anonymous article 'La résistance et la chute du fort de Loncin' in Revue Générale, Juillet, Août et Septembre 1920 was also probably written by him.' Nassens was writing patriotic propaganda and he did not find it necessary to follow the facts or military logic if he could invent a cracking good story about Belgian military prowess, but his account does contain some interesting information, much of it unintentional, such as the frequent use Belgian soldiers made of civilian clothing.
73. Leman, Liège, 150–8.
74. Rudorff, IR 39, 21.
75. Galet, Albert, 104, 325–6
76. Lombard, Sous les Ouragans de Acier, 145–6, 150.
77. Lombard, Sous les Ouragans de Acier, 158.
78. Galet, Albert, 105–7, 326–7.
79. Weltkrieg I, 122, Map 1.
80. Galet, Albert, 107–8.
81. C. Donnell, The Forts of the Meuse in World War I, 53–4. The first source Donnell cites is Crutwell's The History of the Great War 1914–1918. Crutwell supposedly said 'the resistance put back the German timetable by 72 hours, without which the British Expeditionary Force and the French Army would have been destroyed'. In fact, what Crutwell said (p. 15) was that 'it does not seem that the brave Belgian resistance, though unexpected, interfered with the German plans'.
82. Tuchman, The Guns of August, 193.
83. Moranville, Babel, 215–28.
84. Dupont, 'Le haut commandement allemand en 1914' in: Revue Militaire Française, 1er juillet 1921, No. 1.
85. H. Corda, La Guerre Mondiale (1914–1918) (Paris: Chapelot, 1922) p. XVIII.
86. Moranville, Babel, 161–74.
87. Moranville says he is citing 'three excellent articles in the Bulliten Belge des Sciences Militaires by Lieutenants-colonel in the General Staff Nuyten, Lemoine and Schmidt, May and August 1920'.
88. Leman, Liège, 135.
89. Normand, Liège, Namur, 56.
90. K. Deuringer, Die Schlacht in Lothringen und in den Vogesen 1914 (Munich: Max Schick 1929) II, 508. This is the official history of the Bavarian Army Archive. See my translation of The First Battle of the First World War: Alsace-Lorraine 1914.

Epilogue

The only units that benefited from the Liège operation were the German siege artillery. Liège served as a live-fire training test, and the German siege gunners both drew the relevant lessons learned and gained immense confidence. Namur had three weeks to prepare its defence; the positions in the intervals between the fortresses were thoroughly dug-in and reinforced with wire obstacles. The German heavy artillery opened fire at noon on 21 August and by 25 August the fortress had fallen. The battle was an even bigger disaster for the Belgians than Liège. The Germans had almost completely surrounded the fortress and the Belgians lost 15,000 of 23,000 defenders, including 10,000 men from 4 DA, which was destroyed.[1] The Germans reported taking 6,700 POW and 12 field guns. Between Liège and Namur the Belgian Army lost eight of its twenty manoeuvre brigades.

The German siege artillery conducted its next operation, against Fortress Maubeuge, with a self-confidence bordering on arrogance. The Germans employed twenty-one heavy and super-heavy batteries, but only a reserve infantry division and an active-army brigade, against a garrison which they estimated at 25,000–30,000 men. On 8 September, after a ten-day siege, and in spite of severe ammunition shortages, 40,000 French troops marched into captivity. The French had also lost about 5,000 men in combat, for a total of 45,000 casualties, the Germans 1,100.[2]

The German Army had spent about twenty years creating mobile heavy artillery. This involved not only building the weapons, but writing the doctrine and training at all levels, from the individual gun crews to realistic live-fire exercises and fortress General Staff rides. The result was heavy artillery that was technically and tactically proficient, guns that could move, shoot and communicate, and officers at all levels that could use their initiative. This was the foundation of the brilliant successes of the German heavy artillery at the beginning of the Great War.

Appendix

The Testimony of
Abbé Madenspacher

Oscar Madenspacher was the curé at Retinne from 1911 to 1944, when he died. He wrote two accounts of the events in his village during the war, one apparently in 1919 when he was called on to testify in court, as well as in response to a requirement from the Bishop of Liège to report on the spiritual life of the village during the war.[3] The second a personal account of the fighting, apparently written in conjunction with his official report. These were therefore written about five years after the fact, but remain important documents.

In his official report Madenspacher says that the civilian authorities did not take any actions of any kind. The civil population was terrified, and he did all he could to calm them. Caravans of livestock and pigs passed through the village; the Belgian Army requisitioned 'a great many'. The inhabitants of the villages near Herve and Battice fled to Fléron and Liège, as did several families from Retinne. Mass was well attended, and many spent the night in the presbytery, reciting the rosary. This included people 'who had never set foot in the church before the war'.

The Belgians constructed three redoubts, or trenches: one at Haute Retinne (Redoubt 24 which Madenspacher says was not engaged), one at the hamlet of Surfossé (Redoubt 25) 'about 10 minutes from the church', and one at Liéry – the defensive preparations at Liéry were therefore extensive.

To clear fields of fire from the trenches the Belgians destroyed a 'great number' of trees and hedges. At Haute Retinne, on the Rue Ste Julienne, Belgian Army engineers destroyed a farm and two houses, resulting in the death of one civilian. How this occurred is not explained; perhaps he refused to leave his house. The military authorities destroyed several houses and a chapel near Fort Fléron.

In his personal report Madenspacher says that the Belgian 14 Line Regiment was sent to Retinne on 1 August. It was joined, according to his official report, on the evening of 5 August by a detachment composed of elements from 9 L, 12 L (400 men) plus a regiment of artillery, identified as 14 Brigade with artillery and MGs. The church tower was used as an OP.

On 5 August Madenspacher said eight German spies dressed as Belgian gendarmes arrived at city hall in Retinne and telephoned the commandant of Fort Fléron to learn the location of the Belgian troops.

Madenspacher was in the cellar from the beginning of the attack until the next morning, so his account is based on hearsay. He says that at 1900 the Germans made contact with the advance posts of Fort d'Evegnée. This is unlikely: the Belgians were probably just nervous. At 2100, troops from 9 L, 12 L and 14 L (400 in all) took position at Redoubt 25 reinforced by two MGs. An outpost occupied the city hall. The Germans pushed the Belgian security detachments back towards Liéry at 2230, burning down two farms and three other buildings, and the Belgian troops in Redoubt 25 opened fire, with some of the German troops taking cover behind the houses.

At 0230 the Germans installed two artillery pieces and MG near a farm opposite the city hall, but their fire had no effect whatsoever because it was too high. This is unlikely: the German sources do not mention either MG or artillery at Redoubt 25. What the Belgian troops in Redoubt 25 probably heard was Belgian artillery fire at Liéry, which was only 800m away. At 0330 the fire died down and ceased altogether at 0400. Madenspacher says that there had been 2,000 Germans engaged and they took 60 KIA and 200 WIA; there was not a single Belgian casualty. The German dead were buried on site.

At this point the Belgians withdrew towards Saive (north-west). Colonel Simonis strayed too far to the right (left?) with 100 men and was captured. One man, Corporal Laveaux, was killed by MG fire and was buried here by Simonis and several Belgian soldiers.

Now that R 25 had been cleared the Germans pushed on to the west, singing, yelling 'Hurrah!' and sounding trumpets. At Liéry they encountered 4 Brigade with 'a dozen cannon and machine guns', supported by the guns of Fort Fléron. According to Lieutenant Aerts of 14 Line, the Germans advanced behind a white flag, as though they wanted to surrender, then killed Captain Bokarty and several Belgian soldiers. Numerous German soldiers were buried by collapsing walls.

The Belgian soldier who most distinguished himself was named Rutten, who was from Evegnée. He remained crouched by his artillery piece while the other gunners hid. He fired the first round, which killed General Wussow, among others. Wussow was hit by canister in the head, his last words supposedly being being 'Kill and burn!' Rutten also fired the last cannon shell, and then escaped to the 'Renaissance room' in the vicinity, changed into civilian clothes and mixed himself into the men who were burying the dead.

The Germans had great difficulty advancing and lost almost all their officers. A hundred Germans soldiers and twenty Belgians were killed, 200 Germans wounded and five Belgians were gathered at the church, other Belgians sent to Queue-du-Bois. Most of the Belgian gunners fled to Liège, a dozen were captured.

The artillery commander, Major Hontheim, a captain and a second lieutenant hid in a farm and were captured on 10 August. 'A great many' Belgian soldiers escaped because they changed into civilian clothes provided by two local farm families: one of the farmers gave up all of his clothes. The Germans also rousted a dozen Belgian soldiers from the cellar of a house at Surfossé. At a hamlet named 'Rothys' there was an all-night engagement from 5–6 August between fifty Belgians soldiers from 14 L hidden in a house there and 200–300 Germans arriving from Micheroux: five Belgians and a number of Germans were killed, including a German officer named Windmuller who was buried on the spot.

According to several residents, the bodies of the German soldiers were transported by automobile during the night back to Germany; the corpses were mutilated to demonstrate Belgian treatment of German troops.

When the Germans continued on to Liège they took hostages, some fifty men all over the age of 50, some as old as 70. If they did not move quickly enough they were prodded with a bayonet: one man returned with a bayonet wound in the back. One 45-year-old man had to march without shoes and died several weeks later. One 70-year-old man was left by the side of the road; he was taken to the Chartreuse where he spent the night without food and was 'maltreated'. He was then taken to Liège where he was released.

The Germans were known to have lost 500 dead and wounded at Retinne. A rural guard said that he was required to enter the cellars where the civil population was hiding and bring out men under the pretence that they would perform labour service; they were led to a field and shot one by one. The rural guard was to be shot too, but was detailed to transport a wounded German officer and spared. He saw a German soldier bayonet a wounded Belgian soldier sitting on a stoop, and four other Belgian soldiers who had surrendered were lined up against a tree and shot. A woman in Retinne said that two Belgian soldiers hiding in the courtyard of her house tried to surrender but were shot. 'Other civilians were pulled out of their cellars and shot on the road in front of their houses.' In one house the women had to walk past their husbands' bodies. The women and children were locked up in a stable. From time to time they would be forced to kneel in the courtyard as though they would be shot. One woman delivered her baby. They were fed little and released the next morning. Madenspacher lists the names of twenty-four men 'shot and killed' at Retinne, one outside it, one who died of wounds, a woman accidentally killed by a German bullet, and a 60-year-old man, two women, aged 64 and 74, and a 5-year-old child 'accidentally killed by a shell from Fort Fléron'.

Thirteen men from the hamlet of Fêcher were killed at Retinne, according to a young man from there whose name might have been Decortis. Madenspacher wrote, 'It is certain that some of them were buried in the Retinne cemetery; I saw several unknown bodies buried'.

The Germans set fire to a dozen houses and the city hall with all the archives and registers. Several workers' and bourgeois houses were damaged. The Gothic oak main doors to the church were broken in, as well as the door to the sacristy. A Catholic sergeant prevented German troops from burning the church down. The church was turned into a hospital. The windows and *grisailles* were 'somewhat' damaged by bullets. The sandstone mouldings around the window fell down due to the concussion from the German siege guns during the bombardment of Fort Fléron. A German artillery shell hit the attic window of the presbytery. The chapel of Lisse, outside the town, was completely destroyed, apparently by shells from Fort Fléron.

After the battle, life in Retinne proceeded normally. The Germans did not interfere with the religious life of the town; indeed they celebrated military mass at the church on several occasions. Several well-off members of the congregation built a Catholic girl's trade school in some haste, before the city council, majority socialist, constructed a public school. From 1915 to 1919 an octave [eight-day] mass was celebrated the second week after Easter for the victims of the war. In the first year the church was 'packed' each evening, and in subsequent years it 'enjoyed great success'. On the first Sunday of each month a solemn patriotic procession with the Holy Sacrament was conducted around the church. In conjunction with this, patriotic Eucharistic groups were formed for young girls and boys and a League of the Sacred Heart of Jesus for adults, which were well attended. On the other hand, public morality declined 'in Retinne as everywhere: practically every Sunday there were parties and balls'. The young girls, Catholic, liberal and socialist, ran a successful soup kitchen, but it closed before the war was over. A food bank was established in Micheroux, but the mayor, a liberal, was distrusted because he gave special privileges to his friends. The Germans made an inventory of the church bells and the organ pipes, which drew an energetic protest from Madenspacher, which was apparently effective. When the Germans withdrew in 1918 they did not kill anyone, but 'pillaged and stole', including 'several head of cattle and horses'.

Fifty-six men from the parish served in the Belgian Army; fifteen were volunteers, twenty-one were POW (37 per cent!). Two were killed near Retinne in August 1914, one died in 1917 at Dixmude, one died of influenza at Brugge in 1918 (7 per cent fatalities from all causes). Two NCOs were decorated.

In his personal report, Madenspacher said that he had gone to bed at 2200. At 2300 he was awakened by rifle, MG and artillery fire and he could hear impacts against the wall of his bedroom. He dressed hurriedly and went to the cellar, which was already occupied by his servant and the family of his neighbour. The battle lasted until 0400 or 0500. He could hear the whistling of cannon shells and the rounds impacting against the walls, penetrating into the house and knocking the tiles off the roof and bricks from the chimney. He confessed everyone in the cellar and 'we waited for death'. They discussed whether it was better to die in the cellar or upstairs. Madenspacher decided to go to the church. He made it to the sacristy unseen. The door from there to the choir had been broken down, where he heard German voices; he quickly returned to the cellar. All of the houses round about were on fire. They expected the German soldiers at any time.

At 0500 he left the cellar again, accompanied by his neighbour, and saw three German soldiers, whom he spoke to in German. They all entered the presbytery and he offered them coffee, which he had to drink first. His neighbour saw that his cattle were still in the field and against Madenspacher's advice went to bring them back, as 'his cattle were his entire fortune'. He was immediately arrested by the Germans, tied and led off as a prisoner.

Madenspacher put on his stole, took the holy oil and went towards the Belgian field hospital. He had only gone a few steps when he saw two of his adult male parishioners dead in a pool of blood. As they were socialists, he assumed that they had fought with the Germans, not realising that they had been 'pulled from their cellar and shot'. He then saw another corpse, stabbed in the chest with bayonets. It was later established that a wrist had been slashed.

Walking down the Herve–Liège road he encountered a group of German soldiers. An officer grabbed him, saying, 'Here's the guilty one who encouraged the population to fire on us! He preached against Germany!' The troops began excitedly yelling 'Hang him! Burn him! Shoot him!' The officer said, 'We are all honest family men, but you are *Schweinhunde!*' The soldiers searched him for weapons. Madenspacher took the pouch with the holy wafers from his pocket and held it out, saying in German, 'These are my weapons! I have come to offer the Last Rites to your dying comrades and you want to kill me! You are not brave soldiers. I never encouraged anyone to fire on you, nor did I preach against Germany; what I do preach is Christian charity towards all, Germans as well as everyone else'. The soldiers, astonished, stepped back. He was told to sit on the kerb with several civilians and Belgian soldiers. Civilians were marched down the street, hands tied behind their backs. The German soldiers guarding them debated whether they should be shot. Madenspacher continued to defend his parishioners, arguing that they were innocent and had never fired on German soldiers.

In the immediate vicinity was the house of an employee of the Liège city government. He had taken refuge in his cellar, along with the principal and vice-principal of the school and two blacksmiths and their families. That night the men had been pulled from the cellar and shot in front of the house. The women and children had been moved to a stable opposite the house. Madenspacher and the other prisoners were ordered by an officer into the cellar, stepping over the bodies on the way.

An officer ordered Madenspacher's hands untied, so that he could inspect the church and presbytery for weapons. Everything was thoroughly searched, including the coal cellar, except Madenspacher's bedroom, which Madenspacher said was fortunate, because he had a loaded pistol and twenty extra rounds of ammunition in a cigar box on his night table. Madenspacher was told to remain in the church; if he was seen in town he would be shot. The wounded German soldiers would be brought to the church, officers to the presbytery and Madenspacher and his parishioners were to care for them.

The sacristan arrived with his family, having escaped from his burning house (the Germans burned down houses from which they had been fired upon). The officer asked a soldier if they had taken fire from the house. Madenspacher interrupted him, saying that he needed the sacristan to care for the wounded, and added as many other names as he could. During the day he saw several buildings on fire, and German soldiers led men past the church, to be shot in Liéry. From time to time German soldiers would ask him the most direct route to Germany, in order to desert. Fearing a trap, he refused to help them. Towards evening, German solders began to seek him out; all but a dozen were Protestants.

Practically all the houses in Liéry were filled with wounded, who were happy to see a priest who spoke German, 'even the Protestants' (evidently the Germans relented and allowed Madenspacher to leave the church). He visited the women and children at the stable, and spoke with the German soldiers guarding them 'who instantly became calmer and gentler towards them'. Some were released that evening, the rest the next day. In a field there was 'a crowd' of prisoners 'some of whom were not sympathetic towards me: one continually said to the others "you'll see: the priest will have us shot"'.

About 200 German and 4 or 5 Belgian wounded were transported to the church. While this was occurring, a German soldier came to Madenspacher and said, 'Civilians are shooting at us!' He left the church and saw several soldiers aiming at a woodpile, where the Germans said the shooters were located. He was given a stick with a white flag tied on it and told to move towards the woodpile. As he did so, a bullet whistled past his ear, and he hid behind a wall, then moved through fields to return to the presbytery. He said that the Germans used this incident to prove that civilians had fired on them at Retinne. Madenspacher said that no one had actually seen civilians firing. On the other hand, there were still Belgian soldiers hiding in the cellars: the Germans found some on 6 August and again on 9 August.

The social tensions in Retinne come out loud and clear in Madenspacher's account, with serious divisions between Catholics, liberals and socialists. Madenspacher was also clearly dismayed to note that 90 per cent of the German troops, including all the officers, were Protestants, only 10 per cent Catholics. The German troops distrusted the Catholic population, the priest in particular, a sentiment which the Catholic population returned in full measure.

One morning, a German sergeant from Engineer Battalion 4 came to Madenspacher and told him that the troops had wanted to burn the church down (Madenspacher noted that it was now filled with wounded), but as a good Catholic he had prevented them from doing so. He would appreciate a letter to this effect to his wife and curé, who would be pleased. Madenspacher did so, but did not receive a reply.

Madenspacher confessed the man, who asked for a religious souvenir: Madenspacher gave him a medal of the Holy Virgin and one of Ste Julienne, patroness of the parish.

The Germans bombarded Fort Fléron, using the bell tower as an OP. A Belgian shell, probably from Fort d'Evegnée, exploded in the second floor of the presbytery: had it penetrated to the ground floor it would have killed the wounded German soldiers lying there. Four people were killed by shells from Fort Fléron, including a widow of 74, a second of 64, a 60-year-old man and a 5-year-old girl, and several homes destroyed. One dud Belgian shell hit a barn without setting fire to the grain and passed through three houses. Another dud hit the clothes closet in the room of small girl.

Notes

1. Galet, Albert, 144–6.
2. F. Kaiser, *Das Ehrenbuch der Deutschen Schweren Artillerie*, 166–70.
3. Récit de l'Abbé Madenspacher sur les événements d'août 1914 à Retinne. Présenté par Pierre Caberg. From the parish records. Sent to me by Daniel Neicken.

Index

If you enjoyed this book, you may also be interested in…

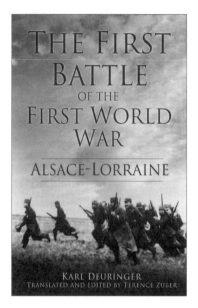

The First Battle of the First World War: Alsace-Lorraine

KARL DEURINGER, TRANSLATED AND
EDITED BY TERENCE ZUBER

978 0 7524 6086 4

On 7 August 1914 a French corps attacked towards Mulhouse in Alsace and was immediately thrown back by the Germans.

On 14 August, two weeks before Tannenberg and three weeks before the Battle of the Marne, the French 1st and 2nd Armies attacked into Lorraine, and on 20 August the German 6th and 7th Armies counterattacked. After forty-three years of peace, this was the first test of strength between France and Germany.

In 1929, Karl Deuringer wrote the official history of the battle for the Bavarian Army, an immensely detailed work of 890 pages, chronicling the battle to 15 September. Here, First World War expert and former army officer Terence Zuber has translated and edited this study to a more accessible length, while retaining over thirty highly detailed maps, to bring us the first account in English of the first major battle of the First World War.